D1553984

FAMILY MATTERS

SUNY Series, Feminist Philosophy
Jeffner Allen, editor

FAMILY MATTERS

Feminist Concepts in African Philosophy of Culture

Nkiru Uwechia Nzegwu

State University of New York Press

Published by
State University of New York Press, Albany

Printed in the United States of America

For information, address State University of New York Press,
194 Washington Avenue, Suite 305, Albany, NY 12210–2384

Production by Dana Foote
Marketing by Fran Keneston

Library of Congress Cataloging-in-Publication Data
Nzegwu, Nkiru.
    Family matters : feminist concepts in African philosophy of culture / Nkiru
Uwechia Nzegwu.
        p. cm. — (SUNY series, feminist philosophy)
    Includes bibliographical references and index.
    ISBN 0–7914–6743–0 (hardcover : alk. paper) — ISBN 0–7914–6744–9 (pbk. : alk. paper)
1. Igbo (African people)—Kinship.   2. Women, Igbo—Social conditions.   3. Philosophy,
Igbo.   4. Sex role—Nigeria.   5. Family—Nigeria.   6. Patrilineal kinship—Nigeria.
7. Feminist theory—Nigeria.   I. Title.   II. Series.

DT515.45.I33N93 2006
306.87′089′96332—dc22

                                                                        2005014077

ISBN-13: 978-0-7914-6743-5 (hardcover : alk. paper)

In memory of my mother
Veronica Umebe Uwechia
died 12.13.02

CONTENTS

ACKNOWLEDGMENTS

Finally, it is done! This book has gone through numerous conceptual shifts and turns before finally taking this present form. I wish to express my utmost gratitude to Jeffner Allen, editor of the SUNY series, Feminist Philosophy, who signed on to the project at its very early stages and provided invaluable advice at various stages of the manuscript. I cannot thank her enough for her generosity, encouragement, and vision. I am pleased to thank Jane Bunker and the staff of the State University of New York Press for believing in this project and working with me to bring it to fruition. Although she is no longer with the State University of New York Press, I would like to thank Lois Patton for first seeing the potential of this book and contracting it for the State University of New York Press. The anonymous reviewers of the press were extremely helpful, and their thoughtful criticisms have made this a much better book. I also thank Lindsey Dominguez Reed for an excellent editing job.

Without doubt, this book is the outcome of the effort of many additional individuals. In the collegial world of academic subcultures and the conferences that support these subcultures, I have found a number of learned and generous colleagues who have assisted this project in numerous ways. I am particularly indebted to Susan E. Babbitt, who insisted early on that feminism would be enriched by the experiences of African women and from seeing reality through their prism. I thank her for the encouragement and for providing this philosophical challenge. As well, I have to thank her for creating numerous academic meetings, conference panels, and workshops that initiated and facilitated the expansion of various sections of this book. Additionally, I would like to thank those whose suggestions and criticisms also helped to make this book a better product: Oyèrónké Oyĕwùmí, for many rewarding theoretical conversations and her special insight on gender; Rifa'at Abou-El-Haj, for enriching intellectual stimulation and unyielding insistence on the importance of historicity; Olufemi Taiwo, for his attention to philosophical content; and Justice Nkem Anunobi Izuako, for providing critical jurisprudential ideas and for procuring elusive court documents. I benefited tremendously from the generosity of Marilynn Desmond, Chinwe Uwatse, Barry Hallen, Lynn Jones, Tejumola Olaniyan, Micere Mugo, Madonna Larbi, Paul Tiyambe Zeleza, Cassandra Veney, Barbara Abou-El-Haj, and many other colleagues and friends too numerous to mention.

I would also like to thank the Institute for the Study of Gender in Africa (ISGA) at the University of California at Los Angeles, for the Senior Research Fellowship I received to begin writing this book. Two chapters of this book are radically revised versions of previously published works. An earlier version of chapter 4 appeared in the *Canadian Journal of Law and Jurisprudence*(1994b) and was also republished in *JENDA: A Journal of Culture and African Women Studies* (2001a). And an earlier version of chapter 1 also appeared in *JENDA: A Journal of Culture and African Women Studies* (2003).

At the foundation of it all is the family. I would like to express my profound appreciation for the unwavering support of my daughters Uzoamaka and Azuka, for whom the book was written, for the encouragement my brother Jideofo Uwechia, and for my mother Veronica Umebe Uwechia, who showed me the possibilities that women can attain when they believe in themselves, but who did not live long enough to see this book of her dreams come to fruition. Uzoamaka, Azuka, Jideofo, and Veronica na m muo ib'ye were all sounding boards for many of the ideas in this book. *Dalu nu o.*

INTRODUCTION
Igbo Family Structure and Feminist Concepts

Feminists have found most forms of family prevalent in history and in the present to be destructive of women's equality both within the home and in all other spheres of life, and sometimes of their basic well-being.
—Susan Moller Okin, "Families and Feminist Theory: Some Past and Present Issues" (1997)

Feminists have conducted a close scrutiny of the family . . . and have seen how oppressive it can be for women.
—Linda Gordon, "Why Nineteenth-Century Feminists Did Not Support 'Birth Control' and Twentieth-Century Feminists Do" 1982)

Contemporary human rights discourse has defined a framework for under-standing African families that pits the rights of individuals against the norms of cultures and traditions. The 1986 African Charter on Human and People's Rights, the constitutions of various African nations, and the United Nations Draft Declaration of the Rights of Indigenous Peoples (Article 12) all protect indigenous cultures under the concept of people's rights while offering strong protection for individual rights. Tensions have steadily arisen between those eager to secure the individual rights of people over the customs and values of cultures that violate those rights. These tensions have coalesced around the rights of women. From the late 1980s, landmark cases in a number of African countries either stripped wives and daughters of whatever rights they had, or determined that they never had any. The 1999 case of *Magaya v. Magaya* comes to mind, in which the Zimbabwean Supreme Court equated the status of adult daughters to that of teenage sons, as well as the 1987 Kenyan case that denied Wambui Otieno the right to bury her husband, Sylvannus A. Otieno (Bigge and von Briesen 2000, Stamp 1991, and A. Gordon 1995). In both cases, the judges in the two countries defined the boundary of the family in accordance with presumed traditional customary practices, restricting the rights of daughters and wives. In cases as these, where cultural norms are privileged, modern constitutional provisions that guarantee women equal rights with men are eroded. Such contemporary appeals to culture and selective invocations of traditions continue to be used in different countries to entrench the gender subordination of daughters and wives and to curb whatever rights they may have under the constitutions of respective countries. Interestingly, most of this curtailment occurs within the context of the family, specifically under the provisions of family law that rest on customs and traditions as well as on cultural conceptions of the family. These conceptions are historically derived from men's notions of customs, their perceptions of values, and their articulations of the structure of the family.

It is indeed true that the consequent problem of gender subordination in Africa over the last sixty years or so can be traced to European colonial policies and African men's views and constructions of the family. Because this male-dominant view of the family has never been challenged, it has gained legitimacy and paramount importance. Modern prejudices about women underlie this view, and such biases have worked to consolidate and protect men's rights within the family and in the society at large. The consolidation of husband's and son's rights has resulted in a patriarchal consciousness in which the subordination of daughters and wives is taken for granted and is assumed to be culturally rooted and based on their natural inferiority. This lends support to the characterization of African societies and African families as historically oppressive to women. Once scholars concede that women in African societies are culturally subordinate to men, it becomes difficult to uphold a human rights charter that simultaneously offers equality to women and safeguards the integrity of cultural traditions. Searing tensions are automatically generated for modern African women seeking to assert their constitutionally protected rights, as this goes against the tenets of the equally protected tradition. Often, to their great chagrin and embarrassment, they face the demoralizing prospects of having their rights struck down in their nations' highest courts by African judges who doggedly privilege the constitutionally protected right of "customs and traditions" over the rights of women in order to keep women in what they see as their culturally assigned roles, that is, in subjugation to men. The rulings of these African male judges have been crucial in configuring the current human rights discourse in Africa as one pitting women's individual rights against the collective right of a people (read: men) to their culture.

Of course, the ruling of the judges in cases such as *Magaya v. Magaya* suggests that African women are not really part of the culture, and so could not have a meaningful role in discussing and reforming any parts of the culture.

Their modern demands are deemed transgressive, even though women were sidelined in important conversations on the constitution of cultural norms and laws that took place over eighty year ago, conversations that treated them as social and legal minors and that resulted in their present second-class status. The present discourses on culture, then, are based on a historical, one-sided male construction of customs and cultural practices that must be re-examined. The issue of what constitutes culture and cultural practices raises the much larger question of who decides (and once decided) on which customs are privileged, and why? And, why must the rights of women be sacrificed?

Male judges in different African nations who rule for women's subjugation rationalize their rulings on the grounds that the community is always larger than the individual, and that traditions and cultural values are vital to the identity, well-being, and continuity of the community. These judges and their political supporters trivialize modern African women's insistence on the protection of their constitutional right of equality as an unacceptable commitment to the ideologies of individualism and feminism, which are characterized as antithetical to the African way of life and ill-suited to govern the distribution of power and resources within the family. Any challenge to what is perceived as "African culture" or "African values" is considered by these judges a direct threat to the vital force of African society and to what it means to be African.

The problem with this stance of male judges is that it fails to examine what we claim to be "the traditional African family" and the entitlements that accrue to members, especially given that the ideology of individualism underlies much of contemporary life and that the processes of modernization have radically reshaped and continue to reshape the very "African society" they are invested in protecting. Historical changes, of which modernization is a large part, have given rise to new forms of family relationships, new value systems, and new aspirations that were never part of precolonial societies, including the "traditional" society they constructed in the first three decades of colonization. Tensions and conflict have arisen in families between the newer and older family ideology, leading to family crises that underlie cases such as *Magaya v. Magaya*. The question that arises, then, is how do cultural proponents determine which social features are worthy of preservation as traditional and which are subject to modernization? Because discussions about the rights of women and the legal status of members of the family cannot take place without an understanding of the sociocultural nature of the specific African family under examination in different historical times, it is imperative to open up discussions on these subjects.

This book examines the modern African family and its corollary social vision in one specific region in Nigeria. It does so in light of Western feminist theorizations about the impact of the family structure on women and the impact of human rights discourse on gender equality in modern African societies.

The area of study is northwestern Igboland, which, prior to colonization and contrary to the popular beliefs of Igbo men, was a nonpatriarchal, nongendered society.[1] In the last 150 years (1854–2004), the Igbo family has undergone vast structural changes as it responded to an intense barrage of cultural forces, including the trans-Atlantic slave trade, late nineteenth-century and early twentieth-century Christian evangelism, colonialism, rapid urbanization, the ideology of individualism and its sacralization of the self, migration to other parts of Nigeria and the world, anticolonial struggles, nationalism, independence, ethnic cleansing, the Nigerian-Biafran war, and contact with various forms of family relationships worldwide. In myriad ways, these economic, social, political, and cultural forces have extensively transformed Igbo families and have shown that the notion and idea of the traditional family is a highly complicated one. In some cases, the impact of these forces resulted in the total disintegration of some family features and forms of conjugal relations, and in other cases it wrenched family relationships grotesquely out of shape. What we are left with today is nowhere close to the late nineteenth-century family structure that predated British colonialism. The questions this book addresses are, what was the impact of all these changes on women's status and their role within the family? And what was the cumulative social impact of these changing family patterns between the second half of the nineteenth century and the end of the twentieth century?

The normative model of family embodied in colonial and nationalist policies and labor relations is radically different from what existed in Igbo society. These policies completely redefined women's identity as that of wife, and produced a developmentalist discourse and a series of nationalist and postcolonial policies that supported a dependency status for wives. This study grapples with the impact of cultural change in Igboland as it studies the norms, beliefs, and ideals that regulate the lives of female and male members of the family in different historical contexts. It recognizes that there is a push-pull relationship between an idealized notion of family and real-life families. It also notes that a similar relationship exists between codified (lawyer's) customary laws and the living customs of the people and between contemporary customs and those of the late nineteenth century. As such, this book is not a study of the idealized family and codified customary laws, nor is it one that idealizes the family and present customs or makes an emotional plea for their relevance. Although it acknowledges the importance of families and customs in the political, social, economic, and emotional life of Africans, it recognizes, too, the dysfunctions of real-life families and customs, the compromises that families require of women, and the customs that regulate these compromises. This study of families broadens out to explain the social structure within which families are embedded and to articulate the sort of male-female dynamics that they define. The objective of this articulation is to raise the question of the nature of equality that exists in such a sociopolitical structure and to contrast it with the intrinsic notion of equality in Western societies—a notion privileged by feminists.

Because there is no single model of family, this book deals with different forms of family relationships, notably, the consanguineal, nuclear, mixtures of the two, polygamous, matrilineal, patrilineal, dual-descent, matrifocal, patrifocal, patriarchal, and matriarchal. A consanguineal family construes the family as composed of kin, while the nuclear treats the family as composed of a man and his wife and children. Polygamous families are made up of a male or female husband with multiple wives. A matrilineal family traces descent through the mother, while a patrilineal one traces descent through the father, and a dual-descent family traces descent through both the mother and the father. Matrifocality describes a family that is based or focused on the mother, whereas a patrifocal family is centered on the father. A patriarchal family is one in which the father has the dominant power in the family, and a matriarchal family is one in which the mother has the dominant power in the family.

In the general field of African studies and the subfield of African philosophy, very little attention is paid to families, and interest in the subject pales in comparison to interest in national politics and the political state. Questions of governance, democratization, the viability of civil society, the importance of rule of law, and the securing of people's provisions of human rights dominate the discourse. I appreciate the importance of these investigations, but I also recognize that the stability of a nation state depends on stable, functioning families. Where families are in turmoil, or displaced to refugee camps in regions of Africa that have experienced civil wars, or ravaged by HIV/AIDS, the result has been widespread post-traumatic stress disorders; collapse of some social institutions; moral meltdown; breakdown of law, order, and security; senseless violence; massive social problems; and a severely overburdened social infrastructure. Because there is a connection between family well-being and a healthy nation, and because family destabilization attacks the very foundations of societies, we ought to accord higher priority to discussions of the well-being of the African family.[2] Greater attention should, therefore, be devoted to understanding the sources of this destablization as well as the impact of contemporary global policies and adopted values on families and how these, in turn, feed social pathologies that are an anathema to good governance.

In setting the parameters of this discussion on the family and its related social vision, it is important that we do not proceed with conceptions of the African family and society that have their roots in definitions offered by early British ethnographers and anthropologists who worked within the subjugation ideology of imperialism (Basden 1966, Thomas 1913–14, Leith-Ross 1965, Green 1964, and Meek 1937). As is well known, the conceptual scheme of that ideology is antithetical to the precolonial Igbo cultural scheme, which was characterized by a different social vision that emphasized assertiveness and empowerment. As such, it is imperative that we go beyond the familial descriptions that these ethnographers produced to serve colonial objectives, and, that still inform contemporary descriptions of the Igbo family. Earlier definitions are flawed not because they were written by white men, but because they misrepresent the precolonial Igbo family. This family was not under the dominant control of men, nor was it one in which the sole duty of women was to minister to the needs of men. Early Western ethnographers, Christian missionaries, colonial anthropologists, and educationists viewed Igbo families and society through their patriarchal lens and the male-privileging value scheme of Western epistemology. Propelled by their interpretive scheme, they made patriarchy the organizing principle of the Igbo family and society and generated ethnographic descriptions that reinforced their interpretations by misrepresenting Igbo families as conjugal units. Consequently, they overemphasized the role of conjugal units, focusing on husbands as heads of households and treating daughters, sisters, and mothers as socially, politically, economically, and religiously irrelevant in the scheme of things. Perceiving all women to be dependents of male heads of households enabled them to define women's roles in terms of three principal tasks: the provision of labor, the production of children, and the provision of sexual favors for men.

Far more critical in this misrepresentation of the Igbo family as a gendered space that is governed by unequal relations of power is the methodological root of this epistemological problem and construction of society as patriarchal. Early European ethnographers, Christian missionaries, and educationists failed to recognize the ways in which their own conceptual schemes and ideological beliefs influenced their work. They did not see how their Christian beliefs about the family influenced their assumptions and interpretations about the Igbo family. Nor did they grasp the myriad ways that colonialism and colonial education pitted the interests of men against those of women in the first half of the twentieth century. These misperceptions resulted in the articulation of a static and erroneous model of Igbo family and society that ignored important relations of power, tensions, and figures of authority that fell outside the Western researchers' conceptual scheme. I hope to avoid the flaws of past studies by centering the Igbo ontological and ethical scheme, as well as the consanguineal logic of family relations, in an understanding of the political nature of the society, and the distribution of rights, duties, and entitlements in the Igbo family and society. Additionally, my study analyzes the family and society from the standpoint of multiple female members of the family, principally, that of *isi ada* (first lineage daughter), *umuada* (daughters), *ndi nne* (mothers), Ikporo Onitsha (Council of Onitsha Women), and *inyemedi* (wives). These multiple and shifting perspectives are seamlessly woven together, revealing crucial issues of family and social life and providing a kaleidoscopic picture of the family and society in their ungendered form. Within Igbo family, all consanguineal kin are treated as persons with rights and powers who are engaged in dynamic interactions with each other. This epistemological standpoint is rooted in the view that adult family members—both females and males—have agency and clearly defined rights and powers within the Igbo social universe. At the social level, this results in the formation of a symmetrical system of governance. The study's location within that universe highlights and critically integrates into theoretical discourse important features that were missing in current and early descriptions of the Igbo family and society, and also offers another way of dealing with the political issue of women's rights.

Feminist Concepts and Methodology

In the past thirty years, mainstream Western feminists have undertaken a similar task to mine, rethinking earlier descriptions of the family in Europe and the United States.[3] The objective of their project was to re-envision the family in light of capitalism, industrialization, and the First and Second World Wars—major historical events that have radically affected familial relations in numerous ways. Reflecting on the impact of these social forces on the structure of the family, white middle-class feminist theorists and philosophers have confronted the pervasive gender inequality and the limiting nature of their notion of motherhood, as well as the limited range of roles for women in the family and their society at large (Jagger 1977, Daly 1973, Okin 1989, and Pateman 1988; Thorne 1982, Nicholson 1986, Ruddick 1989, Nelson 1997, and Hansen and Garey 1998). They consequently raised fundamental questions about gender roles and family boundaries, after decomposing the family into its constituent parts of sex, gender, and generation. Focusing attention on the obvious gender-based inequality in the family, they challenged the idea of a monolithic family that privileged the nuclear family. They also began the exploration of the subjective experiences of power relations and of wives' contributions to the family (Hansen and Garey 1998, Nelson 1997, Thorne 1982 and 1992, and Okin 1989).

Speaking largely about European American families in the United States, including Western European and Jewish families, white feminist political theorist Susan Moller Okin (1997, 14) and white feminist historian Linda Gordon described the ways in which the traditional arrangement of relationships within the nuclear family are "destructive of women's equality both within the home and in all spheres of life" (Gordon 1982, 50). Driving home their point, white feminist sociologists and legal theorists pointed to the unequal power relations between the sexes and the privacy codes that allowed incest, rape, and wife battering to go unchallenged in their families. They also showed the ways in which Western family experiences are determined by gender. To their lasting credit, white feminist scholars and activists in the United States spearheaded radical reforms in the family as they sought to establish more egalitarian relationship between the spouses. The global impact of their efforts has been the profound reshaping of global family histories, the introduction of new concepts governing relations in families, and ideas about how families the world over are to be viewed. Part of the underlying objective of this study is to ascertain the relevance and applicability of some of these feminist concepts, rooted in Western social structures, to the study of African families rooted in African social structures and, in the last century, modified within the crucible of imperialism and colonial racism.[4]

So what are these concepts? A review of the writings of white feminist scholars in the United States identifies a range of concepts that were used to problematize the family. These include, but are not limited to, patriarchy, gender, individualism, sexuality, reproduction, equality, motherhood, labor, household, the public and private spheres of life, and the notion of the family as composed of "breadwinner and full-time wife." Although these concepts are used in other disciplines too, they function differently in feminist contexts than they do in nonfeminist ones, where their hidden assumptions about male-female relations are highlighted. The issue, then, is what is feminism and what makes these concepts feminist when they are appropriated by feminism?

At its core, white feminist philosopher Sarah Gamble defines feminism as a movement that seeks to change a social paradigm in which "women are treated inequitably within a society [that] is organized to prioritise male viewpoints and concerns" (2000, vii). It is a multipronged struggle against women's oppression that embodies an anti-female subordination thesis. In this struggle for personhood and empowerment, feminist scholars and philosophers deploy the identified concepts to address issues about gender in relation to the underlying distribution of power in the family in particular, and in the society at large. Their focus is on rights and power relations because they are concerned about the unequal division of labor within the family, and about who in the family possesses the dominant share of power, who is the weaker partner in the marriage and why, and who controls matters of sexuality and reproduction.

In the important essay "Is There a Feminist Method?" white feminist philosopher Sandra Harding provides a fuller discussion of what constitutes feminist methodology and practice (1989, 17–32). Although she argues against the idea that there is a method, she gives examples of how to determine that a chosen strategy is feminist. There are three key features: the utilization of gender as an analytic category of explanation, the focus on women's experiences, and the placing in full view of both the assumptions and beliefs on the same cognitive frame. The first is the most important feature of the feminist method.

Without it, a focus on women's experiences would not rise to the level required for it to be feminist. Harding observes that there are countless studies on women that are not feminist. The use of gender as an explanatory scheme elevates the discourse to the level of feminism because its built-in assumptions are calibrated to detect constructions of masculinity and femininity as well as of female oppression. It will detect any instances of sexual differentiation that are rooted in male dominance. The second feature of a feminist methodology is that it takes women's experiences as a critical resource. For Harding, this means generating "problematics from the perspective of women's experiences" and then using them "as a significant indicator of the 'reality' against which hypotheses are tested" (1989,14). The third and last feature is requiring that researchers place their beliefs and assumptions about race, class, culture, and gender within the same frame. This allows anyone to apprehend the researcher's concrete beliefs and interests in the analysis, rather than reading him or her as an invisible, anonymous, disembodied voice of authority.

The last feature is not an altogether unreasonable requirement. It is one from which any research method will benefit, as it makes it easier for reviewers to evaluate easily the strengths and weaknesses of a study. Insofar as the second feature is an argument for the legitimacy of generating research problematics from women's experiences, there is nothing theoretically wrong with the position. In fact, it would not have been identified, were it not for the fact that most research themes within the Western intellectual structure of knowledge derive from conceptual schemes that devalue women. If such devaluation were not part of standard intellectual practice, the issue would not even be raised. However, the efficacy of the first feature in ferreting out women's oppression has been both its greatest strength and the basis of its immense popularity with feminists. It is also the source of its greatest weakness. The category of gender crudely reads any instance of sex difference or social hierarchy as an instance of female oppression. It is unable to determine whether an instance of sex difference is the result of some other organizing principle than male dominance and female devaluation. Insofar as the category of gender is a legitimate response to the ideology of women's subordination embedded within Western episteme, the possibility exists that it would become redundant if the ideology of female oppression that is operative in both the cultural and epistemological scheme no longer existed, or if there were cultures that did not share that ideology.

So what if the category of gender is absent in certain cultures? Would the feminist perspective still apply in studying families in those societies? Oyèrónké Oyěwùmí has argued that the organizing principle in precolonial Oyo Yoruba culture is seniority, not gender (1997). Elsewhere, I have argued against Ifi Amadiume that the Igbo society was ungendered and that social phenomena cannot be named as patriarchal in the absence of relevant supporting structures and

practices.[5] To what extent then will the feminist perspective and related concepts apply in studying family relations in such a different cultural environment?
The feminist perspective will not straightforwardly apply as Oyewùmí argues
since feminism and feminist theory is rooted in the Western nuclear family that
is fundamentally different from African forms of family (2002, 3). Feminism, a
priori, injects patriarchy and the category of gender into cultures because its underlying standpoint presupposes the existence of unequal relations of power between males and females. Consequently, it analyzes all relations between males
and females as entailing male dominance and female subjugation. Once the
feminist methodology is applied, the society is assumed to privilege male viewpoints and concerns, and any instances of sex difference will automatically appear as instances of female subjugation.

This is not to say that questions cannot be raised about social hierarchies,
the relationships between males and females and between husbands and wives
in such cultures, or about unequal power in Igbo societies.[6] They must be raised
outside of the feminist paradigm if we are not to slide automatically back into
and engage in gender discourse. It is not always clear that feminism represents
a vision and model of society that is universally true. The mere existence of
unequal power relations such as those between father and daughter, senior son
and junior daughter, or sometimes between husbands and wives, does not prove
gender inequality. Because the focus of this study is on cultural groups, social
institutions, and principles and patterns of social organization in different historical periods in a nongendered society, the questions raised in this study will
not automatically presume the existence of male dominance. Rather, the operative cultural logic in such cultures will be elicited to provide the explanatory scheme through which family relationships, historical events and judicial
decisions will be understood.

Given that the Western intellectual scheme that defines scholarship is
imperiled by the ideology of female subjugation, there is need for caution in
discussing ungendered societies in a gendered framework. We need to be mindful that theoretical work within Western episteme would surreptitiously install
Western concepts and Western cultural dynamic into other cultures, regardless of their differences. Working within a gendered framework robs a researcher or theorist of the requisite flexibility to respond effectively to relations
that are not products of patriarchy. The epistemological challenge for this study
is to avoid the irresistible undertow of the assumptions and concepts of Western epistemology. Thus, in this study, the gender category will not dictate the
terms and trajectory of research so that other rationales and possibilities can
be uncovered. The feminist standpoint and its concepts will, however, be invoked and interrogated simultaneously when appropriate. We are mindful that
the forces of imperialism exported the ideology of patriarchy to cultures the
world over, and as a result, gender has become a legitimate category of analy-

sis for aspects of social life of formerly ungendered cultures that have made the transition into modernity. However, there are cultural remnants of ungendered times that are not susceptible to gender analysis. A culturally focused perspective is sensitive to historical changes. It attunes us to social and ideological convolutions created by the forces of colonialism and local resistance to them. The merit in this approach is that it guarantees that we adhere first to African social precepts and that we treat complex cultural configurations as central rather than as tangential to understanding. Given that some Igbo cultural institutions—the *Omu* (female monarch), the dual-symmetrical system of governance, the consanguineal family principle, and the multi-generational dispersal of power in families—are absent from the Western ontological scheme, this approach allows us to offer appropriate explanations that the feminist viewpoint and its categories cannot grasp because the truths of those ungendered institutions are outside its frame of reference. Thus, the most important reason for prudence in adopting a gender-explanatory framework of interpretation is that the possibilities the gender discourse automatically closes off will immediately open up.

Even in societies that have always been patriarchal, scholars from marginalized cultural groups have mounted devastating critiques on the explanatory scope of feminist concepts and theories because of the way white feminist theorists efface experiences that challenge their point of view. In the United States, for instance, African American scholars have demonstrated in various ways that the category of race and the ontology of racism complicate the pattern of gender relations in their minority cultural group. In some cases, race challenges the relevance of some concepts that mainstream feminists have upheld as universal. That women are restricted to the private spaces of the home while men work is not a phenomenon experienced by black and Chicano families and poor working-class white families. Attending to the cultural variance between the mainstream and black families, some African American women scholars—Patricia Hill Collins, bell hooks, Niara Sudarakasa, Elsa Barkley Brown, Evelyn Higginbotham, Angela Harris and Cheryl Harris—have narrowed the all-encompassing scope of white feminists' claims about the family.[7] The value of these interventions is that they highlight the limitations of feminist discourses and the limited scope of feminist concepts when adequate attention is paid to the categories of race, ethnicity, and culture. By exposing the fact that family experiences are racially and culturally constructed as well, they force us to see the race and class-bound nature of some of the concepts and issues of white feminism. In white, middle-class discourses about gender, the public-private dichotomy, the role of the mother, and the distribution of power among family members do not cross racial and cultural lines easily. This does not mean that the concepts lack relevance; it may be that they are totally inapplicable, or applicable in some way.

However, some African American literary writers, including Alice Walker (1986), Maya Angelou (1970), and Michelle Wallace (1990), complicate this picture of the black family as a safe haven by exposing the sexual abuses of women and the sexual molestation of children that go on therein. This exposure seems to suggest that the strategies recommended by mainstream white feminists may be applicable to black families. Although most blacks would prefer to keep these sexual problems private because of the racist barrage on black subjectivity and the racist bias of these pathologies, Walker and Angelou chose to air these secrets as an effective way of tackling the problem. Thus, while the work of the first group of scholars calls for a cautionary use of white feminist strategies, ideas, concepts, and analysis of the family, the second group of writers are insisting that white feminists' concepts and ideas are both relevant and applicable to African American families, which are embedded in the American experience. The latter group of writers is not denying the validity of the first group's insight about the distinct feature of black family experience as much as pointing out the complexity of black family relations and areas of overlap with the larger mainstream American experience.

Postcolonial Distortions in Reading the African Family

Chinua Achebe's celebrated novel *Things Fall Apart* popularized a model of traditional Igbo family as structurally similar to that described by Western feminists (1958). His formulation of the family, although located in a different cultural environment, recalls the patriarchal families against which feminists have railed. It also contradicts my contention that precolonial Igbo family was ungendered. The Okonkwo model is polygamous. It consists of an overbearing patriarch, subordinate wives, and numerous children. The family experiences of Okonkwo's wives and daughters vis-à-vis the experiences of Okonkwo and his sons were radically different. In fact, they approximated the experiences and type of relations that white, middle-class feminists identified in the nuclear family. Further making the case for patriarchy are some Igbo female writers, such as novelist Buchi Emecheta and legal scholar Uche U. Ewelukwa, who have drawn parallels between a feminist conception of the patriarchal family and the Igbo conception of family (Ewelukwa 2002, 424–486). Accepting the ideological imperative that patriarchy was endemic to Igbo society as other societies worldwide, these Igbo scholars and writers have focused on specific experiences and activities that presented the Igbo family as abusive of female members of the family, particularly wives and widows. Their works suggest that the concepts articulated by white, middle-class feminists are indeed applicable in analyzing Igbo families.

Taking a seemingly opposing view, another group of scholars, principally, Felicia Ekejiuba (1995), Amadiume (1987, 1987b), and Chikwenye Okonjo

Ogunyemi (1996), underscored the strong maternal ethos and the relationship of complementarity that exists in the traditional Igbo family. Amadiume goes much further to make a strong case for the matriarchal basis of Igbo societies in the early stages of their history and for the gender flexibility that exists therein.[8] She argues that Nnobi matriarchy was an "older system that is being intruded upon by patriarchy" (1987b, 11). This viewpoint suggests that the family experiences of Igbo women—mothers, wives, and daughters—were vastly different from those of European, European American, and Jewish women. The suggestion raises the following questions: What then is the correct conception of Igbo family? Why did the maternal pole/axis atrophy while the paternal pole/axis flourished? Why did Igbo society and family move from their historical matriarchal basis to the dominantly patriarchal forms of today? (Chapters 1 and 2 will explore these questions extensively and provide answers to the ongoing postcolonial distortions in readings of African family.)

It is worthwhile to note that in spite of their many differences, the conception of family of the two sets of women writers overlap, not just in their adoption of some feminist concepts and in their attempts to present an accurate view of the culture, but in that they take for granted the thesis that Igbo society was historically patriarchal. The injection of patriarchy into history makes male domination and women's subordination an organizing principle in Igbo societies prior to colonial rule. Thus, regardless of whether the view of family each group of writers defends is a positive or negative account, one thing is clear: the perception that Africa's "traditional past" was dominantly patriarchal prompts an analysis of Igbo societies to uncover the axis of subjugation of women. The flaw in this line of thinking is that it assumes that its description of Igbo family and society is correct. This enables theorists to set up an a priori gendered reference frame and a trajectory of analysis that ignores radical social norms and practices, the complex histories and social structures of African societies prior to and during colonization. By assuming a history and tradition of gender oppression, very well documented in colonial and missionary literature, such analyses reinforce the central idea of their starting position. The circularity in reasoning is ignored in the goal of proving that African families, like all families in other regions of the world, and as depicted in the literature, were patriarchal. The underlying goal of this line of thinking is intellectual conformity to the ideas articulated in anthropological literature as well as in the feminist framework. But how can we assume the global similarity of family systems and the Igbo family's conformity to patriarchal family dynamics prior to closely studying the Igbos' own conception of family?

Feminism has had an inordinate impact on our understanding of the family. It has offered a critical lens and a set of tools for evaluating families and societies at large. It has ensured that the study of the family focuses on the roles and positions of women in families and on the power relations between the sexes so as to eradicate gender discrimination. It has also worked to spread the "fact" of women's subjugation around the world. Meanwhile, in its evangelical mission, feminism had become a colonizing system of beliefs that sought to remake every family and every society in the image of its own. Beginning in the 1980s, a new group of white Marxist and feminist-inspired Africanist women scholars emerged and explained the modern economic dependency and subjugation of African women on the indigenous structures of inequality embedded in African traditions.[9] For them, scholarship on Africa must recognize the oppressive nature of African tradition as well as the fact "that sexism is indigenous as well as imposed" (Robertson 1987, 123). But where is the historical and cultural evidence for this gender oppressiveness of African tradition? The evidence was provided by European imperialism; it was contained in a corpus of ethnographic materials that were used to justify colonial domination.

Scholars who have a facile appreciation of the pernicious, deep-seated nature of colonialism and of the core tenets of patriarchy risk importing the underlying assumptions and prejudices of their Western epistemological scheme into their data collection and interpretation of African culture. Because of the surreptitious ways the assumptions of their epistemological scheme operate, it is absolutely essential that we engage that scheme, the feminist method, and the colonial ethnographic literature with a critical mind. A less-than-critical stance will result (and has resulted) in the insertion of patriarchal relations and feminist concepts into African culture during a period when patriarchy did not exist in our region of study. The high prevalence of the feminist method's misuse and the unquestioning reliance on colonial ethnographic literature has resulted in one of the modern myths of Africa, which is that the traditional Igbo family was patriarchal. Responding to the seductive pull and believability of these myths, scholars—both African and nonAfrican—freely invoke the concepts of patriarchy and gender in their work and project them further back into Igbo history, through discourses that devote only cursory attention to cultural histories and social structures. In the process, as various chapters of this book will show, they generate specious traditions that end up erasing communities' histories as well as material evidence of women's social autonomy in the past.

Exploiting the Concept of Tradition

African philosophy of culture is concerned with the sum total of a people's ways of living, histories, conventions, and practices that have been passed on from generation to generation and that endow them with a distinctive character. This means we have to consider social institutions at different points in time, including the changes produced during and after the colonial period. We need to be mindful that the dialectics of modernity speak about change and traditions in convoluted ways, and that references to tradition are sometimes projections of the present unto the past, projections designed to compel a particular type of action or mark a behavior as authentic. As will be discussed in chapters 2 and 3, certain "traditions" of male privilege were legislated and subsequently produced in order to bring Igbo society in line with European norms.[10] Meanwhile, Igbo traditions of women's autonomy and assertiveness were simultaneously inverted so that referencing them now attracts dismissive comments about their being foreign, as well as feminist in nature.

Historically, the Igbo social structure and philosophical scheme expose the error of presuming that the society is patriarchal. Prior to colonialism, numerous northwestern Igbo communities possessed dual-sex systems in which there were separate political lines of governance for men and women. This separation between the sexes did not imply the exaggeration of differences, a suppression of similarities, the superordinate status of one sex over the other, or the creation of irresolvable conflict between the sexes. Rather the political division of duties and tasks seemed designed to make men and women interdependent. Because sociopolitical powers were assigned to each group, each group required the assistance and collaboration of the other. The relationship between the groups was symmetrical, although within each group it was organized asymmetrically. Owing to the symmetry of the structure, men's interests could not undermine women's interests, proving that men did not have the rights anthropologists and feminists attributed to them.

Igbo family histories and social practices also expose the falsity of constructing Igbo families as exclusively privileging men's interests and concerns. Ekejiuba described practices that her maternal aunt utilized to recharge her life and expand her hearth-hold after a failed childless marriage (1995). Supported by members of her consanguineal family, both male and female, she had a child in an *idigbe* relationship in which she did not marry her male paramour so she retained custody of all the children of the union who became members of her own lineage. To expand her family, the aunt also had children from wives whom she had married in woman–woman marriages. It is important to stress that the institution of *idigbe* and woman–woman marriages entailed a panoply of rights that are inconsistent with the patriarchal paradigm. Besides, a family organizational principle that encourages *idigbe* relationships and woman–woman marriage could not have been patriarchal. Patriarchy is not complementary to or supportive of models of spousal unions that do not privilege the dominance of men. As the 1934 study of Margaret M. Green attests, Igbo societies were not the male-dominant enclaves that contemporary scholars have made them out to be. (How women's subordination was avoided is taken up in chapter 1.) Even though colonial rule had deployed Western gender attitudes in present-day Igboland, the societies did not immediately transform into patriarchal societies. The transformation was gradual and systematic, occurring at both the conscious and unconscious levels, and in both public and private sectors of the people's lives.

During the period of colonial rule, patriarchal traditions were created by the colonial administration and Christian missions. Over the course of forty years and more, the post-World War II generation of educated Igbo elites increasingly aspired to and embraced the patriarchal nuclear family model as the modern, civilized, and progressive model of family. As products of Christian mission schools and Western higher education, these elites adopted the patriarchal ideology inherent in the Western educational systems because of the advantages they believed it conferred on them. Husbands and wives worked assiduously to bring their family in line with it. As this patriarchal structure of family was inserted into the Igbo culture with its strong matricentric ideology, a force of erasure was activated that, over time, expunged an array of daughters', mothers' and wives' tasks, duties, rights, and positions that had secured the autonomy of women. The progression of this erasure and the corollary devaluation of women that followed subsequently led to the rise of reactionary attitudes towards women. By the 1970s, a new generation of women and men had arisen who seemed unaware of the older matricentric ideology that had prevailed in Igboland prior to colonial rule. Because this new generation grew up in Christian homes that were committed to patriarchal values, both men and women learned that the husband is the pre-eminent figure in the household and that the prime duty of wives is to do whatever is necessary to make life comfortable for husbands.

The modern political economy of Nigeria, which privileges the nuclear family model, has difficulty integrating the lingering elements of indigenous consanguineal ideology of kinship that prevailed prior to colonialism. This new political economy and its labor market treat the nuclear family as the basic family unit for all development planning purposes (Fapohunda 1987, 283–287), even as individuals romantically continue to insist on the social priority of kin ties of the traditional African family. Yet, ever since the Christian mission arrived in Onitsha in 1857 and colonialism by 1892, neither the Igbo family ideology nor the Igbo family itself has been the same.

This focus on the nature of the family is dictated by five compelling factors. The first is the prevailing view that Igbo families retained their traditional character and remained authentically African even after the infusion of salient European cultural values. The second is the standard assumption that colonialism and its nuclear model of family created libratory spaces for women. The third is the realization that a combination of colonial and postcolonial marriage policies and Christian marital norms have injected nuclear family values into the culture that are in serious conflict with the indigenous lineage structure of family and the social structures that support it. The fourth factor is the awareness that the prevalent intra-family feuds in varied parts of contemporary Africa and Igboland demand serious investigation, since they are the result of competing family systems in the throes of decomposing, reconstituting, and recomposing elements of their structures. The last is the dubious use of tradition to confer legitimacy on a family model that is rooted in European family ideology and that is especially discriminatory towards women.

The dichotomy between family as defined by nuclear family ideology and family as defined by kinship ideology raises questions about what many assume to be the traditional Igbo family. In taking the Okonkwo model of family as quintessentially Igbo, we miss the fact that other models of family and conjugal units existed, including consanguineal families, woman–woman families, matrilineal families, and dual-descent families. Not only was the Okonkwo model not universal; it was also not traditional. Colonial and contemporary experiences of the state and religiously instituted patriarchal family values blind us to the ways in which the Okonkwo model contravenes the indigenous principle of Igbo family organization. In fact, the central principle of the Okonkwo family most closely resembles the pater familias principle of the nuclear family, save for its polygamous character. In contrast, the traditional Igbo family was primarily consanguineal, based on kinship relations with powers dispersed among members in a hierarchical order. Family heads lacked the sort of jural mandate and autocratic power that characterized nuclear families and that Okonkwo freely displayed. Within this consanguineal model, the "family" is synonymous with kin who do not co-reside, rather than with conjugal units. The so-called traditional Igbo family of Okonkwo does not conform to the dictates of the consanguineal model. It is essentially a conjugal unit in which there are no male or female kin whatsoever. The absence of kin and its demand for proper behavior from members exposes the family as a version of the Christian family that is found in communities set up by converts after separating from their families upon conversion to Christianity. Only in such an environment did Igbo families exist without kin.

Critical examination of families is important given the radical changes Igbo families have undergone. With the introduction of nuclear-family ideology into Igboland, the once prevalent consanguineal ties began to erode. The new ideology increasingly replaced longstanding Igbo family values with nuclear family values, resulting in fundamental changes in the power relations and the distribution of family resources—mainly land, farmland, and homestead. The new family values were based on an ideology of permanent union between a husband and wife, which forced the displacement of the lineage as the central structure of family. For various reasons, the post–World War II reality created a sociopolitical context in which generations of Christianized Igbo males opted for the nuclear-family model of marriage that collapsed women's identity to that of wife and assigned a dependent status for them. Privileging the nuclear model had far-reaching, unintended consequences. It cre-

ated a range of insecurities and pathologies for wives, such as alienation, disenfranchisement, and loss of self-esteem, which the statutory marriage and probate laws did nothing to address. It also narrowed the range of conjugal unions
that had existed such as *idigbe* (in which the children of the couple belong to
the female partner), woman–woman monogamous and polygamous marriages,
men's polygynous marriages, infant son and adult woman marriages, and
girl–man marriages, which have all but died out. Those that still exist do so in
attenuated forms.

Despite these changes, one would not realize that substantial modifications of family relations have taken place, to hear some Igbo men hold forth
unreflectingly about the enduring nature of "our culture and traditions." This
mostly occurs when daughters, wives, and women in general assert their rights.
It is clear that on such occasions, the term "traditional" is being invoked to
modify women's behavior. On closer inspection, however, what is being represented as traditional are patterns of behavior that actually derive from the
Christian ethical scheme that missionaries and teachers utilized to regulate
the lives of these men. Confusing these Christian values with the traditional
Igbo values they had rejected, husbands and fathers typically appeal to false
traditions to justify autocratic powers in the home and their egregious abuses
of wives. In this duplicitous manner, traditions were invented to rationalize
and authorize patriarchal relations of power that served to enhance the interests of men.

Family as a Nexus of Contestation

It is ironic that the historical changes that produced the modern Igbo family
have created a convergence of interests between Igbo men and Western feminists. Although philosophically opposed to each other, both share the central
assumption that the African family in general, and the Igbo family in particular, have always been male dominated. Both are engaged in the enterprise of
casting their patriarchal view of families as traditional and culturally rooted.
Both share the task of representing African women as voiceless and inferior to
men. Both have successfully established as true the myth that African women
lack agency. This book is consequently organized around a series of intercon-
nected arguments addressing and exposing the flaws of this shared misconcep-
tion. It begins by treating the family as a nexus of contestation of cultural forces
of change. Without attempting to present a chronological account of family
development, it examines the evolutionary moments of change that transformed the Igbo family in inherent ways.

Recognizing the strong maternal ethos of Igbo families, chapter 1 explores the form of Igbo family structure in the northwestern corner of Igboland
prior to colonization. It exposes the unwarranted conflation of patriliny and

patriarchy as well as the belief that the family is coterminous with the household. If patriliny is not equivalent to patriarchy, and patriarchy is not the organizing principle of the Igbo family, then it is crucial to consider how powers and responsibilities among consanguineal kins diffuse laterally and vertically across generational lines. By understanding the constituent parts of the Igbo family and centering the ideology of motherhood, we are able to see the understated sources of power and channels of influence of Igbo women. In the past, the convergence of these channels on the mother had checked the development of patriarchal force by significantly curtailing the rights of fathers and husbands over daughters and wives.

The colonial experience initiated the transformation of the Igbo family system into a patriarchal one. Focusing on the provincial and native courts of southeastern Nigeria, chapter 2 explores the processes involved in the creation of patriarchy in Igboland between 1890 and 1940. It attends to how the court system collected and codified a body of laws that constituted the customary laws of Eastern Nigeria. By critically re-reading the oral and written histories of Igbo women, we explicate the impact of these colonial laws, edicts, legal policies, and judicial institutions on the character of Igbo families and Igbo societies in the first quarter of the twentieth century. The objective is to understand the impact of colonial legal policies and ideology on families, especially on the status, roles, and experiences of female members of the family. How far did the collected body of "customary laws" reflect the family ideology and the traditional laws of Igbo societies rather than the family ideology deployed by the colonial state? This question helps to ascertain in what manner the native courts reconstituted women as individuals and brought them into the legal scheme and the sphere of humanity.

If, as is widely accepted, the colonial administration did not recognize the existence of "native" women and made them invisible, then how and when did they incorporate them and their rights into the legal codes? The central contention of chapter 3 is that European colonialism empowered African men to turn the nongendered Igbo cultural landscape into a gendered one, making it appropriate for the utilization of feminist concepts. It focuses on the way the male-privileging customary laws continued to institutionalize the rights of men through the judicial system of postcolonial Nigeria. With special attention devoted to widowhood and the politics of inheritance, I highlight the systemic ways wives and daughters were forced to give up their rights. Family transformation steadily occurred as the precept of gender subordination worked its way through the judicial system. Because of the complex way in which such disenfranchisement occurred, I utilize two judgments, *Nzegwu v. Nzegwus* (1986), and *Nzegwus v. Nzegwu* (1997), to expose how the judicial system facilitated the creation of gender inequality. The investigation highlights the long-term effects of these male-privileging judicial precepts and their creation of dysfunctional modern family relations that are inherently prejudicial to women's long-term interests.

Because discussions in the preceding chapters allude to but do not fully explicate the emancipatory elements of the nongendered Igbo social scheme, chapter 4 undertakes an extensive examination of Onitsha sociopolitical structure in light of feminist conceptions of equality, patriarchy, sexuality, marital relations, power, and women's identity. It does so by means of a docu-drama that sets up a conversation between the Omu (female monarch) and her counselors on the one hand, and Simone de Beauvoir, Germaine Greer, and Helen Henderson on the other. The dialogue highlights the main grounds of difference between female identity in the nongendered Onitsha dual-sex sociopolitical system and female identity in the gendered European mono-sex sociopolitical system. The dialogue is projected back in time to achieve the recovery of a dual-symmetrical conception of equality and to contrast it with one that is explicated from a mono-sex system. The dialogic process facilitates the exposure of tacit assumptions about women, their roles and statuses, and the invisible expectations of each of the socio-political systems.

Underlying most feminist gender analyses is a hidden social ideal of equality that regulates and shapes the direction of research and seeks the elimination of women's subjugation. On closer inspection, one finds that the prevailing notion of equality in these contexts is informed by the mono-sex character of Western political systems. Drawing insights from the docu-drama, chapter 5 examines the conceptions of equality in two sociopolitical systems. The first is the mono-sex system in which biological sex is putatively ignored even though it fundamentally regulates the society along male privileging lines, and the second is the dual-sex system in which biological sex is recognized but does not affect the social valuation of human worth. The dual-sex system challenges the idea that sexual division of labor implies women's subjugation or patriarchy, instead it provides a robust conception of equality that rests on duty and responsibility. By contrast, the mono-sex system provides a conception of equality that does not combat sexist oppression because it embodies an individualistic conception of equality that does not provide much emancipatory potential for the individual. Noting that true equality can be attained when a society is ungendered, I advance a conception of rights that recognizes sex groups in ways that equalize the power relations between women and men. I conclude by testing the efficacy of this group-based notion of rights in the United States.

In concluding, I contend that the emergence of a healthy Igbo culture and political philosophy will require breaking down reactionary dogmas that have arisen in response to the colonially imposed patriarchal structure. Igboland today is imperiled by a culture of violence, brutality, political excesses, and gargantuan social problems. These problems call for imaginatively rethinking the very foundation of the society, and ridding it of fictive traditions and ideologies that forced women to adopt a diminished worldview.[11] Once we know that fictive traditions reinforced the prevailing anti-female ideology in the culture, we need not hold onto reactionary principles and specious traditions.

1

Family Politics

Making Patriarchy in a Patrilineal Society

I must confess that women are not deprived of their rightful status
in society, nor, as in other tribes, doomed to perpetual degradation.
—S. Crowther and J. C. Taylor, *The Gospel on the Banks of the
Niger* (1895)

Among the Egbos, women hold a very superior rank in the social
scale; they are not regarded, as among other tribes as an inferior
creation and doomed to perpetual degradation, but occupy their
"rightful status in society."
—Africanus Horton, *Black Nationalism in Africa 1867* (1969)

Allowing for slight local variations, Onitsha and many northwestern Igbo
communities have been presented in ethnographic literature as having patrilineal forms of family organization and virilocal forms of marriage. By patrilineal, I mean descent through the line of fathers, and by virilocal, the practice of spouses residing with a husband's family. The fact that in these societies
descent is reckoned through the line of fathers led early British ethnographers
G. T. Basden and Northcote E. Thomas, as well as later ones such as C. K.
Meek, to represent the societies as patriarchal.[1] Epistemologically, their
representations rested on the assumption that if paternity was at the center
of kinship formation, then the social and family system must be one in which
fathers (men) were the most dominant members of the family. This conclusion, of course, contradicts Cheikh Anta Diop's contention and Ifi Amadiume's demonstration that matriarchy was the distinguishing feature of African
societies historically and was what separated it from European societies and
families.[2]

23

Thomas, Basden, and Meek's ethnographical representations would be true were it not for the fact that their epistemic schemes derived from and are lodged within a patriarchal framework. That framework treats a wife as incorporated and consolidated into the personhood of her husband, who is her lord and master. As Amadiume rightly noted, "European anthropologists were misled by their own ethnocentrism into insisting on a general theory of male dominance in all descent groups" (1997, 80). There is no question that the Western explanatory system fundamentally influenced the ethnographers' observation of the dominance of fathers, and inevitably reinforced their interpretation that fathers were the rulers of families. In recording what they saw, these early chroniclers of Igbo culture consistently privileged men's experiences, completely respected men's voices and opinions, and methodically interpreted the world through their male-privileging lenses. In neglecting to consider the epistemological consequences of their conceptual framework and the manner in which it may have dictated their research choices and trajectory of investigation, they accepted the veracity of their countless nameless male informants, and pronounced upon the subjugated status of women. But as R. S. Rattray discovered years after his research on the Asante Empire, his acceptance of women's irrelevance, notably the irrelevance of the Asantehemaa, marred his research. Unbeknownst to him, his local male informants were aware that the white man considered women to be inconsequential, and so narrowly tailored their responses to accord with the female dismissive spirit of his questions. This self-administered editing of informants also served to reinforce Rattray's underlying gender assumptions by paradoxically providing for him the natives' own confirmation of the ethnographic "evidence" he desired.[3]

In numerous imperceptible ways, the female-devaluing readings continued as Christian missionary ethnographers and colonial social anthropologists used their own male-privileging epistemic scheme and conjugal models to understand the natives they encountered. Although they took for granted the superiority of the British family system, they nevertheless assumed that fatherhood and motherhood were generic concepts with stable meaning across cultures. Not surprisingly, the single most important difference in their account was that the Igbos were at a more primitive level of development than Europeans and that their notion of parenthood was much more unrefined and crudely drawn. The idea that paternity or paternal relations might not imply patriarchy was not an intelligible one within their epistemic frame. The conception of fatherhood informing the views of early British ethnographers at the turn of the twentieth century was predicated on women's subjection to men and on private property relations. Rooted in the Victorian ideology of late nineteenth-century England, this view of subjection is modeled on the doctrine of coverture that stipulates a wife is completely subject to and the property of her husband. To be an Igbo father then was to be a husband whom

Thomas claims "has considerable power over his wife" (1913–14, 69). Writing about Igbo marital relations, Archdeacon Basden, a Christian Mission Society (CMS) missionary, states that "[a]fter marriage the woman is ranked with the other property of the husband with a proportionate value attached, but little greater than that of the cows and goats" (1966, 69). Meek, a colonial government anthropologist, affirms this view of Igbo wives as property. He states: "There is little doubt that many Ibo husbands do, in fact, regard their wives as, to some extent, a form of property which they can treat as they please" (1937, 279). To secure the validity of their perception, customs were graphically described to conform with and reinforce patriarchal intuitions about native societies. By contrast, the customs that seemed to undermine the thesis of male dominance were either ignored, summarily acknowledged in abrupt ways, or reinterpreted to accord with the patriarchal presumptions of their explanatory scheme.

The ethnographers' correlation of patriliny with patriarchy raises questions about whether or not societies are patriarchal simply because they are patrilineal. The correlation does not provide a forum for explaining the existence of practices such as *idigbe* and woman–woman marriages that are oppositional to patriarchal relations. When such anomalous practices are encountered and theoretically acknowledged, they undermine the legitimacy of the description of Igbo kinship patterns as exclusively patrilineal and fundamentally patriarchal. They also challenged the validity of Western and African feminist claims as well as contemporary Igbo men's assumption that Igbo societies were patriarchal prior to colonialism.[4] The possibility of this falsification raises a number of interesting questions such as whether or not the principle of family organization may be other than patriarchal. If so, what is this principle that disrupts the formation of patriarchal relations? Is it motherhood, as Diop and Amadiume hypothesized? What is the status of mothers in Igbo societies, and what does the prevailing conception of motherhood tell us about family organization? If descent through the father's line does not exclude the offspring of daughters, can such a family still be patriarchal? Is it possible that Igbo societies might not be patriarchal given that the epistemological contour of patriarchy does not overlap with patriliny? If Igbo societies were not patriarchal, as feminists assume, then although patriliny may be a necessary condition for patriarchy, the reverse is not exactly true. How then do we understand Igbo societies?

Challenged by these questions, we will examine, in this chapter, the historical period between 1890 and 1930, during which time matrifocality and the maternal principle in families were downgraded and patrifocality and the idea of fathers as rulers gained ascendancy. I shall argue that prior to colonial tinkering, Igbo society lacked patriarchal features and was not exactly patrilineal. Using the perspective of *isi ada* (senior lineage daughters) and the concept of motherhood, I establish that the necessary conditions required for the transformation of the society into a patriarchal one did not exist. Although fathers were a vital part of Igbo family life, the Igbo concept of paternity and its structure of family relations did not embody the conditions and powers that would have made them patriarchal. Fundamentally social, the Igbo notion of kinship as consanguineal overshadowed the principle of conjugality that governed members' personal life. The family was not the conjugal unit but the kin group. In the late nineteenth century, social roles and ideology shaped kinship relations within which families were situated, and our understanding of familial relationships and social organizations must accurately reflect that fact. After setting the conceptual parameter in part 1, I will clarify the character of Igbo family so as to lay bare the complex diffusion of power in Igbo families that defines the family as nonpatriarchal. In part 2 I will reconceptualize the two conceptions of fatherhood and wifehood in light of the dynamics of the northeastern Igbo family. In part 3 I will examine in detail the role of motherhood in defining a different social dynamic as well as how the idea of mother's social dominance undermines the early British ethnographers' own theses. I will conclude by considering how patriarchal thinking reconstitutes the northeastern Igbo family and society.

Setting the Conceptual Parameter

Clear terminology is important in setting the stage if we are to avoid past epistemological errors of mischaracterizing families and collapsing patriliny into patriarchy. "Patriliny," a widely used term given ample explication in social anthropology, refers to a system of family organization in which descent is traced through the father. This descent may be traced on the basis of biological fatherhood or genetic blood ties, so that all descendants are progeny of the same ancestor or father. This definition of patriliny draws from a notion of family in which fatherhood is conceived of as a biological act, and biological descent is the determinant factor in genealogical reconstruction. Although this is the prevailing definition in the field of African studies, it contrasts with the Igbo notion of fatherhood which emphasizes the social nature of kinship ties rather than the biological nature of ties between fathers and children. This will be explained in due course.

It is useful to make a crucial distinction between patriliny as a form of family organization and patriarchy as the locus of power in families. "Patriliny" does not really identify the locus of power in families because there are different conceptions of father and different patterns of power distribution in families. "Patriarchy," on the other hand, assigns power to fathers and describes a family with one dominant center of power. It bestows exclusive authority in fathers and fosters a social organizational scheme that treats men-as-a-group as having power and rights over women-as-a-group (Lerner 1986, 212). Under patriarchy, women's sexual and reproductive capacities are commodified and controlled by men, and whatever privileges or power women have is dependent on their singular attachments to men (1986, 213–214). Clearly, women lack autonomy within a patriarchal system, and as Lerner points out, even when property relations within the family have developed "along egalitarian lines than those in which the father wields absolute power," the public realm of institutions and government are still structured by male dominance (1986, 216–17). For Lerner, patriarchy is the manifestation and institutionalization of male dominance over women and children in the family and the extension of male dominance in society in general.

Other feminist analysts of patriarchy agree that the single most determinant feature of the system is its culture of male domination. Sylvia Walby sees patriarchy as a system of social structures and practices in which men dominate, oppress, and exploit women (1990, 20). She argues that construing patriarchy as a "social structure" undermines the supposition that every individual man must be in a dominant position and every woman in a subordinate one. She contends that it is immaterial that some men lack power and some women have power, because patriarchy is not a thesis about the social location of individual men and women. It is one in which men as a group are uniquely privileged and women as a group are distinctively disadvantaged.

In her own contribution, Carole Pateman cautions against understanding patriarchy as paternal right, since this literal interpretation misses the other dimensions of that system of power and male domination (1991, 54). She states that the modern variant relocates the basis of men's rights from the family to the political arena of civil society and the state (1991, 59). Modern patriarchy is based on contractual, not natural relations that uphold a masculine right rather than a father's right (1991, 59). This sexual basis of the contract positions men and women in superordinate and subordinate positions based on a system of male domination. At the family level, the system requires husbands to provide protection and access to property to passive, dependent wives who, in turn, consent to provide sexual and housekeeping services to husbands. The personal sexual nature of this contract, agreed upon in and governing the private realm of men's lives, established the doctrine of coverture that limited women's roles and creative powers to private domestic space.

Even if we accept all these refinements and the idea that there are different historical and cultural variants of patriarchy, the question remains, as to whether Igbo society at the turn of the twentieth century was a patriarchal society with a society-wide system of male domination, as the feminist viewpoint states? Did it possess the features of a patriarchal society? I argue that it did not. At the family level, which is the focus of this examination, we will find that its family system of organization together with its extensive diffusion of rights,

powers, and obligation between the sexes is antithetical to the sorts of familial and societal relations that patriarchy prescribed. Indeed, to be a patriarchal
system, the Igbo patrilineal system required an additional set of practices, customs, moral schemes, and structures about power and control. The four key required system-wide features are, first, the concentration of powers in the hands
of men over women as a group; second, the division of a society into public and
private spaces and the restriction of women to the private space of the home;
third, the domestication and exploitation of women, including the control of
their sexual and reproductive powers; and last, the systemic devaluation of
women. These features were absent in Igbo societies prior to colonization. In
the face of massive female opposition, all four features were subsequently injected into Igboland through missionary activities, colonial administration,
and education. The fact that women opposed the ensuing changes is proof that
these features were not an intrinsic part of the culture.[5]

PART 1: THE CHARACTER OF THE IGBO FAMILY

Archeological Excavations: Recovering the Slave Trade History

Aware that misdescriptions arise when one adheres too closely to standard anthropological viewpoints about African societies and families, critical scholars
have called for a radical rethinking of the theoretical framework within which
scholarship on Africa is conducted. Nigerian sociologist Peter P. Ekeh charges
that kinship terms and categories are imprecisely defined in African studies.[6]
He argued that early social anthropologists tended to deploy terms without
"historical examination of societies to ascertain the nature and character of
kinship" (1990, 669). Treating "kinship as constant over time in African societies," these theorists rarely probed "how long it has been in existence, why it
was so dominant in Africa, or whether it was related to the slave trade that ravaged Africa before European colonization" (1990, 669). Ekeh's point is that in
a bid to advance the professional legitimacy of anthropology and to secure the
goals of colonialism, early social anthropologists failed to attend to the specific
logic of African family systems.[7] Once they laid the theoretical bedrock, future
generations of ethnographers built on those foundations without closely examining the assumptions, presuppositions, and conceptual framework on which
their theories were based. The result has been that the categories of kinship articulated by the pioneers of the discipline and their successors have raised practical and theoretical problems for understanding African families.

Before we begin an analysis of the character of Igbo family, we must explicate the type of family that existed in the late nineteenth and early twentieth centuries, before Christianity and the policies of the British colonial ad-

ministration wrought their changes. The explication will enable us circumvent the problem of mistaking an ideological model of family for a social one. Early in the nineteenth century, the trans-Atlantic slave trade had created a turbulent region marked by incessant kidnappings, Igala- and Aro-engineered slave raids, vast movements of people fleeing the raids in search of refuge, and families' heroic efforts to cope with the devastating disappearances of family members.[8] Even though the trans-Atlantic European slave trade officially ended in 1802, the trade still continued unofficially until the end of the century, when the British naval blockade curtailed the activities of other European slavers. Elizabeth Isichei noted that the internal trade in slaves continued because its internal structures were not dismantled (1973, 62–63). Because the process by which captives were procured were by raiding and kidnapping, a state of siege pervaded Igboland. Recognition of this infamous history compels us to attend to the deep psychological scars and extensive social chaos that defined the trade. We have to recognize that the slave trade corrupted social practices, coarsened human sensibilities, and marked a sharp dichotomy between the more peaceful pre-slavery period in which Igbo men and women freely moved around to establish communities[9] and the slavery period that was marked by fear, moral turpitude, and the devaluation of human life. Awareness of this sharp historical divide requires that we examine the strategies adopted by families to deal with an unending attack on their existence.[10] At the very least, such an examination forces us to avoid treating the "olden days" as idyllic, or of reading the present history of social stability and Christianized, patriarchal values back into a chaotic, turbulent period of history.

Historical attentiveness would help us avoid misconstruing families as static and unchanging when improvization and adaptation were the two dominant principles that families had to deploy to survive. Viewing families as dynamic systems enables us to integrate the nature of Igbo response to the two centuries-long period of regional threat, suspicion, and fear. Igbo families were not the static, cohesive, male-dominant systems early European and modern Igbo male writers have represented in the literature. They were dynamic organizations that ingeniously devised strategies of survival to respond to the protracted period of slavery. In the process, they radically modified their structures in myriad ways to survive. From the late eighteenth century, Igbo families in northwestern Igboland fought for their survival as the Aboh, Igala and Aros expanded their riverine and internal trade in slaves until they were forcibly halted in 1929. From late nineteenth century, they also fought against economic exploitation by rogue free traders and officials of the Royal Niger Company, and in some areas, they endured naval bombardment and military campaigns. Between 1890 and 1920, families were caught in the grip of two opposing economies—the internal slave trade and the oil palm trade. They had to live with two very conflicting demands, and so they devised creative ways to cope with these disruptive events the best way they could. In some communities, families responded to the depopulation of their numbers by socially encouraging and privileging high birth rates, while others boosted their numbers and continued their line by absorbing children and adults whom they had purchased in slave marts. Many communities and families also assimilated adult immigrants (*nnatambili*) who settled with them and continued to do so as late as 1950s. In other cases, small families merged with other families when numbers dropped precipitously, and sometimes entire communities moved to merge with bigger or better-armed neighbors.[11]

The assimilation of immigrants entailed resettlement on other communities' and other families' land. These resettlements occurred without "undermining the very foundations of indigenous socio-political organization and kinship solidarity," as S. N. Obi had misleadingly insisted would happen if a daughter's son and husband were to inherit from her family (1966, 74). The reason why no such foundational erosions occurred was that prior to colonialism, land had not acquired commercial value, as historian A. Adu Boahen noted, and families were not committed to excising daughters from their families as they do today (1987,100). Prominent and wealthy families of the period were made up of immigrants, domestic servants, and slaves, as well as *nwa afo* (child of the womb) who were part of the direct line of descent.[12] Over time these various annexes fused to become part of the host's family, village, or ward. Communities that merged with others shared their hosts' narratives of origin, their history, and their identity. This was very much so in Onitsha, where the Egbema, Aboh, Igala, Akpoto, Ikem-Nando, Ogidi, Ozubulu, and Ojoto immigrants merged into and became Onitsha indigenes. The importance of this assimilationist history is its epistemological impact on the notion of kinship. It created a socially constructed notion of kinship as families repaired the physical and psychic assaults in their lives. They created a semblance of normalcy and stability through social kinship ties that were seemingly modeled on biological ties to give meaning to their newly constructed interpersonal relationships. The emergence of these types of families gave a new meaning to consanguinity or kinship.

The Logic of Consanguinity

From 1850 to 1940, the dominant family principle in northwestern Igbo was consanguinity. The family was a consanguineally based, complex, multigenerational lineage system made up of agnatic kins. The minimal lineage is often referred to in anthropologically inspired texts such as Obi's *Modern Family Law in Southern Nigeria* as the extended family. This raises the question of what they are extended from. George Peter Murdock, who first articulated the terms "nuclear" and "extended" families, stated that the extension is predicated on the

nuclear family, which in his view was the elementary, most basic form of family (1949).[13] This implies that any construal of the traditional Igbo family on
the nuclear model collapses the discussion into the Western ontological
scheme that treats a husband, wife, and children as the normative structure of
families. But construing the late nineteenth-century northwestern Igbo families as extensions of, or deviations from, the Western nuclear family imposes
conjugality as the dominant principle of family organization, even though the
Igbo conception of family is fundamentally a social constructivist model of
consanguinity. Equally, too, privileging conjugality as the norm for family relations, as some Igbo scholars have done, misconstrues the peculiar nature of
the Igbo family system and imposes an inappropriate logic upon it. Insofar as
late nineteenth-century Igbo families in the northwestern region were formed
from consanguineal kin groups, all matters about conjugality or derivations
from conjugal unions, such as nuclear or polygamous family, male or female
husbands, or subordinate wife or dominant husband/fathers, should recede to
the background.

   Discussions of the Igbo family must be conducted on its own terms. These
should occur outside of the regulatory principles of the nuclear family and of
conjugality that the twentieth-century Western episteme upholds as the standard for any discourse on family. Serious discussions of Igbo family systems cannot presuppose or continue to draw upon a standard that imposes patriarchal
tendencies into the society being studied. Critical researchers cannot simply
interrogate history and recover facts; they must subject the recovered facts and
the operative concepts and principles of their epistemological scheme to critical analysis as well. When this happens, they will find that they have to avoid
treating the conjugal unit as the basic form of Igbo family.[14] They will have to
initiate a discourse that centers the principle of consanguinity as the operative
principle for analyzing the Igbo family.

   Once the consanguineal logic of family descent is given epistemic priority in understanding Onitsha and northwestern Igbo families, two parallel lines
of kin immediately emerge into focus. These are the line of *umuada* (daugh-
ters/sisters) and the line of *umu okpala* (sons/brothers). At the head of the sororal or female line is *isi ada* (first-lineage daughter), and *di okpala* (first-lineage
son) is the head of the male fraternal line. Descending in a hierarchal order are
a multitude of generational nodal points among which are *umunna* (all adult
children of the lineage), *umuada* (all adult lineage daughters who may or may
not live within the family compounds), *okpala* (adult lineage sons), *umu agbo*
(young unmarried girls), *umu ikolobia* (young unmarried boys), and *umu aro*
(little children). Within this dual/symmetrical family system, power, duties,
and responsibilities radiate out along multiple intersecting paths, coalescing
along seniority lines. As heads of the family, *isi ada* and *di okpala* were consulted
and their approval secured in matters affecting the family. The assumption that

the traditional Igbo family was politically male dominant is wrong. The Igbo consanguineal family system did not assign power to fathers and husbands exclusively. It was not a homosocial, masculinist space. The voices of *umuada* carried weight because their line was a constitutive part of the family sociopolitical structure. [I will intermittently use the Igbo word *ada* (singular of *umuada*) rather than daughters and sisters or daughters/sisters because it best captures the culture's conception of a daughter with its implicit connotation of a sister].

Adhering to the logic of consanguinity, we will find that prior to Christianization, Westernization, and the colonial injection of patriarchal ethos, the Igbo family was the sum total of siblings born into the family/lineage. This family or lineage may have either a father or a mother as the dominant ancestor. Where the father was the dominant ancestor, the siblings were known as *umunna*, and where the mother is the dominant *ancestor*, they were known as *umunne*. Within either of the lineages, all agnatic kin or in-group members were *nwanne* (a gender neutral term that means "child of the mother"). Kin referred to themselves as *nwanne*, even though they had different mothers and sometimes different fathers. Some of them were the children of unmarried adult daughters and others were the children of women whom the sons had married. Linguistically, the terms "sister," "brother," "aunt," "uncle," "niece," "nephew," and "cousin," as well as the relational family separation they defined, did not exist in Igbo language and society. Structurally, there were just two kinds of kinship categories: sons (*okpala*) and daughters (*ada*). These categories created a fraternal and sororal form of family administration in which sororal members weighed in on matters that affected the family. This form of administration was necessary because daughters, like sons, were considered integral members of the family. This explains why the bodies of married daughters were returned at death to be buried with their kin. Okafor Anyegbu contended that if "they were buried outside their people's land, it would be like making them strangers in other people's land" (cited in Isichei 1978, 47).

The principle of consanguinity fostered a consciousness in which members were siblings regardless of who their mothers or fathers were, how they were conceived, and what the conjugal union of their parents was. They were siblings not simply because their bloodlines directly traced back to a particular ancestor, but also because they were part of the legal and moral responsibilities agreed to by this collective of kin at the time of the children's birth or their assimilation into the family. To maintain family cohesion, the organizations of *umuada* (daughters) and *umu okpala* (sons) in either an *umunna* (children of the father) based lineage or an *umunne* (children of the mother) family group functioned as systems of family unification. Senior members of these organizations decided which ancestral line and which personage would receive prominence, which to ignore, and which uterine unit or *usokwu* (the mother force) governed real family relations. These organizations authorized versions of lineage histories that were remembered, retold, and revised in light of changing family needs. It was not unusual that these histories were full of inconsistencies and contradictions, given that they served political objectives and were revised to serve these ends.

Although the common term that describes lineage members, "*umunna*" (children of the father), gives preeminence to the fraternal side of the line by suggesting that all ancestors were fathers, not all founding ancestors were male. The suggestion mistakenly lends weight to the idea that families can schematically be represented with concentric circles in which *umunne*, kin of the same mothers, is the inner core and *umunna*, kin of the same father, is the outer larger circle. The supposition that the mother's circle is the inner circle derives from the idea that Igbo families are polygynous, hence the inner family circle is made up of a number of mothers and their children. Within this polygynous system, the father becomes the overarching figure who unites the children of different mothers, and at the higher level, the ancestral father brackets the families of the different sons. The basic assumption here is that the *umunne* subgroup is always subsumed under the superordinate *umunna* group. This hierarchical structure would turn all mothers into wives and make them as a group structurally subordinate to fathers as a group. The error with this father-dominance structure is that the implicit view of family is predicated on the principle of conjugality rather than on consanguinity. Insofar as this dominance of *umunna* is an argument from conjugality, it does not capture the consanguineal nature of the Igbo family system, and thus must be rejected.

Some prominent families and communities were established by mothers or on a mother's *usokwu* (maternal center), and so a different explanation is required. When families trace their genesis to a common ancestral mother or a mother's *usokwu*, the term *umunne* has a similar epistemic function as *umunna*. It points to the maternal figure as the overarching figure who unites families, wards, and communities. This maternal figure may not have been a wife. She could have been an *idigbe*, the dominant figure in a connubial male–female relationship, and she could have married wives of her own. The functional equivalency of *umunna* and *umunne* is consistent with the principle of consanguinity rather than with conjugality, in which a wife is subordinate. The *umunna* group does not always subsume the *umunne* group; it is sometimes subsumed by the latter. Thus, it cannot always be assumed that *umunna* defines a superordinate relationship to an always subordinate *umunne*.

The idea that *umunna* is the more dominant relationship comes from unconsciously invoking the patriarchal ideology embedded in the Western epistemic scheme underlying African studies scholarship. Many female ancestors of communities are being written out of history as families and communities succumb to the fashionable male-privileging view of history and revised their history to de-emphasize the role and authority of mothers. The inadvertent deployment of the patriarchal concepts of this Western episteme assumes erroneously that the Igbo conception of mother and father corresponds to the Western variant, and is similarly embedded in the same type of superordinate-subordinate relationship that holds in a nuclear family type relation.

Prodded by this male-privileging principle of history, most contemporary discussions of so-called patrilineal families simply reproduce the male-dominant view of families. They rarely address the consanguineal character of family relationships between *umuada* (daughters) and *okpala* (sons/brothers). They generally take conjugal units as the point of departure, as if conjugality and marital relations constituted the normative basis of Igbo families. Such an approach misconstrues the organizing principle of the Igbo family and completely blocks out the proper sphere of female salience in families. Rather than focusing on the daughter identity of women, it mistakenly focuses attention on the wife identity that is a subordinate identity within a lineage. This lends credence to the false idea that all women are wives and that wifehood is their enduring identity. What is missed is that the wife identity is terminable, and is terminated at various points in a woman's life, such as when she shifts to any one of her multiple identities—social, occupational, mother, or natal; or when she ends her marriage. Consequently, the assumption of a one-dimensional identity for wives falsely imposes an enduring, uni-dimensional, subject identity on all Igbo women, and enables researchers to conveniently ignore the political role of *umuada* in family spaces and in founding families and communities.

The Onitsha social system did not foster a family system that assigned a one-dimensional identity on daughters and treated women as a group as subordinate to men as a group. Instead, it devised a parallel system that equally affirms both daughters and sons, and allowed them to assume different substantive identities. As the history of Olosi, Usse, and sections of Obikporo lineages in Onitsha demonstrate, *umuada* contributed to the expansion of their consanguineal family either, by becoming *idigbe* and/or by marrying wives of their own.[15] To become an *idigbe*, these women chose a paramour with whom they had children who remained in their custody and who became members of their own consanguineal family. Those who divorced their husbands and married wives, as did Felicia Ekejiuba's aunt, expanded the number of people in her kin group. Blocking out these actions of some *umuada* makes it seem that all *umuada* married male husbands, and that all their children belonged to the husband's or genitor's consanguineal family. Within a lineage, adult sons and resident *umuada* whose children lived with them in family compounds were in the peculiar position of simultaneously being fathers or mothers as well as siblings (that is, brother/sister) to their own children. By contrast, "away" daughters who lived in their marital homes and adult sons in *idigbe* unions would simply be senior sisters/brothers to the children in their natal lineage, since their own children belonged to other lineages. The point here is twofold. The first is that the children of some sons (and those of some daughters) were not part of their own natal family. And the second is that, regardless of the conjugal choices of lineage members, or of their paternal/maternal relationship to the children in the lineage, all consanguineal kin were first and foremost siblings who shared a common allegiance to generations of siblings who had gone before them and to those yet to be unborn. It is this community of siblings that is misrepresented as fathers by ethnographers in order to justify a reading of families as patrilineal.

Also, blotting out the fact that some *okpala* (sons) functioned as paramours or genitors made it seem that they all married wives and that their children belonged to their own consanguineal family. Underplaying this fact comes from illicitly upholding the principle of conjugality and placing the father at the center of the family system. It is a strategy of exclusion; one that excludes practices and conjugal forms that do not accord with the logic of patriliny. The exclusion of the lives of daughters from the Igbo family system channels theoretical analyses along pathways that facilitate the construal of families as patrilineal and entails the substitution of consanguinity for conjugality as the basis of family formation. The substitution succeeds only because researchers were responding to the underlying patriarchal ideology of their theoretical framework, and have ignored the consanguineal principle of family formation that had provided options to daughters to remain at home either because they had entered *idigbe* unions, their marriages had collapsed, they were widowed, or they had married wives. Moreover, the substitution also conceals the fact that adult sons who were in *idigbe* relationship had children who were not part of their own family but rather belonged to their mother's family. It is important to underscore that the reason for all these misreadings is the operative Western episteme that privileges conjugality, but it also comes from overemphasizing the fraternal line and the fatherhood role of adult male siblings on which patriliny is grounded. This occurs at the expense of the motherhood role of adult female siblings, and of the tie of consanguinity that allowed the children of daughters to be full members of their mother's family once the mothers were not formally married.

The patriarchal intuitions of Western episteme percolated into the bodies of theories in ways that limit the possibilities of daughters as well as the consanguineal implications of the lineage family system. That Richard N. Henderson was operating with such a patriarchal model in his seminal book on Onitsha society is evident in his construal of *umuada* as pollutants, whose sons must be cleansed of their mothers' impurities before they can become part of her consanguineal family. He states, "The maternal linkage in descent is impure, but that impurity can be rectified through dedication to nze" (1972, 425).[16] He goes on to discuss how to obscure any public statement that such a person was a daughter's child. Henderson's interpretation of events clearly ignores the epistemological significance of the principle of consanguinity. He comes to terms with the socially and theoretically disruptive concepts of *idigbe* and of woman–woman marriage by representing them as rarities and aberrant. Given the patriarchal assumption embedded in his epistemological framework, the concept of *idigbe* could not sit well within the male-privileging episteme of his scholarship. Every effort was therefore made to bury it together with any social practice that was antithetical to the patriarchal logic. After all, to acknowledge an idigbe's existence would be to acknowledge that daughters had real and tangible stakes in their consanguineal families and that their children have similar rights to the children of sons. Because the postulates of *idigbe* and woman–woman marriage do not cohere with the validating ideas of Henderson's conceptual structure, that is, with the postulates of patriliny, the Onitsha family could not have been both patrilineal and patriarchal.

The theoretical banishment of *idigbe* provides a convenient way for declaring that the presence of a daughter's children in her lineage is anomalous, even though they were not in the historical period under discussion. By failing to give such "anomalous" social practices the theoretical attention they deserve, their nonexistence was established. Lacking evidence of their existence, younger generations of scholars would swiftly rule that such practices never existed. The circularity in reasoning is easily ignored because it serves political ends. Respected Igbo scholars would go on to insist that Igbo "women have no right to remain permanently unattached (by marriage) to a man and his family" (Obi 1966, 74). In making matrimony the norm for women, all females in the family are then mandated to marry, and all women are easily represented as wives and not really as part of their agnatic family. Female kin are consequently denied their lineage rights on the ground that marriage had extinguished those rights. This definition of women solely in terms of their roles as wives is achieved by falsely explaining consanguineal families on the patriarchal conjugal model, and by making the marital arena the pre-eminent sphere for a discussion of *umuada's* identity and rights. This explanatory model transforms all *umuada* into wives and permanently locks them into a sexualized identity that necessarily places them as a group beneath superordinate (male) husbands and male patriarchs of the family. The formal proscription of the practices of *idigbe* and woman–woman marriage, in the early decade of the twentieth century, also served this political purpose. It obliterated the rights of adult daughters in families and their stakes in family property. The logic seemed to be that if it can be established that "customary laws did not allow daughters to remain permanently unattached" (Obi 1966, 74), then it could justifiably be argued that there was no provision in the culture for the transmission of interest in family property through women (either daughter or wife) to their children. Having brought families and women under a general theory of male dominance, early ethnographers and later scholars of Igbo culture established the platform for characterizing the family as patriarchal and patrilineal.

Prior to this tampering with the Igbo conceptual and social schemes, the consanguineal structure of family formation corresponded more to a dual-descent structure of family in which daughters or sons could be founders of families. It allowed for a range of sororal practices and spousal unions that gave flexibility to *both* the male and female side of the family. Both daughters and sons could marry wives, both daughters and sons could be in relationships in which their children belong to their partners' lineage, and both daughters and sons could establish relationships in which their children were members of their own family. Under the Igbo consanguineal principle, some lines of descent were based on mothers, who may have been living in their lineage as widowed, divorced, or *idigbe* daughters, or they may have been wives in their marital lineage. Under the terms of *idigbe*-ship, Igbo families could not have been patrilineal in the mode that is conventionally described. It is not just that patriliny could not account for all the forms and practices within the Igbo family system in the late nineteenth century, but that the male side of the family did not exclusively control the affairs of the family. The assumption that sons totally dominated and oppressed their sisters is untrue given that the operative principle of consanguinity in Igbo culture did not posit a superordinate/subordinate relationship between sisters and brothers, and given that not all daughters were married or stayed married and that wifehood did not define their sole social identity. Thus, contrary to modern-day representations of Igbo family, the *di okpala* and other male elders of a line (*umu okpala*) did not historically have overall political right and authority over the *isi ada* and the collective body of *umuada*. The relationship that existed between the two sexes was quite radically progressive and postmodern. It was consultative and collaborative. As a group, *umuada* participated in the collective body of family administration, checked their brothers when they acted irresponsibly, negotiated peace treaties before warring communities, and managed their own affairs without the authority of anyone.

In summary, we should note that the family-system feminist concepts most appropriately describes is the nuclear, conjugal family in which husbands and sons were the dominant kin, and mothers and daughters were subordinate. This contrasts sharply with the consanguineal family system that offers complex lines of descent and multiple power centers that does not give males dominant power over females. Within this system, daughters as mothers, daughters as wives, and daughters with wives have founded families, much in the same way that sons did. At the very least, feminist concepts and theories about female subjugation and male dominance are inapplicable in analyzing this family system.

PART 2: RECONCEPTUALIZING FATHERHOOD AND WIFEHOOD

Nna as Social Fatherhood

The interesting question that consanguinity raises for feminists and Africanist scholars is, how do we understand fatherhood? Can there be patriliny with a different notion of fatherhood that does not conform to the notion of father within the nuclear family? The short answer is, yes. There are different varieties of fatherhood according to the family system we are dealing with. Fatherhood in numerous Igbo cultures was not defined biologically, or on the basis of a biologized notion of patriliny, so there is no reason why it should conform to the nuclear family's notion of father that pervades the discipline of anthropology. Besides, it is also well known that Igbo families absorbed wives' children that were not fathered by their husbands as well as children who were not fathered by sons. "Ezelagbo" (one who came from and with the genealogical traits of another family) and "Omenazu" (one born at the back or after the demise of the father) are names that were usually given to children who were not conceived by their mother's husband. A biological notion of fatherhood, therefore, is exceptionally narrow and cannot explain the range of relations that the Igbo notion of fatherhood covers. Using it would have resulted in the end of many families during the traumatic period of kidnapping.

A socially constructed notion of fatherhood enabled families to continue to rear children and to deal with the disappearances of fathers, husbands, and brothers and to regenerate themselves in new ways. The expansive notion of fatherhood overcame the built-in inflexibility of the biological conception of fatherhood by focusing on the rearing of children and fostering the replacement of kidnapped or deceased fathers, husbands, and brothers. This typically occurs when a wife married wives to have more children in the name of her husband; or when she preserved the memory of her deceased or kidnapped husband by having children in his memory.

The forces propelling the development of this flexible notion of fatherhood brought into existence a societal model of fatherhood that families adopted and upheld. Quite unlike the biological fatherhood of the nuclear family system, *nna*, or social father, was a remarkably expansive and noncontrolling being. He might be the most senior brother or uncle in the family who exhibited custodial qualities toward other members of the family both male and female rather than ownership or tyrannical tendencies. Nothing in this definition suggests that *nna* is a biological father, nor does it suggest that all brothers or uncles are *nna*, nor does it stipulate that all males in relationships are fathers. Only the oldest sons, brothers, or uncles are *nna*. Male paramours of *idigbe* do not have custody of their biological children and so do not count as the father of the child. Furthermore, the children of all married males do not necessarily refer to their fathers as father. Within a consanguineal compound, they may call their father by his name while treating the oldest uncle or grandfather as father. This is because *nna* marks seniority and elderhood.

In a context in which a father was not tied to reproductive capacity, *nna* was a protective figure who may or may not have had direct biological ties with the families or conjugal units that were under his protective influence. He was not necessarily a husband (when his protective influence extended over homes that had lost their husband or father), but he was one in his own home. It is a mistake to treat the two—husband and *nna*—as the same, since the category of *nna* does not neatly overlap with that of husband. As an elder kin in the lineage, *nna* does not have spousal relations with the widows and the wives of disappeared men who were within his sphere of protection. On occasion where a widow elected to remarry from her affinal family, the chosen sibling must be the junior of her deceased or kidnapped spouse, not his senior, which minimized the possibility of *nna* marrying his junior siblings' widows and compromising his guardianship status. Because the categories of *nna* and husband do not overlap (even within his own conjugal unit[17]), a *nna* was not a patriarch, given his relationship with his *anasi* (his first wife), who as his confidante was the controller of his conjugal family and compound.

Contrary to ethnographic claims, the status of *nna* as a protector did not diminish the importance of *anasi*, who remained the more formidable figure in the conjugal compound. Because of the manner in which powers were dispersed in consanguineal family systems, *nna* or social father, did not have the moral authority to run both the conjugal and consanguineal families as he pleased. He was first and foremost a coalition builder, and he worked with a collaborative scheme rather than an authoritarian framework. In this position, he attended to his *anasi's* concerns; he responded to the pressures, concerns, and views of his own agnatic male and female kin; he considered the interest of in-laws, who stood in a superordinate position over him and his family; and lastly, he responded attentively to the *inyemedi* (lineage wives) who always used group pressure against the object of their animus. The intricately balanced diffusion of powers and social responsibilities undermined the formation of an autocratic framework and a superordinate ego, the very consciousness that is crucial to the development of patriarchal relations. Without the material conditions for the development of this egoistical streak, *nna*, or the Igbo social father, never became a patriarch.

This concept of social fatherhood and the custodial powers that go with it prevailed for many generations, because other factors too sustained it. One of these would be that prospective in-laws, who needed to ensure the safety of their *ada* (daughters/sisters), would only sanction a marriage that gave her the protective space she needed to preserve her personal autonomy. Parents were not interested in sending their daughter to homes where there was no protective *nna* or father figure and where she would be vulnerable to abuse.[18] Given the regional state of insecurity, brides' families were averse to marriages that either required their *ada* to live far away from home or to join families whose integrity they could not always gauge.[19] They knew that there was a very high probability that a disgruntled or an avaricious husband might connive and sell an intemperate wife to Aro slave traders.[20] Concerns about such possibilities prompted communities to develop marriage norms that minimized potentially egregious actions and to sanction the emergence of *nna* model of fatherhood.

Because fatherhood is not necessarily fused to biology, the prevailing notion of social fatherhood sanctioned the idea of wives or daughters being able to have children for themselves in the name of deceased or kidnapped fathers or husbands, and for husbands, whether or not he was the genitor.[21] Affinal families were appreciative of this practice because it meant they could forestall the closure of their sibling's lines by encouraging a widow or the wife of an abducted kin to have children in his name. For this practice to work effectively, wives had to have sexual autonomy even after marriage. In authorizing this autonomy, societies tied fatherhood to marriage and invalidated the parental claims of a nonspousal genitor. This meant that it was not the act of impregnation that made one a father, rather it was marriage.[22] A child belonged to the family that had received the legal and moral writ to the product of the bride's womb from her family, following her consent. This grant of writ did not cover the entire personhood of the bride; it was restricted just to the child. Setting up matters this way had social implications for fatherhood as well as for wives. First, it detached sexual exclusivity from the institution of marriage; second, it placed wives' sexuality outside the purview and exclusive control of husbands; and third, childbearing became the most important thing that both affinal and consanguineal families cared about. This reproductive responsibility of wives turned childbearing into a prominent social duty for them. For Western readers, this child emphasis may cast wives in the unflattering light of baby producers. We should note, however, that producing children provided them with the basis of their sexual autonomy and the socially authorized pathway to move to an elevated, empowered social level. Women's desire to be mothers was rooted in their positive experience of motherhood, in the social validation of their reproductive labor, and the emotional needs having children satisfied for them.

Onitsha and most northwestern Igbo communities created the right social environment for women to become mothers. They developed social norms and reproductive expectations that authorized wives to procreate whether or not their husbands were around, and whether or not their husbands were capable of impregnating them. They had the right to select partners when husbands proved to be infertile, sexually inadequate or dead; or to opt out of a marriage without foregoing conjugality. In the latter case, the institution of an *idigbe* became the viable alternative. She could select and live with a paramour, changing him for another according to her needs. The moral framework defined by this practice required a different understanding of marital morality and spousal faithfulness. Faithfulness was tied not to spouses' bodies but to the lineage; it was concretely expressed in activities that reinforced and facilitated the growth and expansion of the lineage. Wives, too, benefited from this moral framework, as it did not privilege only the sexual rights of husbands. It accommodated both. Wives (specifically daughters) were assured that no obstacle stood in their quest to become mothers.[23] Somewhat affirming this sexually progressive worldview is an Onitsha maxim that counseled fathers, as late as the 1970s, to "not ask about who impregnated one's wife, but to rejoice that one is the father."

If we center our discourse on the principle of consanguinity, we would have to change our theoretical language and expectations to emphasize both male and female kin in the family. More pertinently, we would be attentive to how social practices and categories shaped the Igbo notion of fatherhood. We would come to realize that the conception of the social father, as a custodial figure, was consistent with the principle of consanguinity because it values all children—both *ada* and *okpala*—both those he sired and those he did not. But the fact that *nna* was a protective figure did not mean that he had exclusive authority over everyone, that his *anasi* and other wives were irrelevant, or that they were valued just a little higher than "cows and goats," as Basden claimed. Although wifehood is a subsidiary category, *nna* was well aware that the marriage norms subordinated husbands as a group to in-laws who had sanctioned the marriage of their daughters to them. This subordinate relationship of husbands to in-laws wrested immense autonomy for wives, whose natal families functioned as a protective bulwark against abuse from husbands and the affinal lineage.[24] We see this in the way Amaeze Obibi community threatened hostilities if their daughters were mistreated or abused. That *nna* did not neutralize the personal autonomy of wives is evident too in the way Victor C. Uchendu's mother combatively challenged her husband's eldest brother even when her husband could not do so (1965, 7).

Scholars in the domain of African studies generally assume that the logic of patriarchy is simply about paternal right of fathers over children. They consequently affirm patriarchy because they believe that children are naturally subject to their father's authority and that a wife is subject to the authority of her husband, who is also the paternal figure. But this is not what patriarchy is about. This construal is erroneous because it confuses a father's parental obligation to his family with a father's political right to dominate his family. This idea of political domination is antithetical to the Igbo family system. In the landmark book on the sexual contract underlying civil society, Pateman makes clear that parental right is not synonymous with patriarchy. She cautioned against this understanding because it misses the dimensions of patriarchy that are truly about male dominance.

Patriarchalism was defined in seventeenth-century Europe as the rule of fathers. This definition married paternal right with political rights, thereby vesting only fathers with political rights and vesting paternal obligation with much more than parental responsibility. Pateman argues that this rigged-up version of paternal rights possesses a greater subset of rights than are normally conceived of as parental rights. On the patriarchal scheme, paternal rights carried the parental power of discipline as well as the subjection and control of a wife. This state of affairs was surreptitiously embedded into what ordinarily passes for political rights to achieve the political goal of women's subjugation, to render them rightless, and to delegitimize them as political actors. The effect was the transformation of politics into a masculine activity. But much more insidious was the extension of the state political system into the home and the configuration of power relationships in the home to accord with the structures of the state.

Pateman further explains that the political right of fathers did not merely derive from fatherhood. A whole set of structures and conditions were required to sanction and make it possible. Because "sons do not spring up like mushrooms" (2001, 126), somebody had to be the mother for there to be sons, which means that in a patriarchially structured society somebody's rights had to have been appropriated by a sexual contract to produce sons for a patriarch. With the appropriation of wives' rights, and the total erasure of a wife's personhood, patriarchy was born. Patriarchy and patriarchal rights lie in sexual rights, that is, in conjugal rights, or in a man's sexual access to the body of a woman and in his control of her personhood. Thus, the foundation of European patriarchal power is rooted in a deeper level of domination, which goes unnoticed because women no longer appear as political beings.

If, as Pateman argues, sexual rights were the basis patriarchy, we need to ascertain the kind of cultural codes that warrants this right. What is the political nature and conditions of this European notion of sexual rights that so clearly differs from the Igbo model of marriage and fatherhood? The underpinning cultural codes of European marriage and patriarchalism appropriate the reproductive capacity and creative essence of wives by defining them as passive or non-beings; "empty vessels for the exercise of men's sexual and procreative powers" (Pateman 2001, 127). Husbands controlled the sexuality of their wives to maintain the purity of their descent line, which resulted in codes of virginity, pregnancy, and illegitimacy that, Barbara Katz Rothman states, ensured "that no other man's seed entered [a wife's] body . . . that she came to the marriage bed unimpregnated . . . [and] that she could not destroy the seed" (1998, 22). These codes bestowed exclusive power over the wife on the husband demonstrating his exclusive control of *his* family. Pateman asserts that the marital rules of this "patriarchal story is about the procreative power of a father who is complete in himself, who embodies the creative power of both female and male. His procreative power both gives and animates physical life and creates and maintains political right" (Pateman 2001, 127). Indeed, the "patriarchal argument refuses any acknowledgement of the capacity and creativity that is unique to women. Men appropriate to themselves women's natural creativity" (2001, 127). The short story is that wives are irrelevant. The subsequent sociopolitical condition prescribes a status of subjugation and negative roles for wives and women in general.

Although there are radical differences between classic and modern patriarchy, the latter preserves intact the ancient idea of women's subjugation by contending that "the man . . . is the nobler and principle agent in generation." Modern constructions of patriarchy also adds to this the idea that women lack reason, and "the capacity to sublimate their passion and are a perpetual source of disorder, [which is why] they must be subjected either to a man or to the judgments of men" (2001, 135). In general, patriarchy—both the premodern and modern versions—view women negatively as "incapable of transcending their sexual passions and particular attachments and directing their reason to the demands of universal order and public advantage" (2001, 138). Contrary to assumptions, patriarchy is not simply about parental authority; it is about the deep-seated mode of domination of women that leaves them with only an identity as a wife. In the subjugated space they occupy, women are hardly seen as productive beings, and are restricted to the private personal aspect of men's lives.

Leaving aside for the moment the description of patriarchy, we need to ascertain whether or not the Igbo notion of husband embodied these patriarchal stipulations. The question, however, is whether elements of sexual rights could have been contained in Igbo marriage norms. In addition, did the "pater" in patriliny accord with the Igbo sense of husband and social father so that the families could still be described as patrilineal? The answer to the first question will be explored in the following section. That of the latter will be taken up when we examine the mother-child dyad.

Patriarchy Undermined: The Sexual Autonomy of Wives

The stipulations of sexual rights granted to men were not possible in Igbo marriage norms because wives were not regarded as procreatively empty vessels.[25] The Igbo marriage contract preserved the personal autonomy of daughters, who had to give their consent to the marriage, and who, as wives, retained autonomy over their sexuality. (By sexuality we mean genital sexuality and the kind of heterosexual desire or behavior intended to satisfy and bring about conception.) The father-husband never received any right to base his political power on the subjugation of his wife. The Igbo marriage norms never gave husbands the right of domination over wives that patriarchy did. For one, unlike in European societies, the jural-legal existence of a woman was never suspended during marriage; hence it was not part of the marriage contract. She was not incorporated into a husband's identity, nor was she exclusively under his protection. Athough wives were structurally subordinate to members of the affinal lineage into which they were married, they were not locked into a state of subjugation.

Patriarchy stands for lack of autonomy of wives, most crucially the lack of sexual autonomy. This was not the case in Igbo society, where wives retained control of their creativity, possessed the right to engage in economic pursuits, and to provide the consumption needs for themselves and their children. Contrary to the patriarchal stance that women had no place in civil society or public realm, Igbo women as wives and as daughters participated in political activities and established political groupings both in the family and the community at large. The existence of their political, religious, spiritual, and economic powers meant that they were not excluded from the sphere of civil society. Moreover, their society and family structure were not organized around the public-private dichotomy that segregated family life from civil society. Unlike the Western modern society, Igbo society did not generate a public space that excluded both *umuada* (daughters) and *inyemedi* (lineage wives) from the political and economic life of the community.

European political discourses on patriarchy make clear that the patriarchal ideology views women as inferior and demands their obedience. The Igbo political scheme and public morality makes no such avowal. Although there are important differences between the status of women under the consanguineal scheme and the patriarchal scheme, modern Igbo scholars still followed the lead of Thomas, Basden, and Meek in characterizing Igbo wives as the property of their husbands, insinuating that they were constrained by the same power and conditions that had dominated European women. These claims of lack of personal autonomy continue to be made even though they are inconsistent with the ethnographers' own findings on the sexual, economic, political, and spiritual autonomy of wives. Thomas wrote in 1913 that "in Awka and the surrounding towns a married woman entertains her lovers with the permission of her husband who is, as a rule, approached by the lover in the first instance with a gift of palm wine" (1913–14, 69–70). Concurring, Basden claims that "in the majority of cases the polygamous husband is not the actual parent of many of the children who call him 'father'" (1966, 103). Disagreeing with Thomas on the fact that husbands' permission was relevant, he asserts that the Igbo woman "has her own particular male friend, independently of her husband, with whom a more or less *clandestine* relationship is maintained" (emphasis mine, Basden 1966, 94). Regardless of whether the relationship is "clandestine" or permission was obtained, one thing is unequivocally clear: wives had lovers. This fact of having lovers had important marital implications that sharply conflict with the core tenets of patriarchy. Speaking from a patriarchal standpoint, it is clear that when wives engage in sexual relations with men other than their spouse and then pass of the fruits of their liaisons as their husband's child, the political right of the husband or father is limited, the father pole is compromised, and patriliny is disrupted. When this breeching of the father's power and bloodline is sanctioned by the community and happens quite routinely, then wives must not have traded their political right in the marriage contract. To a large extent, wives' sexual autonomy was rooted in their motherhood rights and in their economic productivity, food production, and control of the family's food consumption. Wives wielded this power over food in patently political ways to achieve their goals. It is on record that "in daily life they hold a strongly entrenched position, the key of which is food. A crossed woman will torment her husband . . . by refusing to prepare food for him" (Basden 1966, 100). The use of food as a political weapon and the actual deployment of these rights establish marriage as a political space and wives as political actors whose rights had not been circumscribed by marriage. When these facts are added to their possession of lovers, we gain a different understanding of the status of Igbo wives that is antithetical to the sort of conditions demanded by patriarchy. This antithesis highlights the error of describing Igbo family systems as patriarchal or in assuming conditions of conjugality that are unique to nuclear-family systems.

It is public knowledge in respective Igbo communities that mothers had lovers and often switched the bloodlines of their families and reconstituted the "father" pole of families.[26] They did this by engaging in two types of transmarital relationships:[27] those that were sanctioned by the community and those that were not.[28] Community-sanctioned transmarital relationships occurred when, for professional reasons, spouses such as Awka blacksmiths and Nri ritual specialists, undertook journeys that kept them away from their conjugal units for months on end; when a wife married other wives and the male genitor was not the husband (male) of the husband (female); when a husband had difficulties producing sons and a wife had relations with a man known to have a propensity for having sons; when the wife in the previous example of a woman–woman marriage, in turn, married her own wife; when a groom died without the birth of a male child to continue his line, and the widow selected a paramour with whom to produce an heir and continue the line; when young widows with little children chose to have more children in their husbands' name; when the groom was impotent and was unable to father a child, and the aid of an obliging male surrogate was elicited; when the mother of an infant male child married a mature woman for her son and the wife engaged in sexual relations with paramours; when pregnancy did not occur within one year of marriage, and the wife returned to her natal home for "medicinal treatment" that included sexual liaisons with other male partners; when a bride conceived between the post-*uri* and pre-*ina uno* period[29] and arrived pregnant to her marital home; when a much older husband is unable to satisfy the sexual needs of a much younger wife and the wife elicits the services of a husband helper; when a spouse was mentally unbalanced and sexual relations were ruled out for the safety of the wife; when there were ritualized grounds for a bride or wife to take on a lover and she exercised that right; when there was a desirable physical trait that a wife or the couple saw in some man and wanted to bring the traits into their conjugal unit; and lastly, when couples were estranged, but not yet formally separated, and the wife engaged in sexual relationships with other partners. Nonsanctioned but nevertheless prevalent relationships occurred when a wife entered into a sexual liaison with a partner outside of the identified extenuating circumstances, such as having relations only with lovers when a husband is medically and mentally fit as well as available.[30]

Family grafts, the result of transmarital relations, were fairly common in Onitsha and various parts of Igboland in the nineteenth century.[31] They continued to occur for most of the twentieth century, when couples had difficulties conceiving a child, and when a couple decided to bring an admired trait from another family's gene pool into their own.[32] It is no secret that many children in Onitsha families were the product of such relationships and that many family *diokpa* were born this way, long after the demise of their social fathers. In fact, a mid-1970s attempt by an Odoje family to claim a biological son from the family into which he had been born was widely rebuffed on the ground that the entire social fabric would unravel were their claims to be upheld. The case revealed to all and sundry that family grafting was historically prevalent and acceptable. The very fact that there were fears of widespread social instability showed that family grafting was much more common than readily admitted. In fact, a prominent family that today may claim to be Ikpeazu (from village X) may in fact have been the biological child of Ogbuli (from village Y). Meanwhile, the myth that the Ikpeazu line continues uninterrupted was widely accepted until critical questions were raised about the exact genealogy of the line. It is important to stress that the construction of this family myth depends on suppressing the knowledge that one of the mothers in the lineage had changed the bloodlines, effectively using her *usokwu* to supplant her husband, who is the socially recognized father, in family importance. These suppressions are fairly recent events, since these actions were openly discussed less than thirty years ago.

Family myth-making and the preservation of family myths are important political components in postcolonial society. Prior to the infusion of Christian and patriarchal values into Igboland, the social imperative of becoming a mother outweighed concerns about chastity. Motherhood and the desire for children ranked higher than a husband's ego. By virtue of this ranking, the right to motherhood and the terms of marriage curtailed husbands' rights, and emptied the notion of adultery of its meaning. It nullified whatever social reproach could have inhibited a transmarital relationship. Although some categories of transmarital relationships were not encouraged, they were by no means *alu* (abominable) or *nso* (unholy, unclean) and so did not have the fearsome stigma of moral impropriety attached to them.[33] It is for this reason that husbands accepted all the children of their wives, regardless of the circumstances of conception. The implication of this acceptance is that the Igbo concept of husband entailed a notion of wife and panoply of wives' rights that obstructed the development of a superordinate power for husbands as a group.

In postcolonial, Christianized societies, Igbo families have extensively reinvented their histories to bring their families in line with what they perceive to be proper Christian values. The more they embraced the religion's rigid gender categories and ideology, the more they transformed their families to accord with the spirit of Christian gender categories. Consequently, ethnographers and sociologists must pay greater attention to the need of families to represent themselves in conformity with prevailing Christian morality. Prior to the prevalence and adoption of Christian mores, the question of who is the father, and which *pater* constituted the line of descent, was a profoundly complicated question that did not demand a one-dimensional answer. The collective view was that a husband of a bride was the father of the wife's children, regardless of how they were begotten, yet at the level of marriage relations, it was a very big issue because the society prohibits endogamy. Families had to know, in order to preclude the possibility of biological siblings getting married. Consequently, a genealogical screening that focused on the fact that children may not have been fathered by the social father was a critical part of the marriage process. The fact that such screening occurred informs us not only that wives exercised their sexual autonomy, but that the community was aware of this fact.

Thus, against the backdrop of sanctioned and nonsanctioned reproductive relationships, the standard representation of Igbo families as one in which power rested solely on the husband were false. In his magisterial pronouncements, Obi (1966), following the lead of Basden, Thomas, and Meek, was at pains to highlight the authority of the fathers and male members of the family, and the inconsequential role of mothers and adult female members of the family.[34] The error in his work is that his claims ignored the ways mothers actually re-engineered families and introduced other bloodlines into the marital family. Even when they did not re-engineer the family, wealthy mothers effectively overshadowed and sometimes displaced the lines of their husbands, and positioned themselves instead. Her uterine line would subsequently take her as the reference point of identification in tracing their ancestry. Over time she would become the founding or dominant ancestor of the line. It is important to stress that, although this action of mothers in suturing broken lines helped to maintain the myth of family continuity, it profoundly altered the character and dynamics of the family and undermined the validity of patriarchy. Although Igbo male writers routinely represent the culture in ways that conceal these transmarital relationships and family reconstitutions, the relationships cannot be swept aside as insignificant, because they undermine the legitimacy of claims about the patriarchal structure of Igbo families. We cannot pronounce a family system as patriarchal when it comfortably accommodates the sexual autonomy of wife, and it enshrines the disruptive power of mothers. In fact, when both properties occur, it is an indication that family and social relations are nonpatriarchal and nonpatrilineal.

Interrogating Virilocality

If Igbo society in the "olden days" sanctioned the institution of *idigbe* for daughters, absorbed their children into their family, accommodated wives' sexual autonomy, and allowed wives to preserve their natal identity, then patriarchy could not have existed, regardless of how social anthropologists, contemporary male historians, and female researchers manipulate their data. Although northwestern Igbo societies had a structure of family organization and notion of fatherhood that is vastly different from that of the West, the differences are missed by conventional definitions. Virilocality, the practice of daughters moving from their natal family upon marriage, is one of the factors that compelled researchers and feminist scholars to continue to treat Igbo families as patrilineal; in fact it is one of the pivots on which the argument of patriliny rests. Much is always made of the fact that upon marriage, brides relocate to their grooms' homes. In Onitsha, in the recent past, they were escorted there by a phalange of *umu agbo* (young maidens) and *umu ikolobia* (young males) of her ward, who officiated the handing-over ceremony. But the fact is that these marriages were not based on any kind of contract that undermined the multiple identities of the wife or resulted in the appropriation of her rights and identity by her husband.

In communities that are described as having a patrilineal system of family organization, virilocality is seen as a historically timeless phenomenon. But as will become clear, this custom is not as ageless as people want to believe. In over two centuries of slavery raids (and even during colonization), family modifications had taken place in response to safety concerns about young girls of marriageable age. It is quite probable that contrary to assumptions, virilocality may not have been the norm, just as Northcote Thomas's 1911 survey of the Nri-Awka subregion revealed that polygamy was not the dominant mode of marriage there. It would make sense that families and *umuada* rejected virilocality, especially when suitors were from communities that were not located within an acceptable geographical proximity.

Until the late 1940s, Onitsha women had a habit of not accepting marriage offers from suitors they derisively called "*ndi* Igbo."[35] Although their men married Igbo wives, Onitsha women who entered into *idigbe* relationships or married non-Onitsha men did so only after the settlement of the paramour or groom in the town. These foreigners may be from neighboring communities that were barely six miles or more away. Thomas's statistical comparison of Agolo (*sic* Agulu) and Awka also revealed a similar pattern. Awka men would marry Agolo girls, but the reverse (from Awka to Agolo) appears not to have been the case. Although virilocality was practiced in the early twentieth century, as Thomas's description of Agolo-Awka marriage patterns shows, the issue is not that it was practiced, but whether it can serve the weighty theoretical task to which it has been put.[36]

Foreigners could marry *umuada* when they resided in the community, which meant that they permanently relocated to live with their brides.[37] Onitsha women would transmit citizenship to their children and to these men who chose to become a part of the community. In such cases, the conjugal unit would come under the sphere of influence of the wife's family. In eighteenth-century Onitsha, for example, Olosi, the daughter of Obi Chimaevi, married a foreigner who permanently settled in Onitsha, and their descendants today constitute the town's ward of Ogboli Olosi. The same was the case of Usse, whose children formed part of the Obikporo ward, as well as of Umuikem and Mgbelekeke wards. These two wards were created by descendants of men who had come from Ikem-Nando and Igala, resettled, and married Onitsha women. This pattern of marriage and women's bestowal or conferment of citizenship to their spouse and children was also replicated at the family level by numerous Onitsha women in other parts of the town. This often resulted in women founding descent lines in families and other sections of the Onitsha community. The question then, is what is the justification for privileging virilocality over these other spousal patterns, especially when they have been responsible for the formation of large communities?

It could be argued that the regional state of insecurity at the time was the reason why virilocality was not the sole pattern of marriage in this community. Otherwise, it was the dominant pattern of marriage, especially for indigenes who best knew themselves. But we do not know that for sure. Given the general fluidity of communities and their ill-defined boundaries, no evidence exists to show that virilocality was the only pattern of marriage settlement among Onitsha indigenes. But even if it were, the mere existence of virilocality does not prove patriliny. To prove that, we need to show that virilocality excludes conjugal arrangements of the *idigbe*-type relationships (in which male bachelors entered into relationships with widows, unmarried and divorced women) and woman–woman marriages. In the absence of such proof, the issue that needs to be raised is, why are scholars striving to simplify Igbo society? Why is the direction of simplification toward virilocality and patriliny? And what justification is there for privileging virilocality and patriliny as if all marriages conformed to their precepts? The problem with exaggerating patriliny and the fraternal line is that patriliny does not underwrite or explain the various forms of social practices and spousal unions that proliferate in a region with a consanguineal principle of family organization. Patriliny is not complementary to or supportive of models of spousal unions that do not replicate the nuclear family logic or privilege the dominance of fathers (and sons). In fact, the organizational principle that facilitated the development of *idigbe* relationships and woman–woman marriage could not have been patrilineal. When all is said and done, the privileged status of virilocality is really tied to the theoretical function it performs, which is to provide theoretical support to patriliny. Virilocality is really consistent with the interpretive scheme that privileges it, only because that scheme had assumed the very issue that needs to be proved.

PART 3: THE IDEOLOGY OF MOTHERHOOD AND MATERNAL POWER

Oma and the Mother-Child Dyad

If we treat Igbo history as dynamic and accord it the epistemic significance it deserves, where does the principle of consanguinity leave motherhood? The question is pertinent, since wives are deemed to be structurally subordinate to husbands, and patriarchy deprives them of their creative powers. As stated earlier, economic production in a subsistence economy conferred autonomy to mothers, who as Amadiume and Ekejiuba argued, were responsible for their own maintenance and upkeep (Amadiume, 1997, 1987b, and Ekejiuba, 1995, 1966).[38] Their *usokwu* (the wife's dwelling unit and space within the marital compound)[39] was a primary space for procreativity, consumption, and production, and the negotiated relationship between the spouses created a measure of interdependency and relative autonomy for both. Further reinforcing the autonomy of mothers and the retention of their procreative powers is that marriage under the principle of consanguinity did not transfer control of the wife to the husband. Wives embodied a multiplicity of identities, some of which were subordinate identities, while others were socially empowered identities.[40] Whereas wifehood constituted a subordinate identity,[41] motherhood liberated them from that status and accorded them immense powers. Once a wife became a mother and established the mother-child dyad, her status dramatically changed, giving her greater rights that allowed her to reshape her conjugal unit and the larger marital family.

The relationship of the conjugal unit to the consanguineal parallel lines of kin is that the former constitutes the physical space for rearing new members. This space, which may enclose monogamous or polygynous units, was linked to the sororal and fraternal lines, depending on which member established a marital or *idigbe* union in the family. It is important to stress that not all mothers within an agnatic group were wives. Those in *idigbe* unions, and others who married wives of their own in woman–woman marriages, became mothers without becoming wives. The sociological importance of the concept of *idigbe* is that it exposes motherhood to be a social identity that is often and erroneously conflated with wifehood. The fact that an *idigbe* is a mother challenges us to sever the link between wifehood and motherhood. Once this is done, we gain a deeper appreciation of how women did not have to be wives to become mothers and of the range of rights they had. Because they are two separate states of affairs, motherhood is not rooted in a subjugated identity. Unlike wifehood, it is rooted in categories of fulfillment, regeneration, expansion, and plentitude. Becoming a mother, that is, creating a mother-child dyad, requires assumption of an empowered identity, one that itself emerges upon the birth of a first child.

"Nne" means mother. Igbos mark this identity with a new name for the mother. She is no longer called by her name, but as the "mother of X," where X is the name of her child.[42] Within the Igbo universe in which humans constitute wealth, reproduction is a vitally important labor to families and to society. Mothers are the producers of family wealth and social regeneration. All mothers have an *usokwu*, where *usokwu* is her residence either within the affinal family or among her agnatic kin. Every *usokwu* is a nodal point of power. It is the center of child socialization activities. Because the principal function of mothers is to grow the lineage by having children, motherhood is the goal of *usokwu* formation, and the *usokwu* is the seat of mothers' power. Within the consanguineally based family, and within the polygynous conjugal units of members, children of the same mother bond together and define themselves as members of their mother's *usokwu*.[43] Being from *ofu afo* (literally, one womb) they are bound by ties of loyalty. Mother's blood provides the cohesive glue that binds siblings, which men's blood-oaths attempt to mimic. Hers is the true bloodline in the family.

To fully appreciate how *usokwu* and *omumu* (the principle of fertility and reproductive power) create autonomy for mothers, we need to retreat into the Igbo cosmological framework, in which humans were much more than the sum total of their physical parts. They were composite beings with spiritual and physical sides whose interaction affects and shapes their lives. Controlling this interaction requires knowledge of the rites and rituals for manipulating the relationship between the spirit and earthly realms. Those who have jurisdiction over certain rites, knowledge, and capabilities controlled the interaction. The autonomy and power of mothers in affinal families derive from their control of the spiritual powers and rites that lie at the heart of fecundity and procreation. As bearers of children, these powers are vested in them and fall under their jurisdiction.[44]

The spiritual power of procreation and generation was totally under the jurisdiction of mothers. Contrary to the patriarchal conceptual scheme, mothers rather than fathers or paramours controlled the powers and condition of generation. Usokwu, omumu, and chi (the inner spiritual guardian of any individual) constitute the tripod upon which rests the powers of the mother. At the core of usokwu is oma (the spirit of mothers, mother's mother, and mother's uterine sisters) that enables a mother to attract and control the psychic and physical conditions necessary for procreation. Oma harnesses omumu, the principle of fertility and reproductive power, and omumu is activated by sacrifice to mothers and the principle and fountainhead of motherhood. The activation of oma and the associated principle of omumu were believed to manifest once a mother-to-be is in tune with oma. This opens the creative channel of maternal energy to flow through her, clearing whatever psychic obstructions there may be in her path. Energized by oma, the mother-to-be is spiritually placed in a receptive state for conception and to attract the right earthbound spirit. Her chances of safe delivery are heightened if she is in alignment with the protective custody of her chi, and if the prenatal choices she made at her own gestational moment accords with her present goals. It is because wives are receptacles for the power of oma that they are socially encouraged to take whatever steps are necessary to become mothers, including returning home to the safer spiritual environment of her natal family if this is required.

We cannot under-emphasize the spiritual system that legitimizes mothers' powers. "Nwa na eso oma eje" is an Asaba adage that explains that a child inherits his or her qualities from the mother (Isichei 1978, 184). The philosophy enshrined in the adage vests the mother with the power to shape a baby's identity and being. Because omumu is channeled into the usokwu from the maternal line, procreation and reproduction are totally outside the control of husbands, who have to bow to this force. During her first pregnancy, a prospective mother is protectively ensconced within the chi of her mother who, in concert with the oma of her own mother, mother's mother, and mother's uterine sisters, constitutes the protective spiritual cloak for her and the gestating fetus. It is true that every person has a chi, the inner spirit or personal deity that guards and protects one throughout one's life. But because the chi of a new bride lacks maternal experience, she is brought under the protection of her mother's chi during her first pregnancy. Just as the fetus is enveloped in a protective placenta, so the prospective mother is enveloped by her mother's oma. As important as is the birth of the new child is the emergence of a new being, the mother.

At childbirth, the moment the baby is expelled from the protective placenta, the *chi* of the new mother separates from the protective *oma* and becomes *nne* (mother).

Although anthropologists, feminists, and legal theorists are aware that the status of a wife changes once she becomes a mother, they insufficiently acknowledge the implication of that change.[45] As a result, they do not fully apprehend the power and moral authority of mothers in reconfiguring families and in blocking patriarchal consciousness. Even though wives were structurally subordinate to members of the affinal family, this did not mean they were submissive or powerless and possessed no rights. Quite to the contrary, motherhood enabled them to make up whatever structural disadvantages that adhered to their role as wives.[46] After the birth of her first child, the new mother created a shrine to her *chi* and *oma* in the kitchen close by her cooking hearth. She was aided in this weighty spiritual task by her *isi ada* (eldest lineage daughter and priestess) and her *di okpala* (eldest lineage son and priest), not by her husband or paramour or any of his relatives. The latter were, however, aware of what was going on and would have given their consent. The spiritual task of the spirits inhering in the shrine was to guard, protect, and nourish all who feed from her pot. Through the food of which they partake, her *chi* asserted its influence, and her *oma* reached into the very beings and consciousnesses of those whom her food nurtured.

Though Igbo male scholars were at pains to highlight the patriarchal authority of fathers and the subjugation of wives in traditional families, their efforts obfuscated the actual dynamics of Igbo marital relations. Mothers remained the genetically significant line of succession.[47] Patriliny seems to be an ideological construction that does not square with the fact of social fatherhood and the generative powers of motherhood.[48] It was a metaphor that drew its strength from virilocal pattern of marriage but cloaked a modified form of dual descent principle of organization.

Patriliny Contested: The Full Implication of Motherhood

The ideology of motherhood extends to all mothers and constituted the basis for compelling obedience from everyone who gestated in the womb. Its power covers a range of activities that continues long after the birth of the child, the most important of which is establishing the moral parameters for belongingness and loyalty. Those within the uterine circle of life, who emerged from the "same womb" and ate from the same pot, are the truest of kin. They are tied together by the same blood, the same nutrients, the same memories, and the same *oma*. *Oma*, the sacramental power that is a force of unity, inscribes its ideology on the consciousness of all children of the same mother. It defines the boundary of humanness. Morality begins in children's formation of an ego and an awareness of their relationship to the mother. This relationship coordinates the formation of interpersonal experiences that helps the child to define himself or herself in relation to others. Disloyalty to the mother or the break-up of the uterine ties of kinship is tantamount to destroying the last covenant that makes our community human. Mother's force works by binding together *umunne* (children of the mother) in a moral scheme that compels them to act together to further the interest of their *usokwu*.

Among consanguineal kin, maternal ideology sets the terms of the deeper relational family ties. Igbo historian Michael A. Onwuejeogwu recognized this fact when he conceded that "the basic criterion of exogamy is common motherhood" (1980, 53).[49] The ideology of motherhood is what gives siblings and lineages a close-knit sense of loyalty and unity. Although a lineage consists of children of several different mothers, the cement that binds these siblings together is not the paternal tie, as some would like to believe, but the mother or maternal ideology of the founding ancestor. Even where the professed ancestor is male, it is the mother's *oma* or *ibe nne* (the maternal force or power) that provides the superior basis for constructing the ties of *nwanne* (child of the same mother). B. M. Akunne, a Nri cultural historian, puts this in perspective when he describes the power and authority of *oma* or *ibe nne*. He states that "*ibe nne* symboliz[es] the true spirit of unity that binds persons through common motherhood. . . . The term *nne* [mother] symbolically dominates *nna* [father] in specifying degree of relationship between persons." In his view because, "the term and the relation *nwa nna* has no direct blood relation; people who have one father use the term *nwa nne* and not *nwa nna*" (1977, 60). They are united by the ideology of the father's mother, whose authority or maternal force binds them as one. Unlike the patriarchal epistemic scheme that traces life back to the father and the first semen, the Igbo system of morality traces life back to the womb. This appeal to maternal cohesiveness centers on the mother's gravitational pull in the family, and alerts us to the pre-eminence of mothers over fathers in family regeneration.

Within the Igbo cultural scheme, motherhood is not altogether complementary to and ancillary to the unity of the *patri*lineage. Most times it is the nodal point of segmentation and departure from the group. Agnatic kin listen to their mothers and heed their counsel primarily because she provides their long-term memory of the family's history. Her historical account is privileged because it constitutes the relevant compass for negotiating their way amongst nonuterine siblings with competing and sometimes radically divergent objectives. It is a well-known fact that family politics coalesce around uterine or *usokwu* units. Through their *usokwu*, Igbo mothers effectively disperse their influence through the lineage, forcing consanguineal kin to think and act in terms of uterine groupings. In accordance with the principle of inheritance, families segment and break away along maternal lines. Siblings of a breakaway *usokwu* would subsequently reconstitute and form a new lineage, either within the same community or in another location. Although such new lineages and the older ones are today presented as patrilineal, on closer inspection we find that the basis of their constitution, the dominant consciousness, and the most significant ancestor of the lineage is either the ancestral mother herself or the mother of the founding male ancestor. Even in Onitsha, the segmentation of the core Umuezechima group is on the basis of the differing mothers' *usokwu*.

To sufficiently grasp the moral force of *oma* or *ibe nne* is to see that the salient tie of unification, identity, and oneness did not come from fathers, but from mothers. It is also to reverse the view that the family is not a gendered space. Although fathers were undoubtedly important in the scheme of things, they did not carry the moral inscriptor of unity upon which the sanction of exogamy was based. It is for this reason that the principle of family segmentation has always been maternal, and that family cleavages have always occurred along maternal lines. The *oma* (motherforce) that initiated separation from other consanguineal kin is the same *oma* that bound the descendants of uterine kin in cohesive ways, such that lineages that today appear to be *patrilineages* actually trace their kinship or *nwanne* ties either to a specific mother, or to the *usokwu* of a founding male ancestor.

Motherhood's challenge to patriliny derives from the fact that mothers represent the true bloodline of descent. They expose the conceptual limitations of deploying "patriliny," a term that does not truly reflect all that it claims to be, in explaining descent. The use of that label, however, has helped inordinately to characterize and reorganize Igbo families under male leadership and dominance. It does so at the expense of motherhood. When we attend to family dynamics, lines of division, and the basis of family loyalty, we see them coalescing around maternal ties, suggesting that present-day lineages were actually descent lines of specific *usokwus*. Although family narratives have shifted dramatically under colonial influence and Westernization to represent sons exclusively as progeny, Igbo families in the past accommodated progeny of both daughters and sons. It seems that the urge to bring Igbo families in line with the disciplinary schemes of interpretation of anthropology and the Western scheme of knowledge have simultaneously worked to downplay the importance of mothers. Although the Western epistemological scheme keeps referencing the father, patriliny is intelligible only because it collapses into and rests upon maternal ties. The cohesiveness of families and lineage reflect the maternal force, which is why the ultimate appeal to family solidarity is *nwanne* (children of the same mother).

The question some would ask is, if mothers were so dominant, where does that leave fathers? What then, is the basis of the modern Igbo father's power and importance? These questions appear innocent, but they actually invoke a form of explanation that organizes the culture along patriarchal lines. The de-

mand for a much more significant platform for fathers is at odds with the consanguineal structure of family organization that does not emphasize the dominance of fathers as it does that of the heads of families and of kin. A father is
primarily a son and a brother, basically a member of a lineage. That he is a father did not give him any special rights over and above his kin group or over
his child. In fact, a child is not *his* child but *our* child. When we consider that
historically not all adult sons were married, and those in *idigbe* relationship did
not have any claims to their children, we begin to see the more modest limits
of the power of fathers in this system. This is not to say that fathers did not
matter, just that the kind of inflated power the patriarchal scheme assigned to
them did not exist in the consanguineal system.

The question of why fathers are privileged today goes to the heart of colonial history and the epistemological scheme within which theory building
takes place. Colonial policies, Christianity and Islam, Western education, and
contemporary experience teach us that fathers have always been dominant
even though the Igbo culture did not share this view. Further undermining the
theoretical prominence of mothers is the cultural shame induced by privileged
Christian ethical ideals. This propelled the progeny of woman–woman marriages and *idigbe* unions to reconstruct their family history along patriarchal
lines. Many recast the husbands of their mother's female husband into their father. Others presented their mother's father as their father; some turned their
eldest brother into the male ancestor of their line; and others cast their
mother's paramour as their father. In the latter case, the progeny presented
their mother's *idigbe* relationship as a formally constituted woman–man marriage even though they were aware that the relationship was not what it was
billed to be. These transformations are understandable given that they are
strategies for gaining legitimacy in a newly emerging political order that privileged fatherhood and structured laws and policies to reward patriarchalism.
Although some would argue that some lineages trace their descent to some
founding father, what is at issue is not the possibility that there could have been
such lines of descent. At issue are the lines of descent at the founding of the
family before the Western social scheme and the fact that Christian and colonial ideologies represented mothers as inconsequential.

Patriarchal Theorizing: The Reconstitution of Igbo Families

In a range of writings reaffirming the perspective of ethnographers such as Basden, a number of contemporary Igbo male scholars represent "traditional" Igbo
societies as possessing all the characteristics of a patrilineal-patriarchal society.
A leading legal scholar, S. N. Chinwuba Obi, has done so in a number of texts
on the Igbo family system, land tenure, and principles of succession and in-

heritance. In *Modern Family Law in Southern Nigeria*, he defines the Igbo "patrilineal" family as

> a social institution consisting of persons who are descended through the same line . . . from a common [male] ancestor, and who still *owe allegiance to or recognise the over-all authority of one of their number as head and legal successor* to the said ancestral founder, together with any persons who though not blood descendants of the founder, are for some reason attached to the households of persons so descended, or have otherwise been absorbed into the lineage as a whole. (My emphasis, 1966, 9)[50]

Innocuous as this description may sound, it constitutes the ground upon which Obi legitimized the patriarchal and male-dominant basis of Igbo family. In this description, a lineage is no longer a family with diffused parallel and crosscutting lines of authority in which *umuada* (lineage daughters) had important administrative roles. Rather, it is one in which overall authority rested on one male individual, who commands the allegiance of every member of every conjugal unit, and who consults occasionally with family elders, who are all men. Elsewhere, Obi had defined the family as a corporate body with a family head, and a council.[51] His family council "is composed of the heads of the various branches of the extended family."[52] The head is the oldest male member of the family, who may "be likened to a company's managing director" (1966, 18). The idea that this kind of authority coalesces on one individual simultaneously transforms the custodial and priestly role of the male head of family into a sovereign patriarch and eliminates the female head of family. The rest of Obi's description curtails the powers of other family members.

The creation of a sovereign head with an all-male plenipotential council shifts the ethos of the family from one in which rights automatically derive and are guaranteed by birth to one that is based on gender. On this definition of family, patriarchal norms are further inserted into the society so that daughters could never have similar status and right of membership as sons. This transposition of patriarchal values into societies reconstitutes Igbo lineages into an inherently masculine sphere of authority. According to Obi, its smallest subdivision, the household, "consists of a man/patriarch and his wife or wives with their unmarried children and any other dependents such as wards and domestic servants" (1966, 9). Yet, under the principle of consanguinity, the smallest family grouping should be *umu aro* (small children), not a conjugal unit. The question of how *umu aro* came into being is not central to the formal structure and principle of family organization.

Culture has always been the site for epic equity struggles. For this reason, it is important that we treat Obi's representation of Igbo family with circumspection. A close study of his writings reveals that he is engaged in what has been called patriarchal theorizing, that is, a mode of theorizing that is located in a theoretical system that generates an outlook that takes for granted the truth of men's definitions and accounts of the family. Patriarchal theorizing centers on men's experiences and does not concede the existence of women in any significant role, nor accepts the legitimacy of their experiences or opinions. A review of his literature shows that Obi draws substantially on the writings of early male missionaries, colonial anthropologists, colonial intelligence reports, customary court decisions, and his own knowledge.[53] He supplements these with judicial interpretations and the legal arguments of a coterie of Nigerian male scholars.[54] Given his theoretical starting point, it is hardly surprising that no woman was consulted, and that a woman's view did not shape whatever was written. His account of family defines what is or is not possible in terms of customary law. Because "marriage is virilocal, women cease to be members of their maiden family (understood as a political unit) as soon as they marry, but [they] retain their family membership (in the sense of a social unit) in spite of marriage" (1966, 10). In other words, their membership in their natal lineage is primarily ephemeral rather than substantive. Obi cannot really speak for women because his perspective on family, customs, and tradition neither recognizes nor comes to grips with *umuada's* experiences. To purport to do so, however, implies either that they are not worthy of speaking or that their views do not count, or that they have nothing to say, none of which is true.[55]

Writing in the 1960s, decades after colonial impact has drastically affected Igbo societies, the key weakness of Obi's construal of the traditional family was its lack of historicity. He seems to have taken as historically given the gender relations in place in the previous thirty years. Reading these back into history, he treated them as the traditional norms and customary practices of Igbos. It is true that women's peculiar situation did not fall within his scholarly purview, but that did not justify the interpolation of the present into the past, the exclusion of daughters' perspectives, and the failure to crosscheck with them the veracity of some of his data on family structure and customs.[56] Obi's privileging of only men's account of customs becomes the methodological sleight-of-hand that allowed him to exclude viewpoints that fundamentally challenged his interpretation of the society. The exclusion enabled him to privilege contentious practices that were instituted during colonial rule, and which women, in the previous fifty years, had publicly denounced as contrary to the customs and their self-definition. They had contested these "customs" on the ground that their introduction encroached on their sociopolitical rights, curtailed their political agency, and transformed the society in male-dominant ways. Not surprisingly, Obi's preferred version of family dynamics, customs, and traditions ignored these contestations of women; rather he went ahead to privilege their colonial relegation to the category of minors. His account of customs, therefore, continued and expanded the colonial project of disenfranchising women in the postindependent era.[57] With the customs of "traditional Igbo society" presented as stable and unchanging, it is easy to ignore colonial restructuring of the Igbo family. Obi's one-sided male view of the Igbo cultural scheme goes undetected because it captures present-day reality. He represented Igbo families as patriarchal, discounting the transformation that had occurred during colonialism and the fact that the principles of power diffusion in lineages problematize this characterization.[58] There is no doubt that Obi's definition of the traditional Igbo family and his description of practices accord more with the early British ethnographers' descriptions, in which there is only one male center of authority, than with an actual Igbo family that consists of two parallel structures for sons and daughters. His description of the traditional Igbo family is closer to the one that was brought into being by colonial policies and legislation, which is why it underplays the fact that married daughters were very much part of Igbo families, and that through their multigenerational daughters' organization (umuada), they participated in family administration.[59] Lastly, when we consider an important but rarely discussed feature of Obi's definition of family, his narrow focus becomes obvious. This feature is the idea that a legal successor might not be a blood descendant, but simply someone who had been absorbed into the family. A consequence of Igbo social construction of fatherhood is that it contains an element of ambiguity that is at odds with the patriarchal model that Obi invokes. The fact that the father line may be sutured with the help of another bloodline means that we have to pay greater attention to the role of mothers in the family.[60] After all, the family is the product of their sexual decisions.

Amadiume's writing raises a different set of problems, one that involves the use of gender as an explanatory category. She insists on the matriarchal character of Igbo families, directly challenging the validity of Obi's downgrading of mother and matrifocality. In examining the matriarchal basis of Igbo family organization, Amadiume makes the very important point that defining complex multifaceted societies as patrilineal or matrilineal creates the erroneous impression that only men have power in such societies. She states that "the recognition of the motherhood paradigm prevents the error of taking patriarchy as given, or as a paradigm" (1997, 83). For her, an "understanding of matriarchy/matriliny [entails] a shift of focus from man at the centre and in control to the primacy of the role of the mother/sister" (1997, 80).

There are sharp differences between Amadiume and Obi's views on the family, that one could claim that they are diametrically opposed. But her stance on matriarchy notwithstanding, Amadiume's description of family relations overlaps neatly with Obi's conception of family in an essential area. She similarly portrays Nnobi-Igbo society as patriarchal, even as she claims to challenge the patriarchal values that were imposed during colonialism and Christianization. Employing the same problematic language of description that marred the work of early social anthropologists, she portrays Nnobi women as objects and property rather than as subjects. She underscores the second-class status of Nnobi women by stating that Nnobi men assert authority over women (1987, 37); that "[c]apital comprised land, *wives* and *children*"; and that "movable property consisted of . . . human labour, especially women's productive and reproductive powers including their sexual services" (1987a, 30–31, my emphasis). Moreover, her work is replete with phrases such as "wife control," "purchase of wife," or "wife ownership" that comes straight out of the social anthropological framework. This language of description strips Nnobi women of both sexual and reproductive autonomy and represents them as under the domination of men. It also provides justification for the use of feminist concepts in analyzing traditional Igbo families.

The more important point of Obi's and Amadiume's convergence is that, irrespective of their theoretical positions, both conceptualize Igbo families in terms of conjugality, a procedure that shifts the focus back to man at the center and in control, and analyzes husbands as the dominant beings in the family.[61] The more radical element of Amadiume's insight collapses when she tries to pass off the traditional Igbo family as conjugally based. She states, "the paradigmatical gender structures of kinship in the indigenous society are in binary opposition. They are expressed . . . in the *Obi* (ancestral or family home) which is male, and the *Mkpuke* (the matricentric unit or mother and child compound) which is female" (1997, 83). The questions this raises are, why is the dominant structure of kinship conjugal rather than consanguineal? Why are fraternal and sororal kin in binary opposition? And, where are the daughters of the house? If Amadiume's response is that daughters are not at home because they are located in the *mkpuke* in their marital homes, she has collapsed the identity of daughter into that of wife and effectively excised daughters from their natal homes. It is not merely that such a response leaves no substantive identity for daughters, even though the two identities do not overlap, and marriage never cancels out the daughter identity. It is more that her conception of Igbo families misconstrues the organizing principle. When the dominant lens for analyzing Igbo family privileges the identity of wives as mothers to the exclusion of their identity as daughters, we are no longer talking of the traditional Igbo family that is organized around consanguineal cores, but a Westernized, nuclear family that is organized around spouses' connubial relationships.

The quite radical analysis of Amadiume sputters when she tried to marry both matriarchy and patriarchy. Her views on family structure are hardly indistinguishable from the received view of Igbo families that Obi privileged, which overemphasizes the dominance of fathers and the fraternal line to the detriment of the sororal line. Like Obi's model, Amadiume's model of family is similarly rooted in the principle of conjugality, centered on a man, his wife or wives, and children. Any difference between the two models is one of accent rather than of substance. When she represents the ancestral family home as male and the matricentric unit as female, the question Amadiume forgets to answer is for whom are these spaces male and female? The *obi* is not a male space to *umuada* (daughters) neither is the *mkpuke* a female space to *umuok-pala* (sons). Spouses, but not sons and daughters, may think of their spatial relationship in terms of male and female spaces. But as full members of the family, daughters and sons draw the line of distinction on grounds of membership or nonmembership in the family. Thus, Amadiume's paradigmatic gender structure is informed by patriarchal rather than matriarchal thinking, in which the human anatomy rather than the principle of complementary family relations is taken to assign meaning to spaces.

For the most part, the fact that conceptual interpretation of Igbo society by modern Igbo scholars did not always proceed from the inner logic of their society, social institutions, history, and customs did not seem to matter. Both male and female scholars readily assume the legitimacy of their underlying theoretical structure and concepts, though they may disagree with some sociological facts embodied in the structure. But we have seen the sorts of distortions Western-derived theoretical structures and concepts create. In the recent past, the idea that the theoretical orientation of much of Igbo cultural interpretation may be flawed was not systematically questioned, and so the few critiques that have been made are rarely thoroughgoing. Now that we have seen the ways in which received ethnographic views and other uncritical perspectives underplay the importance of daughters and their mothers, we need to be more attentive to our constructions of the indigenous Igbo family.

Conclusion: Path of Reinterpretation

The character of the consanguineal Igbo family exposes the limitations of feminist concepts and methodologies in explaining and analyzing such families. The presumption of female subjugation embedded in these concepts cannot provide illumination on an ungendered family structure and so are not relevant. However, how do we account for the patriarchal interpretations of the Igbo family in the works of male theorists who were born and nurtured in the culture? The answer is inseparable from the history of colonial experience and the educational framework within which they shaped their interpretive scheme. It is also inseparable from the gains that accrued to men during the colonial period and its aftermath. William J. Goode notes that dominant groups tend to "take for granted the system that gives them their status, they are not aware of how much the social structure, from attitude patterns to laws, pervasively yields small, cumulative, and eventually large advantages in most competitions" (1982, 137). In addition to the cumulative advantage that came to them by virtue of their sex, most Igbo theorists were educated under the colonial patriarchal ideology, and they speak the same male-privileging language.[62] In most of their interpretation on cultural matters, most have neither taken the time to view the world from female perspective, nor have they studied the gender impact of colonialism on their social institutions. Consequently, they are ignorant of the ways in which colonialism benefited African men and rewarded them with their present authority over women. Moreover, there is ambivalence to studying this colonial gender history, not least of which is that they would have to acknowledge that men's experiences under colonialism were significantly different from women's experiences, and that they gained their present advantages by colluding with colonialists to exploit their female relatives. Such an acknowledgment would be devastating given that it roots their ascendancy on injustices against women, and it entails the deconstruction of the male identity and masculine privilege. It is far easier to sidestep the damaging scrutiny of seeing themselves as oppressors and to contemplate the restructuring of power relations and present rules of inheritance that follows from that framework.

The question we really ought to ask now is not to what extent these descriptions of Igbo men are accurate, but rather, by what processes and in what ways Igbo societies changed to become male dominant during the colonial era. How did we get from a society that encouraged the growth of women's capabilities and full flourishing to one that constricted their life objectives? In what way are contemporary Igbo men's observations on patriliny and patriarchy self-serving and rooted in colonial history? Because customary laws, codified during the colonial era, were one of the effective instruments for enthroning patriarchal consciousness and diminishing the social worth and importance of women, we must explore these legal processes to understand how African men systematically shortchanged women.

In the next chapter, I will explore these legal instruments and processes that initiated the transformation of Igbo societies into patriarchal ones.[63] I do this by highlighting the invidious role of the native courts and their officials as well as the patriarchal implications of judicial decision of the time. Towards the end of the chapter, I focus on how the newly implanted Western family ideology disenfranchised Igbo women and, in the face of their resistance, effectively transformed their societies into male-privileging ones.

2

Legalizing Patriarchy

Sorting Through Customary Laws and Practices

Towards the close of 1929 riots of an unprecedented kind broke out
with startling suddenness in two of the South-Eastern Provinces of
Nigeria. The rioters were women—not a few enthusiasts, but women
en masse—who formed themselves into mobs, armed themselves with
cudgels, and marched up and down the country, holding up roads,
howling down the Government, setting fire to the Native Court
buildings, assaulting their chiefs, and working themselves generally
into a state of frenzy that on several occasions they did not hesitate
to challenge the troops sent to restore order.
—C. K. Meek, *Law and Authority in a Nigerian Tribe* (1937)

With a focus on the provincial and native courts of Southeastern Nigeria, the
oral and written histories of Igbo women, and a critical reading of the historical period, I examine, in this chapter, the judicial institutions in Nigeria, especially the impact of colonial laws, edicts, legal policies, and judicial institutions on the character of Igbo family and societies in the first quarter of the
twentieth century. First, I determine how the court system functioned in collecting and codifying a body of laws that constituted the customary laws of
Eastern Nigeria. Next, I ascertain the processes by which patriarchal values and
consciousness were legally institutionalized and inserted back into colonized
societies as traditional. The fundamental question that drives this investigation is this: If the colonial administration did not recognize the existence of
"native" women and hence made them invisible, then, strictly speaking, how,
when, and to what extent did they incorporate them and their rights into the
legal codes? To what degree did the collected body of "customary laws" reflect
the family ideology and the traditional laws of Igbo societies rather than the

family ideology deployed by the colonial state? To what extent did the native courts and "customary law" preserve the historic rights of "native" women? In short, the goal is to establish how a society that affirmed women and had a mother-centered ideology became patrilineal and patriarchal. I will conclude by discussing the implication of these issues for the family and society.

PART 1: INDIRECT RULE AND THE NATIVE ADMINISTRATION AUTHORITY

Archeological Excavations: Native Courts and Warrant Chiefs

Prior to the Native Courts Proclamation of 1900, "native courts" were already functioning in Nigeria. These courts were established between 1891 and 1895 by Sir Claude MacDonald, Commissioner and Consul-General of the Niger Coast Protectorate, and his successor, Sir Ralph Moore. The courts were designed to perform judicial and administrative functions, and to provide a basis for select Nigerians to participate in the administration of public order (Adewoye 1977). The administrative and trading company officials who staffed them had no legal qualifications and rendered what has been referred to as "political justice."[1] These administrative officials intricately interacted with and affected the character of indigenous judicial processes. They were injecting Western judicial constructs, legal ideology, and their own assumptions about the family and state into customs and laws they came in contact with.

In 1900, the Southern Nigeria Protectorate was created, following the amalgamation of the territories of the Royal Niger Company and the Niger Coast Protectorate. This amalgamation was accompanied by the Native Courts Proclamation, whose objective was "to systematise the practices and experiences" of the two regional areas under British rule and law. Sir Frederick Lugard, architect of British indirect rule and former governor-general of Nigeria, reconstituted these native courts into four grades—A, B, C, and D— (with jurisdiction diminishing in order of magnitude), and opened the court to native membership (Elias 1956, 24). The court was composed of a president, who the British claimed was either a local traditional male chief (where the community had both female and male chiefs) or a "warrant chief," who was created if the society was viewed as a stateless society with no monarchial structure. The grade D category of native court, which proliferated in Igboland, was authorized to try civil cases that involved fines of up to five pounds (£5), and to assign punishment of up to three-months' imprisonment and public flogging of twelve strokes of the cane (Nwabara 1977, 169). By 1929, fines imposed in civil cases were raised to twenty-five pounds (£25), and land cases were added to the court's jurisdiction.

These courts were supposed to rule in accordance with native law and custom. But from the onset, women were excluded from membership in these courts even though they had always been part of the indigenous judicial system and had adjudicated a wide range of cases. In accordance with the colonial state's view of male dominance, only men were recruited for membership in the courts and presiding were warrant chiefs, who were always men. Together with the traditional male chiefs in states with hierarchial structures of governance such as Oyo, Benin, Sokoto, and Kano, these warrant chiefs presided under the supervision of the district commissioner. Lugard states in his *Dual Mandate in British Tropical Africa* that

> [t]he jurisdiction of native courts is limited to natives, and with the exception of a few specified ordinances which they are empowered to enforce—such as those relating to taxation and native authority—they administer native law and custom, modified or added to by such by-laws as may be made by the Native Authority to give effect to local ordinances. (1965, 549)

In accordance with Lugard's directives, the 1901 proclamation gave native courts exclusive jurisdiction in its geographical area of authority (Adewoye, 1977, 43). They were mandated to exercise power "exclusive of all other native administrations," and the law stated that "no jurisdiction shall be exercised in such district by any other native authority whatsoever" (see Native Courts Proclamation, no. 25, 1901, sec. 12, Laws of Southern Nigeria, 1900–1901). Armed with this executive authority, warrant chiefs were empowered to impose their personal will on communities under their jurisdiction. Effectively, this meant that traditional village councils that had been composed of women and men's councils and the age-grades, could no longer preside over community administrative affairs or execute any judicial functions (Adewoye 1977, 43). (They could only do so when they had the mandate from these chiefs). In fact, by means of this administrative override of local traditions, Lugard laid the basis for the simultaneous subversion of the indigenous value system and its family ideology, and the imposition of Western patriarchal constructs within the societies. Bringing together the power of political administration and judicial instruments, he further admonished that if an ordinance or regulation deemed a practice an offense, then "the native court, by means of a by-law, would recognise the act as punishable, *even if not contrary to native law and custom*" (Lugard 1965, 550; my emphasis). For instance, some longstanding social practices that were part of social and family life fell foul of this directive. These included the practice of women marrying women for the expansion of their own personal families, the institution of *igba n'rira* (a swift process of divorce in which a woman simply relocated to a lover's home from her marital home),[2] the practice of women being the head of families, and the practice of holding their own courts. The very idea that women could marry other women as wives or that a wife could choose both to initiate divorce and to become the wife of her lover without public censure was repugnant to the early twentieth-century European morality and conception of marriage and family. As well, this moral reprehension extended to the idea that women could be heads of families, a notion that the state's patriarchal ideology of family could not accommodate. The upshot was that the woman-affirming practices of the Igbo family scheme that contravened European morality codes were defined as contrary to natural law and were gradually proscribed.

With the European moral scheme as the arbiter of proper ethical conduct, and with family increasingly defined along conjugal and patriarchal lines, legal rulings were soon interpreted in line with European social, moral, and family values. In fact, a systematic assault was launched on matrifocal consciousness. This led to the curtailment of mothers' and women's social relevance and their sexual autonomy. The attack began with policies that construed families as households. It continued with the administrative override of native laws and customs about the family, eventually leading to the insertion of patriarchal values and individualistic ideology into Igbo society. Barnes reveals how this occurred:

> When the Administration wished to change the behaviour of the people ... it could either make a regulation and then empower the Native Court to enforce it, or it could persuade the Native Authority to pass an order to the same effect, which would then be approved by the Administration and, as before would come within the competence of the Native Court in some. (1969, 107)

The colonial administration generally adopted "the second alternative so that it might appear that the regulation represented the will of the people and not merely the dictates of the Administration" (1969, 70). Native Authority officials represented those changes as "forgotten" aspects of people's traditions. Nowhere was the effect of this legal fiction and subsequent social engineering more obvious than in Eastern Nigeria, where the creation of warrant chiefs comprehensively facilitated the promotion of a patriarchal political system and family values. British and Igbo male evaluators of the Native Authority system rarely noted the gender implications of these social changes upon political and family life. Because they rarely discussed the strengthening of men's institutional authority and the weakening of women's centers of power, they represented the resultant transformations as ancient customs and traditions (1969, 108).

In *Local Government in Southern Nigeria: A Manual of Law and Procedure under the Eastern Region*, Philip Harris defied the norm by critically reviewing the Native Authority system. Unlike others, he criticized the "dangerous lack of inflexibility" inherent in the system on the ground that its goals of holding onto customs made little allowance for the fact that in "a fast-developing territory, an institution that was acceptable in 1910 might not be generally accepted in 1930" (1957, 5). Other than this criticism, Harris generally treated colonialism as a positive project. He believed that certain aspects of African culture must give way to this progressive force. He viewed the Native Administration system as antithetical to progress and objected to the fact that "it was established whether or not the traditional institutions . . . apprehended by the early British administrators, continued to be acceptable by the people" (1957, 5). In his view, codifying them into customary laws was counterproductive.

However, because Harris's concern was with the formal conditions of change rather than with the sociocultural consequences of these changes, he focused more on the problem of stasis and fossilization. His critique of European agency underlying and guiding the Native Authority system partially exposed the falsity in the official propaganda that the customary laws and the "indigenous institutions owe nothing to European political concepts."[3] So while he was able to see through the official rhetoric of "authentic customary laws," he missed the more insidious masculinization of the Native Authority project. The problem was not as Harris imagined—that the people necessarily found their customs unacceptable and that the Native Authority was preserving irrelevant traditions. Rather, the problem was that various Native Authority Administrations were creating new laws and customs that were neither British nor native, but that conformed to the patriarchal ideology of the state. They were passing off these new laws and customs as if they were desired by the people, and as if they conformed to ancient laws and customs. The alteration of Onitsha family norms and practices and the introduction of patriarchal ideas of male dominance occurred at this time.

Legal scholar S. M. B. Ibeziako underscored this point when he observed that in ways not immediately obvious that even "the customary law relating to family relations, land tenure, inheritance and succession [had] undergone remarkable metamorphosis under the influence of British law and . . . changing social and economic conditions" (1964, 27). Even when he recognized that the Native Authority Administration did not necessarily preserve the customs, customary laws, and traditions of the people, he failed to articulate the implications of this on family and gender relations. Other male scholars such as A. E. Afigbo, S. N. Obi, and S. N. Nwabara failed to integrate the impact of these historical changes on the family into their analysis of colonial policies. Rather, their interpretations of customs and laws moved towards defining Igbo societies as patriarchal and reinforced the state's position, which claimed an expansive and empowered space for men. In some of the more disturbing cases, these interpretations radically transformed family structures when it was claimed that only a *di okpala* (lineage senior son) could speak for the family to the exclusion of the *isi ada* (lineage senior daughter). This arrogation of exclusive powers to *di okpala* rests on the untenable masculinization of the *ofo*—the Igbo symbol of spiritual authority—and delegitimizing *isi ada's ofo*.[4] Compounding matters was the importation and use of problematic terminologies, such as "dowry," "kingship," and "ownership and alienation of land," whose meanings did not reflect local practices.[5] These terms were systematically deployed in ethnographic literature and political accounts of Igbo societies leading readers to the inescapable conclusion that in the late nineteenth and early twentieth centuries Igbo cultures were patriarchal.

That Harris, and later African legal theorists missed the dissimulations caused by the Native Authority system showed that his knowledge about the nature and dynamics of gender relationships in African societies was limited. His failure to note the growing individualism and male-privileging character of social change points to his narrow cultural scheme of reference. The fundamental problem of the change unleashed by the Native Authority system was that it simultaneously subverted women's social relevance and inflated that of men. This reordering of social reality was overlooked because the change conformed to the assumptions of Harris and other theorists about the dominant position of men in all societies. In their eyes, the reinterpretation of laws and customs seemed natural and true, not because it had the legitimation of "traditional" chiefly authority, but because it conformed to their conception of society in which men are the sole political actors. With authority being defined as male and invented tradition being construed as authentic, critics such as Harris ignored the fact that these chiefs and authority figures were created by the patriarchal ideology of the colonial state. The colonial administration and its team of colonial anthropologists wrongly assumed that the pronouncements of Igbo male Native Authority officials accorded with the spirit of local customs.

The problem with Harris's thesis of change is that although it acknowledged a specific phenomenon of change, the implication of that change was never seen to have social effect either in theory or in praxis. If Harris's thesis of change is treated seriously, then one of the social consequences of the Native Authority system was its devaluation of women's lives and activities and the enhancement of men's lives and institutions. Harris (and others after him) failed to recognize that Igbo women of the time found the powerful remaking of the Igbo conceptual scheme and social institutions along European patriarchal lines unacceptable.

Patriarchy-Bearing Concepts and Processes

Today, Igbo legal theorists may contest the fact that the colonial judicial system radically reshaped societies. For them, whatever impact there may have been was quite minimal. The strategy is to safeguard the authenticity of a tradition that has rewarded them with innumerable privileges. Adewoye's detailed examination of the structural weakness of the Native Authority Administration provides ample evidence of how European political concepts were inserted into the Igbo conceptual scheme through the court system. His study validates Harris's intuitions about the impact of European political and judicial concepts on African society, although he did not spell out the character of that change on women's lives. It is indisputable that European concepts were effectively deployed during colonialism. They were inserted into the culture so that their patriarchal ideology eroded oppositional structures. Native court officials conducted judicial adjudication on the basis of these concepts and their social ideology. According to Adewoye, "it was the common practice of native courts to ape the judicial procedure of the Supreme Court and, under the influence of the court clerks to administer a corpus of law, 'neither British nor Native,' that hardly met the standard of justice of the supervising administrative officers" (1977, 203). Although colonial propaganda made it seem as if "these courts . . . [kept] as closely as possible to the indigenous laws and customs", he showed clearly that they did not:

> The supervising administrative officers of the native courts were Englishmen born and bred in a different cultural context. When called upon to pronounce on the equity of customary law and practices, they inevitably brought their cultural framework to play, for "the only justice and equity they knew was English justice and equity." (1977, 208)

Consequently, British gender norms and ideas about dowry, bride-price, leadership, alienation of land, vagrancy, larceny and theft, marriage, adultery, and imprisonment, which were upheld in the courts, began to reshape the society (1977, 203). For example, these ideas and the Victorian standards of morality underlying the entire administrative system initiated the transformation of how Onitsha people and other Igbo communities thought about their own social and customary practices. The insertion of British morality codes into marriage practices and gender relations began in Onitsha as early as 1857 with the establishment of the Anglican Christian Missionary Society (CMS) and the opening of its primary schools for boys and for girls in 1858. In 1885, the Roman Catholic Mission arrived under the leadership of Father Lutz. From 1885 to 1900, the pace of Christian evangelical activities accelerated as the

CMS and the Catholic mission fiercely competed for souls and territorial influence. This competition resulted in the dissemination of Western moral values, and in 1900, paid off in the appointment by the colonial government of the first Christian Obi of Onitsha, Samuel Okosi.[6] From then on, a series of laws were introduced by the Christian Obi and Ndichie to curb the escalation in the amount of bridewealth that husbands were required to provide to the bride's family and to curb the high rate of divorce by Onitsha women (Nzimiro 1972, 106–8). By 1915, the Christian missionaries and Western-educated male elites pressured the Obi and council to ban *Ije Urie* (a practice where by a betrothed girl paid extended visits to the suitor and his family) on the grounds that it encouraged immorality. These reforms instituted Christian marital norms and morality into the culture and encouraged the curtailment of wives' sexuality by tying it to procreation and making extramarital relations a prosecutable offense.

The flexible nature of local customs allowed new inflexible ones to be created and the old flexible ones discarded. In his study in East Africa, Chanock (2002) noted that such transformations occurred when customs that were previously flexible guidelines for conduct were transformed into rigid rules for settling cases. Treating them as rules within the colonial judicial system drastically simplified the adjudication process by reducing the range of possible options that preserved the ideal of ambiguity required in an adjudication process that strikes a balance between redress and reconciliation. The new rules jettisoned the ambiguity ideal, preserved men's interests and authority, and reinterpreted Igbo customs to accord with the male-privileging ethos of the Common Law. Either way, native court officials successfully imposed new laws on communities while claiming to be working with local laws.

In Onitsha, the appointment of Obi Okosi I resulted in the introduction of the concept of autocratic leadership that subverted the system of checks and balances of Onitsha political structure. The Obi (male monarch) became the head of the Native Authority and assumed colossal new power to make laws with his council and male members of the ruling age grade.[7] Historically, an Obi was a spiritual recluse with limited political power.[8] The Native Authority Administration altered the local balance of power by inflating the power of the Obi and conferring executive powers on him. Upon appointment as Obi of Onitsha by Commissioner Bedwell, Samuel Okosi exercised his new powers in dictatorial ways to appoint his brother Gbasuzor Okosi to the post of Onowu or Prime Minister (Nzimiro 1972, 200). Prior to that, he had refused to perform a range of installation rites that conflicted with his Christian beliefs. He worked with an educated, Christian, all-male Onitsha Improvement Union that was committed to the Christian moral scheme. They introduced and passed a series of laws that began the social transformation of the community into a "progressive" society that emphasized male dominance and patriarchal family values. Influenced by their Western education and Christian beliefs, they abolished institutions they deemed to be unprogressive and morally reprobate. One institution that fell afoul of their policies in the early 1920s was *idigbe* (*adagbe* or *idegbe*), which allowed a daughter to enter into a socially legitimate union with a man of her choosing (1972, 107).[9] Because this union was not a regular marriage, she could dissolve the union whenever she so desired and retain full custody of her children who become members of her natal family, with equal standing in the family to that of her brother's children.

Educated and Christianized Onitsha men saw the institution of *idigbe* (and a whole host of other liberal practices) as immoral and antithetical to the new "progressive" society they were striving to build. They saw the options that were valid under the older morality code as "unnatural" and as giving far too much freedom to women. Women who desired this option were ridiculed as harlots, and over time the ridicule achieved the goal of presenting patriarchal marriages as the only valid model of connubial relationship for women.

Various conceptual changes were ongoing during this period as well. In the 1930s, G. I. Jones, a government anthropologist working in the Eastern Provinces, was already seeing the effects of the introduction of Western concepts into Igbo society by the Native Authority Administration and the native courts. Jones stated that there was "complete divergence both in theory and practice between Native law and custom and the law actually administered in the Native court."[10] Earlier in the century, between 1910 and 1915, Archdeacon George T. Basden had given a graphic account of one way that native courts were restructuring communities' notions of justice in line with Western values. He recounted his intercession on behalf of a friend in a trial presided over by the district officer. He was alarmed to hear the charge: "Rex versus C.— 'You are hereby charged with intent to conceal a felony contrary to the Larceny Act of 1863' by receiving money in compensation, heavy truly, no less than £3 10s. for a stolen fowl." According to Basden, "what the accused had done was quite normal under native custom, [but was] wrong according to the new law being imposed upon the country" (1938, xv). Although he succeeded in clearing the accused on that count, the accused "did not escape, because *the charge was changed* to one of extortion, or alternatively, false pretenses, and . . . [he] was sentenced to six months' hard labour" (1938, xv).

This account exposes the supervenient force of British law and the hypocritical nature of claims that local customs were guiding judicial processes in native courts. What it most cogently reveals is the persistence of the court in securing convictions that traumatized communities and viscerally reminded them that their own value schemes had been displaced in favor of imported ones. The range and consistency of the convictions hastened the adoption of the Common Law ethical scheme. The message to all was to adjust immediately to the new value scheme, to embrace the new concepts that were dictat-

ing new forms of knowledge and new patterns of social and family relationships, or be punished. For Igbo societies that never had the notion of punishment by incarceration, the policy of imprisonment was psychologically devastating. It wreaked emotional havoc on individuals and families, and threats of
it forced compliance with the changes desired by the colonial state. Even when
communities knew that the native courts were violating local customs and normative social relationships, it was imprudent to challenge those violations,
since this meant challenging the colonial state and attracting the wrath of its
security arm.

By the third quarter of 1907, the native courts in the eastern provinces
of Nigeria had officially handled 4,493 civil cases and 3,246 criminal cases
(Afigbo 1972, 551). The real number is undoubtedly higher, because the warrant chiefs, court interviews, messengers, and policemen unofficially handled
cases that never became part of the court record. But even if we take only the
officially recorded cases as the valid ones, communities by that time had received 7,739 examples of how to modify their behavior in accordance with the
new laws. The disciplinary mechanisms of the court had instructed them 7,739
times that penalties would accrue if they did not do the biddings of the court
clerk and the court messengers, and if they did not abide by the stipulations
laid down by colonial law. Imprisonment and public floggings of elders and
adults were especially traumatic to Igbo, who never used those methods as a
means of law enforcement. However, they served their purpose well. By pun-
ishing certain behaviors and rewarding others, the colonial government skillfully altered the traditional worldview, set new standards for what constituted
acceptable behavior, and compelled communities to comply strictly with the
law. Where communities were tardy in complying with the expected dictates,
they were subject to military expeditions or they were collectively fined. The
chilling effect of all these reinforcing punishments was the alteration of society's norms and customs.

By 1924, there were 134 native courts in the eastern provinces, and the
number of cases and the effect they had on communities expanded exponen-
tially. During this time the notion of theft, the concept of family, the meaning
of justice, the law of debt, the process of arbitration, the forms of marital relationships, and people's ideas about spirituality, bodily integrity, and personal
dignity were undergoing radical revision. The point here is not simply that the
court cases themselves or native courts as institutions were the sole authority
that compelled change in Igboland. The point is that once judicial decisions
were made, the courts defined the direction of change and the Native Authority Administration deployed all its processes to enforce it. Communities
had little choice but to comply in modifying their customs and behaviors in
accord with new regulations, edicts, and by-laws. Given that only men served
in these judicial and law-enforcement positions, women's voices were muffled,

and their perceptions and interpretations of cultural norms and conventions were factored out of rulings. Years after these changes, generations of Nigerian men who had benefited immensely from colonial rule and its patriarchal ideology bought into the myth that their customs had remained intact.

PART 2: FROM FEMALE-AFFIRMING TO MALE-VALIDATING IDEOLOGY

The issue we ought to focus on is not what the impact of the arbitrary and imperious powers of court officials on the administration of justice was, but how societies that were female-affirming shifted to become primarily male-privileging. We need to understand how a sociopolitical culture of legitimation for males was created.

Igbo historian A. E. Afigbo provided a pertinent answer in his richly documented book on the warrant chiefs and the convergence of colonial political directives and law-enforcement policies. As early as 1898, soon after the formation of the Native Authority Administration, he noted that warrants were issued to locals who became the administrative agents of the colonial government. These male functionaries who sat on the native courts derived their power exclusively from the British authorities, not from any indigenous political institutions. As Afigbo showed, the vast majority of these local collaborators "were either scoundrels or just ordinary young men of no special standing in the indigenous society," and so they were not concerned with preserving the old sociopolitical order (Afigbo 1966, 541). By virtue of their social elevation, these collaborators acquired extraordinary political powers. They became first and foremost servants of the colonial state and were totally accountable to the government, not to their kith and kin (Afigbo 1972, 257). For example, in Ihiala, a non-Aro community, an Aro man was made a warrant chief of the community, because he had collaborated with the colonial government to enforce the disarmament of Ihiala (1972, 63). In Ihitte in Okigwe, a reluctant collaborator believed he was outwitting the British when he put forth one of his slaves to take his place as a warrant chief without consulting anyone in the community. In another community in Obowo in Okigwe district, a scoundrel who had been sold as a slave by the community, seeking to rid itself of his antisocial activities, became the community's warrant chief through what could best be described as a comedy of errors (1972, 63). In Owerri, a major slave trader and local big man was coerced into working for the British and was eventually rewarded with a warrant chief certificate. Because all these warrant chiefs were not part of the traditional order of authority, they felt no moral, political, or social obligation to abide by or preserve the spirit of any local customs that did not suit their personal goals.[11]

Thus, at the very outset, the officials who became the key functionaries of the Native Authority system had no special incentive to uphold local laws and customs especially the female-affirming ones. Backed by the dominant power of the court, they were more interested in changing the society to create a permanent political order for themselves. Being men of no significance in the old sociopolitical order, they happily accepted the issuance of "warrant" chieftaincy, unconcerned about the radical political consequences this had for their communities. Not only did their rule overturn the traditional political order, but it also gave each appointee powers that were unprecedented in the political history and social organization of these societies. As warrant chiefs, they became both "judge and executive officer; and [their] court clerk without analogue in the indigenous system, was policeman and prosecutor" (Barnes 1969, 110).

Operating outside of the local political structures, a warrant allowed chiefs to "conscript anybody ostensibly to work on government roads or stations whereas in practice it was to do [their] own private bidding. When holding court they could seek the aid of elders who were in their good books, but they were not bound to accept even their unanimous opinion" if it conflicted with their own (1969, 110). These warrant chiefs used strong-arm tactics to get their way and frequently overruled the local councils of male and female elders. Very much in the manner that Aro slave traders used military threats to subdue communities, warrant chiefs, too, used threats of calling in the colonial military patrols to back up unpopular decisions. Drawing justification from the military power and patriarchal ideology of the colonial administration, warrant chiefs reinterpreted local divorce customs and conventions to make it difficult for women to divorce their husbands.[12] They gave these interpretations legal weight and used them as precedents in other cases, effectively nullifying the legitimacy of other interpretations of once flexible customs. A former warrant chief disclosed that they could do this because they were more powerful than any institution within the indigenous system. Warrant chiefs "feared the Government more than the people [because] . . . the latter could not unseat a chief but the Government could."[13] Realizing that "as long as [they] enjoyed the confidence of the government" they were accountable to no local centers of power and were immune to prosecution, they ruled as they liked and did whatever was necessary to maintain their positions (Afigbo 1972, 257). This included colluding with court clerks, interpreters, and the police to ensure that no petition could be sent to District Officers (1972, 280).

The reason for drawing attention to this multifarious problem is neither to call attention to the endemic nature of corruption in the Native Authority system nor to catalogue the extortionist practices of the officials of the native courts. The objective is, first, to show the ways in which societies that had earlier affirmed females were forced to shift their value system to privilege men exclusively; and second, to understand the historical reasons why Igbos began to identify authority, privilege, and power with men. Contrary to Amadiume's assumption, the latter had nothing to do with the ontological structure of Igbo society or the purported flexibility of Igbo gender constructions.[14] The male-privileging identification was a consequence of colonial history.

In an achievement-oriented society such as the Igbos', warrant chiefs and court clerks became new models of power and success that the Aro slave-trading chieftaincy could never have hoped to become (Afigbo 1972, 254–255). Ambitious young men not only noted the power, authority, and prestige that accompanied the modern (European) way of life, they also saw the lavish lifestyle and patriarchal values of warrant chiefs and court officials. They defined these as the benefits of the new civilization. Morally upright community elders disapproved of the thuggish ways in which warrant chiefs and court officials accumulated their wealth, but impressionable ambitious young men sought to model themselves after these individuals who were perceived as the new "gor'ment in town." By the early 1920s, the male-dominant emphasis of the colonial government, the labor market, and Christian missions had become apparent. Young men did not have to convince their families that they offered the best hope of bringing the rewards of the new European system to the family. Aware of the male-privileging values of the colonial economy, some mothers and fathers sent their sons to primary schools and on to either secondary schools or teachers' training college, and sometimes to England for a professional degree.

Parents sold family land they had received from their lineages and tapped the services of female relatives to educate their sons. Such services were ungrudgingly given because in a labor market that favored only males, kin looked forward to their share of wealth, prestige, and the good life once these sons and brothers became lawyers, doctors, and engineers. It is true that not all men followed this path, but the lure of the ideal was so strong that families went all out to encourage sons and brothers to succeed. Although fourteen Onitsha girls and thirty boys were in the first CMS schools for boys and for girls as early as 1858, by 1912, the Annual Report on Education showed that boys had outpaced the number of girls in schools.[15] There were 6,445 boys and 585 girls in a total of 117 schools. The basic curriculum was reading, writing, and arithmetic, but in the intermediate class, the girls focused on domestic skills—cooking and needlework—and the boys went to trade classes that included woodwork or agriculture.

The first Anglican grammar school for boys in Onitsha, Dennis Memorial Grammar School, was opened in 1925, and the Catholics opened their own, Christ the King's College Onitsha in 1933. Reflecting the general lackadaisical attitude toward girls' education, the Catholic secondary school for girls was not opened until 1942, and the Anglican Church did not establish any for girls in the province.[16] In 1938, the enrollment figure for schools in Onitsha province was 11,335 boys in government and government-assisted schools, 3,930 girls in similar schools, and 30,654 students in nongovernment-assisted schools.[17] Although there is no breakdown along sex lines in the latter figure, the ratio of girls to boys would be much higher than in government-assisted schools, because for-profit schools catered to the needs of the male-privileging labor market and required parents to pay fees. This gender gap widened in the work environment, where employment opportunities for girls were stymied by the inherent gender bias of employers. Consequently, daughters socially and educationally lost out to sons and brothers, who became the new privileged class after they were sent on to grammar schools, teacher's training colleges, and higher institutions abroad.[18]

Paths to social advancement and employment were closed to equally capable and ambitious women for whom the colonial system relentlessly portrayed as mentally inferior. With limited employment opportunities, they had limited avenues of social and political advancement. In general, the social position of daughters and sisters declined as families deferred to educated sons who increasingly lived by the patriarchal codes of modern colonial life. Only two options were available to daughters: The first was to labor actively for the success of brothers, with the general expectation that their labor would be rewarded after their brothers became gainfully employed.[19] The second option for socially ambitious Onitsha women was to marry, or to marry off their daughters to upwardly mobile men. Only in their role as dependent wives sharing in husbands' successes and social prominence could women attain social significance.

Christianity and colonial policies promoted patriarchal values in the family as well. The long-term effect of occupying a subordinate position led to the normalization of women's secondary status, the social diminution of daughters and sisters, and an inflation of the value of brothers. As Guyanese historian Walter Rodney put it, "No group of people can be privileged over another for decades without developing an exaggerated sense of superiority" (1982, 88). Similarly, no group could be devalued for decades without developing a sense of inferiority. Not surprisingly, after decades of enduring the ideology of subordination, Igbo women found themselves defining authority, power, and prestige as male, and increasingly relegated to subordinate spheres by colonial policies, their male relatives, and male court officials. For men, in contrast, the normalization of masculine privilege reinforced the idea that sisters, wives, and the less-privileged female relatives would defer to them automatically. By embracing a nuclear family ideology and pursuing their personal fulfillment, the primary allegiance of educated men went to their conjugal unit, no longer to the family lineage. Their elite status and wealth shielded them from the anger of consanguineal kin who felt that their ethics of individualism undermined traditional family values. (The effect of the principle of individualism will be explored in chapter 3).

A. E. Afigbo's seminal study of warrant chiefs effectively showed that Native Authority officials manipulated local rules, customs, and laws to serve personal objectives, and what they represented as traditional legislation was fundamentally at odds with local norms and laws. What he failed to show, however, was the social cost to women and the society-at-large of the changes that were taking place, especially the diminution of women's spheres of authority and the constriction of their self-worth. Critically studying the effect of the native court system on women, one can see that these social changes created a political culture and a political consciousness that privileged maleness. This emergent culture of maleness encouraged the repression of women's rights and the erosion of a daughter's right to family and communal property. It provided the basis for the argument that the rights of daughters were automatically extinguished through marriage.

The Creation of Fictional Customs

In *The Nature of African Customary Law*, published in 1956, Taslim Elias, Nigeria's constitutional jurist and lawyer, sought to sketch the character of African legal theory. He argued that legal fictions provided the means for giving legitimacy to new habits, new rules of governance, and new norms. He analyzed the "basic concepts underlying African law and the interpretation of these against their social and juridical background" (1956, v). Though he was responding to the dominant debate of the time—that Africans were primitive people who lacked these legal tools—he explained that Africans were familiar with the concept and use of legal fictions "in changing substantive rules of law" to fit new demands. For Elias, "[w]ithout the use of legitimate fictions . . . legal transition from tribal into marginal society and from marginal into urbanised (or industrial) society, would be haphazard and non-synthetic" (1956, 185–86). He believed that "legal fictions occur when social norms, patterns of life, and beliefs that regulate the laws of societies are altered or modified, but the alterations are concealed by passing off the changes as enduring, traditional features of the society" (1956, 186). He saw them as functional and useful in social transitions and transformations. What he neglected to determine was the view of those who were completely shut out of the process of "social transitions and transformation." The question Elias did not consider was, whether these legal fictions, created by male colonial officials for local men and by local men for their communities, were as benign to women as his language suggests.

Reading Elias's contribution in a positive light, only African men would say that the changes and fictions that were introduced during colonial rule were for the collective good. Igbo women of the time did not appreciate this onerous "progressive" change and declared that fact in numerous demonstrations. Although Elias had assumed that such changes were positive for all and that what favored men automatically benefited women, Africans in the colonial system were not working for the benefit of all Africans (both female and male).[20]

Historical records show that by the late 1920s in Eastern Nigeria, the fictions created by the native courts had pushed women into a marginal space of nightmarish existence. Staffed as they were by egoistic grasping scoundrels, native courts had acquired notoriety as "hot beds of intrigue, corruption and injustice." As Adewoye noted, "Corruption was rife . . . the courts are . . . far too prone to sell justice to the highest bidder or to favourites. Too many cases are adjourned for decisions after the evidence has been recorded and too many persons are seen privately in the houses of court members and clerks before, during and after the hearing, but before judgment is delivered" (1977, 180). Governor Hugh Clifford knew of this deplorable situation as early as 1921 and condoned it.[21] Part of the problem was that the "warrant chiefs" lacked any training in both the Igbo principles of resolution and reconciliation and the Western liberal democratic principles of law and jurisprudence. The other part of the problem was the poor administrative supervision by the colonial office.

The district commissioners, who exercised supervisory powers over these courts, were not always around because of their other administrative duties. As a result, the semi-literate native court clerk, the only official who sat permanently in the court and who generally was not from the community, became the arbiter of law and procedure and the master of the court in parts of Eastern and Southeastern Nigeria (Adewoye 1977, 180). He had "control of the books of licenses, passes and certificates of various kinds, and of rubber stamps which more than anything else symbolized the delegated power of the Administration" (Barnes 1969, 110). He knew the way the judicial process worked, including the appeal process that stacked the odds against women. Colonial administrator C. T. Lawrence acknowledged this extraordinary powers of court clerks when he stated that court clerks "issue[d] every summons without any reference to any Chief, [gave] orders for arrests, control[led] the court messengers, [took] charge of prisoners and convey[ed] to the . . . Chiefs instructions sent from the Divisional officer."[22] As the vital link between the court and the administrative officer, court clerks wielded power out of proportion to their duties and their low educational achievement.

According to Afigbo, "Native Courts were not only places where chiefs and clerks had given many an unfair verdict, they have also been used in many places as centers for the collection of tax," some of which were illegal (Afigbo 1972, 242). By virtue of their unique position and manipulative ways, six court clerks in Onitsha province had amassed personal fortunes and had purchased motorcars by 1928. The excesses permitted by the massive scale of this corruption resulted in the insertion of a male-dominance ideology into the very structure of the courts themselves. The ideology guided the courts' ruling on family matters. In a speech delivered to the Legislative Council on March 6, 1933, Sir Donald Cameron observed that the "native administration which we have created and recognised is based on a system of European medieval polity dependent on the *relation of vassal and superior*" (Harris 1957, 5; my emphasis). Because of the hierarchical and patriarchal nature of this power, native courts functioned as agents of oppression of women. P. O. Onwughalu, a former interpreter, revealed that court officials shrewdly circumvented disciplinary measures by shielding all their nefarious activities: "what the District Officer saw in the judgement book as the proceedings was often what the Clerk . . . decided to put down rather than what actually was said in Court" (Afigbo 1972, 275). But even when District Officers witnessed acts of dishonesty, they tended to ignore them on the grounds that chastising court officials "would have considerably undermined the chief's [and the clerk's] judgement" (1972, 277).

Writing in 1922 to rationalize this official ineptitude, J. Watts, senior resident for Owerri Province, stated with resignation, "Impartiality and purity of justice are high ideals which can be obtained among these people only after the passing of many generations" (cited in Adewoye 1977, 180). By giving tacit legitimacy to these acts of dishonesty, officials such as J. Watts allowed the exploitation of the judicial system by the warrant chiefs and court clerks for their own benefits. Women, especially, were very vulnerable in this male-privileging system that did not even recognize them as social adults. Residents' and district officers' acceptance of these violations resulted in the codification of a litany of fictitious male-privileging customs as the laws and customs of peoples of Eastern Nigeria. In shaping the character of customs, the codification sent a powerful message to communities that this patriarchal ideology of the family and state was what the new political dispensation desired. The social implications of all these male-privileging laws were the corresponding diminution of matricentric consciousness and the autonomy of the *usokwu* as communities changed to reflect this ideology.

These transformations raised the ire of Igbo and Ibibio women and in 1929 culminated in the historical event known as *Ogu Umunwanyi* or Women's War, which Lord Lugard described as a "strange phenomenon" (Lugard 1937, vi). As the managers of this new male-privileging system, strategically placed Igbo males arrogated to themselves the right to redefine the value system of communities along male-privileging lines. Powerful and increasingly corrupt, egotistical, and selfish, these male officials were hardly perturbed by the erosion of women's social and political rights. In their mind, this was progress. It is important to note that these men were not only directing the destabilization of the Igbo social scheme and determining the areas to be subverted, they were also the sole beneficiaries. Afigbo did not realize how true his words were about women's situation when he stated:

It must not be thought that the thirty years or so of Warrant Chief rule left no scars on the indigenous system. Continued survival was achieved at a price. Indisputably what was revived in the 1930s as the indigenous system would have appeared as only pseudo-indigenous to any native of this area who died about 1850 had he been able to return ninety years latter. For one thing the oracular and other spiritual agencies which in pre-British days occupied a very prominent place in village government had by 1930 lost much of their importance. . . . The generation which was born between 1900 and 1930 grew up with a Native Court mentality. (Afigbo 1972, 293–94)

PART 3: THE IGBO FAMILY AND THE
NATIVE COURT CULTURE

Legislating Patriarchy in Families

It has been argued that some of the difficulties that women faced in colonial society can be traced to the manner of penetration of the Western legal mode into African social systems (Chanock 1982, 53). Although cultural defenders as well as legal theorists such as Obi, Okoro, and Ibeziako, and historians such as Afigbo, are sufficiently informed about the slights men suffered, they are less informed about the discrimination suffered by women at the hands of the colonial state and Igbo male officials of the Native Authority Administration. As well, they are totally oblivious to the corrosive impact of colonial gender ideology on Igbo women. In various analyses of customary laws, they ignore the impact of the male-dominant ethos in the formation of Nigeria's political and legal history.[23]

In the 1960s, when Obi, Okoro, and Ibeziako were writing, they hardly realized the extent to which they were dealing with the legacies of legal fictions that had transformed Igbo society into a male-dominant culture and that continue to this day, to strip women of their social worth and significance. These writers mistook the socially transformed customs they encountered in the 1950s and 1960s in their respective towns and villages, as well as the codified customary laws of Eastern Nigeria, as having existed since "olden times." In their re-reading of the works of early European anthropologists, they are critical of the latter's racism but not of their sexism and religious bias. Thus their discussions of Igbo family structure, inheritance, and land tenure make it seem as if the customs they were discussing were unaffected by both European and Christian gender ideology. They treat them as "authentic documents of the past," and use them to prove either that women never mattered, or that they were not entitled to family land or had no access to family resources. Yet, "the sources of customary law today are the various judicial decisions recorded in different law reports, All England Law Report, etc., the statement of natural rulers and chiefs, and various societies, the works of textbook writers, both lawyers and anthropologists" (Ibeziako 1964, 18). The unifying factor in all these sources is that men produced them at a time when women were removed from political significance.

Obi and Okoro fail to consider the full impact of earlier colonial regulations and legal decisions on cultural values and of how these colonial policies had devalued women. One immediate reason for this oversight is, perhaps, the objective of their work. Obi's project is an expository work dealing with "the subject of customary law relating to property in Iboland" (Obi 1963, vii). Although he recognized the impact of Western culture, statutory laws, and case laws on customs, his aim was to present "customary law in its purity as much as possible" (1963, vii). By contrast, Nwakamma Okoro's objective was to "treat the subject from a lawyer's point of view," because he reasoned that "a study of customary laws which fails to take into account the influence of the general law on customary rules is inadequate" (1966, vii). Consequently, his sources were "(i) statements in existing literature written by lawyers and social-anthropologists; (ii) the decisions of the general customary courts; (iii) legislation; and (iv) information obtained by [him] between April and September 1962 from Judges (who are the authorities on the subject) of the various Customary Courts in Eastern Nigeria" (1966, vii). Because both scholars' objectives were framed by legal concerns, they missed the fact that these are the very sources in which the words and interpretations of women are sorely underrepresented. For Obi, this under representation appears to have been inconsequential given that he unproblematically classified women as persons under legal disability (1963, 68).

Like Obi, Okoro did not fundamentally question the sources and body of laws that he drew upon, because he did not see the need to do so. Neither scholar seriously attended to how the laws were collected and codified during the Native Authority period. Neither scholar undertook a critical historical reading of customary laws and their damaging impact on women's ownership of land. It seems they imagined that Igbo customs somehow remained uncontaminated and untouched during colonial rule. They hardly saw the ways the legal precepts and concepts had altered family dynamics and male–female relationships in various Igbo communities. They missed the role played by the chiefs and the native courts in introducing and disseminating patriarchal principles to southeastern Nigeria. As a result of the trajectory of their investigations, both Okoro and Obi mounted only an immanent critique, not the radical one that called to question the very legitimacy of the customary laws and the "customs" they wanted to investigate. One might argue that it is for this reason rather than sexism *per se* that they paid no attention to the violation of the principle of equity in the corpus of laws. But we must add that their lack of attention to these matters speaks of their location in a nationwide system of power that privileges their male identity and generates a definite philosophical outlook toward women and women's subordinate place in society.

Patriarchal Impact on Marriage

To highlight the presence of the patriarchal ideology of the colonial state in Igboland, we need to carry the investigation to the matrimonial realm. The starting question in this regard is, how and in what areas did women actually lose ground? First, women's loss began by being locked out of positions of relevance in the Native Authority Administration.[24] Their absence resulted in their being stripped of their historic rights, and over time, memories of those rights and traditions of political organization faded for future generations. The generation of women who were born in the late 1960s generally had no memory of these indigenous political structures and organizations. As the male–female relationship skewed more to men's advantage, educated male members of the families upheld marital rules and regulations for wives, daughters, and sisters that accorded with the patriarchal norms of the state, their Western educational experience, and their Christian religious beliefs. These norms suited their goals and crosscutting interests and greatly inflated their importance. Wives were no longer autonomous beings with whom husbands had to negotiate living, feeding, and sexual arrangements; they were dependent beings who had to abide by master's orders. Unfortunately, treating the invading patriarchal ideology as progressive and enlightened, Igbo families subsequently embraced this ideology and extended a subordinate identity to all females regardless of their situational position. Whereas in the indigenous familial ideology daughters and sisters did not share the same category as wives, and did not stand at the same structurally subordinate level. In the new patriarchal reality, however, there was no difference between wives, daughters, and sisters once they were all lumped into the category of "woman." Because the patriarchal scheme construes "woman" as coincident to "wife," the utilization of the term "woman" to describe daughters and sisters resulted in the latter's loss of ground, although not all in the same way. And so we must guard against homogenizing women, because the use of the term in family discussion obscures the social location of daughters and conceals how much ground they lost.

Following the creation of native courts and the appointment of warrant chiefs, a model of marriage akin to slave marriages became common. Warrant chiefs and court officials began a practice of marrying wives by coercion. Court clerks, interpreters, messengers, and warrant chiefs forcibly compelled women plaintiffs and defendants or daughters of male plaintiffs and defendants to become their wives if they were to avoid the crippling financial cost of protracted litigation.[25] Some of them had forty wives (Aba Commission of Inquiry 1930, 739), there were those that had close to seventy wives, and according to Nwanyieke of Ahiara, some had two hundred wives (Aba Commission of Inquiry 1930, 253). Families accepted these injustices in the hope they would be protected from capricious court clerks and judges. They hoped in vain that marital ties would buy them security and spare them further miscarriage of justice (1930, 738–739, 745). As husbands, warrant chiefs and court officials exploited their positions to strip widows and young heirs of their properties.[26] They were able to get away with these excesses because they were imbued with magisterial powers, often they were the "arbiter of law and procedure," and whatever they recorded was final (Adewoye 1977, 180). Nnenda Nwoji explains that these magisterial powers were guaranteed by district officers who routinely "support or uphold the judgment of the chiefs" when appeals are made (Aba Commission of Inquiry 1930, 745).

There is a tendency to think of Igbo families as stable and unchanging. But there have been radical shifts in the structural principles of families that they should no longer be considered as traditional. Coerced marriages and the values they fostered were deviations from the status quo. They were generally modeled on the sexual unions of "those-who-do-not-have" people (that is, captive women, female slaves) and their male captors or owners. Coerced marriages gave court officials undisputed authority over wives in a way that proper marriages did not. Disempowerment, a condition defined by lack of a supporting family, forced coerced wives to endure whatever treatment was meted out to them. The inherent inequality between husbands and such wives forced the latter into a deferential mode. In Onitsha, for example, such passive behavior was at odds with the behavior of Onitsha wives, who were reputed to be audacious, independent, and assertive. Consider the marriage of Odu Isaac Anieka Mbanefo, who by the time of his death in the 1990s had become the undisputed patriarch of the Mbanefo family of Odoje in Onitsha. He inadvertently confirmed this assessment of Onitsha wives in his memoir. By his own admission, his marriages to Onitsha women were very turbulent, indicating the women's refusal to tolerate actions they found demeaning to their dignity and prejudicial to their welfare. They were not prepared to accommodate his pretensions to authority just because he was part of the colonial economy and earned a salary. According to him,

> [m]y wife [Azuka, daughter of Ogbuefi Bosa of Umu Dei] and I kept on having domestic erruptions (*sic*) which made it quite stormy. . . . Our parents could not even make peace prevail between us for any reasonable length of time. Indeed the volatile nature of our life was beginning to strain the relationship between her parents and mine. . . . After three years of our marriage without another issue, I married Nwankie, daugh-

ter of Etukokwu of Ogboli Eke in 1924. That marriage turned to be a disaster. We parted in less than one year and went our separate ways. (1990, 48–49)

The ideology of male marital dominance was by no means the normative model of marriage in Onitsha prior to the enthronement of colonial ideology and value. Mbanefo finally attained marital "peace" when he married young foreign Igbo wives. The reason for this is that marriage to an older man in a community that is perceived to rank higher than one's own, and "being young, immature foreigners"[27] created a dynamic of disempowerment. Alienated in a foreign land, without critical family support, they were placed in weak, vulnerable positions, akin in status to captive wives. From the colonial male's point of view, these disempowered women made excellent wives. First, their subordinate status amplified their husbands' authority over them; second, their families were hardly nearby and rarely intervened, since at the time it was prestigious to have Onitsha men as in-laws; third, the families counseled their daughters to endure marital abuses on the ground that their lots would dramatically improve once their children became adults; and fourth, faced with limited options, these Igbo wives accepted a deferential position as a survival strategy.

The issue here is not that Onitsha men were bad husbands but that subordination becomes the lot of women who are marooned in communities where they lack kinship support. Colonialism, with the help of Christianity, created a new model of wives, whose court official husbands upheld patriarchal rules of conjugality. The wives had few rights, lived in subservience to their master-husbands in large polygamous compounds,[28] and endured their husband's derision as well as his contemptuous treatment of them. Co-wives were often at each other's throats as they took out their frustrations on each other and sought the favor of their master. Physically and emotionally insecure, they sought to produce heirs for their master to guarantee the longevity of his line and to secure their rights in his household. Unlike daughters in the new colonial reality, sons do not move to a different location upon marriage, and so these wives bided their time until their adult sons restored their rights.

Reinforced by a Western value system, Western education, and Christianity, the model of coerced new wives became the dominant model of marriage for aspiring professionals by the late 1950s. These children reproduced their parents' marriage as the Onitsha marital norm marriages. Because sons of foreign Igbo wives were socialized to be like their fathers, they expected wives to be as deferential as their mothers had been, believing that subordination was the proper customary or traditional behavior of wives. Naturally, intense marital stress developed when they married women whose mothers were not foreign Igbo wives, and who had been socialized to be assertive.

Children of these marriages compensated for their mixed culture by overemphasizing the importance of the father. The manifestation of patriarchal tendencies in these children of foreign Igbo wives constituted a major pathway through which male-privileging bias entered the culture and reshaped Onitsha families. As male bias flourished, the elimination of some female-privileging practices that were contrary to modern (i.e., patriarchal European) family norms and values accelerated. The subsequent erosion of the matrifocused consciousness of Onitsha culture gained momentum under missionary pressure. Christian converts, who perceived Onitsha marital practices as promoting moral laxity, established public morality brigades.[29] Its patriarchal ideology began to erode the authority of the *usokwu* (hearth hold) and its matricentric consciousness. Even the naming pattern of children came under assault. Up until the 1930s Onitsha children bore their mother's name as their identifying name. But as they enrolled in schools from 1858, school authorities compelled them to identify by their fathers' names. Thus Bey Nwamaka became Bey Agbakoba and Aniemeka Mgboli became Aniemeka Ibekwe. The gradual infusion of Western patriarchal consciousness shifted the society away from its matricentric pole.

Though this matricentric ideology has seriously been eroded, it was not completely overthrown, as Helen Henderson, a white American anthropologist discovered in the mid-1960s, when she conducted research in Onitsha. She found residual elements of this matricentric ideology in the assertiveness of the women and in men's perception of them. An elderly Onitsha man waxed eloquent on the nonpassivity of Onitsha women. According to him: "We say never argue with women. Let me have a dispute with men but never with women. If you enter their trap you will not come out again. Forever after, you go to the stream, they will call your [sic] names. This woman goes to market, she talks my name, that women talks my name; here and there and my name is all over in the town. No! We keep peace with women" (Henderson 1969, 171).

Patriarchal Impact on Divorce

The judgments of the native courts facilitated the transformation of customary marriage laws into patriarchal ones. Forms of marriage that did not conform to the new patriarchal model were outlawed. Concerned to prove that Africans were not primitives and that men ruled the roost, native court decisions stressed the subordination of wives and the role of husbands as head of the family. The rights of women in the community were curtailed by limiting the possibility of their autonomy and subverting their right to abandon oppressive marriages. Philip Igbafe described extensively the sorts of manipulation undertaken by Benin chiefs that occurred too in Igboland. In one particularly egregious example, Chief Obaseki, the vice president of the native court, claimed and collected payments for damages and personal injury from the beaux of his fifteen runaway wives (1970: 87). Ahudi of Nsidimo describes an Igbo equivalent in which chiefs refuse to pay the full bridewealth of their wives, but would insist on an outrageously inflated compensation from the ex-wife and her new beau (Aba Commission of Inquiry 1930, 114). Nwadaru of Owerrinta also disclosed that court clerks and warrant chiefs punished women by subverting their divorce cases. They did this by keeping the portion of bridewealth that should have been returned to the husband to conclude the divorce (Aba Commission of Inquiry, 1930, 588).[30] They knew that if a husband did not receive the requisite portion of the bridewealth, the woman would still be married to him and he could claim spousal privileges. This interference by court officials created many problems for women, since they unfairly tilted the advantage to husbands, who could then harass wives.

To further complicate matters, husbands seeking to punish ex-wives took to suing their wives' partners for adultery, claiming that they had caused their wives to run away. Flora Kaplan recounts cases of men who went to court to recover wives and bridewealth ten to fifteen years after their marriage ended (1997, 267). Not only were such cases motivated by the urge to punish errant wives, but they were undertaken to extract financial compensation from male paramours. Such punitive measures prompted warrant chiefs to invent fictional customs designed to control wives' sexuality. They had the effect of representing sexual relations between a wife and her paramour as adultery, and as meriting punishment. For example, a former warrant chief from Isikwuato, Onuoha, claimed that:

> Under traditional law and custom a man found guilty of [adultery] not only gave seventy shillings to the injured husband, but also produced a dog for sacrifice in propitiation of *Ala*. But in the Courts introduced by white men the outraged man got nothing, nor was the pollution of *Ala* removed. (cited in Afigbo 1984, 265)[31]

That this was an invented custom to assuage the dignity of the cuckolded husband is conveyed by the computation of the penalty in *shillings*. The ex-warrant chief failed to disclose why "traditional law and custom" specified penalties in the British currency system, not the Isuikwuato currency system of brass rods and cowries. S. N. Nwabara's (1977) work suggests that this computation may have been based on the conversion of the local currency system into the British system. But the idea that seventy shillings was, in fact, the traditional equivalent of the fine, lacks merit since the local economy at the time could not have sustained such heavy fines prior to its expansion during colonial rule. As Nwabara's analysis on colonial taxation showed, most men of the time could not pay the assessed rate of 5 shillings 9 pence let alone a fine of 70 shillings (1977, 176). The argument could still be made that prohibitive fines were customary and deliberately set to curb adultery. But that argument lacks credibility. What does "adultery" mean in a context where transmarital relationships are permitted?[32] And, how do we understand "adultery" when relationships that the court viewed as such were not conceived of in that light in the local culture? Afigbo perceptively disclosed that the attempt to ensure that "'native law and custom [were] not repugnant to British ideas of justice' led to the growth of a body of laws which, from the point of view of the people, was far from indigenous" (Afigbo 1972, 264).

Furthermore, one cannot really take the word of the ex-chief from Isikwuato on adultery as true. An understanding of the Igbo ethical scheme reveals the absurdity of making adultery a punishable offense and a sacrilege to *Ala*. This is an ethical framework that permitted practices which violate the English/Christian matrimonial codes, as we saw in chapter 1. The ethical scheme expected an adult wife of an infant child to have children with other men; it expected wives who had difficulty conceiving children with their husbands to have relations with other men to "seek a child."[33] The nuclear family model of "faithfulness" was an idea that native court judges sought to inject into the culture so that it could become a prerequisite of Igbo marriages. Once they did this, adultery became an offence that attracted lucrative compensation for husbands and corrupt judges.

Meanwhile, at the opposing side of the spectrum, European writers of the period presented colonialism as holding out material benefits to African women. Concerned to justify colonialism, Amaury Talbot (1915, 89) and Northcote Thomas (1913, 24) argued that "the white man's law" gave Igbo women a strong basis to resist unfavorable and oppressive marriage. Nothing could be further from the truth. Prior to the diffusion of restrictive mores underlying divorce laws, Onitsha women could easily end their marriages, and some of them used *igba n'rira* to terminate unfulfilling marriages more quickly.[34] *Igba n'rira* occurred when a married woman entered into a clandestine relationship with a paramour. As the affair intensified, the couple might decide to get married. The woman, who was already married, "eloped" to the paramour's home rather than following the more extended procedure of returning to her natal home, ending the marriage by returning a specific portion of the bridewealth, and subsequently remarrying. While some may see *igba n'rira* as a messy process, it had the effect of expediting the end of a marriage and the beginning of a new one.[35]

In light of this history, it was erroneous for European writers, who were hardly knowledgable about the culture, and male officials of the native courts to characterize divorce as nonexistent in Igbo cultures. That divorces were common in Onitsha is seen by the fact that its social norms included provisions for accomodating returning daughters. Even as late as the 1960s, when the white American anthropologist Richard N. Henderson studied the society, he was able to observe the residual elements of that tradition. He found that "[marital] separation must have been common; villages expect to have a core of daughters in residence and to provide them with houses" (1972, 235).[36] The fact that families expected to have a core of adult daughters at home tells us that marital separations were nothing new and that daughters' rights to shelter were never extinguished. In patriarchal societies, by contrast, women stayed married, even when their marriages were intolerable. Their families expected them to do so, and they had to because they did not have the requisite family support to abandon oppressive marriages. This was not the case in Onitsha.

It is simplistic to assume, as is so routinely done, that colonialism emancipated African women from "repressive" traditions. It is equally simplistic to assume that Igbo women and men were disadvantaged the same way or that there was unity of purpose in opposing colonialism. Colonialism worked to the advantage of a variety of interest groups by pitting one group of Igbos against another. In the area of family relations, it secured its exploitative goal by empowering Igbo men—specifically husbands and fathers—to become direct oppressors of their wives and daughters. Notwithstanding Afigbo's excellent historical account of warrant chiefs, we cannot but note his failure to interrogate ex-warrant chiefs about their discriminatory practices toward women. Although he was sensitive to the slights warrant chiefs suffered at the hand of British colonial officials, he failed to acknowledge how the warrant chiefs' rulings adversely affected women and subsequently altered male–female relations profoundly. Chanock's (1982) work proves that a critical interrogation of the gender biases of male court functionaries is possible. By being sensitive to the plight of women under colonialism, he was able to expose the male-privileging nature of court rulings. He could see that they resulted in the gender reconstitution of local institutions and cultural values. Because he focused on the nature of male–female politics in judicial arbitration, Chanock was able to note that women were not seen as the offended party. This meant that customs had to be invented or manipulated to suit whatever some men hoped to gain.

It should not be assumed that women condoned this state of affairs. They resisted in various ways, they asserted their rights to end their marriages, many ran away from husbands, and others retaliated by refusing to return their bridewealth until they found another husband willing to fund it.[37] Strapped by their wives' departure and the withdrawal of their labor, husbands further pressured native court officials against being soft in their rulings. Sensitive to this appeal, native court judges began to construct and apply punitive definitions that they made out were traditional practices. As Chanock observed in East Africa, the judges increasingly "emphasiz[ed] not the offense against the husband, but the need to punish the women" (1982, 63). The new divorce laws that emerged from these punitive native court rulings became the customs that today are enshrined in customary laws statutes.

PART 4: PATRIARCHAL IDEOLOGY
AND WOMEN'S RESISTANCES

"A Strange Phenomenon": Women's Resistance against Patriarchy

If all these historical examples of women-affirming practices are true, one might ask, why didn't women protest the erosion of their power, rights, roles, and responsibilities? In fact, they vigorously resisted the usurpation of their traditional structures of governance and the distortion of customs they entailed. Because resistances such as the Women's War have been cast as an economic protest by Meek, Jones and Afigbo, the assumption is that they are not political protests and any anti-patriarchal interpretation illicitly reads contemporary political concerns back into history. Meek, the colonial anthropologist sent to study the cultural roots of women's uprising immediately after the event, described the protests as "primarily due to an unfounded fear [of] direct taxation" (1937, ix).[38] He downplayed the women's hostility to the colonial administration, the Native Authority Administration, and its system of warrant chiefs and native courts. In fact, he claimed that "no objection had been taken to these courts as such" (1937, x). If Meek's account is correct and the Women's War had nothing to do with issues of patriarchy, then we cannot legitimately characterize Igbo women's grievances as spurred by resentment of patriarchy.

Meek's characterization of the causes of the Women's War casts the women as irrational, an act that slickly conceals the legitimate grounds for Igbo women's uprising.[39] No only did it portray them as politically immature, he refused to accept that their fears of taxation were legitimate.[40] He makes very little of the fact that the global economic climate had drastically depressed the amount of payment they received from British trading agents for their palm oil produce that was the basis of their personal wealth and the region's economic wealth. At the same time the women were coping with these economic difficulties, the patriarchal policies of the British administration were pushing them out of the economic arena. As avenues to wealth opened up for men, they were being closed for women. They could not grow their trade, not because they lacked initiative, as Jones' (1989) analysis seemed to suggest, but because the resources they needed to grow their trade, such as land for collateral and wives as helpmates, were no longer available options. To make matters worse, they had to divert their trading capital to pay the taxes of sons and husbands, as well as a host of other illegal fees that court officials imposed on individuals and communities.

The women's vehement reactions in 1929 and their animus toward the colonial symbols of their grievances was as much a protest against their economic impoverishment as it was against the looming threat of taxation. Because of his dismissive view of women, Meek's reading of the 1929 Women's War failed to appreciate that taxation was not a bogus threat, but one that added another layer of burden onto already existing ones.[41] Afigbo undermines Meek's attribution of irrationality to Igbo women by revealing that utterances of some district officers showed that plans were afoot to implement such a taxation policy.[42] He further explains that "taxation on men had in fact in places meant taxation on men and women [since] women helped their husbands with their earnings and some widows paid for their sons of sixteen years or thereabouts" (1984, 239). Igbo women were in a position to do so because the only profitable commodity in the region at the time was palm oil (Jones 1989, 97). This meant that, although only men were on the tax roll, it was women who were being taxed since they provided the money for the taxes from their palm oil trade.

So when Meek made it seem that Igbo women were politically ignorant, not only was he invoking the Western patriarchal scheme that depicts women as lacking rationality and political reason, he was playing fast and loose with the truth. Igbo women were very much aware of political issues and the impact of economic events on their livelihood. They controlled the region's produce of palm oil that contributed a disproportionate amount of revenue to the colonial treasury (Jones 1989). Although they were unaware of the exact nature of the global economic system, they were experiencing the effects of its price fluctuations on their palm oil trade. Contrary to Meek's claims Igbo women were very clear about the economic and political issues galvanizing their protests. They knew they were being forced to subsidize husbands, sons, fathers, and brothers without political representation and adequate compensation. One could say they were resisting incorporation into a system that exploited their labor, and then publicly devalued their contribution by treating them as invisible.[43] Because Igbo women had always been political actors, they could analyze these exploitative issues and their political reasoning led them to challenge this attempt to exact their labor without compensation. They used all the traditional political instruments that were available to them to conduct what has become known as *Ogu Umunwanyi* (Women's War).

The Women's War provided a vivid picture of Igbo women's indigenous political instruments. In Aboh, they defined Oputa, the Obi and warrant chief of Aboh, as a collaborator and informant of the administration. Exercising their traditionally sanctioned rights of discipline, they "kidnapped" Obi Oputa and forced him to sing humiliating songs all over town (Mba 1982, 72). In Ogoja province, Afikpo women en mass besieged the district officer for two weeks, demonstrating against the impending imposition of taxation without representation.[44] In Abakaliki division, Izzi women forced the village heads who had accepted tax discs (proof of payment) from the district officer, to throw them away on the ground, in defiance of a taxation that they believed was a perfidious plot to cause sterility among women and ruin their yam crop (Mba 1982, 73). The idea of sterility was, of course, a metaphor for women's growing disempowerment and social irrelevance in the new political dispensation. In Onitsha, the imposition of a water rate without community discussion brought out the women who protested against the already heavy burden of taxation they had to pay.[45] Declaring that they knew of no place where people's water was sold back to them, they demonstrated outside the station magistrate's office, singing scurrilous songs about then resident officer, Captain Dermot P. J. O'Connor. Taking the issue one step further, they launched an economic boycott of the European firms and sought to starve the Europeans by refusing to sell foodstuffs to them and their cooks. In Opobo, where women traders were hit exceedingly hard by the 1929 financial crash and the drastic slump in commodity prices that followed, they vented their anger at their growing impoverishment in a series of mass demonstrations against the district officers and the economic policies of European trading companies (Mba 1982, 75). At a meeting in Umuahia in December 1929, Umuahia women sought to impress upon the agents of the trading firms the importance of opening discussions on commodity prices. Obowo women went a step further and presented their own position and price list to the European merchants (Mba 1986, 75).

Igbo women's strategy for dealing with the economic issues proved their political acumen as well as their relevance in the political scheme that predated colonialism. Resorting to the political strategies of protest marches and direct confrontations, the women advocated for the rejection of the new political system. They insisted on the restoration of the traditional judicial system that had affirmed women's voices. In their view, this would allow everyone, including the poor, to obtain justice without facing financial ruin at the hands of the colonial system of justice with its corrupt warrant chiefs and court officials. Rather than heed this call for reform, district officers spent valuable time trying to ferret out the troublesome men behind all the "disturbances." Clearly, in their patriarchal minds, Igbo women, like women elsewhere, lacked the critical faculty, organizational skills, and ability to assess their political reality for themselves. It is not surprising that British colonial officials, Meek included, could not see the political dimension of the women's uprising, even after the conclusion of the tribunal investigation of the causes of what they called "women's riots."[46]

Between 1925 and 1935, Igbo women incessantly organized protest rallies that targeted the oppressive symbols of colonialism. They dumped refuse in the courts, placed obstructions on the roads, roughed up collaborators, and picketed the offices of colonial officials to wrest from them some form of representation. In Eastern Nigeria, for instance, there were numerous village-level and province-wide demonstrations by women against the erosion of their powers and rights. The first recorded evidence of widespread women's unrest was the Nwaobiala (The Child Has Come) Movement, misleadingly tagged the "Women's Purity Campaign" by administrative officers who could not conceptualize women as political actors (Onitsha Province Annual Report 391, 1925). Nwaobiala movement interrogated specific colonial policies and, remarkably, initiated political reform through using the context of dance. Traveling in bands from fifty to three hundred, members of the Nwaobiala Movement radiated north to other communities to pass on the good tidings. They delivered their message after purifying the compound of elders (both male and female) and performing the Nwaobiala dance. In the face of stiff government opposition, the movement, which had begun before October 25, 1925, spread swiftly to the entire Owerri province, Onitsha province, and parts of Ogoja province (a distance of about 6,000 square miles) by December of the same year.

Reconstructing this historic 1925 unrest from colonial records, scholars reveal that the native court was the object of the women's animus (Mba 1982, Amadiume 1988a, Oriji 2001). Women filled the local courthouse with refuse, signifying their disgust with a flawed structure of governance that had marginalized them. Military escorts were sent to quell the "disturbances" in Abakaliki, Okigwe, and Nnobi. This first phase of Igbo women's political unrest, a prelude to the Women's War, was a protest at the ongoing political changes and social distortions. In a pragmatic move, women in the three provinces of Owerri, Ogoja, and Onitsha sought to recover their former political relevance, and tabled for reform sets of issues that were most pressing to them. In Bende and Umuahia in Owerri Province, they demanded that women's prostitution be stopped. By contrast, in Awgu in Enugu Province, the protesters underscored the right of women to control their sexuality and become sex workers (Mba 1982, 70–71). They urged women not to charge too much for their sexual services, and demanded that married women should be allowed to have consorts without fear of being taken before the native court (1982, 71). The patriarchal attempts of the native courts to curtail women's sexual autonomy in early 1920s prodded women to request a return to the old system, in which there was no criminalization of transmarital sex, and in which it was not grounds for divorce. In the older ethical scheme, transmarital sex did not have this negative connotation, and hence had not been regarded as a cause for marriage dissolution (1982, 71).[47]

These protests exposed court officials' utilization of the coercive powers of the state to enforce patriarchal morality norms and codes. The women's responses showed too that the imposition of a gender framework was inconsistent with local norms. In the women's view, these patriarchal codes undermined their autonomy and agency as well as the principle of matrifocality that underpinned their worth as mothers. The use of the courts to control women's sexuality and to limit their power created much resentment against the native court, and turned it into the focus of their anger. It is instructive that women were angry that such controls limited their rights and closed off their life options since it showed their unfamiliarity with that value scheme. In their value scheme "the world depends on women"–after all they are the ones who multiply its population (Enyidia of Mbiopongo, Aba Commission of Inquiry 1930, 80). Igbo women's demands in the three provinces converged on their opposition to the warrant chiefs because the newly created class of powerful men of the courts was corrupt and they victimized the poor. That they felt politically empowered to seek relief from their tyrannical rule and male-privileging ideals unequivocally shows they were unaccustomed to this sort of political treatment and domination.

In the second phase of Igbo women's political unrest in 1929, combatants of the Women's War named the conflict as such because they were at war with odious colonial policies that impacted negatively on their lives. Proof of this awareness is evident in the fact that some wives and daughters of warrant chiefs led the revolt against their husbands and fathers who were political rather than economic figures, and whose implementation of colonial policies affected their lives as women. Their status as women entailed political obligations as community mothers that outweighed any personal relations they had with husbands or fathers. Deploying their sanctionary powers and the conflict-resolution mechanism of "sitting on the object" (ino kwasi ya ani) of annoyance the pan-community Women's Council forced their grievances into public discussion. First, they "sat on" Mark Emeruwa, the assessor who had been sent by the highly unpopular and corrupt Okugo, the warrant chief of Oloko, to count items of women's wealth. And second, when several women were injured by Okugo's thugs, trying to secure the release of Emeruwa, women from Umuahia, Owerrinta, Nguru, and Ikot Ekpene converged on Oloko to "sit on" Okugo. Faced with this mass uprising and women's insistence that Okugo's cap be removed, the British district officer promptly put Okugo on trial, where he was convicted and imprisoned for assaulting the injured women. Because the political dimension of this 1929 crisis was sharply drawn, Okugo's warrant chief's cap was taken from him.

News of this success energized women, who came out en masse to press their political objectives and to mount a region wide attempt to topple the warrant chief system and remove all corrupt warrant chiefs. The uprising spread over an area of 6,000 square miles, throughout Owerri and Calabar provinces. Mary Onumaere led three-thousand women to enter Owerri town on December 14, 1929 (Mba 1982, 83). Nnete Nma in Obioha near Azunmini led local women who burned the native court. Edure, daughter of Nda, a court official, led Etchi women to destroy the home of a court member (1982, 84). At Utim

Etim Ekpo in Oron, one of the wives of Chief Akpan Umo beat the drum that summoned women to the demonstration (1982, 84).[48] At their wits end, the colonial administration ordered troops into the region to quell the uprising. Fifty-five women were shot dead at Opobo, Utim Etim Ekpo, and Abak; another fifty women were wounded, ten native courts were destroyed, and houses of native court officials were damaged. Despite the women's heavy casualties, the end of the war did not signal the end of the protest movement and their agitation for political representation. Barely six months later, in May 1930, Okposi women in Afikpo division assaulted and kidnapped a village head, demanding that he return taxes he had collected. Again, the demonstration soon spread (cited in Mba 1982, 95; Ogoja Province Report 2/1/90).

Although Igbo women were appreciative of some of the benefits of colonial rule, such as better medical care and transportation networks, they wanted better financial compensation for their produce. They did not want to pay taxes, given that their sons and husbands provided the unpaid labor that constructed the roads network, and their oil trade was attracting all kinds of government duties. At the very least, they wanted to preserve their historic rights to generate wealth and to attain political prominence and prestige in their communities. Because their former political framework had provided them with avenues to be politically relevant, they could check the powers of men and call them to order. They wanted an equal space with men in the new political order and sought to reform the new colonial order to provide corresponding opportunities for women. To this end, they proposed that the tenure of warrant chiefs be limited to three years of service, and that women should be appointed to these positions and be consulted in the selection of officers for these posts.

The Anti-Patriarchal Edge of the Women's War

The question could now be asked, did the war have anything to do with Igbo women's opposition to patriarchy and the colonial administration's patriarchal ideology? Other than scholars' suggestions, what evidence is there that Igbo women found that ideology odious? The evidence can be found in the women's testimonies at the tribunal investigating the causes of the Women's War. At the root of their responses was a clear awareness of the destructive aspects of the administration's patriarchal ideology. The women spoke of their oppression by the new political system and its local agents. Mary Okezie's letter to the tribunal made clear that "the tyrannical ruling of the chiefs [who are all men] over their subjects" did not sit well with women (Mba 1982, 87). In her petition, Nwanyiriwa pointed to the corruption and extensive oppression of Igbo male court officials (Mba 1982, 91). She petitioned to have "white man in every Native Court because our black men are [treating people] too badly."

Nwoto of Okpuala queried the white men if they really "came to bring peace to the land . . . [because] if this oppression [of the native courts, warrant chiefs, and court clerks] continues, how are we to praise you?" (Aba Commision of Inquiry 1930, 805). Mary Onumaere summed it up, "We women are the mothers of Europeans and the Chiefs, and we don't wish women to be oppressed. . . . We have not been treated well . . . we don't wish to be oppressed by our menfolk" (Aba Commission of Inquiry 1930, 239-340).

The women's responses exposed the government's sexist ideology and revealed women's unwillingness to accept the damaging consequences of that patriarchal ideology. Warrant chiefs, court clerks, and messengers were the direct recipients of their anger because they were the enforcers of offensive policies at the local community level. Although there were economic motivations for the war, Igbo women's unrest during the years 1915–1930 was tied to the steady erosion of their sociopolitical powers. They perceptively grasped that the erosion was tied to the Native Authority system and a gender ideology that placed women outside the boundaries of what it means to be social. Treating the Igbo as lacking political institutions, British officials failed to see that within the Igbo sociopolitical tradition, women were one of the politically constituted groups. They possessed powers to back up their demands and objectives. Within this political culture, lack of representation, *ewe onu okwu* (not to have a voice/say) meant powerlessness; it also implied loss of personhood. We can then begin to understand the intensity of women's anger when they discovered that they had been politically reclassified into the category of the enslaved.

The depth of women's resentment towards the warrant chief and the invading patriarchal ideology came to light at the Aba Commission of Inquiry's probing the combatants of the war.[49] Olenga, a combatant from Umuakpara, excoriated the arrogance of these chiefs and indicted their administrative abuses for triggering the uprising. One of the major grievances of Igbo women was that the new political ideology overturned the indigenous political structure and eliminated the political institutions of women. Olenga explained, "instead of coming home to consult women [i.e., working in a consultative manner with their women councils as in the past], they [the chiefs] generally agree with the District Officer straight away. They would not consult us." (Aba Commission of Inquiry 1930, 665). Her explanation contained an expectation of women's political right that echoed Ahudi's (of Nsidimo) contention that women must have equal rights with men to approve candidates for warrant chief. Ahudi had argued that "If a new man is appointed then all the women should be present and all the men should be present and *both* should approve his appointment" (Aba Commission of Inquiry 1930, 115, my emphasis).

Olenga and Ahudi were pointing out that women's political expectations were hardly met by the new colonial order. Pinpointing this expectation is highly significant. It showed that Igbo women were, indeed, political actors,

and that contrary to claims that "tradition" treated them as minors, they had
participated in the governance of their communities. Furthermore, they were
accustomed to participating in a political process in which "all the women" and
"all the men" were involved in making community decisions. A petition by
women from the twenty-seven towns of Nguru made clear that they expected
to be accorded access to political leadership. This expectation underpins their
recommendation to the colonial government to cancel the warrant it had issued to chiefs because they (the women) were not consulted and they had re-
pudiated the chiefs (Owerri District Report 1/14/49 cited in Mba 1982, 88).
Their natural confidence in their own political rights explains why they objected vehemently to the male-privileging shift taking place in the society.
These shifts were eroding their political autonomy and destroying their basis
of authority, and as Nwanyieke of Ahiara bluntly put it, the protest was their
way of telling the government that their warrant chief system was unacceptable because "the chiefs have been oppressing us. [They] have oppressed us a
lot" (Aba Commission of Inquiry 1930, 254).

Another way to read Olenga's and Ahudi's testimony is to see it as a statement that patriarchs did not rule the indigenous political culture. Women were
not the social minors that the colonial government or a number of contemporary Igbo men now perceived them to be. Prior to the installation of the colonial administration, the Igbo political process and culture were not male dominated. The Nwaobiala movement and Olenga's response at the tribunal tells
us that the patriarchal ideology was at odds with the indigenous cultural ideology and inimical to the latter's conceptualization of women as social adults.
A number of scholars have made this point in other ways when they stated that
the warrant chiefs were ruling in contravention to local laws, norms, and customs.[50] The problem, however, is that they did not factor this insight into their
general history of the region, the character of local political systems, social institutions, and the implication of the native courts' rulings. Although Mba and
Amadiume recognized that women's frustration called attention to the way
male privilege was being upheld at a cost to women, they concluded erroneously that patriarchy was exacerbated by colonialism rather than introduced
at the time. To avoid reading into history, they should not have assumed, without sociological evidence, that patriarchy was endemic to the culture. They
should have recognized that patriarchy was just beginning to make inroads into
the culture.

The lack of a clear understanding that Igbo society shifted to become a
male-privileging society from one that had equitably distributed powers between the sexes explains why the depth of women's anger in 1929 still eludes
many scholars. Mba and Amadiume did not convincingly explain why Igbo
women were really upset with the patriarchal policies of the colonial administration if they were already familiar with the ideology of patriarchy. Afigbo's

claim that Igbo women's anger was over taxation does not fully comprehend the scope and depth of their frustration, which they expressed in frequent demonstrations against the colonial government in towns and villages from 1925 to 1929 and thereafter. Although I accept the notion that taxation was the proverbial straw that finally broke the camel's back in 1929; nevertheless, it was not the sole issue that galvanized women's anger and the numerous local and regional protests.[51]

Igbo women were angry for a number of reasons. Nwoto of Okpuala (Ngwa) clearly articulated some of these at the Commission of Inquiry: "We had cause for grievances before the taxation was introduced. It is a long time since the Chiefs and the people who know book [educated people] and the Nkwerre people have been oppressing us. . . . We are annoyed because men are born by women and they marry women. . . . We are telling you that we have been oppressed. [The chiefs] don't treat us well at all . . . the new chiefs are also receiving bribes" (Aba Commission of Inquiry 1930, 805). Rachel Nenenta put it bluntly: "We women are sick of various troubles emanating either from Mr. Jackson [district officer] himself or from Government as a whole" (1930, 742). Igbo women were angry because, unlike in their indigenous society, the newly installed warrant chiefs, who, after all, were born of women and married women, were treating them disrespectfully. To their chagrin, the government of the white men, which they thought had come to bring peace to the land, dismissed them, the mothers of the community. Worse still, it treated them as if they were politically irrelevant, a situation that was odious to them.[52] Their resentment showed that they were new to this kind of ideology and its depreciatory treatment of women. Igbo women of the time were decidedly outraged that *they* were receiving oppressive and cavalier treatment from their own sons, proving that their sons and husbands were not given to this type of behavior in the past. Having identified the warrant chiefs and their patriarchal ideology as the root cause of their grievance, Ahudi told the Commission of Inquiry what it will take to resolve the problem:

> [T]hese disturbances will go on perhaps for fifteen years unless these chiefs are decapped. All the Chiefs, when they appear before you, say all sorts of things to impress you that they are good men. All the chiefs whom we ask to be deposed should be deposed, otherwise the trouble will go on. . . . You may take evidence for many days, but *unless you come to a conclusion which will satisfy the women,* we will follow you wherever you go. . . . [W]e never made demonstrations in this manner, but we do so now in order to show you that women are annoyed. . . . We will continue fighting until all the Chiefs have been got rid of, but until then the matter will not be settled. (Aba Commission of Inquiry 1930, 114–15, my emphasis)

For Ahudi to set up women's satisfaction as the only way the social un-
rests would stop is to speak as one who is not accustomed to men thinking for
them, making decisions for them, and telling them what to do. She was speaking from the position of a politically conscious being who is cognizant of
women's full political rights in their various communities. The self-assured image she projected revealed that the basis of the women's outrage was the patriarchal ideology, which conflicted with their very clearly defined social and
political identities as well as the goals of the women's councils. Further aggra-
vating matters was the fact that their economic activities, which secured their
political autonomy, were being transferred to men, as the colonial administration directed all its economic and administrative resources to men.[53]

Lessons of the Women's War: Remaking of Igbo Society

Cultural misreadings can be traced to the explanatory framework and conceptual tools used by contemporary scholars. These sometimes occlude theoretical vision and prevent researchers from apprehending the African cultural
landscape as it was prior to the impact of the male-privileging ideology of colonialism and Christianity.[54] Thus, under the universalizing impulse of feminism
and its expansive claims that historically all women were dominated by men,
the conceptual tools of the discipline define the direction of research. A sea-
soned researcher is propelled to miss vital clues that will offer a different reading. Meanwhile, any instance of sex difference and social hierarchy would automatically be projected back into history as indicative of patriarchy. The
reduction of sex differences to a precolonial patriarchal scheme in Igboland
overly simplifies the region's social institutions and history. Not just because
the simplification treats new phenomena as endemic to the culture, but because it diverts attention from countervailing evidences as well as the dynamics of social changes that occurred during colonialism.[55]

In reality, the Women's War was a direct response to the installation of
the patriarchal ideology in a region unfamiliar with the provisions of patriarchy. An important lesson of the war was that it disclosed the existence of a
different political culture in which women viewed themselves as equal stake-
holders in communities' political processes, and participated in the governance
of the community through their Women's Councils and Assemblies. Historically, Igbo women had a strong conception of self; they were aware of their right
and duties and they expected these to continue after colonization. When they
did not, these women "armed themselves with cudgels," and as Meek reported,
"marched up and down the country, holding up roads, howling down the Government, setting fire to the Native Court buildings, assaulting their chiefs, and
working themselves generally into a state of frenzy that on several occasions
they did not hesitate to challenge the troops sent to restore order" (1937, ix).

The sharp contrast of Igbo women as political activists and their contemporary picture as subjugated individuals tells us that the latter resulted only after decades of systematic erosion of their rights and relentless attacks on their sense of self and capabilities.

The causes of the Women's War make it clear that Igbo men of the period did not possess the sorts of rights and overriding authority that they claimed for themselves during and after colonial rule. In the indigenous system of governance, women had clearly defined institutions and roles, socially validated strategies for curtailing male excesses.[56] With the diminution of women's political structures during the early stages of colonization, Igbo women could not effectively check the excesses of men appointed by the colonial government during the latter stages of colonial rule. If "native" women were not considered individuals with legal, social, and political rights, they were not later reconstituted as individuals and brought into the legal scheme and into the sphere of humanity. As colonialism progressed, the losses of women became permanent as the patriarchal ideology threw a masculine veil over customs: a new cadre of politically powerful men emerged who defended and entrenched this ideology by inventing fictive customs to which they then appealed to ground their newly won privileges. Simultaneously, too, a new breed of Igbo women emerged, products of mission schools and the Western view of womanhood, who accepted the subject status of women as progressive. Even after independence, the mechanisms for endowing them with legal and political rights were never activated, and their social, political, and family rights have not been fully restored.

The problems of women were compounded by the passage of government policies, by-laws, and laws that legitimized male authority and effectively eliminated their traditions of seeking consensus from both men and women. A perceptive Rachel Nenenta noted the existence of this masculinist ideology underwriting the collusion of the white male district officers and the local male warrant chiefs, if "you are not satisfied with the judgment and ask for a review or appeal the case . . . the District Officer . . . will not ask you what you have to say in the matter but he will simply say, 'Let the judgment of the chiefs stand'" (Aba Commission of Inquiry 1930, 742). This explains why women such as Rosanah Ogwe could not be heard when they complained that "Court messengers [who are all men] would only throw 4d. [pence] on the ground for an article which should fetch say 3s. [shillings] and go away with the article. If the owner resists or talks in any way about the matter she is assaulted by the Court messengers" (1930, 740). The long-term effect of inflicting state-sponsored violence on women was the normalization of power as violent and male, and of powerlessness as female.

The colonial offer of modernity and progress to Igbo women was of a life of violence and gender domination. Colonialism imbued Igbo fathers with rights that far outstripped what the consanguineal family system had ever accorded them. This imbuement had three political effects. First, it transformed conjugal units that were marked by two households—the mother's and the father's—into one single household with the husband and fathers as the exclusive head of that household.[57] This transformation reshaped the Igbo family from a consanguineal family system to hybrids of the nuclear family in which a family is a man's personal domain, where he rules as head and his wife or wives are subject to his laws, and overall supervision and control.[58] Next, it assigned to husbands/fathers the civic duties of maintaining law and order within the family units, effectively, transforming fathers and husbands into quasi-administrative officers who implemented in family spaces the wage and tax policies and the local ordinances and edicts of the colonial administration.[59] And lastly, this transformation secured the intrusion of the government into homes and the necessary administrative basis upon which to hold husbands/fathers (and all adult males) responsible for families' tax obligations.

The concept of "head of household" divided Igbo cultural landscape into a public and private sphere. What occurred in the household was now deemed to be private and under the jurisdiction and control of husbands/fathers, and what occurred outside of the household was seen to be within the public space of colonial authority. This private/public division barred women from the new colonial definition of public space and the economy and labor market that operated within it. The ensuing gender-based exclusion of women allowed the state to admit only husbands and fathers into the male-privileging public space. Within this newly configured public space, men were empowered to claim a monopoly of power, to speak for their conjugal units and the community at large. Although recent critiques of the household in Africanist literature have focused on the wrongful representation of households as discrete entities, they have not focused on its patriarchal ideology, probably because they do not see the relevance of this critique.[60] Yet, the theoretical articulation of household in African studies ignored the way the concept inserted patriarchal relations into the society.

Prior to colonialism, Igbo wives were rarely dependent on husbands and there was a clear separation between husbands and wives in areas of income, expenditure, and activities.[61] By means of edicts, public policies, and pronouncements that determined families' income and tax burden, the colonial administration deployed the concept of household and turned Igbo husbands into sovereigns. The deployment not only obscured the economic and labor activities of their wives, it also undermined the equitable conjugal relations that had given wives the requisite autonomy to engage in their own self-directed activities, and in the past had blocked the transformation of husbands into patriarchs. As wives, daughters, mothers, and sisters became dependents, they were treated as extensions of the head-of-household's identity. They could not obtain medical treatment without the approval of husbands or fathers, they could not receive education without the consent of fathers or husbands, and they could not open bank accounts without a husband's permission. The political consequence of recognizing only husbands' spousal and paternal rights was that it fostered a male-dominant consciousness that restructured the non-patriarchal Igbo lineages along patriarchal lines.

It is incontrovertible that colonial anthropologists, missionaries, and colonial administrators never really saw African women as fully formed beings, with politically defined rights and roles.[62] What is less appreciated is that the inflation of Igbo men's importance occurred at the expense of women's social status and diminished their social worth. As products of the late Victorian and Edwardian middle-class culture, most British administrators, missionaries, and anthropologists in Nigeria from 1900 to 1940 assumed that all women were wives and that their places were in the home, not in the economic, political, or judicial domain. Many seemed unaware of the matricentric principle of the society, and hence failed to integrate it into their conceptual analysis. Whenever they were confronted with women's demand for rights and social roles, they devised strategies that further excluded them from public space.

Conclusion: A Case for Radical Reform

Igbo women's fears became reality as over time local men grew accustomed to seeing only men in positions of power, and schemed to preserve that status quo. The questions that this state of affairs raises are, why should fictions about customs and laws continue to define contemporary Igbo cultural values? Why should they continue to provide the basis for relegating a section of Nigerian women to second-class status? As if anticipating contemporary desires to overthrow these customs and laws, Meek argued in 1937 that all that was needed to resolve their "shortcoming" were corrective measures (1937, 1). Lately, legal law theorists are singing the same refrain. Ulrike Wanitzek states that law theorists like Hellum, Bentzon, et al., and Armstrong, et al., draw a useful distinction between "lawyers law" (the codified customary laws used by lawyers) and ordinary customs that they refer to as "living law" (Wanitzek 2003, 4). According to her, they believe that since communities have continued to live in accordance to customs that are distinct from lawyers' law, this corpus of customs or living law is judicially relevant especially since they are changing to meet new social conditions, needs, and circumstances (2003, 4). While Meek foresaw the possibility of reforming and preserving "lawyers law," contemporary theorists opt for working with "living law" rather than "lawyer's law."

One shortcoming that living law theorists have not considered is that much of what passes today for "ordinary customs" had, in the first quarter of the twentieth century, been invented, reshaped, or affected by the patriarchal ideology of colonial rule and the Native Authority system. While studying East African legal history and court records, Martin Chanock noted that the reinterpretation of "customary laws" and the consequent recasting of societies was "the most effective way in which African men could exert power in the colonial polity" (1982, 53). J. A. Barnes noted too, that to legitimize these reinterpretations, the new changes were "sometimes presented in the guise of good tribal customs of long standing that unfortunately had been neglected of late but should be revived" (1969, 108). Simultaneously exploiting the allure of "authentic traditions," Igbo male functionaries of the colonial administration, and Western educated ones, had collaborated with colonial officers and systematically pursued policies and edicts that privileged men's goals.[63] Continuing in that tradition today, contemporary male political leaders, scholars, and legal theorists have engaged history from that male-privileging perspective even as another group of scholars presented evidence of Africa's matricentric ethos that radically challenges the colonially induced patriarchal transformations of Igbo culture.[64]

After a century of masculine myth-making, contemporary Igbo women have still not recovered many of their old rights. As generations of older women pass away, cultural amnesia sets in, and serious doubts are cast that women ever had any rights in Igbo tradition. Meanwhile, extensive social damage is done to their social, political, and economic interests by the male-privileging postcolonial institutions that the lawyer's law and the living laws had fostered. From 1914 onwards, these living laws worked at the ordinary, everyday, local level to disenfranchise women both in the late colonial period and in postindependence Nigeria. As Igbo men become extremely masculinist in orientation and consciousness, they are skeptical of the idea that their tradition was once astonishingly liberal and progressive. Unable to see the forest for the trees of patriarchy, they assume that granting equality to women is inconsistent with their so-called traditions and customs that since "olden times" or "time immemorial" had given rights and material advantages to men over women. In the zero-sum world of post independence Nigeria, what is so easily forgotten is that the array of rights that men claim today as theirs by virtue of tradition were based on constructions and legal fictions that were deployed to bring Igbo society into compliance with the patriarchal norms of the colonial state. The social alignment that followed this compliance disenfranchised women and relegated them to a subordinate category. Thus, to address the issue of gender inequality at the heart of contemporary Igbo life, we must radically rethink so-called ordinary customs and living laws that are the bane of much of current social inequality. Now that we understand the role of the native courts and the Native Authority Administration in inserting patriarchal customs into cultures, in the next chapter, I will make the case for radical cultural and social reform by examining how the inserted patriarchal consciousness continued in postindependence Nigeria to disenfranchise women and to create dysfunctional families.

3

Customs and Misrepresentations

Widows and Daughters in Inheritance Disputes

This chapter explores the way inheritance laws that privilege males were deployed in postindependent Nigeria to promote the ascendancy of men and to relegate women to the category of social and legal minors. The goal is to highlight the significant ways gender inequality began to work through the judicial and legal system to institutionalize the right of Igbo men to appropriate and control family's economic resources to the exclusion of female relatives. An examination of the colonially injected patriarchal worldview reveals that well-educated Igbo men utilized statutory laws and their administrative positions in government, the clergy, the private sector, the police and army, and the university to advance their interests. In the process, they stripped sisters, daughters, and wives of family rights, proving that they valued neither the consanguineal nor the nuclear models of family and the laws governing them. Availing themselves of the male-privileging statutes and laws of the colonial government, they created a male-centered, postcolonial society and family structure that is neither consanguineal or nuclear. Their postcolonial world transformed the traditional sexual, social, and economic relations that had nurtured a consanguineal model of family and the principle of complementarity into a hybridized nuclear family model.

Because of the complex way in which the disenfranchisement of both wives and daughters occurred, I will utilize the judgments of two court cases—*Nzegwu v. Nzegwus* (1986), and *Nzegwus v. Nzegwu* (1997)—to study how the court became a venue for the entrenchment of gender inequity. The subtext of this examination is the family. The investigation will highlight the negative impact of the male-privileging judicial processes and of the law on the family as well as how it created dysfunctional family relations that are inherently prejudicial to daughters' and wives' long-term interests. The goal of this analysis is to make a case for the radical overhaul of gender discriminatory "customs" and "customary" laws—of both the living law and lawyer's law versions—that were created in the early stages of colonial rule. Because wealth in Igboland is built through inheritance of land, and because current inheritance laws proscribe women from inheriting land, in part 1, I will analyze the myth that funds the disenfranchisement of women's property rights and the legal processes that reinforce it. In part 2, I will present a number of judicial cases on gender discrimination in families to show how socially embedded judges drew on these myths to render judgements that enthrone male dominance; and in part 3, I will examine the implication of the judges rulings, pointing out the sorts of misinterpretations that were required to bring them about. In part 4, I will re-read some of the customs underpinning these cases and raise questions about the courts' understanding of fairness, fatherly responsibility and fraternal love. Before concluding, in part 5, I will interrogate the role of Igbo mothers in upholding a discriminatory gender ideology for their families, in general, and their daughters, in particular.

PART 1: WOMEN, LAND, AND INHERITANCE

A Male Myth: "Women Don't Own Land"

The idea that Igbo women do not own land has a long history in Igbo male imaginary as well as in social anthropology. As early as 1921, G. T. Basden stated, "Bond and free have one characteristic in common viz., they are the burden bearers of the country. Women have but few rights in any circumstances, and can only hold such property as their lords' permit" (1921, 88). It is difficult to tell to what extent Igbo male imaginary and the views of social anthropologists are mutually reinforcing. Both have played pernicious roles in creating a climate of male domination. However, given the pervasive practice of preventing widows and daughters from inheriting, it is crucial to examine the belief that reinforces this practice, since it has been utilized to disinherit women. Men who wax eloquent that women do not inherit land fail to explain how and when the idea of land ownership began in Igboland. Why it is that only men inherit land? And when did men begin to own land? A brief historical exegesis is required at this point.

After the 1879 naval bombardment of Onitsha, and prior to the relocation of the trading factories from Asaba to Onitsha, land did not have the commercial value that is has today and it was readily available for use by members of the community and even by nonindigenes. Under the Onitsha usufruct principle, no one had absolute ownership of land. Land belonged to families and, prior to the injection of European ideas on property and alienation of land, it was rarely sold. The gradual adoption of the English idea of "fee simple absolute in possession" (Elias 1962, 97), that is, absolute ownership of land, began with the treaties the Royal Niger Company signed with local rulers for the establishment of Crown land. In 1900, the *Lands Registry Proclamation No. 16* was enacted to register all instruments (wills, copies of court judgments, and certificate of title) affecting lands in the former Protectorate of Southern Nigeria (Elias 1962, 319). The proclamation brought all land under the *Registration Ordinance No. 9 of 1895*, which was later replaced by the *Registration Ordinance No. 9 of 1901* and the *Land Registration Ordinance No. 12 of 1915*. These ordinances established the modern practice of registration of documents relating to and subsequently of absolute ownership of land (Elias 1962, 323). The main legal consequence of registration was that it gave official backing to land claims, in effect, conferring legal ownership of land. Nonregistration left one vulnerable to the adverse claims of others such that one could loose one's land to the registered claims of another (1962, 326).

Historically, families controlled vast tracts of land for farming and protected it from encroachment. They assigned this resource to members to use for agricultural and residential purposes and the land reverted back to the family when it is no longer used. Sometimes families lost their land rights to stronger communities who migrated to the area and wrested the land for their own settlement needs, as did the founders of Onitsha. Because the history of Onitsha is a history of major and minor migrations, its land tenure policies changed in light of the prevailing social forces of the time and of the land values of assimilated populations. In the first phase of settlement, the community consisted of discontinuous settlements at Ndende, Okpoko, Oze, and present-day Obosi. In that first century and half of the founding of Onitsha, women played important roles in the establishment of its nine wards, and in the subsequent colonization of land which that involved. Obikporo (literal translation—the residential space of women) was founded in the reign of the second Obi of Onitsha by widows, who settled close to the residence of Obi Oreze to take advantage of his protection (Bosah 1979, 24). Later, other groups merged with them including the Igala entourage that accompanied back Usse (the daughter of Obi Aroli) and her son from Igala. As well, Olosi, the only daughter of Obi Chimaevi, the third Obi of Onitsha, founded Ogboli Olosi, one of the nine wards of Onitsha.

Pressures from Aboh, Igala, and Aro slave-raiding activities led to the contraction of the town as inhabitants were forced to relocate to the present day Inland Town. Between 1800 and 1850, Odoje, Isele Awada, Obio, Obikporo, Ogbeotu, Ogboli Eke, and Oze wards resettled in their present locations.[1] The increased pressure for farmland that followed this contraction changed some practices concerning land, including the allocation of land to daughters during marriage. The present family land of the Modebes was gained through

such a transfer. It was the bridewealth of *ada* Melifonwu of Isiokwe, who became the wife of Modebe. Instances of such allocation of land as bridewealth
are part of people's family history, and such practices continued sporadically
into the early twentieth century. Even S. N. C. Obi (1963, 71) acknowledged
that the ante-nuptial allocation of land as bridewealth was not unusual. Onitsha indigenes have confirmed that either a grandmother or great grandmother
received land from their natal family at the time of marriage.[2] It is not necessary at this time to ascertain the number of brides who received land as part of
their bridewealth, or the number of *idigbe* who received land for personal use,
or of divorced or widowed daughters who received land upon return to their
consanguineal family. What is crucial is that the principle of land allocation
to daughters existed in Onitsha and other parts of Igboland as part of their cultural traditions (Obi 1963, 69–72). Historical evidence shows that it does.

It is important to underscore that not all sons/men received land allocation. Those who entered into long-term relationships with *idigbe* and lived off
the woman's farmland did not have their own land with their kin group. This
did not mean that they lost their usufruct rights; under the Onitsha principle
of land use, they would receive allocation when they needed it. Important
land-tenure developments also occurred at this historical time that minimized
the effect of not assigning land to brides. The Mgbelekeke family that occupied the riverside area of the town evolved a kola land-tenancy system that accorded use and occupancy rights to either a male or female grantee, which upon
death, transferred to the male or female children of the deceased without discrimination.[3] A kola tenant enjoys rights of an absolute owner, and is not restricted in the use to which the land may be put. In the early days of colonial
rule, this kola tenancy facilitated the land ownership of prominent Onitsha
and non-Onitsha women merchants such as Nwanyiemelie Mgbogo Nwonaku
(wife of Ifeajunna Okwugbele of Umuasele),[4] Umejeli (wife of Akunne Mba-
mali of Ogboli Olosi), Emengini Ughakwesi (wife of Mbanefo of Odoje), Lucinda Okwunne (daughter of Bachi Olodi Akpe of Ogboli Olosi),[5] Iyaaji
Nwadigwu, Nwabogo Oba, Iyaaji Enwezor, Ejiamike Okosi (wife of Obi Okosi
I), Okwuenu Nwaezebona, Omu Okwei, Ileanwusi Egwuatu, Mesdames
Eleanor Brodie-Mends, Nnoruka, Obianwu, Romaine, and Araka. Ironically,
these properties are viewed today by their male progeny as "family land" that
only sons can inherit.

Although Obi discussed the rights and interests of women under the category of "persons under legal disability," he nonetheless challenged the general
myth and Margaret M. Green's (1964, 33–34) contention that Igbo women do
not own land. He provided an array of women's direct and derivative rights and
interests in land that further reinforced C. K. Meeks's (1957, 186) evidence on
women's land rights in Nigeria and Cameroon. Igbo women, in particular, acquired land "in a multiplicity of ways—by purchase, lease, pledge, loan, gift, or

inheritance" both before and after marriage (Obi 1963, 69). Obi also rebutted Daryll Forde's and F. Scott's (1946) claim that women had no such direct rights to land as well as their attempt to constrain the range of these rights. According to him, Igbo women owned land in their own right, which they may have acquired before and also while married (1963, 69–72). As part of their ownership of or direct rights to the land, they may cultivate it with hired labor, allow their husbands to plant his crops on it, or permit their children to use it as farmland. On their death, however, the land devolves to their children or a member of her natal family, until the colonial legal system began to privilege the rights of one set of children over another.

Between 1890 and 1918, extensive changes took place in Onitsha that pushed patriarchal consciousness deeper into the society. By 1919, land registration accelerated in Onitsha as the town had become a major trading center and was classified as a second-class town under the Township Ordinance (Mabogunje 1968, 113). With this designation came the constitution and administration of the town in accordance with colonial policies of governance. The Township Ordinance established forms of land use and tenure, and property rights were subject to the provisions of the Land Registration Ordinance. Although customary practice was against the outright transfer of land from families to individual members, male heads of households responded to the security assurances inherent in the Land Registration Ordinances and surveyed and registered their plots of land to give them legal title. While the language of the land policies appeared gender neutral, the implementation of the ordinance was not. It accorded with the patriarchal value and male-privileging ethos of the colonial legal system. The result of these colonially-inspired registrations was that husbands', sons', and fathers' "rights of use . . . hardened into permanence" (Chanock 1991, 73). Because at this time the colonial ideology discriminated against women who were not seen as landowners, the land holdings of wealthy women were registered under the name of sons or husbands, who then gained title to those lands. Registration of such land by daughters was discouraged by a colonial ideology that viewed women as "impediment[s] to the development process," and that accepted the Native Authority Administration claims that women do not own or inherit land (19191, 73).[6]

These changes to the Igbo principle of usufruct neither served nor protected women's interests. Takyiwaa Manuh observed in the case of Ghana that as "the existing flexibility in marriage, labor arrangements, and property relations was removed, more rigid formulations of what constituted . . . access to land and other resources emerged" (1995, 335). In southern Africa, Chanock noted that "while husbands retained rights in the land they had cleared, they also began to assert ownership of land cleared by women on the grounds that it had been done as part of the performance of the duties of a wife" (1991, 73). In Ghanaian courts, as Woodman demonstrated, judges were ruling that "individually owned property . . . acquired by the deceased with the assistance of his wives, sons or daughters" are not owned jointly by the man and his wife or child. "They presume that the wife's or child's contribution was given in pursuance of their duty to assist the husband or father in his private enterprise, and was not intended to benefit the contributor" (1974, 270). Woodman's analysis of the matrilineal Akan makes clear that these rulings successfully disinherited widows and children, first, by construing the conjugal family and the individually owned property in opposition; second, by construing the individually owned property as lineage property; and third, by treating the labor of wives and children as exploitable and alienable. A spouse or father owes no obligation to widows and children once he dies.

In her research on colonial Lagos, Kristin Mann showed the consequences of colonial land registration policies. She uncovered that "fewer women than men obtained alienable, individually owned land and houses in the scramble for landed property" (Mann 1991b, 705). This is significant, since failure to own land and houses put women at a social and economic disadvantage. It "limited [their] access to credit and hence to the capital needed to trade" and it "restricted their ability to control their own labor and resources and to mobilize those of dependents." Worse still, it increased their "dependence on men for housing and assistance [and] gave men potent means of controlling and disciplining women, [thus] heightening their subordination" (1991b, 705).

Exploiting all the legal advantages offered by colonial land policy, Onitsha men surveyed and registered properties as individually owned, effectively acquiring legal force over them. Court cases and local histories show that male relatives used this means to disinherit female relatives of their rights to share in the family land or to own their own personal property.[7] They consolidated their gains by representing to the colonial government and to anthropologists as well that "traditionally" women never owned land. Widows with daughters were especially vulnerable to this representation in a justice system where corruption and miscarriage of justice was prevalent. In a 1934 case discussed by Elias, *Nwugege v. Adigwe & anor.*, six chiefs gave evidence about land inheritance that describes the inheritance of an *idigbe's* property.[8] They stated that "where a man marries a woman who has a house and lives with her as man and wife in that house, [the house] goes to the wife's family on her death" (1962, 243). Because the court misinterpreted an *idigbe's* connubial relationship as marriage, the chiefs did not alert the court of its error but contended "that under their custom it was unheard of that a man marrying a woman should live with her in her house" (1962, 243). This led Justice Graham Paul to insist that he cannot accept as legitimate the inheritance custom governing an *idigbe's* property. He subsequently ruled that the property belonged to her "husband." The effect of these sorts of misrepresentations coupled with the negative colonial attitude toward women's ownership of land wrought dramatic changes in the society. Within a period of sixty years in Onitsha (1900–1960), a collective memory of male dominance and privilege developed that resulted in male members of families refusing to give landed properties to daughters. The standard defense was that under customary law and custom, women never owned land. Having established this as a custom, the collective amnesia it induced prevented many from realizing that so-called family lands were either the land allocated to their *idigbe* mothers, the bridewealth of their mothers, or the lands which their mothers had acquired for farming needs (the latter was the case with the Enwonwu family).

But even if it were true that daughters did not own land, nothing in that historical record proscribes their inheriting land today. The record is there that Onitsha has continually transformed and reinvented itself (Harding 1963, 34).[9] Prior to that assessment, Basden wrote that since 1900, "Native law and custom has been almost completely disrupted. . . . To put the situation plainly ancient native law and custom cannot exist side by side nor intermingle with the principles of Government" (Harding 1963, 34). People then were aware that the policies of the colonial government meant that "there is no longer any fixed law or custom" (1963, 34). They were also aware that changes have occurred to suit contemporary realities without resulting in the obliteration of the society. They were aware that contrary to custom, Obi Okosi I had been appointed to the post by Commissioner Bedwell of the colonial government even though large sections of the community had opposed it on the ground that he was a Christian, and had renounced the customs and spiritual traditions of the community (Nzimiro 1972, 199–200). Later, they accepted the appointment. A more recent example of changing customs is that the proscription of Daike Anyo lineage from producing an Obi has been breached following the recent installation of a descendant of that lineage as the twenty-first Obi of Onitsha. The point is that everyone is well aware that there is no static custom in Onitsha, and so the argument from custom that bars women from owning land is totally unacceptable.

As the nature of trade changed in 1920, Onitsha women increasingly lost their former dominant roles in the economic sector. Part of the reason for this loss was the closure of economic opportunities and the rising gender ideology that upheld the ideal of women as subordinate to men. Whereas in the past daughters were deployed to trading operations, from the 1930s onwards, they were prepared for marriage with the local elite, who increasingly opted for girls who were products of the missionary schools. Trading no longer carried the prestige it once had, and was viewed as unprogressive, something that educated girls did not do. Merchant queens hired Igbo male workers, and increasingly transferred their wealth to sons, who they believed had a better chance of succeeding in the new economy. This partly explains why Isaac Mbanefo's mother positioned him to make a career in trading, while his sister, Nnonye Uyanwa, was prepared for marriage.

The importance of this transference of mothers' wealth to sons is that as male relatives gained control of their mothers' land, they represented them as open to inheritance only by sons exclusively. The construction of male-privileging customary laws ensured the exclusion of sisters and daughters. Consequences of this disinheritance of females can be seen in the quarrels and litigation over land as ambitious male segments of the family sought control of local resources by increasing their land holdings. As Woodman indicated in the case of Ghana and Mann of the Lagos family, the courts ruled in favor of the evidence and remedies presented by men that minimized the credibility of women. The result is that too many erroneous conclusions have become embedded in the fabric of legal principles (Woodman 1974, 268) as well as in the social consciousness of people. What the courts and the land registration policy conferred by way of rights was not always compatible with what the usufruct principle of access to land had once required. Because there is no justifiable reason for condoning injustice on the basis of sex, there is compelling reason to discard and radically remedy the myths and stories we tell ourselves.

Historical Amnesia and the Deployment of Fictional Customs

In the postindependent period, the Nigerian Supreme Court has continued to rule on gender discrimination, upholding problematic native court rulings of the first quarter of the twentieth century that claimed that local customs denied wives and daughters inheritance rights. These problematic "customary laws" were used to buttress cases in the high, appellate, and supreme courts. Formal proof was not required for customs that had already been judicially noted by the courts, but the burden of proof of any custom that had not been judicially noted was on the person invoking that custom. This meant that customs that supported women's autonomy, which corrupt native court judges had ruled to be invalid and which colonial justices refused to accept as valid customs, did not have the weight of the court behind them. In fact, the native court administration guaranteed the subordination of women by establishing a legal basis for their inferiority. The elimination of all customs privileging women, or even according them equal rights in inheritance matters, created a climate in which men had total social dominance, and in which their right to dominance was safeguarded by the courts. The over eight decades (1920–2002) of consolidating and reinforcing men's advantages in society has produced a range of judicially noted customs that have embedded the precept of gender subordination into the culture. This normalization of male domination, even as women in different life situations contested the process, has underwritten the subjugation of women in modern Igbo society. It also underwrites their dispossession of land and their losses in other economic matters. As more and more men gain access to education, economic resources, and administrative recognition, women's social worth has plummeted, and essentially, they have been defined out of significance.

Judicially validated customs have sped up the process of discrimination by institutionalizing the idea that treating wives and widows as subordinate beings is normal. This process was especially evident during divorce and inheritance proceedings. The all-male cast of judges regularly ruled in ways that entrenched the subordinate status of wives and widows, while strengthening the rights of husbands and brothers-in-law. Until the *Mojekwu v. Mojekwu* ruling of 1997 (this case will be discussed shortly), judges rarely used the repugnancy clause to invalidate customs that treated wives and daughters in discriminatory ways. The repugnancy clause states that customs, norms, and practices that are repugnant to equity and good conscience should be struck down. Instead, Igbo judges strengthened these repugnant "customs" by relying on them in rulings such as *Nnezianya v. Okagbue & 2 Ors.* (1963), *Onwuchekwa v. Onwuchekwa* (1991), and *Eze v. Eze*.[10] The supreme court led the way in subjugating women by steadily upholding patently discriminatory customary laws against women (Ewelukwa 2002, 463 n. 133). Taking their cue from the Supreme Court, justices of lower courts ignored the fact that the "age-old" customs reinforcing these rulings were part of a complex of discriminatory customs that were codified during the Native Authority era, and that today are nullified by social transformations in contemporary Igbo life. Although judges such as Justice Eze Ezobu recognized that "[m]en played a dominant role in the formulation of customary law and practice . . . [in that] they are the judges and witnesses," they remained indifferent to the fundamental issue of equity and justice that is at the heart of the utilization of these discriminatory laws.[11] Modern Igbo male judges appear unconcerned that some outmoded policies of the inherited British judicial system and the native court-derived customary laws allowed wives to be treated as property.[12] If anything, they trivialize the fact that these policies and laws are inconsistent with the notion of equality inherent in the 1979 constitution.

The research of legal scholar A. B. Kasunmu (1977) revealed that postindependent courts carried over the precept of gender subordination and continued the project of rolling back whatever rights wives, daughters, sisters, or mothers had prior to colonialism and the introduction of patriarchal values. On occasion, the court blocked women's attempts to exercise rights that would have allowed them to achieve gender parity. Negative attitudes about wives and belief in the subordinate status of women in general underlay and shaped judicial decisions. Displays of gender biases from the bench occurred quite frequently. In *Onwuchekwa v. Onwuchekwa*, for instance, Uche U. Ewelukwa reported that the presiding judge dismissed as not repugnant to natural justice a wife's claim that to deny her interest in a jointly acquired property deemed her and her money the property of her husband (Ewelukwa 2002, 451). In the judge's view, she *was* the property of her husband. Judges routinely talked down to wives and lectured widows on the importance of good behavior without calling the other party to order. In *Orakwue v. Orakwue*, the presiding judge rejected a widow's request to be named co-administrator of her husband's estate, and sternly rebuked her for bad behavior and hostility to her in-laws. Such uneven-handed treatment further encouraged the maltreatment of widows. To make matters worse, judges often placed widows under the authority of some male member of her affinal family, invoking questionable customs to legitimize the systematic transfer of a deceased's property to these male members of the family. Through various means and strategies, they deployed the judicial powers of the bench to effectively block the right of widows and daughters or sisters from inheriting a husband's, father's, or brother's estate. As judicial rulings piled up, they created a gender-discriminatory judicial system and a gender-biased inheritance system. Both systems make it exceedingly difficult for wives, daughters, or sisters to obtain relief in courts, or to reverse onerous rulings.

Thus, in a certain sense, the Nigerian court is male; its ideology and language of doing business privileges men. Male judges strategically used the bench to further the collective interests of men and ruled in ways that did so. They routinely did this in divorce cases by mixing two radically different models of law, or by refusing to rule in ways that would compel husbands to live in accordance with the rule governing their marriage. One such divorce case was adjudicated by Udoma Udo Udoma, a respected jurist and adjudicator of equity and judicial fairness. In his ruling, he pronounced:

> It is almost unprecedented in this country for a wife having divorced her husband to turn around and seek maintenance from the same husband. The very idea of maintaining a wife after divorce appears *to me* to be *foreign* to the African conception of marriage and divorce. A situation like the present cries aloud for distinct Nigerian rules. (Emphasis mine; Kasunmu 1977)[13]

Udoma found the idea of wife maintenance untenable, even though the divorce case under his purview was of a statutory marriage contracted under the Marriage Act. His contention that greater consideration ought to be given to an "African conception of marriage and divorce" shows a frame of mind intent on playing fast and loose with the law. He saw as problematic the stipulations of the Marriage Ordinance Act that a husband should support his wife and children should the marriage dissolve because an entirely different model of marriage releases a husband from this obligation. Given that the couple had agreed to the terms of their marriage knowing fully well what the odds were, Udoma erred in having entertained the husband's claim that African customary law of marriage and divorce makes no provision for supporting an ex-wife. Although it is true that husbands have family obligations outside of their nuclear family, which they help support, so too do wives. Besides, it is not the place of an impartial judge to assist a divorcing husband to pick and choose which elements of his matrimonial vows should apply.

The practice of switching from statutory law to customary law is important, as it exposes the deep-seated prejudice of many Nigerian male judges towards according wives any entitlement that would give them economic autonomy. The disregard for the plight of wives and widows shines through in rulings that refuse to acknowledge that wives and adult-female relatives have been treated unfairly and are still being disinherited by grasping husbands and male relatives. In refusing to acknowledge the legitimacy of women's grievances, judges are deliberately ignoring the colonial and postcolonial history of female disempowerment by the states. They are refusing to see the sociopolitical culture that facilitated the dominant economic standing of husbands and male relatives, which contributed to the inferior economic standing of wives and female relatives. The disinheritance of wives, widows, daughters, and sisters directly benefited male members of the family both in the amount of family resources that accrued to them and in releasing them from duties they may have found unpleasant. By contrast, wives, daughters, and sisters found that access to resources—such as land, high-paying jobs, and credit facilities, which open up the world of economic opportunities—was seriously limited.

PART 2: JUDICIAL CASE STUDIES OF GENDER DISCRIMINATION

The following consists of two case studies that will help us think through the issue of women's disenfranchisement in Nigeria. The first highlights a 1997 landmark ruling by the Appeals Court that invalidates the legitimacy of a particularly egregious custom, which has been used to erode the rights of daughters and wives. The second is a narrative account that centers the family as locus of a complicated chain of events that ultimately ended up in the courts. This particular case reveals the family as a complex site of hierarchies, shifting interests, negotitations, and principles that are not easily discernible.

Case 1: A Gender-Sensitive Appellate Court?

Thirty-seven years after the rulings of Udoma, I returned to the United States from a research trip in Nigeria, where one of my many accomplishments was obtaining a copy of the appellate court judgment on the *Nzegwus v Nzegwu* suit. In my mailbox was a news article a feminist colleague had sent, knowing that one of my many areas of research is law and inheritance. The article, "Inheritance Judgement Spurs Women Activism in Nigeria," by Toro Oladapo of the Pan African News Agency, Lagos, made a compelling case regarding the prevalence of patriarchy in Nigeria. According to her:

> To Nigerian women activists, a recent landmark judgement on inheritance cannot be celebrated enough, if only to demonstrate that the spirit of the 1995 Beijing International Conference on Women empowerment is alive in Africa's most populous nation. "We do not need to travel to Beijing to know that some of our customs . . . are repugnant to natural justice, equity and good conscience," Justice Niki Tobi said in his ruling at an Appeal Court, sitting in Nigeria's eastern city of Enugu in September 1997. (Oladapo 1998)

My first inclination was to ask: Is there an ongoing revolution in Nigeria, in which judges with the mind-set of Udoma were being replaced by progressive judges? Could this new breed of justices really be outraged by the fast-spreading tradition of discrimination against women in the country? According to the news report, Justice Niki Tobi might be doing just that as he attacked the insensitivity of some customs, forming the corpus of lawyer's and living customary laws that had underpinned many rulings on family law. Reading the judgment later, I discovered that he directly engaged the issue of female subordination in his judgment:

> Is [*oli ekpe*] custom consistent with equity and fairplay in an egalitarian society such as ours where the civilised sociology does not discriminate against women? . . . we hear of and read about customs which discriminate against the womenfolk in this country. They are regarded as inferior to the menfolk. Why should it be so? All human beings—male and female—are born into a free world and are expected to participate freely, without any inhibition on grounds of sex; and this is constitutional. Any form of societal discrimination on grounds of sex, apart from being unconstitutional, is antithesis to a society built on the tenets of democracy which we have freely chosen as a people. . . . On my part, I have no difficulty in holding the "Oli-ekpe" custom of Nnewi, is "repugnant to natural justice, equity and good conscience. (*Mojekwu v. Mojekwu* 1997, 304–5)

The facts of the *Mojekwu v. Mojekwu* case are as follows. Augustine Nwafor Mojekwu had taken the widow of his late uncle Caroline Mgbafor Mojekwu to court for championing the inheritance rights of her grandson,

Emeka, who was born long after the death of her son, Patrick Adina. In accordance with Nnewi custom, Caroline had married a wife in the name of her deceased son, who then had Emeka, whom she wanted to inherit her deceased husband's estate in the metropolitan commercial city of Onitsha, in Eastern Nigeria. Augustine sued to void the rights of Caroline and Emeka on the ground that widows do not inherit property under Nnewi native law and a dead man could not possibly father a child. Augustine ignored the fact that his uncle, Okechukwu, Caroline's husband had two daughters by his first wife, Janet. He did not champion their inheritance rights even though the kola tenancy law under which their father had acquired the disputed property in Onitsha permitted daughters to inherit kola properties. He believed that daughters too had no right of inheritance. In fact, he asked the court to rule in his favor since, according to the *oli ekpe* custom of Nnewi, he was the next male in line of inheritance.

Esther Okakpu, the niece of Caroline's husband, felt it was unjust to void Caroline's and Emeka's rights since Nnewi custom also deemed Emeka a legitimate grandson of Caroline and Okechukwu Mojekwu. The Nnewi custom that Okakpu invoked was the one that allowed wives to have children for deceased husbands. After Caroline won the case at the lower court, Augustine appealed, hoping to overturn the judgment. Unfortunately for him, the Appeals Court took a different view of the matter. In the lead judgment, Justice Tobi struck down the two Nnewi customs that simultaneously voided wives' and daughters' rights of inheritance and permitted dead men to have children. Writing on behalf of the other two appellate court justices, Akintola Olufemi Ejiwunmi and Eugene Chukwuemeka Ubaezonu, Tobi ruled that the ninety-year-old widow, Caroline Mojekwu, should inherit the property even though this was not backed by the pleadings. His judgment effectively affirmed the rights of widows, whose marriages were contracted under native law and custom, to inherit their husband's properties. Tobi claimed that he had no difficulty reaching his decision, since the *oli ekpe* custom in the couple's Nnewi society was inconsistent with the world in which we live today. He appeared to grasp the inherent principle of inequality propagated against wives and daughters in Igbo society and seemed intent on stopping it.

The *oli ekpe* custom holds that, in the absence of a male child, the brothers of the deceased are the next in line of inheritance, followed by his nephew. It does not really matter that the deceased has daughters. Their right to inherit their father's property is voided on the ground that they are female. It is important to underscore that none of the principal female characters in this case were of the view that women had inheritance rights and should inherit the deceased's estate. Caroline's and Esther's energies were directed toward securing the rights and interests of some man, Emeka, whom they felt was the legitimate heir. Tobi's bold judgment took everyone unaware. Hailing the ruling as unprecedented, Oladapo contends that in ending a discriminatory practice against Nigerian women, "Mojekwu's victory, ironically delivered by a male judge against a fellow male respondent, after more than thirty-nine years of legal tussle, has come to be seen by Nigerian women as victory for the womenfolk" (Oladapo 1998). Equally significant in the reporter's view was that Okakpu, the niece-in-law of Caroline, broke ranks with her family to stand by her as a primary witness throughout the case. This breach of tradition by Okakpu was seen as crucial to Mojekwu's defense and to the successful outcome of the case.

Analysis begins where the news report ended. The report makes it seem as if the traditional culture was discriminatory, contrary to my earlier claims that it accorded women rights that were taken away in colonial and postcolonial society. The question the report and the courts did not ask was the genesis of such "traditional" laws. Had such a question been posed, we would have had to confront a whole corpus of customs that were invented under the colonial patriarchal scheme to respond to colonial patriarchal experience. Since it was not, I will argue later, the *oli ekpe* was one of such constructed custom. For the moment, however, I want to focus on the travesty of justice in the case that was not part of the report at all.

What kind of a justice system exists in Nigeria that allows a case on inheritance to drag on for thirty-nine years? It is true that Mojekwu was declared victorious, but could she really be seen as victorious when she spent the better part of her adult life litigating a case and waiting for judicial relief? The important questions Oladapo did not ask are, what about the rights of the daughters? Why does the Nnewi notion of fatherhood mandate the dispossession of daughters and the abject treatment of widows? Given the very history of the founding of Nnewi, why does it view daughters as lesser than sons?[14] Oladapo's analysis makes the most of Okakpu's decision to break ranks with her natal family to support Caroline, the wife of her uncle. As told, the tale is a moral lesson on what women could achieve if they stood together. But it does not quite capture the dynamics of Igbo family relations at the center of the legal drama. It did not grapple with the complicated politics between uterine family units with the larger consanguineal family. The reason why Okakpu choose to break ranks with Augustine, her half brother, is not unconnected with the politics of mothers and maternal ideology.[15]

After reading the article, I struggled to reconcile Justice Tobi's new activist image on this issue of *oli ekpe* with the reactionary image with which I was familiar. This was the same Justice Niki Tobi who, five months earlier, had displayed no moral qualms about striking down the ruling of a trial judge against the Onitsha variant of *oli ekpe*, known as *oku ekpe*, in *Nzegwu v. Nzegwus* (1997). Although the appeal had been dressed up as a case about the appellant's "mother's house," Tobi, in his own independent judgment, joined his "learned brother" Ejiwunmi, JCA, to rule that the facts given in evidence before a court of law by the respondent [the widow] were not backed by the pleadings; and that the trial judge had erred in failing to note some "contradictory evidence." By so ruling, he had effectively upheld a far more egregious form of the same "customary" practice that he now declared in Mojekwu's case to be "repugnant to natural justice, equity, and good conscience." In the former, it was not a nephew who was the predator, but an uncle and a cousin, their father's elder brother of full blood, and his son. The closeness of the relationship made the uncle's eviction of his nieces even more insidious.

Oladapo's newspaper article raised more questions than it resolved. In the prevailing social climate in Igboland, in which memories of the once ungendered culture was dying out, and in which attitudes were hardening around male privilege, Tobi's ruling offers some hope for reserving this trend. However, while others were hailing the victory, I could not help but wonder why Justice Tobi chose this moment to break ranks with "his fellow male respondent" to rule against the *oli ekpe*. Would his male colleagues allow his judgment to stand, and how would they move to shore up the breach? More to the point, how do we account for this newfound empathy and clarity of vision regarding the plight of a widow and her daughters? What could explain his sudden hostility to this decades-long Igbo "custom" of extinguishing the rights of daughters and the more recent "custom" of ejecting widows from their marital homes? What role did ethical values play in his judgment? Was it concern for an aged widow? If so, why could he not muster a similar concern toward an eighteen-month-old baby and a thirty-month-old child who were being stripped of their father's estate, first by a man who should have been a father to them, and after his death, by his son, a man whose education had been paid for by the deceased? Was it the thirty-nine-year length of the legal battle that caused his epiphany? Whatever it was that shook Tobi out of his male-privileged complacency, more of it is needed to alter the conceptual scheme of his other colleagues, especially those in the supreme court.

Case 2: A Personal Case Study

Historical Background

To really understand the murky world of family politics, it would be useful to visit one family drama that eventually played out in court. Events are played out in ways that do not always highlight the gender discriminatory basis of the case. The following narrative is told in the voice of the wife of the deceased.

Twenty-two years ago, on October 8, 1980, Godwin Nzegwu, a lawyer and former Special Assistant to the Administrator (the equivalent of a state governor), died intestate. His sister-in-law, a pharmacist, was the only person in his bedroom when he died. By her own admission in court, she slipped out as soon as she realized what had happened and notified members of the family without notifying me, the wife. Meanwhile, I was attending to the needs of my two daughters, aged two-and-a-half years and eighteen months, in another section of the house. I was not told of his death. Within minutes, family members from within the larger compound were streaming into and from the bedroom of my husband, speaking in hushed tones. Some were sobbing silently. I subsequently emerged from where I was to behold a horde of family members. What was going on? Their faces and body language, as they slipped by, communicated that something very ominous had happened. What urgent news did they receive that they literally had to come in to share it with him in the bedroom? Eventually, I learned that Lawyer, as everyone called him, had died. Was this a joke? We had been up all night talking with his personal physician and friend, whom he had asked to come over to give him some pain medication. He had hit the upper part of his leg on the coffee table and was moaning for a strong pain reliever! After having gone through the pain of childbirth, I found this low threshold level of pain rather pathetic. He had then dispatched his personal assistant to summon his personal physician. Believing that there was an emergency, the doctor had come in the hospital's ambulance. He hastened into the bedroom, only to find his "patient" snacking on some fruit and in a deep conversation. We laughed over the misunderstanding, and he joined in the midnight snack and conversation after he had taken the precautionary step of checking the blood pressure of his patient.

Prior to departure, the doctor advised Lawyer to come to the hospital the next day for a full medical exam. He felt it was time that he came off all his high blood pressure medication. At 3:00 a.m. the doctor left to get the pain-relief medication and sleeping medication that the patient had requested. He returned, administered the medication, waited awhile to be sure the patient had gone into normal sleep, and then departed. Ten minutes later Lawyer woke, grumbling that the dosage was ineffectual, not the higher dosage he had expected to receive. We sat up the reminder of the night, talking until about 6:00 a.m., when one of the kids woke up. By 7:00 a.m., as I was preparing my daughter for day care, he died, with Lillian, the wife of his brother, alone in the room with him.

According to her testimony in court, Lillian did not tell her husband Alexander, the deceased's only brother of full blood. A few months earlier Alexander, a civil engineer with his own construction company and a local Romeo, had become partially paralyzed by stroke during one of his trysts. He was a shadow of his former self, and it was difficult not to feel pity for him. By mid-morning, after he had been notified of his younger brother's demise, Alexander demanded a full explanation from me of how and why his brother had died. I could only discuss events that had transpired during the night; I had no idea why he died. I was neither a doctor nor God. As we talked, he reminded me that, since he was still ill, he would need spending money for the funeral. What was I expected to do? He knew I did not have a job. It did not even occur to me then that there was anything untoward in this request. I promised him that there would be money. Leaving the meeting, I retired to write for financial help to a number of clients and to the then leading constitutional lawyer in the country, under whom Lawyer had practiced in Lagos.

The following day, Alexander requested that I hand over to him the keys to Lawyer's bedrooms and law office, keys that I had in my custody. He claimed that his brother had some guns and firearms that he must retrieve. That excuse did not ring true. This was a man who could barely walk or talk, given the severity of his paralysis. What did he need a gun for? He certainly was not going hunting. And if we needed home security, surely we did not need a dead man's guns to do that, and certainly he, Alexander, could not provide it. It did not seem right to hand him the keys so that he could send people to rifle through the personal items of the deceased to find the instrument. It seemed reasonable to refuse the request. That was when the stories began to fly that I certainly had a hand in his brother's death, that I must have colluded with the doctor to kill their brother. The campaign of calumny expanded to stories that I had taken all his money, and that I had instructed my relatives to cart away vital documents from his room. From then on the battle line was sharply drawn.

The objective of Alexander and his nuclear family was gradually becoming clear. Friends of the deceased who had come to offer their condolences saw through the request of the gun. They surmised that what was going on was that the elder brother and his wife were positioning themselves to gain immediate control of the deceased's documents and assets. The letter I had written to some clients and friends netted some results. By the evening, the strategy had changed. The brother decided to play hardball. With the help of his wife, he convened a meeting of some members of his lineage and formally demanded the keys to his deceased brother's bedroom and law office. By this time, members of my family—male and female—had arrived and designated a spokesperson, versed in the nuances of Onitsha culture and politics. I was instructed not to speak to anyone alone, and to permit no one to speak to me alone. It was absolutely crucial that there be witnesses to any conversation, and from their perspective, it was crucial that I not be placed in a position to be pressured. In responding to the key request, I went in the company of elderly women, and my spokesperson, my paternal aunt, officially put it to the group that there were proper procedures and protocol that ought to be followed, and that undue hastiness in bringing up inheritance matters was in bad taste. She stated that the first objective in such matters was the burial of the deceased. Next was the completion of the burial and funeral rites, and only after all duties had been performed should the issue of inheritance be raised. Put in this manner, the point was inarguable. The compatriots of Alexander murmured their agreement and acknowledged that custom should be followed.

The battle of attrition began and spilled into the law courts a month later, after I was threatened with eviction with a masquerade. At the behest of the deceased's brother of full blood, a family meeting of my consanguineal family and their consanguineal family was called, in which I was publicly charged with the death of his brother. I was accused of the heinous crime of going into Alexander's deceased brother's bedroom (that is, my husband's), of rifling through his things, and of using my relatives to cart away boxes and boxes of documents and money. I was indicted for insubordination for refusing to hand over to him his brother's guns and the keys to his bedroom. For these sins, Alexander pronounced that I was to remove my two children and self from the premises, and that the status of the children would be revisited, if they survived into adulthood. To drive home his order, he threatened that if I failed to do so within three days, he would not be held responsible for whatever happened to me. His reason for this drastic action was that he held me responsible for his brother's death.

Unfortunately for Alexander, a high-ranking Onitsha chief, Onoli Oguda Chude, had attended the meeting as a friend of the family. After witnessing Alexander's tirade, this male chief skillfully intervened and took over the direction of the meeting. He called attention to a serious lapse in procedure. In his view, no order of such severity could be made without hearing the accused. I was then called upon to respond to the charges. This unanticipated intervention allowed me to present my side and thereby counter some of the disinformation that had been circulated. At the end of my response, the audience, especially members of Alexander's consanguineal family, was deeply conflicted, since most of them had not heard from me before and did not have the full picture. Sensing his advantage, the chief pressed on, saying that since the welfare and future of two small children was at stake, the meeting should be adjourned to the third day, so that members of my family would have time to consider the charges and frame their response. The meeting adjourned, and on my way to my seclusion quarters, I was attacked by Alexander's wife Lillian, his two daughters, and a niece. I took the matter to the police.

Before the night was out, male members of Alexander's consanguineal family, whose mothers were from the same ward as mine, met with members of my family and disclosed the full plans that Alexander and his cohorts were devising. They confirmed that masquerades were to be used to give customary sanction to their act, and to forcibly revoke my marital ties. The choice of masked spirits was particularly significant, since they would achieve a divorce through the process of eviction. An eviction by means of masked spirits implied a formal and lasting severance from the family, one that leaves a woman voiceless and without relief.[16] Marriages such as mine, which are formalized under Onitsha law rather than the Marriage Ordinance Act, could be abruptly terminated this way by the male members of the family. Lest it be assumed that only men have the right to this sanctionary mechanism, let me note that women too possess a similar right, though they do not use masked spirits as men do. Dispensing of the need to appear with symbolic forms, *umuada* would carry out their eviction by invading their "brother's" home and packing out the wife's belongings. In 1997, for example, the Obi of Onitsha, Ofala Okagbue, had his marriage to his Obosi wife abruptly terminated by the *umuada* (the daughters) of his family who invaded his private home and evicted his wife of many years' standing. The Obi was not in support of the eviction, which nonetheless progressed without his sanction.

Alexander's game plan was the immediate enforcement of the *oku-ekpe* custom, through a preplanned eviction, designed to take place within seventy-two hours. His calculation was that using masquerades would be most effective since I, an uninitiated female, would have no alternative but to flee. Unbeknownst to them, some male members from my father's and mother's sides of the family who had got wind of their plans, began their own preparation, promising to be on the scene with their own masquerades. It was going to be the mother of all battles, a monster battle of masquerades. Faced already with one physical attack, and not knowing how many more to expect before that third day, I sought immediate redress in the customary court at Onitsha, roughly forty days after the demise of my husband. To forestall the threatened ejection notice, I filed a suit the next day, requesting that the court prevent my husband's immediate brother of full blood, Alexander Nzegwu and six others, namely his wife, Lillian Nzegwu; his uncle, William Nzegwu; his half-brother, Chieka Nzegwu; his two daughters, Akonam and Chineze Nzegwu; and his niece, Rita Onyejekwe, from ejecting me and my daughters from my matrimonial home. The specific terms of relief sought in suit No. CCON/88/80 were:

a. An order of Court that the defendants allow the plaintiff go into the 1st Defendant's building and collect her personal belongings, including those of her late husband.
b. An order of Court restraining the 1st, 3rd, and 4th defendants from ejecting the plaintiff from the plaintiff's husband's house at Onitsha.
c. An order of Court that the defendants pay to the plaintiff N2000.00 (two thousand naira) general damages for the battery committed on the plaintiff by them on the 26th day of November 1980.

I laid out the facts of the case in the accompanying statement of claim. I indicated that I was the only wife, with two minor female children, and that I was ordered by Alexander to pack into the still uncompleted building of my husband for the purpose of performing burial ceremonies. Other paragraphs of the statement explained that after the burial ceremonies the defendants and their agents, privies, brothers, and servants had begun to make life difficult for me; that while still in mourning, I had been physically attacked; and that I had been refused access to my personal property and that of my husband. Owing to the urgency of the plea, the customary court heard the case the following day.

All the named male defendants in the suit failed to appear in court, hoping to subvert any order that might bind them against using a masquerade to achieve their eviction objective. Customarily speaking, masquerades were seen as under the purview of men, and uninitiated females could not receive orders for the masquerades. So even though in her own section of Onitsha, Lillian, wife of Alexander, was not subject to such proscriptions; she could not receive directives for the masquerades of her husband's people.[17] By their absence, the male defendants indicated that they were indeed going to use the masquerades for my eviction, and did not want any judicial restrictions placed on their plans. Aware of the political implication of this "no show" and to avoid a miscarriage of justice, the court reconvened in the bedroom of Alexander, who had sent in a note that he was bedridden. After listening to Alexander's objections to the motion for an interim order, the court overruled his objection and granted my motion for interim injunction. The Order restrained the defendants "from molesting and ejecting" me from the premises, where I was then residing in the Nzegwu compound, and from using any type of masquerade in ejecting me from the house.

After the granting of an interlocutory order, I appealed for court protection in the high court to go into Alexander's house to retrieve my personal belongings. The order was granted by Justice F. O. Nwokedi. Shortly afterward, the plaintiff applied to have the substantive case transferred from the customary court to the high court at Onitsha. The application was granted as suit No. 0/78/81. The protracted case lasted six years! Judgment was finally rendered on July 24, 1986, by the presiding High Court Judge, Justice Obunneme Onwuamaegbu. As the terms of relief stated, the pivot of my case was not inheritance but access; a request not to be ejected from my husband's own residence, which he had not completed before his death. [The house that Alexander made the subject of dispute was situated on a property that belonged to Lazarus Nzegwu, a famous court clerk, the father, brother, and grandfather of the defendants.] Lazarus Nzegwu's property is community property, vested in the family. Individual sons had acquired subordinate interests in the land, but because of the collective family nature of the property, individual sons did not have separate and inalienable rights to the property. This usufructary principle of land guarantees that "the right of a member to make use of and enjoy family property never ripens into ownership" (Okoro 1966, 21). I was aware that as a wife, I could not assert a right of inheritance, since I was not part of the Nzegwu family or "in-group." However, by virtue of being in the in-group, my daughters had the rights to exercise or stake a claim for usufructary right of residence in their father's share of Lazarus Nzegwu's property.

The Judgment Five-and-a-Half Years Later

After an extensive period of fact-finding, Justice Onwuamaegbu delivered his judgment (*Nzegwu v. Nzegwu*, 1986). He ruled that:

> It is admitted on both sides that on the death of her husband, a married woman has the right to continue residing in a house built by the husband, even if the woman had only female children for her husband. The 1st Defendant qualified this by saying that such right existed only as long as the woman was of good behaviour. I have no doubt at all and I find as a fact that a married woman, under Onitsha native law and custom, is entitled to reside in the house erected by her husband and that on the death of her husband that right ensures for her benefit and that she must have committed very serious wrong for her to be deprived of that right. The complaints made by the 1st Defendant against the Plaintiff were not reasonable at all. It was painful enough to her to be asked to move out of the apartment where she had been living with her husband from the time they became married. It was even more painful that she was asked to move out at the time she had just lost her husband, and when she most needed comfort and companionship of the 1st and 2nd Defendants. It was understandably heartbreaking for her to be asked to surrender the keys of the apartment for the 1st Defendant (who did not indicate that he had any particular things therein) to be sending people to ransack at will.
>
> It was quite reasonable for the Plaintiff to have refused to surrender the keys at that stage and counting her refusal as a wrong committal [*sic*] by the Plaintiff was most unreasonable for the 1st Defendant.
>
> I must say that from the evidence before me and from the demeanour of the 1st Defendant at the time he was testifying, he was a man of ungovernable temper who was agitated at anything he felt (whether justly or unjustly) that amounted to questioning his authority as the *pater families* [*sic*] of his own household. At a stage when he was asked the innocent question about his accepting the Plaintiff back into the Nzegwu family he threw himself into such frenzy of anger that shook his fragile frame from head to toe and it was with great difficulty that he was calmed down and then he replied that he would not accept her. The 3rd Defendant, William Nzegwu, spoke the truth that he would have told the 1st Defendant that his reasons were not sufficient to ask the Plaintiff to leave the Nzegwu compound.

One other reason given for asking the Plaintiff to leave the Nzegwu compound was the anxiety of her mother to take her [the plaintiff] away and her [the plaintiff's mother] abuses on the Nzegwus. Even if that was true, they were not the acts of the Plaintiff and in law the wrongs of mothers are not visited on their daughters. I am satisfied from the evidence before me that the Plaintiff was threatened with ejectment [*sic*] from the Nzegwu family by use of masquerades. I believed her evidence on that issue and did not accept the denials of the 1st Defendant and the other witnesses who testified to the contrary on that point. I am satisfied from the evidence adduced that it is disastrous for a married woman to allow herself to be ejected from her husband's compound by a masquerade and that it is more reasonable for her to move out by herself than to wait to be ejected by a masquerade.

From the evidence before me I find as a fact that the Plaintiff was forced to move out of the Nzegwu compound after the death of her husband to avoid the odium attached to being ejected by a masquerade. I am satisfied that she had the intention of going back to the Nzegwus after her right has been established. The Plaintiff is entitled to remain with the Nzegwus during her lifetime. Her two daughters are entitled, by Onitsha law and custom, to live in the house built by Godwin Nzegwu within the Nzegwu compound and she should not be ejected from such house, if any, without the due process of law. Similarly, her children, females as they are, cannot be ejected without the due process of law.

It has been argued with great force that the Plaintiff has not asked for an order that she should be allowed to return to the Nzegwus and that she cannot be granted a relief which she has not sought. It is basic rule of litigation in our courts that a party should not be granted a relief not sought. A number of cases, including *Olumo & Ors. v. Okure & Ors.* (1985) 3 NWLR 372, and *Animashaurun v. Onuta Osuma & Ors.* (1972) 2 ECSLR 274 emphasize this point. In the Animashaurun case, the Supreme Court (par Fatayi Williams J. S. C., as he then was) stated as follows, at p. 283:

As we have pointed out on a number of occasions, it is not the function of a Court of trial to raise for the parties issues which they had neither pleaded nor relied upon. The case should be decided on the issue properly raised in the pleadings.

See also *Registered Trustees of Apostolic Church v. Akindele* (1967) NMLR 263. It is also true that any evidence adduced, even if in cross-examination, but which is not material to any issue raised by the pleadings, may be disregarded by the Court; see *Abimbola George & Ors. v. Dominion Flour Mills Ltd* (1963) ANLR 71, *Overseas Construction Co. (Nigeria) Ltd v. Creek Enterprises Co. Ltd* (1985) 3 NWLR 407 at p. 418 and *Ransome Kuti v. A. G. of the Federation* (1985) 2 NWLR 24E or (1985) 6 S. C. 246. It is equally true that the Court should not allow technicalities to tie its hands to such an extent that if [sic] would fail to do justice to the parties before it, because every Court has a duty to strive to do justice to the parties in a case.

There is no doubt that in this case the Plaintiff has the duty of proving that her husband was the owner of the house in dispute. Furthermore, as laid down in a number of cases including the case of *Julie Nnezianya & Anor. v. Okagbue & 2 Ors.* (1963) 1 ANLR 352, and as revealed by the evidence in this case which I accepted as true, under Onitsha native law and custom, a woman cannot inherit her husband's landed property. She may occupy the landed property of her deceased husband but she cannot assume ownership thereof or alienate it.

In this case the important question is, "who was building the house in dispute?" Three answers are possible, namely:

1. Godwin Nzegwu, during his lifetime,
2. the 1st Defendant, and
3. both the 1st Defendant and Godwin Nzegwu.

There was evidence that both the 1st Defendant and Godwin Nzegwu were so close together that they did a number of things in common. It was therefore possible that both of them were building the house together. Neither of them had any other brother or sister. But neither the Plaintiff nor the 1st Defendant pleaded or testified that the building was a joint venture of the Plaintiff's husband and the 1st Defendant. The third alternative is, therefore, not supported by any evidence or the pleadings.

The 1st Defendant and other witnesses for the Defense maintained that the house was that of the 1st Defendant himself. Exhs. 5 to 5J were produced in an attempt to establish that fact. Exhs. 5 to 5J bore the name of the 1st Defendant but on the face of it, it did not show that it was an approved building plan. Moreover it was a modification of a former plan which was in existence. That former plan was not tendered to enable the court to determine who made it and in whose name it was made. Therefore Exhs. 5 to 5J could not assist in deciding who was building the house.

Although the 1st Defendant and the other Defendants stated that it was not Godwin Nzegwu, but the 1st Defendant who was building the house, that piece of evidence must be weighed with other facts adduced in evidence. It was proved that the Plaintiff's husband was burried [sic] in a room in the house in dispute and that by Onitsha native law and custom a dead man is not buried in the house of some other person. This was not challenged. It was evidence to prove ownership of the house in dispute by Godwin Nzegwu. Furthermore the evidence of PW3, Dr. Umeh, that Godwin Nzegwu was usually taking him round the house whenever he visited, and as stated by the 2nd Defendant that he caused the original building plan to be modified, pointed to a probability that he was building that house. Furthermore, there was evidence that persons in the same age grade with him were building their own living houses. That he was once carefree about building and marriage, but he later married. He was said to be a prominent lawyer. There was evidence that the 1st Defendant has erected a building in the Nzegwu compound and that it was the youngest brother who, by Onitsha native law and custom, would take over the mother's "Usokwu" and that the first son would get his lot from his father's portion. I accepted these facts as true. All the facts proved in this case have led me to the irresistible [sic] conclusion that it was the Plaintiff's husband who was building the house in dispute before he died.

But it was also proved that the Plaintiff could not inherit that house. I agree. She was not claiming any right to inherit it but not to be ejected therefrom. The 1st Defendant stated that a widow's right to occupy the house of her deceased husband was subject to the widow's good behaviour. I also agree, but the bad behaviour must be persistent; one single act may not be enough. It was established that the Plaintiff had been of good behaviour and the wrong which she was said to have done was the refusal to surrender the keys to the 1st Defendant soon after the death of her husband. That was not a wrong at all and construing her refusal as a wrong was most unreasonable.

The 1st Defendant will eventually take over the house in dispute if the Plaintiff remarried and the two daughters of Godwin Nzegwu be given away in marriage or if both the Plaintiff and the two daughters be dead, but he cannot take the benefit of the death of Godwin Nzegwu and reject the liabilities attached thereto: See the case of *Solomon v. Gbabo* (1974) 4 E.C.S. L.R. 457.

The defendants appealed the judgment, and a year after filing the appeal, Alexander Nzegwu died. His first son Okechukwu, who was not a party to the initial suit, and whose education in the United States had been paid for by Lawyer, stepped in to represent his father and to inherit his uncle's property in lieu of his children.

PART 3: JUDGES AND JUDICIAL INTERPRETATION

The Courts and the Ideology of Male Dominance

The deep-seated sexism prevalent in the postindependent Nigerian judicial system had empowered both male and female judges to rule in ways that treated widows as incompetent, sometimes placing them under the authority of juveniles who happen to be sons, and sometimes depriving them of rights to properties they jointly acquired with their husbands. I am not suggesting that all male judges are necessarily sexist, or that all judgments are rendered from a sexist framework or that all widows are good women. I am contending that in cases of divorce and inheritance disputes, the prevailing norm and axis of justice tend to privilege male relatives. Even where customs had existed that vested inheritance rights exclusively to the eldest son, the courts had intervened to secure rights for other sons and invalidated former practices that allowed the eldest daughter to succeed as head of the family until she can have a son where there is no son or if the eldest son dies without issues during his father's lifetime (Elias 1962, 241). The negative attitudes toward the idea of women's autonomy often prevail in the adjudication of a substantial number of cases.[18] African American Harvard law professor and former Chief of the United States Courts of Appeal for the Third Circuit, A. Leon Higginbotham, Jr. made a pertinent point about the judicial decision-making process that bears repeating because of its relevance to the subject of gender discrimination in the Nigerian judicial system. He reminded us that

> courts do not dispense justice in sterile isolation, unaffected by the prevailing political, social, and moral attitudes and currents of the broader society in which they operate. Judges, prosecutors, and other lawyers are not immune to the unconscious influence of—indeed they may even consciously subscribe to—the group of negative stigmatizing assumptions . . . characteristic of the ideology of racism. Thus the broader societal racism, may consciously or unconsciously, infect the attitudes and behavior of judges and lawyers in the courtroom. (1996, 30)

Higginbotham's statement is particularly useful in thinking through the ideology of male dominance in the justice system and the broader societal problem of gender oppression. Those who think of judges as impartial, must be mindful that judges are members of the society, and as such, they carry societal biases and attitudes about gender. Very few of them are interested in gender-based judicial reforms. It is to be expected that their rulings will be informed or affected by their stance on the question of gender equality. The ideas that men should control valuable family property and that wives should be subordinate are ingrained in the psyches of most male judges as well as in the justice system. Consequently, many male justices approach matters of inheritance from the position of custom and tradition, which rule that males must be the overseers of family property.[19]

As we saw in the previous chapter, the rulings of the Native Authority Administration nurtured a patriarchal consciousness that entrenched new family values that collapsed the category of woman into wife. This conflation led to the identification of women as wives and to the devaluation of all women, since women were no longer perceived through a consanguineal or maternal lens. Even though for most men, women were wives, but sisters and mothers were not women, the deployment of the concept of "woman" resulted in the establishment of attitudes and policies that were prejudicial to adult females' interests as a whole. These manifested in how females were perceived in courts, not as mothers and sisters who had autonomy and status, but as women who were sexual beings and who were subordinate to men and subject to male control "at home." The more adult females were perceived through the sexualized identity of wife, the more the feeling gained ground among male relatives that, properly speaking, adult females must be subject to male authority. Men often forget that the rules they invent to constrain wives (who are perceived as nonkin) have the unintended effect of constraining their mothers, sisters, and daughters who are kin.

Younger, rather than older wives bear the brunt of gender discrimination during divorce cases and in probate hearings. The younger the age of the widow, the greater the belief that she must be placed under the authority of some affinal male who will control and guide her in making the right decisions.[20] When this prejudice is coupled with the customs derived from native court rulings, the devaluation of wives' worth and legal status follows suit. Their legal status as minors means that they cannot be trusted to look after themselves and their children, or to inherit or manage any landed property. Although, historically, widows' sexuality was perceived positively as crucial to the growth of the consanguineal family, as Igbos adopted the Christian moral framework, their attitude toward female sexuality changed.[21] The negative perception of a widow's sexuality now provides a public platform for brothers-in-law to launch a pre-emptive appropriation of a deceased's estate.[22] The brothers-in-law's goal is camouflaged by representing a widow's sexuality as destructive to family cohesion. The widow is painted as a predatory jezebel, who will take the family resources and drift on to another man. Of course, what the campaign of calumny is doing is defining the ground on which the affinal family concedes the widow's right to manage her sexuality, provided she gives up her right (and her children's right) to her husband's economic resources. So, when a widow contests her brother-in-law's power of attorney, it further confirms his accusations that she is indeed eager to "divest" the consanguineal family of their brother's property (which was never theirs in the first place) and to embark on a life of sexual wantonness.[23] The sum effect of this campaign of calumny is the creation of new customs for widows, although nobody saw them as such, at the time.

Rarely do male judges see that the family problem is usually created by male relatives who are either invested in appropriating the deceased's estate, or in establishing sexual relations with the widow. What the judges tend to see and privilege (because they inevitably see themselves and their own lives reflected in these cases) are the brothers' profuse declarations of family unity and "brotherly" love—sentiments that are not necessarily consistent with their true objectives. So at probate hearings, widows spend an inordinate amount of time fending off patronizing questions that derive from images of widows as predatory and hypersexual. Widows are thus forced to prove their loyalty to their marital family, and the only available proof is their acceptance of a brother-in-law's hegemonic authority. Herein lies the paradox of modern life. The brother derives his right to appropriate his deceased brother's property on the ground that they are maternal siblings. But the validity of this uterine tie is continually being eroded by the male-privileging ideology that governs modern Igbo family life.

Ironically, while affirming the value of maternal ties, the contemporary perception of widows as problems is tied to the overall negative valuation of women (mothers included), and the establishment of patriarchy as the foundation of the Igbo family. Male judges find a woman's grievances believable only if there is a responsible male figure "guiding," "supporting," and "stating" her cause. In the eyes of the court, only men are authorities on matters of custom and tradition. It does not matter that they may not know as much as they claim, or that there is no one definitive reading of social practices. In the male-affirming eyes of the court, women cannot be experts on customs because, by definition, women are social minors or irrational beings and hence incapable of being knowledgable experts. Thus, in trials, women are belittled if they express their knowledge, especially when they are presenting aspects of social practices that challenge men's claims to patriarchal dominance. It does not matter that their versions may be more accurate than those of the recognized experts. The corollary effect of the court's "preference for patriarchal authority figures" is that women expert witnesses are rarely called upon to testify about local customs, and widows are forced to rely on male figures who seem sympathetic. The problem with this reliance is that these male advocates are continuously editing and reconstructing "tradition" along patriarchal lines to entrench the larger group interests of men. Using male authority figures as expert witnesses has the effect of forcing women to conduct their cases on grounds that reinforce sexism and paternalism.[24]

Because male-privileging policies were a standard part of a complex of discriminatory activities in the judicial system, it was easy for the appeal court justices in *Nzegwus v. Nzegwu* (1997) to ignore the wealth of materials generated during the trial—an area map of Lazarus Nzegwu's property, testimonies of other witnesses, admissions of defendants, the fact of the deceased's burial in the house—that the trial judge had carefully noted in ruling on the ownership of the disputed residence. The appeal court judges chose to decide the case on some perceived contradiction between the widow and one of her male witnesses. It did not matter that the widow had researched the customary laws governing her own circumstances. Judges correlated age with knowledge, and since she was a young woman, she could not possibly know. The appeal was allowed to stand because her testimony seemed to contradict the view of her elderly male witness. Because the judges had chosen to ignore much of the evidence that emerged during the trial, they readily made much of the perceived contradiction. But was there really a contradiction? The matter will be taken up in the section on the meaning of *usokwu* later in this chapter.

Meanwhile, the respondent's counsel attempted to undercut the gender discriminatory leaning of the court and to make a case for the right of daughters. He alerted the judges to the consequences of striking down the trial judgment. But according to the majority judgment written by Justice Akintola Olufemi Ejiwunmi:

> The . . . learned counsel contends that any law or custom of Onitsha which deprives a daughter of any interest in the property of her deceased father merely on grounds of [sex] is unconstitutional and therefore null and void. He also contends that any law or custom in Nigeria including Native Law and Custom of Onitsha which requires that a widow is not entitled to the properties of her deceased husband merely because she begat no male child for him is unconstitutional and therefore null and void. In essence the submission of the learned counsel for the respondent (in brief) is that the Native Law and Custom of Onitsha is inconsistent with the provisions of section 39 (1) 2 of the 1979 Constitution as amended. The inconsistency being that it constitutes a disability or deprivation on the part of the widow and children of the deceased on grounds only of sex contrary to the provisions of the Constitution above cited. (Ejiwunmi, *Nzegwus v. Nzegwu* 1997, 23)

In the majority ruling, and in Tobi's separate page-and-a-half judgment, all the judges rejected the argument of counsel on the unconstitutionality of depriving daughters and widows of their interest in the estate. Tobi's terse response began with this perfunctory statement:

> It is elementary law that facts given in evidence before a court of law must be backed up by the pleadings. Facts given in evidence which are

not vindicated by the pleadings will go to no issue, and a court of law will not make use of them in the evaluation of the evidence before it; not to talk of giving a judgment based on such evidence. (Tobi, *Nzegwus v. Nzegwu*, 1997)

His judgment follows:

In paragraph 13 of the Amended Statement of Claim, the respondent declared as follows:

According to Onitsha native law and custom the house where a mother lived was called her "Nkpuke," and if the mother died leaving more than one son her "Nkpuke" was usually occupied by the youngest son.

Although the respondent gave evidence in line with paragraph 13 above, her witness, PW1, gave contrary evidence when he said:

In this respect "Usokwu" is used figuratively to mean mother. On the death of a mother her "Usokwu" goes to her male issues according to Onitsha Native Law and Custom but with the proviso that the senior male issue will be in charge of the "Usokwu." On the death of a junior brother without a male issue the "Usokwu" devolves on the senior brother exclusively.

Apart from the fact that what PW1 said was not pleaded, it is clearly contrary to paragraph 13 of the Amended Statement of Claim and the evidence of the respondent. PW1 was the witness of the respondent and she must stand and fall by his evidence.

Where the evidence of witnesses is in material contradiction, a court of law will be in difficulty to assign credibility to such evidence. The court cannot salvage the contradictory evidence in favour of the party. (Tobi, *Nzegwus v. Nzegwu*, 1997)

After further drawing out the implication of this contradiction, Justice Tobi went on to acknowledge that "whether a contradiction is material or immaterial is an exercise to be undertaken by the trial Judge at the evaluation stage of the evidence. Because the trial Judge saw it all, he is in a better position to determine the materiality or otherwise of the contradiction" (Tobi, *Nzegwus v. Nzegwu*, 1997).

Although the trial judge, Justice Onwuamaegbu, had determined that there was no contradiction, Tobi ruled in favor of construing the property in question as *oli ekpe* or *oku ekpe* (in Onitsha dialect), and in favor of the right of the defendant/appellants to disinherit the daughters of the deceased. All the Appeal Court judges—Ejiwunmi, Tobi, and Okey Achike were very clear on the gender discriminatory consequences of their ruling. In his ruling, the trial judge had summarized the evidence of Alexander, the uncle of the children, contending:

> Under cross-examination . . . that the children of [the deceased] could not inherit any category of his properties because they would be married away, in due course. He claimed that under Onitsha native law and custom widows are left to fend for themselves. . . .

As part of his ruling, Justice Ejiwunmi accepted as legitimate the appellants' argument that the orders of the trial judge "were made in clear breach of the Onitsha Custom" (1997, 23). He found it believable that Onitsha custom deprived widows of access to their matrimonial home and stripped daughters of their right to their father's estate, effectively abandoning them to fend for themselves. Because such a law was acceptable to him and his fellow jurists, he did not see it as repugnant or in clear breach of the 1979 Constitution that stipulated that daughters had rights to their father's estates equal to that of sons. Since there were no sons, it stood to reason that the daughter should be the *sole* heirs. It is most telling that Justice Ejiwunmi decided that a custom should prevail that infringes on a daughter's right to equity and equality. To facilitate this act, Ejiwunmi drew judicial wisdom from a 1963 case that was decided before the 1979 Constitution, to uphold customs that clearly violate the fundamental principle of equality enshrined in the constitution.

Justices' perception of the role of the court is vital in understanding their rulings. Where trial judges perceive the court as instruments for social justice and redressing social wrongs, they may ignore technicalities and reject spurious arguments from tradition, as did Justice Onwuamaegbu, and later, Justice Tobi in the Mojekwu case. But when justices subscribe to a passive view of the court, they rule conservatively, upholding customs and practices that promote gender inequality.

Far more ominous in the ruling of the Appeal Court is not the refusal of the judges to see the judicial system as a means of redressing societal ills, but their tacit stand not to uphold the provisions of the Constitution that proclaimed gender equality. Although it is commendable that Tobi and Ejiwunmi attempted to correct this in the Mojekwu case, but one could still legitimately argue that their stance in the Nzegwu case is an affirmation of patriarchal ideology. The argument would be valid because the appellate justices embraced improbable rationalizations to subvert those provisions in order to entrench male dominance. Not so surprisingly, discriminatory customs that are subordinate to the constitution are used to override the latter when the two conflict on matters concerning the social equality of women. Interestingly, arguments from custom are routinely rejected when they infringe on the powers of men to control or subjugate women. This selective application of customs and norms provides undisputable evidence of a concerted effort to uphold male dominance and to keep women in a subordinate state.[25]

Although it is legitimate to observe that the legal system installed during the colonial period laid the basis for the inherent weaknesses of Nigeria's present judicial system, we cannot but recognize the failure of Nigerians themselves and of Igbos especially, to radically reform their system. Once the issue of responsibility is raised, we begin to see the limitations of blaming colonialism for the current ills of the judicial system especially since the British had radically revised their own laws, and made them gender sensitive. The reluctance of the Igbos to do the same exposes their disregard for their daughters and wives. The colonial and postindependent retention of nineteenth-century British laws and invented local customs that promote an oppressive climate for Nigerian women are not made by white men but by Nigerian men, specifically fathers, sons, brothers, uncles, husbands, judges, administrators, and civil society activists, for whom the West's colonial domination of Africa was abhorrent. It is instructive that these same champions of African emancipation and Nigerian independence sanguinely claim the right to oppress their women specifically, wives, daughters, sisters, and mothers as a normal order of reality.

Reflecting on these judicial machinations, we accept Charles Warren's point that "the court is not an organism dissociated from the conditions and history of the times in which it exists. It does not formulate and deliver its opinions in a legal vacuum. Its judges are not abstract and impersonal oracles, but men whose views are necessarily, though by no conscious intent, affected by inheritance, education and environment and by the impact of history past and present"[28] (Warren 1926, 4). Because there is merit in Warren's observation, it is incumbent on us to review the "conditions and history of the times" if we are to combat the pervasive culture of gender oppression endemic in modern-day Nigeria. In the following section, I will expose how Nigerian judges interpret tradition to legitimate, reinforce, and perpetuate the ideology of male domination.

Colonialism and the Origins of *Oku Ekpe*

Because the Mojekwu and Nzegwu cases raised questions about *oli ekpe* or *oku ekpe*, it is imperative to examine this concept in greater detail. *Oku ekpe* is the motivating factor in Alexander Nzegwu's assertion that the children of his brother could not inherit any category of things, because they are female and would be married anyway. He drew moral strength from this custom to put himself at the top of the inheritance line, ahead of his deceased brother's children.

To ensure that his *oku ekpe* rights would be immediately preserved, Alexander represented his appeal as an inheritance dispute, even though he knew that such *oku ekpe* rights come into effect only after the children are married and the widows are dead. Moreover, his misstatement of the ground of the trial in his appeal documents deliberately ignores the fact that this is not a case of inheritance, as Onwuamaegbu correctly stated, but instead concerns daughters' and widows' entitlement. It is after the conditions that warrant entitlement have lapsed—that is, the remarriage or death of the widow, and the marriage of daughters—that the property actually comes up for inheritance. This means that correctly understood, *oku ekpe* rights cannot revoke or abruptly terminate the rights and entitlements of daughters and widows.

Pertinent questions may now be raised: Why did Tobi nullify the legitimacy of widows' and daughters' entitlement provided by Onitsha custom? What explains the haste to rule on the issue of inheritance that was not the subject of trial? Why did the appellate judges persist on this course, knowing full well that the children were minors? Even after their attention was called to the fact that the Constitution had declared such customs unconstitutional, why did they commit to settling the issue of inheritance in gender-oppressive ways and in direct contravention to the Constitution? To answer these questions, we have to unravel the logic guiding the Appeal Court's decision in *Nzegwus v. Nzegwu* (1997). Two questions immediately arise: Why did the trial judge not see the contradiction that Tobi claims is "the fulcrum of the whole case"? And could it be that there was no contradiction in the first place?

Part of the answer may be that being Igbo, the trial judge was familiar with the conditions under which *oku ekpe* rights arise, whereas Tobi, a Yoruba, was unfamiliar with this practice. But since Tobi's judgment rests on a logical ground, a critical part of the question goes beyond the issues of the judges' ethnicities. Given that an understanding of *oku ekpe* (or *oli ekpe*) is important for apprehending the legitimacy of Tobi's insight, and for resolving the issue of "material contradiction," I will now explain the *oku ekpe* practice and its principle.

Oku-ekpe states that in the absence of a male child to inherit a father's estate upon his death, the late man's brothers are the next in line of inheritance, followed by his nephews. But this is after the widow has died and all the daughters are married.[26] In the early stages of colonialism, when the combined forces of Christianity and educational ideology were pressing daughters to marry, daughters undercut the principle of *oku-ekpe* by breaking up their marriages and returning to live as *idigbe* in their natal home. Any children they had after their return inherited the property. Widows also undermined this *oku ekpe* provision by having more children themselves, or by marrying a wife or wives for a deceased son, as did Caroline Mojekwu. Contrary to supposition, *oku ekpe* was not an enduring, long-standing custom. It emerged in the colonial socioeconomic context in which land was acquiring value and becoming the basis of family wealth. The developing patriarchal value system turned against *idigbe* unions that had been the basis for the children of daughters to inherit family property, and thereby established a rule to guide the appropriation of a homestead in which the wife had died and in which there was no one in direct line of inheritance. Prior to the commodification of land and escalation of land values, such a homestead would typically fall into ruin, once the daughters were married and the widow had died. It would revert back to the lineage family land and would later be reassigned to a family member who needed it.

Whereas in the past no one had more land than they could use, the introduction of the colonial labor economy and idea of absolute ownership of land resulted in the accumulation of real estate as wealth and for economic purposes. With the beginning of land commodification at the turn of the twentieth century, new social practices, ethical values, and residential patterns were introduced to respond to this social phenomenon. One of these allowed homesteads in which there were no inheritors to go to the eldest son of the maximal lineage rather than reverting back to being family land.[27] However, when a man died with no sons to succeed him, a widow still within her childbearing years had several options. She could choose to end the marriage and return to her own family, and could later remarry. Or she could marry the junior brother of her late husband and merge her home with that of the new husband. Or she could continue to reside with her daughters[28] in her conjugal home and have children in her late husband's name. If she opted to continue as a wife in her husband's name, she was entitled to live in that homestead for the rest of her life. In the interim, if she bore a male child, that child became the deceased's heir.

The accuracy of this interpretation is evident in the case of *Nnezianya v. Okagbue & 2 Ors.* (1963), which Ejiwunmi misused to support his judgment. In this case, the widow lived and died in her husband's home, and the issue of inheritance arose only after her death. Other cases in which widows lived in their husband's name for the rest of their lives include Chuba Ikpeazu's mother (whose father was born after the death of her husband), the paternal grandmother of the appellants' counsel; Odu Mbanefo's sister, Nnonye, wife of Patrick Orefo Uyanwa; Madam Nwanolue, mother-in-law of PW1; Madam Azuka Aduba, first wife of Chief George Nzegwu; Ma Nnukwu (Big Mother), wife of Lazarus Nzegwu; and Nne Katie Egbunike, wife of Chief James Egbunike, among others.

As was the case with the paternal grandmother of the appellant counsel, a widow who had a child after her husband's death had the social support of the community. Prior to the change of this policy in 2001, the community readily accepted the child as the legitimate son or daughter of the deceased. The fact that such children were conceived and born well after the death of a husband is proof that a widow's entitlement to reside in her matrimonial home was then uncontested. Such children were viewed as the children of the deceased, hence were legitimate members of his lineage. If any of them were male, their inheritance rights automatically superseded those of the deceased's brother, uncle, or nephew. The latter usually had no qualms about the termination of their rights because they were invested in the continuity of the memory of their deceased brother, uncle, or nephew and in the expansion of his lineage.

There were two other ways in which longstanding social customs allowed and even encouraged women to circumvent this fairly recent tradition of sons-as-heir that emerged during the very early period of colonial rule. First, the widow might marry either a wife or wives, who would then bear the son. This was the option chosen by one of Lazarus Nzegwu's wives, Ma Nnukwu. She married a wife, in a woman–woman marriage, who bore a son named Emmanuel. He inherited her *usokwu* or homestead within Lazarus Nzegwu's compound. The same is true of Lazarus Nzegwu's first daughter Eselu Agadi Nzegwu, wife of Chief Richard Uwechia. She had two daughters and married two wives in a woman–woman marriage that resulted in sons. The second option occurred before the proscription of the practice in 1923 by the first Christian Obi of Onitsha, Samuel Okosi. In this latter option, a daughter might end her marriage or reject marriage altogether and opt for the institution of *idigbe*. Under this practice, she lived at home and had children with a paramour of her choice. Because she did not marry the consort, the children were full members of her own agnatic family, not of the paramour's family.

These options, which had been available to women, began to disappear between 1899 and 1920, due to the increasing influence of Christian ideology in the social life of Onitsha indigenes. Within the Christian ethical scheme, such options—*idigbe*ship, woman–woman marriages, women's polygamist relations, and marriages for deceased sons—were morally reprobate. Church officials proscribed them for members and refused medical treatment in mission hospitals to women who were engaged in these relationships unless they renounced these practices. They also refused to enroll the children of such relationships in schools, which were usually the only schools available. By so doing, they effectively penalized the child for the actions of the mother which the community deemed legitimate. Some mothers succumbed to the pressure to avoid jeopardizing the futures of their children in the new labor market, which required its workers to be educated. Although the entire community did not convert to Christianity, by 1895 a noticeable change was occurring in the values of the community as the children who had gone to school and became Christians, became adults. With the female-friendly option of *idigbe* closed up, widows continued, up until the late 1950s, to work with their only surviving options: they either married wives for themselves in a woman–woman marriage, or they married wives for deceased or infant sons as did Caroline Mojekwu, or they had more children themselves.

By the 1960s, these options were further reduced, following the massive acceptance of Christian marital ideology. Widows had to have the sons themselves, and many exercised this option even though it may have been detrimental to their health. Fears about the future forced them to continue having children as they sought to solidify their entitlement and to convert their access to a right of inheritance. The ongoing social transformations and the political upheavals of the time sufficiently distracted the community from focusing on the emerging social problems of the time and to respond to them effectively.[29] Women community leaders failed to address publicly the ways in which the spreading patriarchal ideology was disempowering wives, widows, and daughters and pressuring them to have sons because residential rights and access to land now depended on having a son, and most of women's past options had been foreclosed. No attempt was made to relax or discard the emphasis on sons as the only way of solidifying wives' right of access to their matrimonial home. Rather than empower wives to expand their options, the society placed greater obstacles in their paths. The rise of nuclear family ideology and the strict sexual restrictions it prescribed for women placed a further burden on wives and mandated that they bear the sons themselves. Unlike in the past, when they could marry wives to bear sons for them, the nuclear family ideology eliminated such options.

The rise of individualism and the nuclear family consciousness increasingly led to the diminution of the multigenerational lineage consciousness. It was not that the lineage became less important or irrelevant, but that emphasis was placed on the nuclear family rather than on the lineage. The more educated and professionally successful men privileged their nuclear family over the lineage when it suited them, but at other times they would subordinate their wives to their kin to mollify their kin for their own aloofness. With lineage cohesion being exploited to serve crosscutting personal goals in the period prior to the Biafran war, and as cohesiveness rapidly broke down afterward, skyrocketing real estate values created searing family tensions in Onitsha. Widows' attempts to protect their husbands' resources for their children were increasingly defined as antithetical to the interests of the family (i.e., the interests of the brothers' of the deceased). By 1970, when the Biafran war ended, major conflicts began to erupt over inheritance rights, as the notion of family vacillated wildly between lineage and nuclear. In these pendulum swings, widows tried valiantly to respond to rapidly shifting value systems, drawing on historic models that were familiar but fast becoming obsolete. Meanwhile, male members who were in line of inheritance resisted what they defined as the delaying tactics of widows aimed at preventing the distribution of a deceased brother's property. As widows asserted the rights of their children to the nuclear family estate of their father and of the couple, brothers-in-laws shifted from a value scheme that urged the preservation of their brother's memory to an individualistic one that endorsed the appropriation of their deceased brothers' estates for their own personal use. Not only did they seek to undercut widows' historic entitlement to residences and access to land, but they also sought to extinguish the rights of minor children. From the 1980s, the overriding concern of some male members of the family was how to appropriate a deceased's property as quickly as possible. Whereas historically the absence of a son did not initiate the eviction of the widow, in the high real estate market of Onitsha, the ideal of brotherly love was jettisoned as modern men succumbed to the lure of hot real estate market and aggressively pursued their own personal wealth and property.

The staggering rise of real estate values in Onitsha in the latter half of the twentieth century, and the immense population pressure in "Inland Town" (the ancestral home of Onitsha indigenes), propelled impatient *diopkas* (eldest lineage sons) to drastically shorten the timeframe within which properties could become *oku ekpe*. The Nzegwu case provides a prominent example of the practice of ejecting the deceased's daughters and widow to shorten the time in which a property became *oku ekpe*. The truncated timeframe enabled an elder brother to make a pre-emptive bid for his deceased brother's property. To guarantee the success of the bid, the deceased's house was represented as the brother's mother's home. This misrepresentation was designed to extinguish the children's rights. The strategy allowed Alexander to circumvent the culturally established principle that protected a widow's right to reside in her husband's house. Characterizing the building as "his house" situated at "his mother's *usokwu*" meant that he did not have to wait for the devolution of the property.

In light of the modifications and aberrations to which the custom of *oku ekpe* has been subjected, Igbo feminist legal activists such as Joy Ezeilo readily denounced *oku ekpe* as "archaic" (Oladapo 1998). What they miss in their quick denouncement, however, is that we are dealing with a distortion of a fairly modern custom that was devised to respond to colonial economic policies affecting the value of land. Scholars of African material culture tend to assume that all customs must be ancient and unchanging. This frame of mind prevents them from seeing that some customs were historically recent, having been introduced to cope with new social changes emanating from the new patriarchal value system. Contrary to suppositions, the *oku ekpe* is not an archaic custom but a modern response to land commodification. Nevertheless, Ezeilo is right in asserting that it is the "unrelenting efforts by male chauvinists in pursuit of their preference for their own economic resources that created the cases" (Oladapo 1998). As the preceding analysis showed, three factors were responsible for the travesty: the closing off of options which women had used to balance their family, men's attempt to gain monopolistic control of land; and the community's failure to address the implication of the new value systems that created numerous social problems.

Although *oku ekpe* may have been the strategic response of *diokpas* (the male heads of families) to acquire more landed property in an economy that supports land ownership, the present socioeconomic reality that requires daughters and sons to function at the same economic level of labor and wealth generation mitigates the need to disenfranchise daughters and undermines the contemporary relevance of the principle of *oku ekpe*. Besides, the consanguineal structure of family that once gave it legitimacy no longer exists. In a society governed by an individualistic and nuclear family ethos, young children have a more effective guardian in their mothers than uncles whose primary interest is their own nuclear families. The only reason the *oku ekpe* and similar principles are invoked at all as they were in the Mojekwu and Nzegwu cases, is that grasping male relatives seek to acquire more properties for themselves. If we do not confront the fact that these customs are being used to entrench gender inequality, we will fail to see that modern Igbo men are upholding a framework of gender domination and are claiming that these recently introduced customs speak eloquently about a historical past and authentic tradition.

PART 4: READING CUSTOMS AND DEFINING FATHERLY LOVE

A Note about Tradition

Kwame Gyekye (1997) puts this politics of customs in context while making the excellent point that there is nothing static or stable about traditions and customs. He argues that the root of the problem lies in the way that present generations have chosen to preserve their customs or traditions. According to him, "the preservation of [a belief or practice], in part or in whole, would depend very much on the attitude the new generation adopts toward it. . . . This means that the continuity and survival of a pristine cultural product depends on the normative considerations that will be brought to bear on it by subsequent generations" (1997, 221). Gyekye's point is that customs are rarely received and preserved in their old forms. This tells us that our focus should be on the attitude and normative values that Onitsha men have brought to bear on receiving and deploying these customs, rather than on the customs themselves.

In light of this, it would be most beneficial if we direct attention to the attitudes and normative values of male family members. Doing this will allow us not only to see the flexibility of Igbo cultures and how liberatory spaces were created for female member of the family, but also to undermine the classic ploy of blaming tradition. Contrary to supposition, Igbo tradition had given childless widows and widows with daughters a range of options with which to mitigate their structural disadvantage and guarantee their accommodation, access to land, family support, and social status. Problems began with the modern elimination of the society's provision for women that narrowed their motherhood options, if they did not have a male child, without offering them a viable alternative. Because access to land was still contingent on having a male child, wives' vulnerability was dramatically enhanced, yet the overwhelming pressure they faced could have been ameliorated had the emphasis on sons been waived.

Careful sociological scrutiny reveals the different ways in which customs hardened, showing that they have hardly been static and unchanging over time. Highlighting the ways in which customs acquired gender inequality overtones can isolate the specific occasions when male members of a family embraced misogynistic values and the closing off of resources to female members of that family. Although the actions of such male relatives were guided by self-interest, over the years, such acts of appropriation had the deleterious effect of narrowing widow's abilities to educate their children to their fullest potential as well as impoverishing their daughters. The failure of present-day Igbo male leadership comes from ignoring the implication of all these changes, which have radically reshaped families. Once the collective ethos of the lineage family was eroded by the individualistic ethos of the nuclear family, public debate and family reform should have commenced. Such debate would have triggered reforms that could respond to the fact that the consanguineal notion of family was no longer the dominant notion in the changing times. However, in failing to engage in public debate and re-examine the implications of these individualistic values, the Onitsha community could not respond cogently to the forces of modernization, and so were trapped in living a family ideal that had been undercut by the exigencies of modern sociopolitical life.

Thus, when Alexander testified in court "that the children of [the deceased] could not inherit any category of his properties because they would be married away . . . [and] that under Onitsha native law and custom widows are left to fend for themselves" (*Nzegwu v. Nzegwus*, 1986, 15), he was not stating the custom. He was manipulating customs for purposes of personal aggrandizement. He was aware that this manipulation was antithetical to the older societal framework within which lie both the notion that family unity was paramount and the concept of *oku ekpe*. We should note that by representing his position as deriving legitimacy from custom, he was following the standard ploy of native court clerks of conflating their personal interests with lineage interests in order to appropriate the assets of anyone in their crosshairs.

Understanding the Meaning of *Usokwu*

Surviving Igbo customs have continued to be distorted to serve contemporary objectives, as the following misreading of *usokwu* (hearth-hold or mother pole) shows. Contrary to Elias's statement that Onitsha has a primogeniture principle of inheritance (1962, 242), the community has a matri-segmentation principle of inheritance, which is the division of land among wives, with children as nominal heirs. This matri-segmentation principle is preserved in the Onitsha maxim *ekesia na iba eke na usokwu* (literally, that after the division at the level of *iba* [the father pole], the next level of division is that of *usokwu* [the mother pole]). The division of a father's estate proceeds by determining the number of wives within the family, and the property is divided according to the number of mothers. Upon the death of the mother, each mother's (or *usokwu*) section is then divided among her children. However, with the rise of the male-privileging ideology, the principle of division was based on the number of wives with sons. This meant that if there were three wives and only two wives have sons, the family land was divided into two, regardless of the number of sons each widow has. Each portion is represented as the share of each *usokwu*. The wife that does not have a son does not participate in the division, but her physical *usokwu* or residential dwelling is left intact. She is entitled to live out the rest of her days in that residence, and upon her death the land is allocated to the *usokwu* that had received that share of land at the first level of division. This is what it means to "matri-segment" or share at the level of *iba*.

The next level of division, which is the *usokwu* level, follows when the sons of each *usokwu* divide their own allocation so that each one receives a share. At this point, the oldest son of the deceased may or may not move into his father's home, which becomes that family's *iba*. All the sons divide up their mother's allocation. The younger son of each unit takes the spot that used to be the mother's dwelling home or the *usokwu*. In typical Igbo compounds, this spot is typically located toward the rear of the father's compound. Although the matri-segmentation maxim "*ekesia na iba eke na usokwu*" suggests that there are two levels in which sons receive their inheritance (at the paternal and maternal levels), the truth is that each son receives just one share, not two.[30] Once the division of the estate has taken place, it becomes mischievous to describe the allotment of the younger son as *usokwu*. This creates the erroneous impression that the physical *usokwu* is still in existence or that the younger son's home is really the mother's residence, not his allocation. The representation further suggests that the younger brother already has his own allocation elsewhere, and that the mother's *usokwu* is a separate, additional portion that the sons of the mother would share equally.

Using this diversionary strategy, the counsel of the appellants made it seem to the two Yoruba judges that "the custom . . . is that all the sons inherit the Usokwu, with the proviso that the eldest male child shall act as the custodian" (Ejiwunmi, *Nzegwus v. Nzegwu* 1997, 4). In successfully creating the impression that the land on which this property stands is not part of the father's compound or the younger brother's legitimate share, the appellants and their counsel laid the basis for the older brother's appropriation of his deceased brother's property *as if it were still the mother's home*. In fact, that an older brother could think in this manner reveals the depth of his ill intention towards his brother. In the ruling, both Tobi and Ejiwunmi, two Yoruba judges, accepted the validity of the appellant's argument that the plaintiff/respondent's witness had, indeed, undermined the respondent's case. Because of their lack of familiarity with Igbo social practices, they believed that when the witness asserted that "on the death of a mother, her 'usokwu' goes to her male issues according to Onitsha Native Law and Custom but with the proviso that the senior male issue will be in charge of the 'usokwu.' On the death of a junior brother without a male issue the 'usokwu' devolves on the senior brother exclusively" (Tobi, *Nzegwu v. Nzegwu* 1997, 1), he was stating that Alexander was the owner of the house in dispute. The witness was not responding to a question about the ownership of the house that Alexander was claiming. He was responding to a question that sought to establish the Onitsha principle of property division. At that material time, the house in dispute was no longer the *usokwu*, because the two levels of property division had been completed. The house *was* the deceased's own home. Had the deceased died without a son *before* the completion of the property division, and had all burial and funeral rites been completed, then and only then would the devolution occur as the witness stated.

Prior to the formal division of Lazarus Nzegwu's estate, the sons' spheres of influence were limited to their mother's *usokwu*, in which case the senior son, as the elder, was in charge of the entire estate. Once the first level of division was completed, the eldest son of each *usokwu* was in charge of his mother's share. The next level of division occurred when the sons of each mother divided up their portion to obtain their own individual allotment. The distribution of Lazarus Nzegwu's compound had been completed several years before the court case, and the deceased was building his own house on his allotment, which was the site his mother's *usokwu* had once stood. As the first son of his mother, Alexander had chosen a more prominent location as his allotment and had built his own home. The house that Alexander was claiming as "his mother's house" could not be characterized as such, since it was the deceased's own share of his father's estate.[31] That Alexander chose to reference it as such is proof that he intended to appropriate that property for himself and his nuclear family by fudging the line. This point was definitely clear to the Igbo trial judge, Obunneme Onwuamaegbu, who saw through this fudge, which was why he did not see any material contradiction in the statement of the plaintiff's witness. But this subtlety of Igbo inheritance principle and the multiple ways in which *usokwu* is used was lost on the Yoruba appellate judges, Ejiwunmi and Tobi. Okey Achike, the sole Onitsha judge in the group, permitted the reading to stand because he was engaged in a similar act of appropriation in his own family. He was struggling to supplant the senior *usokwu* of his father's first and legal wife with his mother's junior *usokwu*.

In his judgment, Onwuamaegbu revealed that he paid close attention to Alexander's dishonorable intention toward his brother's property. He stated:

> He [Alexander] admitted that Godwin's companions were building their personal houses when he was alive and that it could be that the Plaintiff would know if Godwin was building any house and that the house which is the subject matter of this action was being built on a site which was their mother's "Usokwu." He admitted that the eldest son of a man would inherit the father's "Obi" but it was the youngest son who would inherit the woman's "Usokwu." He admitted that both he and Godwin were the sons of Lazarus Nzegwu who owned the compound where he was living. That each son of Lazarus Nzegwu was given a place to live in within the compound of the [*sic*] Lazarus Nzegwu if such son asked to be given a place. He also admitted that the compound of Lazarus Nzegwu was the communal property of his sons and no son could sell the plot given to him to build on. He said that Godwin was buried in the house where he was laid in state and where the Plaintiff was confined during her mourning period.[32] (*Nzegwu v. Nzegwus* 1986, 15–16)

For Onwuamaegbu, Alexander's assertions contained the three principal facts that established that the property is the deceased's, and not his own. These are (1) that the property was part of Lazarus Nzegwu's property, (2) that each son's land allotment was clearly marked in the survey map of the compound indicating that all the principles of division had been satisfied, and (3) that the deceased was buried in the house. No one is buried in a house that she or he does not own. An ancillary point that Onwuamaegbu also noted as proof that the home belonged to the deceased was that the deceased had the economic resources to build his own home.

Thus, the material contradiction that Tobi harped upon was really not a contradiction, if we understand the Igbo principle of property division, if we recognize that the statement of PW1 was made in the context of eliciting a general rule, and if we are fluent enough in the cultural norms to understand that PW1 was speaking both literally and figuratively about the *usokwu*.[33] Literally, the *usokwu* is the physical abode of the mother. Figuratively, it defines the mother pole in the family as well as references maternal consciousness. Because PW1 was speaking figuratively, his comment about the senior son "being in charge of an *usokwu*" did not mean being in physical possession of her physical residence that no longer existed, but metaphorically being the authority figure of the mother's segment of Lazarus Nzegwu's family. This "being in charge" merely represents the older son as a custodian of his mother's maternal section of the family, not as the owner or as a despot. In fact, on the death of the junior son (where there are only two sons), the responsibility of safeguarding and caring for his brother's conjugal family falls primarily on the senior brother. As a custodian, his role is to protect his brother's share from being absorbed by others, not to absorb it as his own personal property. Because Tobi and Ejiwunmi were oblivious to these cultural nuances, they interpreted *usokwu* in the most literal manner of a physical house, in contravention of the PW1's claim that "'Usokwu' is used figuratively to mean mother." It was their flawed interpretation that caused them to imagine a contradiction where none existed. Thus, when the widow asserted her right to live in her deceased husband's house, that assertion did not nullify the senior brother's responsibility to care for all who are under his mother's *usokwu*. That Ejiwunmi, Tobi, and Achike refused to acknowledge this interpretation is proof that they had already prejudged the issue, and were approaching the case from the ideological framework of gender domination.

For a variety of personal reasons, not least of which seems to be their deep-seated attitudes towards younger widows, Justices Ejiwunmi, Tobi, and Achike allowed themselves to be played.[34] They then utilized analytic contortion to construe the deceased's house as *usokwu* and to hand over to the son of Alexander (who had died by this time) a resource that should have been used to raise the deceased's children. Bent as they were on upholding male privilege and fraternal love, the justices neglected to ask the appellants/defendants what it means to be a father. They did not interrogate the appellants on the extent to which they had been fathers to their deceased brother's daughters, and how their love for their deceased brother translates into the eviction of his children. Clearly, being responsible for one's maternal *usokwu* and professing love for a brother does not mean stripping a younger brother's assets for one's personal gain and then throwing away the children as liabilities. That is certainly not Onitsha custom.

Questions about Fatherhood and Fraternal Love

Writing on the legal aspects and implications of customary law, Takyiwaa Manuh makes the welcome point that people make a distinction between their own laws and the judicial or lawyers' version of customary law. What people regard as the customary laws are "often fluid and adaptable rules, and what emerged from the declarations of judges and courts" are hardened inflexible rules that are used in other decisions "even where mistakes have occurred to the actual content of the customary law" (1995, 335). Knowing that people are aware of the divergence between judicial customary law and the local one, this seems the right occasion to raise the question of what the appellants understand to be the responsibility of fathers. Does being a father entail the rejection of daughters and the discarding of them as liabilities? Is lack of valuation of daughters a part of Onitsha history? The appellants and the Appeal Court judges seemed to offer affirmative answers to the questions, implying that the responsibility of fathers must always be narrowly qualified and negotiated to suit the objectives of men, while the educational needs of daughters were trampled upon.

To justify their ruling, Ejiwunmi, in his majority ruling, invoked the 1963 case of *Nnezianya & Okagbue & 2 Ors.*, in which a widow with an only daughter (who died before the mother) willed the property to the children of her deceased daughter just before she died. In subsequent appeals, the Appeal and Supreme Courts sided with the view that the widow's possession of her late husband's property "can never be adverse to the rights of her husband's family, and those who claim through her are affected or bound by this" (Ejiwunmi 1997, 26). What Chief Justice Ademola of the Nigerian Supreme Court effectively stated in that judgment is that a daughter and her children are not part of the family and they are not entitled to benefit from their father's and grandfather's estate. It is important to state that the children to whom the widow willed the property were the direct descendants of her deceased husband, his grandchildren by his daughter. So when Ademola revoked the will in 1963 and asserted that the Federal Constitution of Nigeria cannot correct this anomalous conception of families and daughters, he was consciously limiting the range of the Constitution and justifying the excision of daughters from families.

It is unclear why Ademola chose to subsume a higher and superior legal instrument (the Constitution) under the lower-level Onitsha customary laws that were codified during the native authority era. If this is a case of protecting an indigenous culture from "western" values and laws, women are part of the culture and deserve to have their rights protected. Moreover, the argument that oppressive aspects of people's culture must prevail does not hold, given that Onitsha customs have always been a flexible set of norms rather than a set of inflexible rules. The convoluted logic of Ademola's ruling raises the more fundamental question of the Chief Justice's conception of the Constitution and the family, and of what he understands and envisions as the status of daughters within it. If the Constitution protects daughters and sons equally, and if daughters are part of the family and of the same culture, what justification is there for declaring a daughter's children to be nonfamily members within the provisions of the Nigerian Constitution?

The absurdity of Ademola's ruling is amplified if we tease out the implications of his "argument by tradition" which construes tradition as infallible. Ademola ignored the fact that customs were created for a different historical time, and that over time, people had been subjected to the influences of Christianity, colonialism, modernization, and the politics of the native courts and native administration authority. His reluctance to consider that customs are fluid and adaptable is disturbing, since they are not static rules that resist modification in different sociopolitical conditions. If we situate Ademola's argument within the context of the United States, it would be tantamount to advocating that the slavery laws and the jurisprudence of the southern United States that treated blacks as property and as outside the human family must continue. The implausible idea being defended is that because these laws had the jural weight of tradition, the Constitution of the Union should not correct this egregious error. Even if Onitsha was historically a sexist society, nothing ties the hands of the Chief Justice of the Federation or prevents him from providing judicial remedy by bringing this section of the customary law into conformity with section 22 (1) of the 1955 High Court Law of the region under which the appeal was made. Section 22 (1) stated that "the Court shall observe and enforce the observance of every local custom and shall not deprive any person of the benefit thereof, except when any such custom is repugnant to natural justice, equity and good conscience or incompatible, either directly or by its implication, with any law for the time being in force." Clearly, the construal of a daughter and a daughter's children as nonfamily members is repugnant to natural justice, equity, and good conscience. Ademola ought to have known that ruling as he did construed daughters and widows as nonpersons who are outside the family. That he was able to rule as he did meant that he had closed his mind to the humanity of daughters and widows. Only using a framework in which daughters are defined as nonpersons would the ruling be judicially consistent. It would then not be repugnant to justice, equity, and good conscience, because it did not deprive *any person* of benefit or rights.

Even if we accept the argument that there is nothing peculiar about gender discrimination given that it has existed worldwide in different historical times right down to the twentieth century, the longevity of sexism, or the pervasiveness of the practice, is hardly the point. The moral should be that it is repugnant to treat one set of children as lesser than another because of their anatomy. At issue for Ejiwunmi and Ademola is the central premise that daughters and widows are nonfamily members because they are nonpersons. The premise is even more pernicious when fathers, brothers, and uncles actually think of their own daughters, sisters, and nieces as nonpersons. Thus, for Ejiwunmi to embrace a morally flawed viewpoint, as if no constitutional provisions challenged that position, is to combobulate the corrective role of the law in matters of equity and justice. To the extent that a warped construction of the role of law provided Ademola and Ejiwunmi with the shaky ground on which to base their ruling, they have engaged in a miscarriage of justice. Focused as he was on his mental calisthenics, Ejiwunmi (1997, 23) glossed over the crucial difference between the two cases *Nzegwus v. Nzegwu* and *Nnezianya v. Okagbue & 2 Ors.* Mary, the widow in *Nnezianya v. Okagbue & 2 Ors.*, lived her life and managed the estate of her deceased spouse. The major issue of litigation was that she could not will the estate to her grandchildren, who were the grandchildren of her deceased husband. In the case of *Nzegwus v. Nzegwu* (1997), the widow and the daughters of the deceased were not even allowed to live in the deceased's house. The judgment seemed to agree with Alexander Nzegwu that they "could not inherit any category of his properties because they would be married away, in due course. [And] that under Onitsha native law and custom widows are left to fend for themselves" (*Nzegwu v. Nzegwus* 1986, 15). Ejiwunmi thus played the infamous role of Justice Henry Billings Brown in the *Plessy v. Ferguson* (1896) case, which instead of sanctioning male dominance, sanctioned racism. Justice Brown dismissed Plessey's argument that the Louisiana statute on segregation violated the Thirteenth Amendment of the United State's Constitution on the grounds that segregation did not amount to servitude or a state bondage for African Americans (Higginbotham 1996, 112–13). Justices Ejiwunmi and Tobi dismissed the widow's argument that she is entitled to live in her deceased husband's house on the grounds that widows and daughters are left to fend for themselves and do not have any entitlement to their husbands' and fathers' estate. To tighten the grip of male dominance, Ejiwunmi, Tobi, and Achike overruled the trial judge who "found as a fact that a married woman, under Onitsha native law and custom, is entitled to reside in the house erected by her husband and that on the death of her husband that right ensures for her benefit and that she must have committed very serious wrong for her to be deprived of the right" (*Nzegwu v. Nzegwus* 1986, 17). Effectively, they ruled that daughters and widows were not discriminated against, because Onitsha customs and tradition defined them as nonpersons.

It is important to underscore that not all male judges share the views of Tobi, Achike, and Ejiwunmi. The trial judge, Obunneme Onwuamaegbu, came to a different ruling partly because of his familiarity with Igbo customs. He could tell when the defendants were playing fast and loose with their accounts of custom, partly because he had been sensitized, through a daughter's experience, to the sorts of machinations wives face from members of the affinal family. Tobi and Ejiwunmi's rulings, based as they were on their inability to grasp the subtleties of Igbo customs, raise questions about the relevance of customary laws in multicultural Nigeria, and about the much-vaunted fact that the Nigerian Constitution can override repugnant provisions of customary laws. There is no question that Justices Tobi, Ejiwunmi, and Achike are familiar with the provisions of section 39 (1) 2 of the amended 1979 Constitution, which declares sexist customs and laws unconstitutional. It is also clear that their stance violates Nigeria's international legal obligations to respect the equal rights of women, since the country is a signatory to the Convention on the Elimination of All Forms of Discrimination Against Women (CEDAW) and the Universal Declaration of Human Rights. It seems that for them, justice is decidedly passive, and that repressive customs and reactionary interpretations of customs are permissible as long as they apply solely to women. To the extent that Tobi, Ejiwunmi, and Achike were at pains to accept repugnant interpretations of customs for women, their failure to uphold the Constitution underlines their subscription to the ideology of male dominance and female subordination.

PART 5: PATRIARCHICAL IDEOLOGY
AND WOMEN'S POLITICS

Hunting with the Hounds and Running with the Hare

During the court case, Lillian, Alexander's wife, testified:

> The widow [plaintiff] and her mother did not show any distress that day, and were even eating a plate of chicken with one of the friends of the Plaintiff's mother. . . . The Plaintiff's mother was saying that arrangements for the funeral should be hurried up, so that her daughter would go out and get another husband. (*Nzegwu v. Nzegwus* 1986, 12)

Generally, patriarchy is construed as the coalescing of power in men and their subordination of women. But patriarchy also deploys women in its agenda, offering them rewards that shore up specific interests they have been positioned to defend. Iris Marion Young correctly notes that "the problem of male domination is not that women are prevented from acting upon and within institutions, but that the benefits of their contribution are systematically transferred to men (Young 1984, 141). This is evident in the closing off of women's options, and in wives (or sisters-in-law) choosing to stand fast with their husbands (or brothers-in-law) when these men are engaged in morally objectionable acts. It does not matter that Alexander publicly humiliated Lillian on numerous occasions with his sexual escapades during the course of their marriage. What matters, some may naïvely believe, is that she publicly assume the role of the dutiful supportive wife.

But Lillian's role cannot be neatly understood in this manner, since she did not stand firm because of love for her husband, or because she wanted to be perceived as a dutiful wife. Rather she did so because of the benefits that would accrue to her sons. As with other middle-class, Christian, educated women who found themselves within a male-dominated nuclear family, Lillian's interest was governed by her objective to secure the best inheritance property for her three sons, and to advance her own *usokwu* and to minister to her family. Within "Inland Town," the geographical zone Onitsha indigenes call home, land has become a very scarce commodity. Rather than move to less densely populated areas where more land is available, families have taken to crowding homes onto slivers of land. This attachment to "Inland Town" is not entirely sentimental but is linked to the high premium that land in this zone commands.

Against this backdrop of land politics, it behooves any reasonable parent to do whatever is necessary to secure land that can be passed on to one's sons, since only sons now inherit land. Put this way, it is hardly surprising that Lillian would be more concerned about her own parental obligation of catering to the material welfare of her own sons than about the welfare of two minor children who were, after all, girls. Besides, everyone knows that daughters do not inherit land. So it is not as if she were dispossessing them. She was not responsible for their being girls or for their father's death. Had he truly cared and wanted to provide for them, he could have written a will to make his wishes explicit; after all, he was a very experienced lawyer. She should not now be blamed if the death of the girls' father opened up the opportunity for her sons to have ample land and homes within their grandfather's estate. Their interests were really not her business; her sole business was the welfare of her own children.

Lillian had worked out that her first son would inherit his own father's house, the second son would subsequently move into his uncle's property, and the last son would make do with the building between the two properties. Additional resources that her brother-in-law's death fortuitously transferred to her own *usokwu* included an extensive law library, which became a vital resource for a daughter who was studying law, and an automobile that was immediately converted to her personal use and that of her nuclear family. The point here is that in the context of scarcity and diminished economic opportunities, wives are engaged in a struggle for survival, and lofty ethical considerations rarely factor into their decision-making process. The scope of their ethical framework and their moral responsibility extends only to the well being of their immediate family. Even when the family is a long way from poverty and destitution, as is true of Lillian's family, the primary concern of mothers and wives remains the material welfare of their own children, not the appropriateness of their action within a higher moral framework.

This is not to say that every mother lives by this amoral framework. Some have publicly rejected it, preferring to live by a higher, more inclusive moral scheme. The lack of an expansive moral scheme is evident in the way some wives jubilate in other wives adversity and collude in the appropriation of deceased brothers-in-law's estates for the benefit of their children. But in garnering and transferring resources to sons, they neither consider the material welfare of their own daughters nor do they reflect on the appropriateness of privileging one child over another on the basis of sex. The patent unfairness of this differential treatment never seems to enter modern Igbo parents' consciousness. They rarely ask the larger question about what will become of their daughter given the prevailing social emphasis on transferring family assets only to sons. Because their focus is primarily on sons, these parents undertake the dispossession of their own daughters, rationalizing their action on the ground that the daughters would marry under the Marriage Act. In their minds, statutory marriage will secure a husband's property and share of his family land for their daughters, a condition that keeps the daughter exclusively dependent on her spouse.[35]

With the exception of a few families that have bucked this trend, the prevailing Igbo view is that daughters are unworthy of inheriting family property. The idea that daughters should look to an outsider (a prospective husband) for property and assets does not strike Onitsha parents as problematic. Rather, the disinheritance of daughters continues to be rationalized on the unsavory and tenuous ground that a husband will provide for them, if they have a son. But Igbo parents are well aware that marriage provides no such security. They are aware of cases where after years of trying, a married daughter still does not have a son. That was the fate of one of Lillian's daughters, who died in the desperate bid to have a son. Also, what if a husband grows tired of his wife and throws her out of *his* house, what happens then? She will then have to rely on the charity of brothers, to whom the entire family properties have been given, and who may not see their sisters as entitled to "their personal property." The critical question parents have to address is, why is love for a daughter demonstrated through disinheritance?

Let us suppose that a husband does not throw out his wife for failing to produce an heir, and that he lives with her until his death. What will her lot be when he dies? Suppose he does not die, but physically and emotionally abuses her, what should she do? Leave the marriage and step into penury, or spend her life in purgatory? Alternatively, suppose she bears a son who then dies in childhood?[36] Or, she has sons but is still shabbily treated, as many wives are? Or, the husband dies when the sons are minors and their uncle moves in to appropriate the husband's land and property? The possibilities are endless, yet they represent a sampling of what modern Igbo women are experiencing. The fact that things frequently go wrong should have spurred parents to revisit the issue of disinheritance of daughters, and to rethink the kind of family values they are promoting. The latter should have prompted family reforms that would have required them to value their children equally.

Chikwenye Okonjo Ogunyemi has chastised white American feminists for employing an interpretive frame that "ignores African sociopolitical complexities and is at odds with the ideology of complementarity, of coexisting" that characterizes African societies (1996, 114). She contends that this ideology of complementarity is one in which women still love their sons, brothers, and fathers, even if they are not romantically involved with their husbands." In her sharp rebuke, she reminds Western feminists that "women rarely perceive men as implacable enemies to be fought to the death" (Ogunyemi 1996, 114–15). She points out that the "need for coexistence in countries made up of heterogeneous ethnic group militates against uncompromising attitudes, particularly with the gender crises subsumed under continental turmoil (1996, 115). Elsewhere, I too, have written about this spirit of complementarity, identifying it as the distinguishing trait of Onitsha society prior to the introduction of patriarchal relations and its ideology gender relations (Nzegwu 1995). But for most of the last quarter of the twentieth century, the combined forces of state policies, Western education, ideology of individualism, employment practices, economic obligations to the family, and nuclear family consciousness have drastically modified families in important ways. Much more importantly, they have led to the concentration of land and wealth in the hands of men. In light of the preceding discussions on the systemic erosion of women's autonomy and the disinheritance of daughters, Igbo women scholars and women of Onitsha need to interrogate their subscription to this ideology of unreciprocated complementarity. For the sakes of their daughters in contemporary globalized world they need to question this concentration of wealth exclusively in the hands of sons.

To help this process along, Amadiume offered a way out, as she voiced a minor disagreement with Cheikh Anta Diop.[37] Where Diop had upheld a "harmonious dualism" between men and women in this relation of complementarity, Amadiume prefers to see tensions and conflict and the controlling tendencies of men. In her words, "in whatever system, men incessantly sought to control women and their services, and succeeded more often than not" (1987b, 84). As if to temper the severity of this criticism, she states in the following sentence that she agrees with Diop, and probably with Ogunyemi too, that "there was never the hatred of men as was evident among Eurasian Amazons" (1987b).

Earlier, in the section on *oku ekpe*, I argued that Onitsha women have steadily witnessed the elimination of practices and institutions from which they had derived their autonomy. Although it is regrettable that all these closures occurred, what was, perhaps, most disheartening was that no son, brother, or father objected to the corresponding diminution of the value and life options of their mothers, sisters, or daughters. The proof that the principle of complementarity no longer exists is seen in the fact that no male relatives are clamoring for the reform of male-privileging social values that had rationalized the disinheritance of their female relatives. None has protested that older customs did not sanction these forms of gender discrimination we are witnessing today. None has worked to put in place or preserve old spaces of autonomy that mothers and daughters had in the previous century. And none have worked to surplant female discriminatory customs with female-affirming ones. Against this backdrop of insensitivity to women's plight, we cannot but observe sons, brothers, and fathers' inattentiveness to, and lack of sympathy with, the damaging effect of these male-privileging policies on daughters and sisters. Rather, what is witnessed is the eager manner in which male relatives stepped into the new roles that the colonial and postcolonial judicial, administrative, and economic systems opened up for men. As Amadiume put it, they "incessantly sought to control women and their services", and enthusiastically contributed to the diminution of women's lives (1987b, 84). The question mothers, sisters, and daughters have to ask themselves is why they should keep channeling love to sons, brothers, and fathers who have undermined their autonomy? Why should they continue to uphold an ideology of female domination that keeps them in a perpetual state of subordination?

Amadiume's point about tensions and conflict becomes relevant here. It notes insightfully the nature of social dynamics at play between women and men for most of the twentieth century. Sons observe their fathers' disrespect in beating their mothers. They fail to respond because the fathers remind them that they are the head of the family, that this is their house, and that they would run it as they please. Some mothers/wives endure the abuse because they know that their brothers have converted the family's estate into their personal property and would be reluctant to assist them in their hour of need by making some of those resources available. Some who are forced to leave abusive marriages receive empty declarations of support from brothers whose sole concern is the comfort of their own nuclear family. In the prevailing male-privileging climate of contemporary Igbo societies, brothers would declare their love for their sisters but would vehemently object to any suggestion that these sisters should receive any share of family land. Lastly, fathers profess love for daughters but have no moral compunction about discounting them, and transferring all valuable assets of land and economic resources to sons. They assuage their guilt by claiming that the sons would carry on their name, and that they would take care of sisters should the need arise. It is as if they do not know that once the property is alienated, it is no longer fiduciary property.

The idea that daughters are unworthy of having property bequeathed to them and should be taken care of only when they are in need defines the basis of some of the tensions and conflicts in modern Igbo families. Of course as Ewelukwa pointed out the escalating phenomenon of land sales undercuts the legitimacy of the argument against female interitance (2002, 443). Land bequeathed to sons is sold and does not necessarily stay in the family. Modern Igbo women find that the battle is two pronged, given the way the odds are stacked against them. First, as daughters, they have to contend with the male-dominant attitudes of their parents and agnatic kin who find them unworthy of inheritance; and then as wives, they have to contend with a similar attitude in husbands and the affinal family. In considering the impact of these tensions on daughters, it behooves us to urge daughters not to be "good wives," whatever that means. Modern Igbo mothers need to mobilize actively for their daughters' autonomy and against discriminatory marriage, divorce, and inheritance laws. They need to uphold and give teeth to section 42 (1) (a) of the 1979 Constitution.[38]

Because Igbo husbands, like other Nigerian men, rarely leave wills, some widows have sought relief in the judicial system. They enter such inheritance battles at great financial and emotional disadvantage, given that the attack is always made at their most vulnerable moment. The bulk of the family resources are frozen by probate laws until Letters of Administration are obtained. In her discussion of the situation in Uganda, Mary I. D. E. Maitun states that in times of such conflict, "most enlightened widows leave the administration of Estates of their dead husbands to the Administrator General to avoid problems with their relatives-in-law. The women who are ignorant of the law just move out and suffer with their children." She concludes from this that "education of women and society in general about the law of Succession would help to alleviate this problem." Maitun's evaluation of the situation echoes the summation of one who has never experienced or witnessed the vindictiveness of recalcitrant relatives-in-law and the violence they can wreak. She does not disclose the fact that her complete faith in the law is premised on the assumption that there is rule of law in the country and that everything works, as it should (Maitun 1985, 155).

Woodman challenges the tendency of some to exaggerate the effectiveness of the principles enforced by the court (1974, 269). He identifies a number of procedural steps a litigant must go through to seek relief, and each one is bedeviled by a number of pitfalls. Even after one is aware of one's right, one can meet with opposition from the family, who, in filing legal challenges to the property, deters the Administrator General from moving forward on estate administration. Additionally, the question Maitun does not consider is how effective is recourse to the law when one is living in the midst of a hostile affinal family, and where law enforcement agents bow to the "economic principle" of serving the highest bidder. How does education help the widow protect herself from violence? Theorists need to understand that "moving out" is not always a sign of ignorance; it may be the most prudent course of action to save one's life. Pronouncements of ignorance cannot be made in the absence of knowledge about the complexities of the situation and the life goals of the widow. Some of the greatest manipulators of the law are educated people, and they do so because they have the education, power, and wealth to achieve their objective. Educated relatives-in-law with wealth and power can tie up probate issues in protracted litigation, as was the experience of Caroline Mojekwu.

Without adequate economic resources to pursue the case, education will take one just so far. Lack of economic means is the greatest obstacle to obtaining relief in Nigerian courts. As Maitun correctly stated, women are not economically independent, and this hampers their ability to attain their objectives. They rarely have any pre-nuptial monies, wealth, or land to fall back on. Relatives-in-law understand keenly that the most effective time to launch an offense is either immediately before or after the burial. A widow is disoriented, still reeling from shock, and she has to attend to the emotional and material needs of children. Most important of all, she lacks access to her deceased husband's income and resources and cannot draw on them to protect her children. In most cases, the widow may not have an independent income for a variety of reasons—she may not have been working outside the home, she may have lost her job, or she might have been unable to find employment. Whatever the reason, her economic resources and standard of living have dropped precipitously, and she lacks the flexibility to wage an effective defense. She has to rely on the charity of her family and friends. While her relatives would be morally supportive, she has to find the means to quickly rebuild her life, feed her children, focus on their education, and if she can find the money, pay for legal representation. Given the dire economic climate in most African countries, families are often not able to assist financially, and even if they are, they are not willing to jeopardize their "personal" property to support a protracted legal battle.

Every Nigerian knows that the Nigerian court system is set up to be punitive and is hostile to widows. [39] It grinds excruciatingly slowly and it frequently grinds up the victims, too. There is no reasonable time frame within which cases are tried. They could go on for years, thirty-nine years as in the case of Mojekwu. Lawyers stretch out the case by means of endless adjournments. They demand travel expenses to appear in court, hotel bills, court fees, and their legal fees as well. Before seeking relief in the court, a widow has to consider her conditions of employment, and whether or not she will have the time to devote to the case. This can include managing witnesses over a period of time, ensuring that they are able to keep their court dates, prodding them to keep their court date, and bringing them back the next court date to which the case had been adjourned. In light of what such cases entail, social pressure is typically brought to bear on the widow to move on, but never on the affinal family to back off. One thing is clear, the lack of equal property rights is a major handicap for daughters and is the cause of the impoverishment of widows and children, especially as land continues to be a valuable resource.

Maitun is right when she points out that women's lack of ownership of land is a hindrance to their empowerment and progress. A review of such cases shows that this is the basis on which challenges to widows' right to inherit land and property are launched. Even when we take the formula under which the Ugandan law of Intestate Succession disposes of a deceased's property, a widow will not receive land. Under the formula: 15 percent of the property goes to widow/widows, 75 percent to children—both legitimate and illegitimate; 9 percent to dependent relatives, and 1 percent to the customary heir (Maitun 1985, 155). In this postindependent period of individualistic, money-based society, the issue of equity between daughters and sons, and wives and husbands in terms of land and property has become absolutely crucial. Daughters and wives are doubly disadvantaged through patrilineal and spousal disinheritance. As CEDAW notes, in its *General Comment 21*, par. 3, "Often inheritance rights for widows do not reflect the principles of equal ownership of property acquired during marriage."

Conclusion

Undoubtedly things must change. It must go beyond the piecemeal efforts of Justice Tobi in the *Mojekwu v. Mojekwu* case. For that to happen, we must ensure that women's equality is not simply a legal or judicial matter. Notional rights in the constitution do not translate into substantive rights. This is not to imply that legal challenges should cease, but that we should create a condition that discourages the reinforcement of daughters' and wives' subjugation. This would happen when daughters and sons have the same right of inheritance so that daughters would have the same opportunities as sons to own, manage and grow their wealth. The creation of "same opportunities" calls for the adoption of the principle of equality between the sexes. But what do we mean by equality? It is usually assumed that equality implies sameness between the sexes and the language of CEDAW reinforces this view. But we need to know what this sameness consists of, and what the meaning of sex equivalence is. Because legal precepts are not formulated in abstraction, but presuppose a social view of reality, we ought to turn our attention to the underlying social system within which equality issues arise. Any attempt to resolve the problem of women's social inequality and to discuss the meaning of sameness must take into consideration the male-privileging value-system that underlies liberalism and modern African societies. The latter's ideological framework construes equality in terms of women receiving the privileges available to men. This raises two pertinent questions, both articulated by Ann Phillips: "Why should equality mean women shaping themselves to a world made for men? And why shouldn't the world be made to change its tune?" Phillips intervention problematizes the precept of equality as sameness underlying the equivalence principle (1987, 19).

Contemporary feminist objections to the equivalence principle are tied to the gender unfairness of social institutions that are inherently masculinist. Feminist scholars such as Catharine MacKinnon (1987, 1989) and Zillah Eisenstein (1988) recognize that there are crucial reproductive events in a woman's life that do not occur in a man's life, and these differences are not positively served by denying them and forcing women to live by men's rules.[40] They point out that the bodies and physiological events in the lives of women and men are neither the same nor interchangeable, and so difference cannot be waived in favor of sameness. Because general discussions on gender justice and equality do not sufficiently come to grips with the underlying structure of the societies, the following chapter undertakes an extensive examination of a different conception of equality when a society recognizes sex difference.

4

The Conclave

A Dialogic Search for Equality

This chapter articulates a model of agency, rights, and political consciousness that allows us to envision a model of equality that would be crucial in reforming contemporary Igbo reality. The model has the advantage of being derived from Igbo tradition. Interestingly, it is radically progressive and politically robust. Its cultural rootedness enables us to bypass any charges that the reforms we recommend for Igbo societies are Western-derived, hence culturally illegitimate. One may still query whether there is an indigenous tradition of sex equality in Africa and whether any concept of equality really derives from Igbo tradition. This skeptical frame of mind derives from the fact that feminist literature on Africa since the 1980s has progressively underscored the subjugated and oppressed state of African women [Mikell (1997), Stamp (1991), Stichter and Parpart (1988), Robertson and Berger (1986), and Cutrufelli (1983)]. By all these accounts, women in Africa have always had very few rights within families and in their societies. The inescapable conclusion is that they are all jural minors and nonpersons.

The celebrated case of Virginia Edith Wambui Otieno is usually deployed to make this point. Christina Jones (1995) does this in her evaluation of equality in Africa. She argues that women's equality in Africa should not be contingent on preserving family obligations, since the institution of family is the very place where women endure the greatest subordination. For her, the fact that Wambui Otieno did not have the right to bury her deceased husband, as he would have, had the circumstances been reversed, or that Otieno's daughters could not claim their father's body for burial, as would a son, showed that sex equality is absent in Africa. Jones favors the principle of interchangeability that would guarantee "same rights" for women as men. She believes that the absence of the interchangeability principle proves gender inequality since recognition of sex difference opens the way for the introduction of a regime of sex inequality.

However, discussions on the structure of Igbo family in chapter 1 alluded to a different notion of equality in which sex difference was factored into the notion and understanding of equality. On this model, individuals are not interchangeable and interchangeability is not an ideal. To decide on the preferred model, it is crucial to explicate this difference-recognizing model of equality, to understand what it consists of, and how it works. Using the Socratic approach of critical dialogue, I will explicate the Onitsha version of this model by posing questions from the Western feminist standpoint on issues of rights, autonomy, agency, conception of self, and political consciousness.[1] Answers will be offered from within the epistemological scheme of Onitsha society, paying special attention to the historical changes and social transformations that occurred in the society in the last one hundred years, from 1890 to 1960. I chose a Socratic dialogue format to give a heightened sociological experience of the lives of Onitsha women. This one-hundred-year temporal span does not invalidate the dialogue, since stories of nineteenth-century Onitsha women have percolated down to us as part of family histories and some of the social practices are still in existence today.

Docu-Drama: Making Contexts Visible

The dialogue is between Omu Nwagboka,[2] Onowu (her Prime Minister), and Onyeamama, on the one hand; and Simone de Beauvoir, Germaine Greer, and Helen Henderson on the other.[3] It is a slightly reconstructed version of the one I had in the late 1980s with Veronica Uwechia and the late Chinyelugo Nneka Chugbo, two of the five advisors in the inner cabinet of two Onye-Isi-Ikporo-Onitsha,[4] the late Umekwulu Odogwu (who deputized for Udezue Emembolu), and the late Nwalie Egbuna. In this intercultural discourse, historically situated women raise pertinent issues about community relations and family law that derive from the social roles and locations. The format reveals the crucial lines of disagreement and the complex ways cultural perspectives and worldviews shape people's conceptions of equality. It is important to remember that equality is not an objectively neutral concept; it is always complicated by the social ideal of a society.

I should state that de Beauvoir, Greer, and Henderson are complex cultural types. They represent as well, contemporary Igbo men and women who share similar views. Though most of what I attribute to these writers was derived from their writings, in contexts that are radically different from the one presented here. Henderson's comments were derived from her 1960s study on the ritual roles of Onitsha women at the time the office of Omu had become defunct.[5] The three women de Beauvoir, Greer, and Henderson represent the different levels of Western women's knowledge of African social life: the uninformed, the fascinated, and the informed. They also present an amalgam of attitudes shared by many Western feminists, which some African scholars perceive as typifying both feminism and feminists' interpretation of women's roles. Although tremendous political gains have been made since de Beauvoir's *The Second Sex* (1990, 115–22), Greer's *The Female Eunuch* (1972), and Henderson's doctoral thesis (1969), the underlying conjugal model of marriage, nuclear family structure, patriarchal assumptions of family, and masculinist impulse of the mono-sex system reign supreme and still pervade much of second-wave feminism and Africanists' ethnographic writings about contemporary African family life.[6]

On the other end of the spectrum, Omu Nwagboka and Onyeamama are equally complex cultural types. They embody the matri-centric consciousness and logic of the dual-sex system, which are routinely ignored or mischaracterized in mainstream Western feminist literature. The selection of Omu Nwagboka and the formal institution known as Ikporo Onitsha (Council of Mothers)[7] is based on the fact that they stand as symbols of this consciousness. Shortly before her death in 1890, Omu Nwagboka had led Onitsha women in a mass resistance action in which women withdrew completely from their social, family, and political duties, and shunned social interaction with men. The main objective of the withdrawal was to impress, first, upon the male monarch Obi Anazonwu and, secondly, on the community at large, that no society can function without the reproductive labor and economic, spiritual, and familial duties of women. Begun as a response to a constitutional impasse with the male monarch, the boycott not only underscored a society's dependence on its womenfolk, but it also revealed the intricate interdependent nature of social relations and family obligations.

The part played by relational identity must be mentioned. The withdrawal tactic is a longstanding strategy of peace-making and conflict resolution. Withdrawal by the aggrieved signals the existence of a conflict and invites appeasement and propitiation from the transgressor. Combining the significance of this disengagement strategy with an understanding of the relational nature of human identity, Omu Nwagboka and Ikporo Onitsha exploited the relational expectations of any social being to establish the terms of their contributions, their social worth, and to expose the interdependent nature of the society. Following the Omu's directives, Ikporo Onitsha, comprised of adult women, strategically withdrew *en mass* from their roles as wives, mothers, sisters, daughters, and consorts, leaving everyone in the lurch. The Omu knew that no society could handle the trauma and disruption entailed by wives', mothers', sisters', and daughters' sudden disengagement from their conjugal and agnatic interactions. Because a society is an intricate network of family, friendship, and organizational ties, and since being social entails expecting and valuing the emotional, sexual, administrative, counseling, feeding, commercial, spiritual, and jural benefits accruing from those ties, sons, grandsons, husbands, fathers, brothers, uncles, cousins, and nephews could not cope with the exit of wives, mothers, daughters, and sisters from familiar roles. In response, they, rather than the activists, pressured Obi Anazonwu to sue for peace.

By relationally positioning the Obi as the transgressor, Ikporo Onitsha portrayed the Obi as a disrupter of social harmony and violator of traditionally validated norms of engagement. Successfully casting themselves as the aggrieved party, they effectively mobilized the whole community against the Obi. This strategy was repeated again in the mid-1970s. Although the Omu's directive and Ikporo Onitsha's action collectively and directly affected sons, grandsons, husbands, fathers, brothers, uncles, cousins, and nephews, the action did not earn them the animosity of the rest of the community. Rather, it strongly restated the autonomy of the institution of Ikporo Onitsha and exposed the error of viewing women as socially inconsequential. The reason for the lack of animosity is that this was a legitimate constitutional process of grievance in a political system that accorded women a governance role. Onitsha men's lack of identification with the Obi, in a matter that may be seen as gender based, is best explained by four factors: their familiarity with the leadership role of Ikporo Onitsha in matters of state; the righteousness of the actions of Ikporo Onitsha fell within the sphere of their political rights; their respect for daughters', sisters', and mothers' multiple roles, constitutional agency, and jural rights; and the absence of a gender ideology that accords women a subordinate inferior status.

Because Ikporo Onitsha had customarily functioned as a constructive, governing institution, and because the maintenance of social harmony reposes with its members as community mothers, Onitsha men saw the entire event as directed towards the overall good of the community rather than at men *per se*. Unfortunately, as Olufunmilayo Ransome-Kuti asserted about the Yoruba, and as many scholars are increasingly finding today in other parts of Africa, this affirming ideology is fast being eroded by the patriarchal values introduced and circulated by missionaries since the 1860s in Onitsha and reinforced by the colonial state from the 1900s.

For the moment, I shall ignore the wide historical gap between Omu Nwagboka and the rest of the cast. This historical lapse does not fundamentally alter the validity of the dialogue. The political duties of the Omu exist in attenuated form and are vested in the *Onye-Isi-Ikporo-Onitsha* (Head of the Council of Mothers). The major difference of the two positions is the low-keyed nature of the office of *Onye-Isi-Ikporo-Onitsha*, a contrast to the elaborate protocols and courtly life of the Omu-ship. The emphasis on the Omu is designed to jolt collective memory and to initiate a remembrance of women's contributions in the histories of communities in West Africa. Also, it spurs interrogation of the present patriarchal values widely subscribed to today by an ever-increasing number of women. It aspires to recover women's social histories and to present a viable social model for combating the continuing subordination of women.

INWE ONU OKWU—HAVING A VOICE

[*1883, Omu Nwagboka's Court.*] Dressed in white cotton to reflect the sanctity and spiritual state of her person, Omu Nwagboka sits on the dais in her palace, surrounded by women councilors known as *Otu Ogene*. On her lap is an *otinri*, a long horsetail whisk that symbolizes ritual mourning. As a spiritual entity who is aware of her own mortality, the Omu must meditate upon and mourn her death each day for the rest of her life. Nearby a little girl stands with *mma abani*, the ceremonial sword, while the Omu's *azuzu* (leather fan) rests on the gaily cloth-covered *ukpo* (dais). Omu Nwagboka is from Ogbendida ward of Onitsha, and her lineage title is *Kpari*. Her throne is an elective one. As Omu, she is the watchdog of the community and Ikporo Onitsha, and she is chosen on the basis of her *ada* (daughter) identity. An Omu is not related to, or accountable to, the Obi, the male monarch, and once crowned (by a Nri priest), she cannot be deposed. Her residence is a place of refuge, which the Obi and his chiefs cannot violate. The Omu rules by virtue of her political savvy, the spiritual purity of her vision, and the respect she derives from women and the community.

In the audience is a feminist delegation that has just arrived from Europe. In accordance with traditional rites, kola-nuts are presented. The visitors introduce their agenda after prayers and the breaking and sharing of the kola-nuts. Discussions follow.

Act I: On Marital Norms: The Home as a Public Space

DE BEAUVOIR: Omu, we have come to tell you that throughout history women have always been looked upon as the Other. They have always been subordinate to men. The reasons for this are numerous. Our studies show that women lack concrete means for organizing themselves into a unit that can stand face-to-face against men. They have no past, no history, no religion of their own; and they have no solidarity of works and interest such as is possessed by proletariat workers. They live dispersed among males, attached through residence, housework, economic condition, and social standing to certain men—fathers or husbands—more firmly than they are to other women. It is not clear to us what is the historical event or series of events that resulted in this subjugation of the weaker by the stronger. What is the case in Onitsha?

OMU: *Onye amuma, nno* (Visionary One, welcome). You have a won-derful message, and we thank you for it. But we believe you have come to the wrong place. We do not share your view that women have always been "the other"; and we do not believe that humanity is male and that man defines women. We have our own problems with our men, but they are not of the va-riety you have described. Just a few moons ago I asked Ikporo Onitsha to shun men and to curtail interactions with them. They complied; and the Obi and his henchmen quickly came to their senses. Our quarrel with the Obi and his group is that they don't stand firm. They are too easily swayed by emotion and the good things of life. They too easily forget themselves, their traditions, and their heritage. They are always in haste to explore new ideas. We refuse to have them belittle us.

DE BEAUVOIR: But the category of the Other is as primordial as con-sciousness itself. It is a fundamental category of human thought. We know that today humanity is male and man defines woman, not in herself but as relative to him.[8] Furthermore, our men have put in place a social arrangement that has relegated women to the private space of the home, while they rule the public space of work and the marketplace. This private/public dichotomy gives them complete power over our lives. The laws of our land support them, too, by rec-ognizing only their rights. In the private space of the home, they are lord and master, and our laws will not intrude to protect us and our children when things are going wrong. Can women here organize to fight this?

ONOWU: [*Interjecting*] This private/public business that you speak of, were you sleeping when it was made? Which men made it? What did your Omu or *Onye-Isi-Ikporo be unu* (Head of the Council of Mothers of your place) do when all this was going on? Didn't she intervene?

GREER: We don't have an Omu or a Council of Mothers. We have a pow-erful Queen who rules everyone. She represents everyone, not just women or their interests.

ONOWU: It's a pity you do not have an Omu or an organization to rep-resent your interests. Here in *obodo* (nation) Onitsha regulations are generally discussed before they become laws. We, Ikporo Onitsha, have to know about them. The Obi and his *Ndichie* cannot decide alone for the entire community. We must have our say too.

ONYEAMAMA: You say your homes are private places. Ours are public places. Many of us live there with our co-wives, children (if grown, their wives, too), grandchildren, husbands, relatives, and helpers. There are so many people coming and going that at times it seems like a market. When there is a quarrel between *di na nwunye* (husband and wife), everyone in the compound will know about it. In fact, people will jump into the matter to help them sort it out. You can deny an Onitsha person food, but not speech. They will voice their opin-ion. The good thing is that the elders of the family—the mothers and fathers[9]—

will try to resolve the conflict. *Ikenye ada'ano nu'uno ewu amua no 'gbuli.* (Elders cannot be home and a tethered goat gives birth.) They will calm ruffled feathers and issue impartial judgment. If one party is too hot-tempered, the conflict might escalate. If the problem is of a serious nature, *umunne* (siblings of the same mother) of both the wife and conjugal partner would gather to sort it out. If the trouble touches a wider community, *umunna* (male and female members of the lineage), or *inyemedi* (lineage wives) or *ikporo ogbe* (women of the ward) will weigh in. The point is, no one lives in the kind of exclusion you are describing that a *di* becomes the lord and master of the compound.

OMU: Should a husband think to become a tyrant, he would do well to remember that *inyemedi,* and *ikporo ogbe* respond collectively to the ill treatment of their members. They have a range of weapons of which the most devastating is *akuku* (snide verbal abuse) that is publicly administered to harass a transgressor to death. Finally, when *ndi ogo onye* (one's in laws) are aware that their daughter is being ill-treated, they too will demand accountability and join the fray. Anybody here will tell you that, regardless of who is at fault, it is worse for the person if *umuada* (lineage daughters) step into the matter.

GREER: You mean you do not submit to the corporal punishment of spanking or whipping from your husbands?

ONYEAMAMA: *Ewuuu* [expressive sound of pity] . . . and you offer your body to him to flog?

GREER: Well yes. In our culture, husbands and wives treat this matter of punishment as a normal sort of proceeding. They recognize that wrongdoing should be punished. They both agree that the simplest, most convenient, most effective, and most natural way for a man to punish the faults of his woman is to spank or whip her (Greer 1972, 210).

ONOWU: And what if he is wrong?

GREER: He's the master, he's never wrong!

DE BEAUVOIR: A man is in the right in being a man; it is the woman who is in the wrong (1992, 116).

OMU: [*Looking at the visitors in bewilderment*] This private/public business of yours is tragic! You white women are really in *ugom* (prison). You really are the properties of your husbands! Where are your *ikwu na ibe* (kith and kin) when all this is going on? Did they sell you to your husbands?

GREER: We used to have what is called the doctrine of coverture. As the Bible counsels, this doctrine pronounces spousal unity. It requires a husband and wife to be one person. Legally he is the "person," and the wife, in cleaving to him as one, becomes his person. Things are changing—albeit very slowly. It used to be that wives could not own property. They had no rights over their children and no control over their own bodies. Their husbands could rape and beat them without fear of legal reprisals. When they were not confined to the home, they were forced by growing industrialization to join the lowest levels of the labor force.[10] Although this doctrine is no longer in use, its legacy still survives today in many societies and in marriages.

OMU: You have a strange custom. And because the husband is the "person," nobody can come to your aid in distress?

GREER: Exactly!

ONYEAMAMA: [*Incredulously.*] Don't you have *aka odo* (wooden pestles used for pounding grains and food items)?[11]

OMU: [*Eyeing her to keep her peace.*] Onyeamama's reputation as a fearless fighter means that no one tangles with her. It is a pity that nobody is protecting the collective interest of your women.

DE BEAUVOIR: Omu, how can you say that women are not properties in your culture? How can you claim that women's oppression is not part of your problem with your men? From our readings, we know that men and women are not equal. We have profound proof of sex discrimination and female subjugation in your national and family lives. Richard Henderson, a Yale-trained anthropologist and fine researcher, studied your culture and this is what he wrote in *The King in Every Man*. I quote:

> A husband has inviolable and exclusive rights of sexual access to his wife . . . he may beat her . . . [she] has no grounds for refusing her husband's sexual overtures except when she is menstruating or performing child care. (1972, 213)

Here's another:

> [a] wife is under the authority of her husband . . . [he] controls her wife's spiritual condition, for he may declare her guilty of forbidden acts or abomination, and . . . fine her for violating the rules of household life. (1972, 212)

And lastly, while examining your marriage customs he discovered:

> the act of marriage is socially defined as "taking a wife" (*inu nwunye*), a process in which a man and his agnates negotiate with a woman's parents and her other kinsmen while the woman herself plays a predominantly passive role as an object of value. A woman may refer to her own participation in these activities as "taking a husband" (*inu di*), but publicly the process is defined from the husband's point of view. (1972, 207)

Now, what do you have to say, Omu?

ONYEAMAMA: *Afuam alu!* (I've seen evil!) [*Hitting her chest and jumping to her feet in temper, she strides to where the visitors are sitting and combatively ges-*

tures towards them.] What did you call that *akili aki* (clerk, writer) of yours? Richard? *Onulu asusu* (Does he understand the language and culture)? Who did he talk to? Surely not to us women! *Welu* (take) has now become *inu* (marry)! [*Turning dramatically to the audience and walking back and forth.*] Ikporo Onitsha (Council of Mothers) take a look at this. Since when did we begin to say *inu iko* (marry a cup) for *welu iko* (take a cup)? [*In rising tones with hands on her hips.*] come, tell your husband that Onitsha men have always married wives not taken wives! Women are members of a family, they are not "items of trade" to be haggled over or "taken."

OMU: Take it gently, Onyeamama. They are visitors, and they have much to learn about our ways. [*Turning to the visitors.*] Visionary ones, there are things you need to understand about our culture. Wives are not under the spiritual authority of husband. They are under the spiritual authority of their *di okpa* (eldest lineage son and priest) and *isi ada* (eldest lineage daughter and priestess) in their natal family. They have numerous occasions to refuse sex.

First of all, when a wife is in *uju* (having her menses), which may last up to six days of every month, she is in a state of *nso* (taboo). As your Richard pointed out, she has a valid reason to refuse sex, and no husband will press his wife for sex when she is in this state. He has to restrain himself or he will be sanctioned. Secondly, when a wife is in *omugo* (a postpartum period of two-and-a-half years) and is breast-feeding, sexual abstinence has to be observed. Historically, during *omugo*, a wife who yielded to her husband's demand for sex was severely penalized by her *inyemedi* for failing to rebuff him. All that frolicking is not good for her. Do you know what it means for a woman to go through nine months of pregnancy and then give birth? The last thing she needs is sexual pressure from her husband. She needs to rest. She needs to heal her body and to care for her child. She has social support to rebuff her husband. As for the sex-hungry husband, he has to seek out other avenues of satisfying himself. If he pressures her and it is publicly known, he will be roundly condemned, and mercilessly too.

GREER: He won't force himself on her? He won't rape her?

ONYEAMAMA: [*Perplexed.*] Why would he do that?

ONOWU: No, he won't. Men are not unreasonable, although you make them out to be predators. There are other occasions when husbands lack sexual access. A sick wife can refuse sex, and a husband who demands it risks having his *umunna* and *inyemedi* sit in judgment over him. Matters never get to this point because husbands are not inconsiderate. However, if one is married to one, the harassed wife is empowered to complain. Mind you, wives have separate rooms from their husbands, so all she needs to do to stop his unwanted advances is lock her door when he comes.

GREER: What if he shouts and tries to break down the door?

ONOWU: Everyone in the household will wake up to see what is going on. Nothing puts a damper on the aroused penis than to have everyone in the vicinity, including little children, wake up and demand to know what is going on. If he were drunk, or the rare shameless one, she too would have learnt how to handle him by now. She would be hurling invectives at him at the top of her voice. Usually at this point, his male kin would step in to deal with his disgraceful behavior.

GREER: But shouldn't the couple be sleeping in the same room?

ONYEAMAMA: [*Bemused.*] Now that's where you women put yourselves in trouble. There is no buffer or space to keep him at arm's length when you sleep on the same bed. All he has to do is roll over.

ONOWU: Why would you put yourselves in such a position? Let us suppose that some of our young women are now living this way. How would she rebuff her husband's overtures? If she wants to be discrete, she would invite a trusted senior member of the family to caution her husband. But she doesn't have to be discrete. She can make it public matter. Everyone will be on the husband's back. Marriage is an open relationship, not a closed one in which one person has absolute power over another. Wives do not tolerate this kind of abuse. They will either fight it out with him or leave, ask Onyeamama.

OMU: [*Hastily cutting in.*] Another time that sexual access is curtailed is when both parties are involved in a quarrel; or a wife is exhausted after a particularly stressful day and cannot entertain her husband's demands. Marriage is about negotiation, so he'll work out a different time with her. However, if he tries to force the matter, he risks waking up the entire *ogbe* (village) because she will raise her voice, and rightly too. This is the kind of juicy gossip co-wives and *ikporo ogbe* (women of the village) thrive on. With *akuku* (snide verbal abuse) they will publicly shame him for creeping around at night and thinking that he can force himself on his wife. And then again, there are times when a wife or wives would conspire to deny their husband sex, and there's nothing he can do. They barricade themselves in their rooms and refuse to listen to his entreaties as he shuttles from door to door. We know of cases of wives who, as they get older and after having the number of children they want, practically retire from marriage.

GREER: Retire from marriage? You can retire from marriage?

OMU: Yes, you can. Wives who do curtail or rule out sex entirely. Some may rule out intercourse just with their spouses, but not with other men. They then actively encourage the husband to marry another wife to meet his needs. They live in the house and may or may not run the household. You know what, the husband does not receive much sympathy if he complains that she rebuffed his advances. Rather, he is interrogated as to why he wants to break his wife's waist by hoisting himself on her. So, when Richard writes that a husband "has inviolable and exclusive right of sexual access to his wife," he is not even describing our marital relations. He is molding it to accord with what he imagines it to be.

ONOWU: [*Cutting in.*] Omu, I am not taking the speech from you, but what Onyeamama said earlier is true. Did Richard talk to *inyemedi?*

OMU: Well, yes, he should have talked to them to get a full perspective. He would have gotten an earful. We are tired of wanderers who come to write about us and then make us out to be shadows of men. Richard's comments on our marriage institution shows that he is focusing more on the views and desires of husbands than of wives. What about the views of wives? What about husbands' obligations to wives, or you think they don't have any?

ONOWU: Simone, what you quoted to us sounds like what would exist under your doctrine of coverture. It seems Richard is trying to turn our marriages into your own marriages, or maybe he is using your mores to understand our own. Either way he is wrong. Onitsha wives are not chattel. If a husband takes to beating his wife, he risks bodily injury from her and members of her family. Not only would she feel no restraint about knocking him out with a pestle, or decorating him with bites, or grabbing and pulling hard on his penis, but she also may hurl him to *Ilo Mgbeleme* (women's judicial square where their dreaded medicinal powers are buried), where he will be publicly sanctioned.

ONYEAMAMA: [*Muttering.*] Don't your women know how to fight?

OMU: Look, the main sexual problem that wives have complained about is not the excessiveness of husbands' sexual demands, but their lack of it. Many men, especially the older ones, cannot keep up sexually. Most times, it is the wives who demand sex from husbands who have difficulty fulfilling these needs. It is worse with those who have many wives. Because they tend to be older, their energy level is not what it used to be. Very few can keep up with the heavy sexual demand of their wives. When this happens, a younger wife who must have children would find a husband helper. Either these wives take on a lover on the side, while still in their marital home, or they relocate to their natal home euphemistically to "drink medicinal potions" and "look for a child." While home, they would publicly enter into liaisons with consorts with whom they would have children. After having the desired number of children, such a wife would send notification of her intention to return. She would then move back to her marital home with her children.

DE BEAUVOIR: How strange! Why would a woman take the children she had with another man to one whom she'd left and no longer loves? Isn't this proof that wives are properties of husbands? Couldn't she leave the husband permanently and marry her love?

ONYEAMAMA: Love? What is that? *Oyi'm* (my friend), is that the madness that is clouding your eyes? Clear it away! You do not have a child; you want one. For whatever reason, your husband cannot make one with you; what should you do? You look to the loin of one who can. What has love got to do with making a child? First, you tell us that women have no rights; then when you find them taking charge of their lives, you complain about it. What's with you?

DE BEAUVOIR: We raise these issues because bride price is a problem.

ONOWU: [*Puzzled.*] How did we get from wives' sexual rights to "bride price"?

DE BEAUVOIR: We think bride price is wrong because it amounts to the selling of women! It forces a wife to stay with a husband she does not care for. It turns her into property, and gives husbands enormous hold over wives. Insofar as this payment gives a husband control of his wife's reproductive labor, then your marriage is slavery. What greater proof of oppression and women's subjugation do you need! A wife's powerlessness is underscored by the fact that she has children with another man and cannot stay with the father of her children. Because your bride price amounts to the selling of women, a wife is forced to take them back to the estranged husband to provide essential labor for him. As I said earlier, women have always been men's dependents the world over, if not his slaves. The two sexes have never shared the world in equality and what you are describing proves the point.

ONYEAMAMA: *Madu ka ekwu!* ("These too are people!" Striding towards de Beavoir) If bridewealth is equal to slavery, how come the "slave owner" is supporting the upkeep of these children knowing that they will inherit his family's estate Is this the kind of thing slave owners do? Did the slave owners in your country allow the children of their female slaves with other men to inherit their wealth? Did they ever do that?

DE BEAUVOIR: No.

ONYEAMAMA: I didn't think so. So you don't know it takes a particular kind of selflessness for a husband to appreciate that if he cannot have a child with his wife, he has to stand aside, knowing that there is someone else who can assist her to fulfill her motherhood goals? And when these children are born, he steps in to raise them as his own. You call this man a "slave owner"? Give credit where credit is due. It takes a particular kind of world to value motherhood over a husband's ego and to ensure that all men accept this state of affairs. Can this happen in your country where your men believe they own their wives?

[*Tuning away and muttering.*] Onowu, please talk some sense into these people; I need some air! Where did you say they came from?!

ONOWU: We call it bridewealth, not bride price. First of all, Simone, bridewealth is not the same thing as the sale price of merchandise. It is part of a set of activities that constitutes the formal commitment by a prospective groom and his lineage to establish marriage ties with the lineage of a prospective bride. Marriage is a union of two families. A prospective husband backs his declaration to marry with appropriate gifts of appreciation to the lineage of his prospective bride and the bride's mother. Far from being a bill of sale, bridewealth is a token appreciation of the family's efforts and labor in raising a daughter, of whose presence he (the prospective husband) would soon be depriving them. It does not compensate the family and it does not give the groom and his lineage proprietal authority over or ownership of the bride. She remains a vital part of her family, visiting them whenever convenient, and returning to them if the marriage breaks up.

Secondly, I want you to understand that a wife who goes to her natal compound to have children does not have to go back if she does not want to. The marriage can be terminated. All she has to do is return the portion of the bridewealth that tied the marriage.

OMU: [*Gazing at the visitors impassively.*] We do not sell our daughters, and nobody sold us. We've heard you say that it is the men who decide everything in marriage: one set comes to "take a wife," the other set "hands over a wife to them," and the girl goes meekly! That may be how you do it, but it is not how we do it. You do not know the young women here. Families and the spouses must have time to know each other and prepare for the marriage. The bride will spend time with the groom's family under the supervision of the mother-in-law; in turn, the groom will come often to work for his in-law. We do not simply pack off our daughters to some stranger's home without working to unify the two families, or letting her know that she can come home if she is threatened. If we did not do this, our daughter may not stay; and even when we have taken all precautions, the marriage may still break up. *Okwò azi* (these young ones), they cannot be coerced. If they do not really agree, you will find your daughter home in a twinkling of an eye.

ONYEAMAMA: Omu, tell them about Nwalameje and others like her. She married and divorced over seven times. If her parents "sold" her, do you think she would be able to move from one man of her choice to the next? If husbands have the sort of absolute control you imagine them to have, how do you account for her marital journeys? Remember Ma Okwune. She even married herself to a white man when her family refused to sanction the marriage. They did not even accept bridewealth from him! If a bride is merchandise, as you say, don't you think the family will try to collect everything they can from that white man? He was the owner of a trading company, G. W. Christian! Before I forget, recall *Chiokwu nkem* (my own Chiokwu). She decided that her husband not longer befits her and took off with her lover. And me? I decided that I'd had enough with Akunne and went home.

ONOWU: Friends, we can do this because we are not objects or property. Our sexuality was never constrained. Those who remained in their marital homes and had children with consorts, or those who went home to "find children" and took these children back with them to their marital homes, did so because of the spaces provided for them to fulfill their motherhood prerogatives. Why is it a problem if a woman wants a child and the husband cannot fulfill the need and somebody else helps out? Is that why the marriage should end? A husband should be thankful that someone came to his assistance. Besides, when you ridicule a man for seeing only the economic advantages of his wife's children, have you considered that he labored to raise these children as his own?

ONYEAMAMA: [*Visibly puzzled.*] What is this thing called "love" anyway that it should cause a husband and wife to dissolve their marriage? Why should a helper to conception become a husband? You're not making sense!

HENDERSON: Surely, a woman must have affection for the father of the child if she sleeps with him?

ONOWU: Why should that be the case? I am not saying that she has to sleep with someone she finds distasteful, but why should she have this feeling you call love? It is only physical, and they both know it. She is not estranged from her husband. She is only looking for a child, so she does not regard the man who impregnated her as the father of the child. You know what, we do not. You may call him whatever you like, but he is not the father. The father of the child is the man to whom she is married. He performed all the rites that unified the two families. He is the one with paternal rights.

ONYEAMAMA: [*Whispering loudly to Onowu.*] That's not really what they want to know. They want to know if our daughter "loves" the husband helper?

HENDERSON: Yes, actually we do.

ONOWU: Why does that matter? He is merely serving a purpose. After the purpose is served they will both move on.

HENDERSON: But . . .

ONYEAMAMA: Don't even think it! Don't even try to apply your standards on us. We've had enough of it from your mission men who call us loose. Leave your morality out of this. Focus on the ideological, religious, political, and economic forces that allow us to live our lives without having tyrants on our backs.

ONOWU: An Onitsha man would not think of saying his wife is loose under the circumstances. Besides, I do not know of any Onitsha in-laws who would condone such an unfit language from a son-in-law. In fact, not only would he be told where his *chi* (personal spirit) burnt him, but he also would find himself without a wife! Whoever amongst men says that Ikporo Onitsha are not of worth, bring that person to us at *ilo mgbeleme*[12] and we will see if he formed outside a uterus (*akpa whulu*).

End of Act 1.

Act II: Marrying Wives: Polygamist Women and Their Wives

OMU: [*Turning to de Beauvoir and others.*] You really have to put aside your ideas about family and consider our own family structure and its ties of interrelationships. This is the only way to comprehend fully our concept of marriage, and our relationship with our in-laws. For us *ogo onye bu chi e* means that in-laws are (like) one's guardian spirit. Marriage is not simply about marrying off a daughter or a son marrying in a wife; it is about uniting two families. Unification comes with a complex set of obligations. A prospective husband works for his in-laws (*ije olu ogo*) to earn the privilege to marry their daughter. Discourtesy to a wife is tantamount to discourtesy to one's in-laws. If a husband is so irresponsible as to act in a discourteous way, his relatives will quickly call him to order and demand that he apologize for the behavior. Should the bad behavior continue, the discourteous man proves that he lacks the maturity to be a husband. He cannot continually disrespect his wife and in-laws and expect to have a wife. The woman will simply return to her natal home. These obligatory ties that bind in-laws together are trivialized when your scholars represent our marriage system as a commercial transaction. You cannot strip social institutions you hardly know of their cultural and symbolic meanings and then claim you have adequately understood and represented them.

ONOWU: I do not know how things are in your country, but here, families value their daughters and grandchildren; children and husbands' lineages value these women as mothers and wives. Nevermind the caustic comments women and men lob at each other. We quarrel and we fight, but we are still families. Our male kin and our children pay tribute to our worth and industriousness. To underscore this fact, we have traditionally given as names, *Nwanyibuife* (women are of worth), *Nneka* (mother is supreme), *Nneamaka* (mother is wonderful).[13] Even *Agbalanze ozo* titles signal the important stature of mothers, as shown by the popularity of the title *Akunne* (the wealth of the mother). In fact, before the Biafran war, one in every three *ozo* men had the title of *Akunne*. The point is not that we are perfect, but that you have to understand the cultural meanings of our institutions to offer opinions about them.

GREER: You speak so eloquently. You make things sound extremely wonderful! But is this not the same society in which men marry many wives? If men really had respect for women, why would they marry more than one wife? We know that women in this society do not really have the same opportunities to live as men do. For instance, they cannot marry more than one husband at any single moment.

ONYEAMAMA: [*Impatiently.*] My friend, you've missed it! The correct parallel is not "marrying wives" for men and "marrying many husbands" for women. Rather, it is "marrying many wives" for both. Why would I want to compound my headache and marry many husbands at once? No! I would rather marry many wives and, as you would say, gain the same advantages that men have. That is the real test for male/female equality. You will be pleased to learn that marrying wives is not something that only men do here; we do it too. We marry multiple wives when we can afford it or when we have a need to. Examples abound: *Nwanyi Kpalu Ego* (woman-who-accumulated-wealth); Nwonaku Mgbogo Ifeajuna had many wives; Eseluenugo Agadi Nzegwu, fourth wife of Onyia Chief Richard Amene Uwechia, married two wives; Ma Nnukwu, wife of Nzegwu, married a wife, Nwabundo Igweze, wife of Ikwueme, married a wife. The list is endless.

GREER: But it's not the same thing.

ONYEAMAMA: Why not?

GREER: Because men sleep with their wives and, as I understand it, you don't. Some other man does.

ONYEAMAMA: So when you asked the question about polygyny, you were only thinking about the sexual act, not about the social institution of marriage and what "marrying many wives" socially implies.

GREER: Sex is a critical part of marriage, is it not? And if procreation is a critical part of your marriages, then there must be sex.

ONYEAMAMA: Not necessarily between the partners. Besides, there are so many different kinds of marriages that do not involve sex between the partners. Examples are woman–woman marriage; woman–child marriage when a mother marries an adult female for her infant son; or when a wife is married to care for an old feeble man or one who is mentally deranged.

GREER: So you mean that there are all sorts of reasons for marrying and all kinds of marriages, so that you cannot reduce the social act of marriage to the sexual act.

ONYEAMAMA: Exactly. You should know that "being a husband" is not equivalent to "being a man." Women are husbands, too, and they relate to lineage wives, or their own personal wives as husbands. If the point of your question is to determine whether women can have sexual relations with multiple male partners, my response to you is "count your teeth with your tongue." What do you think?

ONOWU: [*With a guileless smile.*] Onyeamama, we may be on to something here. Ask them why women would want to have more than one husband (in their own understanding of husband)? If the yardstick is "marrying wives," why do they keep talking about multiple husbands for women? We already do that.

GREER: Well, it seems to me that if men have the opportunity to marry many women as wives, women should have the same opportunities to marry many men as husbands.

ONOWU: We already do. All the men in the family, lineage, and ward into which we married are our husbands. But are men able to have husbands?

That is the issue you really should be pursuing. Why cannot men marry a husband and have many husbands in the same way that women can marry their own sex (be a husband) and the opposite sex (be a wife)? You should be more concerned about why this flexibility and opportunities exist for women rather than trying to limit us to the narrow lives of men.

OMU: Women here have proven that we can marry wives, as men do. We can do this even when we are married to some man. The question is, can men do the same as women? Can they marry or be married to other men who will be their husbands? Go and ask the men why they cannot do what women are able to do. It is time for you to apply your equality standard consistently.

ONOWU: Let's be clear. To ask whether or not men can have husbands is not to imply that sexual activity must occur between them. If being a female does not bar me from having a wife, why should being male bar a man from having a husband? Your investigation should try to reveal why it is that men cannot have husbands. If women have all this social flexibility, and men are trapped in one social role, what is it that limits their social options and expands women's horizon? Why do you want to use men's impoverished lives as a yardstick for women?

ONYEAMAMA: [*Strutting toward the audience excitedly with arms outstretched, she comes to an abrupt stop, swivels, and retraces her steps in* mpete, *improvisational steps of lead dancers. Approaching the podium she plants herself in front of Onowu; rocking from side to side, she invokes the latter with praise names.*] *Onowu akatawhuma!! Uka na gba oji* (the-force-that-riddles-and-destroys-the-iroko-tree). *Kwusei nya ike!* (voice it loudly). *Nwa chi na emelu ife!* (child-whose-personal-guardian-force-labors-for-her). *Nwa obute aku!* (child-of-one-who-garners-wealth). They think it is me and my un-nuanced logic.

OMU: Relax, Onyeamama, we haven't finished.

GREER: All this talk about wives, husbands, marrying, and children shows that there is great emphasis on having children in this society.

ONYEAMAMA: Yes! What would a mother be without a child!

GREER: That's my point! What if a woman is unable to have a child? How would she fare in this place? She would be made to feel incomplete, she would know that she has failed in some way through no fault of her own. There is no way around the matter. If she cannot have a child, she cannot enjoy the social privileges that seem to go with motherhood, here. What do you say to these women? What do you do with them? What is their lot?

ONOWU: Actually, it is not as miserable as you think. No doubt, the women would feel very disappointed with their fate, after doing everything possible including drinking all kinds of medicinal potions and trying out with all kinds of men. But that does not mean that they cannot be mothers. They can still be mothers, but in a different way. Here's what some of them did before church people declared some of our practices morally repugnant. Some of the women married their own wives who would then have children for them. They maintained these women as their wives and provided for their welfare. When the child was born, they become the primary or big mothers. In this stead, these women are in the same social role as men who cannot conceive, but have children by means of marrying a wife.

DE BEAUVOIR: And the society would accept such children?

ONYEAMAMA: Why would they not accept them? They do not have two heads. They are normal children.

HENDERSON: What my friend wants to know is, would these children be ostracized in any way? Would they fit into any family?

ONOWU: What do you mean "fit into any family"? They are already in a family. They were born into one. This is how it works. If the woman who married the birth mother is still living with her own husband, then he becomes the father of the children, especially if he was responsible for their conception. But the status of those children to his other children with another wife, is that of a grandchild. Although he is the biological father, he cannot be the direct social father, because he did not marry their mother. Insofar as his relationship to them is through his wife who is the Big Mother, he is one step removed from them. Because Big Mother is married to him, the children's social identity and patrilineage would be his own.

GREER: This must be terribly confusing for children.

ONYEAMAMA: Not at all. It's actually very simple. We live in compounds with numerous kin, mothers, siblings whom your friends identify as cousins, aunts, nephews, nieces, but whom we identify as *nwanne* (children of the mother). At night everyone retires to different residences because there are different mothers to whom everyone in the compound is tied. Children are familiar with the concept of different mothers, so what is one more mother and one more child to them? Little Ogugua knows that she or he has a small mother and a big mother who takes care of everyone. The small mother is of lesser importance when big mother is around. But then big mother may be junior in rank to *anasi* (the first wife) in the compound, so what does it matter that small mother is subordinate to big mother? If there are many people living in the compound, they will not all be of the same generation. Children understand the concept of hierarchy and they are comfortable with the idea of many mothers. As they grow older they will learn about their situation, and there is nothing embarrassing about it. The main thing is that everything is normal from their perspective.

DE BEAUVOIR: Do all women who cannot have children have to marry wives? And are they all able to do so?

ONYEAMAMA: No. my mother's sister, Nne Chiokwu,[14] did not marry. She became a mother when her immediate younger sister, Nne Nwando, sent Chiokwu to live with her. Chiokwu was unbelievably difficult. When she was still a toddler, she would cry until she was in the company of my aunt. As soon as she weaned, her exasperated mother packed her off to her sister, whom we now call Nne Chiokwu. Later, my aunt took over the children of her co-wife after the latter died. Nne Chiokwu is a mother. She never gave birth to a child, but she raised a number of children to whom she is a mother.

GREER: [*Turning to Onowu.*] What do people call women who do not have birth children?

ONOWU: Aga.

GREER: [*Turning to Onyeamama.*] So your aunt, the aga . . .

ONYEAMAMA: *Oromaka jei nye i oromaka dei!* [*Moving belligerently toward Greer.*] Don't you dare call Nne Chiokwu that! I will tear those jaws of yours apart. [*A couple of women from the audience dashed and grabbed her by the waist, frantically restraining her as she fought them off.*]

ONOWU: [*In consternation to Greer.*] Why would you do that? Why would you fling someone's malady to her face? What did she do to you?

GREER: I didn't mean to offend . . .

OMU: Don't ever do that again! You do not call people names especially when their relatives are about, or you will have a war on your hands. To disrespect Nne Chiokwu is to disrespect Onyeamama. We fight for the honor of our relatives. Their battle is our battle.

GREER: I am sorry. I thought that was the proper word to use.

ONYEAMAMA: [*Snapping.*] Well it is not!

OMU: [*To Onyeamama.*] It's enough. [*To all.*] Improper speech gave cause to improper response. Let us be mindful of our words and actions. Onowu, could you tell them the other ways women deal with this misfortune?

ONOWU: Women have a high fertility rate in our country. Women who have infertility problems may either marry wives or, as earlier explained take on custodial mothering. This may happen in two main ways: they take on the children of their maternal sibling whom they raise as their own; or they may become stepmothers to the orphaned children of their co-wife.

DE BEAUVOIR: You make it all sound so easy, as if those women don't feel the pangs of their barren state.

ONOWU: You seem to want it to sound bad and complicated. We are discussing pragmatic solutions to women's difficulties, not miracles. Nobody is minimizing the gravity of their pain, but if they cannot have a child, then they cannot. That's what they agreed to with their *chi*.[15] They don't have to kill themselves. What is important is what the society has done to make life bearable for them. It created the social space that empowered them to seek treatment, to try out with different male partners, to marry wives and have children by this means, and/or to become custodial mothers.

OMU: Actually Onowu, now that you've spelt it out the way you did, I have to say that we have a pretty good situation here. The issue now is whether our daughters would be able to preserve much of this legacy we negotiated for them.

End of Act II

Act III: Confronting the Underlying Masculinist Yardstick

OMU: Visitors, before you jump to find fault with our lives, you need to think more deeply about the rules and regulations that your own societies have for women. Next, you may want to consider the logic and pattern of reasoning behind your questions.

ONOWU: After listening to you all day today, I have one main question for you. Why are you so male fixated? You don't even try to understand another culture's logic before you launch into your critique. You think you know, when in fact you don't know. You seem driven by unhappy experiences in your culture that make you think women everywhere are equally mistreated in the same way. This clouds your vision and makes you sound illogical. You are continually shifting the standard for women, devaluing who they are, and what they have achieved. You assume that whatever position a man is in, it is the most desirable and the most powerful. Let us go back again to what your son Richard wrote about Ikporo Onitsha in his book. He claims that "Onitsha women are strongly trade-oriented," and that their men are so worried about the high divorce rates that as soon as *nwa-ada* (daughter) marries they begin to prepare for her homecoming (Henderson 1972, 235).

HENDERSON: That is true.

ONOWU: Here again is the crooked logic that I am talking about. If, as Richard says, Onitsha women are under the authority and control of our husband, then really we "have no voice." In effect, we have no power. We must lack social strength. Right? So how does he account for the high rate of divorce in Onitsha, which as he suggests, stems from our strong trade orientation? If we grant that our trading practices are the cause of our divorces, then he is actually saying that our husbands have no authority and control over us and our trading activities. This means, of course, that we Ikporo Onitsha manage our lives, that our husbands, our fathers and brothers too are helpless over the situation. What I'd like to know is, are we under the control of men, or are we women in control of our lives?

HENDERSON: My research shows that Onitsha women . . . have some influence over the affairs of men. For example, an Onitsha king's daughter who had been converted to Christianity strongly influenced her father's attitude to the mission (Crowther 1871, 126), and an Onitsha woman married to an Igala man encouraged her son to bring in troops from Igala to support her village's kingship candidate (Crowther 1873, 21). Women were also . . . active in religious matters; they took part in various public sacrifices; they offered sacrifices to the Niger River to drive off sickness (1873, 95–96).

OMU: So all this talk about Ikporo Onitsha being "under the authority of husbands" who also "control their spiritual condition," where did it all come from? Did we tell him we have your law of coverture? If Richard seriously considered that wives too have rights of sexual access, he would have noted that, when husbands cannot perform their duties, we are totally justified in finding a partner or leaving the marriage. At the very least, he would have seen the two-way street in our marriage institution. It is the one-way street in yours that makes it possible for husbands to be monarchs with exclusive power over your lives. Placed under his will by your marriage vows—"to love and obey, till death do you part"—you are stripped of your individuality and fused into the husband. You may say things are different today, but you still live under the weight of that legacy.

HENDERSON: The cited historical examples are not intended to indicate that Onitsha women are equal to men in position or power, only that, considered in the context of other Nigerian groups, they appeared to the traders and missionaries to have a relatively high status (Henderson 1969, 96).

OMU: The problem with your lens is that it is too calibrated to devalue. Even if our equality jumped up and slapped you across the face, you won't even know what hit you. You remain preoccupied with men, their rights and their conjugal status. That is not where to begin, if you want to understand Onitsha women, their families, and the society. You begin with their identities as mothers and daughters. Their identity as mothers displaces their status as wives. You ask what they are doing and what they have achieved. Their status as daughters will point out their social and ritual roles. That is when you will learn the political relationship between *diokpa* (first lineage son and priest) and *isi ada* (first lineage daughter and priestess) in running the lineage. After you have understood that women's identity is based on their natal identity, then you can begin to grasp their behavior in their marital home.

HENDERSON: When I did my fieldwork I saw that *diokpa* and *isi ada* both have functions that they can perform and cannot refuse. I saw that there was equality of access to lineage shrines, but wives do not administer estates except under certain circumstances. Elderly female lineage members are asked for advice and counsel, but do not normally attend meetings with men (Henderson 1969, 116).[16]

OMU: And did you see elderly male lineage members being asked for advice and counsel, but not allowed to attend meetings with *umuada* (lineage daughters). Did you not see the meetings of *umuada*, or you simply assumed that those meetings were unimportant? What do you know of the duties of *isi ada*?

HENDERSON: Well, I know such a woman cannot be refused a place in her natal compound if she leaves her husband; and if she is *isi ada*, a separate house will be built for her. If the estranged husband fails to support her children, her brothers will assist. On her return to her lineage, she must be shown an area for her garden and farm. Even her children are entitled to use farmland and to build a house, and eventually, if they so wish, to take *ozo* title in the mother's lineage. She has no household duties in the (natal) family compound, and her brother is not entitled to a share of her trade profits. But I also know that wealthy *ada* finance their brother's *ozo* (spiritual title) and cater for his family, though they are under no obligation to do so (1969, 117).

ONOWU: So how do you understand and characterize what you have just described? On one account *umuada* are irrelevant in the scheme of things, and on another account, their *umunna* are running around and doing all they can to support them. Would your own brothers do what our own brothers routinely do? Have you stopped to ask yourself why this is the case? Do you think they would do what you've just described, if they perceived their sisters as socially and politically inconsequential? And how did they come by this sister-centered consciousness? What kind of power relations do you think underlie this relationship? What else are you looking for to satisfy your sufficient condition to grant us our relevance and agency?

HENDERSON: But women are under a husband's *ofo*?

OMU: Every person is under the *ofo* of the father's lineage. In some cases, they may come under the *ofo* of their mother's lineage. Spiritually, we cannot be incorporated under the *ofo* of our place of marriage; we are not one with them, as your marriage vows compel you to be. Our identity endures even after marriage. Ask *Otu Ogene* and the officers of Ikporo Onitsha; after we are married we remain under the *ofo* of our lineage. The primary location of our spiritual condition is the *iba* (ancestral house) of our lineage. It is there that we participate in the spiritual invocation and prayers with our *diokpa* and *isi ofo*, and our *umunne* and *umunna*. Because of this spiritual autonomy, we cannot be incorporated under our marital *ofo*. This is why, traditionally, we established our own personal shrines with the help of our *diokpa* and *isi ada* in our matrimonial home. On these shrines are three major items: *oma* (the symbol of our continued relationship to our mothers), *okposi* (the four ritual objects that symbolize the *chi* of our ancestral fathers), and *chi* (five ritual objects that symbolize the overarching guardian forces of our destiny) and *ikenga* (principle of initiative and success that is closely connected to our first pregnancy).

Husbands do not play a role in this matter. The person who officiates in the ceremony of "bringing in the mother" and constructing the *oma* mound in our marital home is the *isi ofo* of our lineage; not our husband. In the ceremony of "bringing in the fathers" into our marital home, our *diokpa* officiates in dedicating the *okposi*, not our husband. And in setting up the symbols of our *chi* and *ikenga* in our marital home, a *dibia* (diviner) officiates, not our husband. However, as mothers, we respect the spiritual forces of our marital lineage and join them in prayers and activities.[17] But we never become assimilated. In our role as mothers, we make our children aware of this relationship with their fathers and fathers' people, but we instill a strong matri-centered consciousness in them and bring them to worship at our own personal shrine and at the *iba* of our lineage.

ONOWU: Omu, I'm not taking the speech from you, but you forgot to add, too, that in our marital homes we maintain our own economic autonomy and keep our own economic counsel. We do not hand over our earnings to a husband, even if he funded the economic venture. When they acquire wealth, women such as Emengini Uyakwesi Aniebo, the late Odu Mbanefo's mother, financed the *ozo* titles of their husbands, sons, and brothers and built homes for them. Such sons and brothers then honor their mothers and sisters by taking the honorific name of *Akunne* (wealth that came from the maternal line). There are countless cases of sisters and wives who financed the *Agbalanze* titles of their brothers and husbands. In the mid-1980s, *ada* Melifonwu of Isiokwe, Menkiti's wife, underwrote the cost of her husband's initiation into the *Agbalanze ozo* society. In the 1960s, Nwabundo Igweze, *nwanyi nwe lu ife* (woman of wealth and substance) and wife of Ikwueme in Ogbeoza, underwrote the cost of her brother's *ozo* title. At the same time, there are numerous cases of husbands, sons, and brothers who paid for the *Otu Odu* title of their wives, mothers, or sisters.

ONYEAMAMA: But what do we get for our efforts? Writers who insist on devaluing us in numerable ways. Take Richard, for example; he attacked our sexuality and that of our children as well. In his writing, he described the period after betrothed girls "have carried back the pot" (*ibu na ba ite*) as a time "of licentious activity" (1972, 227). It seems that the traditionally sanctioned post-betrothal period of sexual freedom proves our "sexual wantonness (1972, 206)." And if this denigration is not enough, he describes our daughters as "sexual outlets for the community's unmarried males" (1972, 203). What language is this? What did our sexuality do to him?

AUDIENCE: [*Rowdy, restless, and snickering lewdly.*] Maybe he wants some of it!

ONYEAMAMA: This is not a joking matter.

AUDIENCE: Neither are we joking! It is our sexuality that is being ridiculed. We have a right to respond. Why shouldn't we explore our sexuality during this period, as our mothers did? What is his problem with our experiencing what *Osebuluwa* (Supreme Being) gave us?

ONYEAMAMA: [*Retreating to high moral ground with a lament.*] Alu emem! An abomination has been done to me! You know that the *akili aki* called his book on Onitsha *The King in Every Man!* There you are! There's your answer!

[*Striding back and forth excitedly with hands apart.*] Richard was talking about a place where men are kings, where every *oso aka* (wastrel) and *efuluefu* (ragamuffin) are kings. This explains why the husband of my friend here, could not see Onitsha women. He could only see us from the eyes of kings. Not the Obi of Onitsha, mind you, but their own kings who, I hear, treat people like slaves. Let me tell you [*pointing impolitely*], don't quote us anything from your lie-lie books again. If you want to know about our lives, come and talk to us. In Onitsha, our Obi are spiritual entities, limited monarchs. As the custodian of norms and tradition, the Obi must respect Ikporo Onitsha because of our vital roles and duties in the community. Let him not respect us and our *isi ada*, and we will pluck him from his throne, put him on our backs, and deposit him on the wrong side of the border. Or we will stride into his palace in our nakedness and dethrone him by sitting on his throne. [*Strutting around.*] Ikporo Onitsha, is it not as I've said?

AUDIENCE: Onyeamama! It's as you've said. Say it louder! Onyeamama!

OMU: Onyeamama . . .

ONYEAMAMA: No, your son is wrong. Our tradition specifies respect for women. Richard cannot be talking about our kings. (Stomping around) He must be talking about those kings of yours who rule, who rule . . .

OMU: (In a stern voice) Onyeamama, take your seat.

ONYEAMAMA: Omu, I've repossessed my seat.

End of Act III

[*Intermission: Refreshments are served. The visitors and the Omu and Otu Ogene confer separately. Discussion resumes soon after with the hosts attempting to decipher the definition of equality.*]

Act IV: Political Structure and the Quest for Elusive Equality

OMU: *Ndi amuma'm* (my visionary ones), coming back to your assertions on oppression and equality. You have talked a lot about equality. What exactly do you mean by it, anyway? What do you understand by "*i ara nra anya*" (to be equal)? Does it imply *ibu ofu* (being one)?

DE BEAUVOIR: It means being denied what is granted to men. It means having the same powers and rights as men in the society, and being able to do the same things. It means not being told that motherhood is the only career option for women. It means not having to choose between motherhood and a career. And when we work, it means not being relegated to menial jobs and positions because one is a woman. It means sharing the same sets of attributes, not one set for women and another one for men. It means having the same social opportunities, the same social expectations. It means not being declared subordinate because one is a woman, or having one's rights and life options limited. It means not treating biological sex as a basis of systemic disadvantage. For instance, do Onitsha women have the same rights as men to participate in the governance of the community? Do their words count as much as men's? Would a woman of the same age and maturity as a man be considered a distinct individual in the same way he is? Would she command the same respect as a man?

HENDERSON: Before you answer, Omu, I'd like to give a good example of women's diminished role in the political scheme. In my study of the ritual roles of Onitsha women, I found that most of the important extra-kinship political institutions in Onitsha are largely closed to women. One of these, the masquerade society, is directly involved in suppressing them. No woman under the age of menopause can know the secrets of masquerade and none can ever wear a mask. Further, women did not traditionally belong to age sets like the men's, which were one of the major arms of the town-wide political action. They were therefore excluded from the ruling age set, which, together with the king and chiefs, passed laws for the town. The *ozo* title symbols such as the staffs, boxes, etc., are not owned by women, and only a few specially designated ones dare touch them. Women do not become chiefs and therefore do not sit in judgment over cases involving the death penalty. The ultimate in restrictions on females is reached in regard to the king, whose wives do not live in his house and who are limited in the times they may see their husband. The king's family daughters have less a role to play in his life than do those of any other man, being largely replaced by males from the village (*Olosi*), which according to tradition, was founded by the daughter of an early king (1969, 250–51).

ONOWU: Let us begin with the point on the masquerade society. I hope you realize that it was a woman, Usse, who brought the *mmuo* institution to Onitsha. That is why *umuada* (daughters of) Ogbeotu and Obikporo are born into the *mmuo afia* (tall spirit) tradition. They accompany the dreaded *mmuo ogongo* (tall spirit), the most serious of spirits, from a very early age. *Umuada* are not men; remember that they are females. Given their membership into the society and their close proximity to the masked forms, it is reasonable to assume they know the secrets of the *mmuo*.

You say that the age sets are male-exclusive. It is true that female memberships in age sets began in the early 1950s, with the formation of *Odoziaku* Age Grade, but that was not the only "major arm of the town-wide political action."[18] Where do you place the political office of the Omu and Ikporo Onitsha? Why do you expend so much energy trying to make whatever men do appear so much more important than it is and more significant than what women do?

ONYEAMAMA: Onowu, the woman has consistently been measuring us on the standard of men. We are not good enough, because we are not members of *ozo*, and this is predicated on the fact that only men are *ozo* members. We are not good enough because we are not part of the meeting of *umunna;* this rests on the assumption that only men are members of this body. We fall short, because we are not members of the masquerade, again because it is imagined that women are excluded, and postmenopausal women are not women! Come out and say it, Helen, we are not good enough, because we do not have penises! I suppose that there is no point showing you our two breasts to the one penis of a man. You still will not accept that we have more to offer? Really, there is no point underscoring that men will fall short if you measure them by our "two-breast" yardstick? If you cannot see what you are doing and saying, what is the point of continuing the conversation?

HENDERSON: But the fact of the matter is that it is men who make all the political decisions!

OMU: [*Clearly irritated.*] Take a good look at me, and at the position I oc-cupy: Omu (female monarch) of the community and *Onye-Isi-Ikporo Onitsha* (Head of Ikporo Onitsha). These are major political institutions with exten-sive political obligations. You continually think, talk, and act as if they are triv-ial positions. If you acknowledge that they are not, then why do you think that the ruling age set is necessarily more important and more dominant? Histori-cally, Ikporo Onitsha is much older than the ruling age-set phenomenon that began in the 1920s. When the Christian Mission first came to Onitsha in the early 1860s and asked to see Obi Akazu, because of the political character of Onitsha political system, the Obi ensured that my predecessor, Omu Onyearo Nkechi,[19] and her *otu ogene* were there to take part in the deliberations.[20] We were not only consulted, but also our consent was crucial to the decision that was made. When the trading mission of Whitford arrived in 1877, we were cen-tral to the deliberation and the decision making process, even though the pa-triarchal lens of Whitford saw us only as the "old women of the board of trade."[21] Again, when Adolphe Burdo arrived in late 1870s, he followed the lead of Whitford and referred to us as the "female trade commission" (1880, 134–35). You know that my place is an asylum and that the Obi and his *ndichie* cannot invade it.

The question you should ask is what caused the rise of the political in-stitution of the ruling age set? What made it possible for the Obi institution to have more powers than the Omu? What forces convened to bring about the decline of the Omu institutions? And what forces are working today to bring about the demise of Ikporo Onitsha? It is the male-privileging disease that came in the age of Europeans. Let us go to history When did the political in-stitution of ruling age-grade emerge? Not too long ago, you know. In the 1920s, during the colonial period. The Omu-ship and Ikporo Onitsha are far older in-stitutions. But because they were women-controlled organizations, the gov-ernment of the day dismissed them as irrelevant. When it because clear that the age grade would have political preeminence, Ikporo Onitsha mobilized to ensure that the age grades became integrated. This happened in the 1950s. You have to realize that the role of the ruling age set is consultative, not dictatorial. To be effective, they have to factor in the views of the entire community, otherwise they will not be relevant. Because of this consultative role, you cannot plausibly say that it is only what men say that becomes the law of the land.

I find it disturbing that there is a systematic devaluation of whatever women do, including their political roles and spiritual responsibilities. By contrast, whatever men do is automatically valorized without any attempt to understand whether they are really important and to see how we interact with them. Thus, even though Ikporo Onitsha has always had tremendous influence in the community, and what we say shapes community opinion and political decision, you trivialize it. You don't even see it as a political institution. It is not written about as an important political breakthrough in national governing structures. By dismissing it, you erroneously assume that in our political processes the Obi and the ruling age grade have absolute powers and that they can do whatever they please. But far more important is that you ensure that the political significance of Ikporo Onitsha is never known, nor considered by others as a viable working alternative to the problems of gender inequality. History bears us out that the Obi and the ruling age grade do not have that kind of authority. They do not have the power you are trying so hard to invest in them. Whatever community-wide pronouncements were made, were arrived at by consensus.

ONYEAMAMA: [*In exasperation.*] Omu, I have been asking all day where did these people come from? Why are we wasting time with them? Now they are telling us, the owners of the history, that the daughters of Ogbeotu and Obikporo, whose interaction with their *mmuo afia* (Tall Spirit/masquerade) starts from childhood, are not women! They are also arguing with us that postmenopausal women are not women! *Oyibo ndi ogu* (Europeans, people of war). What shall we not see!

OMU: What does it matter if only postmenopausal and not premenopausal women are admitted into the masked spirit institution? Why is the timing of this knowledge for some group of women so crucial? Moreover, how did you arrive at the conclusion that the role of the masquerade is to suppress women? Which man told you that, since you could not have gained that knowledge yourself? Ask him if they use the spirits of their ward to suppress their *umuada*? I know that they do not use it to suppress Ikporo Onitsha, because that is not its role and objective.[22] It seems that you came here to find flaws, and if you cannot find any, you will try to twist things to prove your case. Are we trying to say we have a perfect society? No. But your obsessive focus on men and your attempt to use them as a reference frame is tiresome and not particularly useful to us. For us to have a meaningful conversation you should try to understand the complex social and religious forces that converge to accord motherhood a privileged position. This line of interrogation would enable you see the privileges and prerogatives that structurally accrued to mothers. It is a pity that you do not want to examine spaces where men are absent or subordinately situated. You want to study only the spaces where you think that men have an advantage, because you see those spaces as important. Try to go beyond your set agenda, so that we can have a more fruitful discussion.

ONOWU: Let me go back to what Helen said a moment ago, that "the funeral role of the king's family daughters has largely been replaced by males from *Olosi.*" That observation is not entirely accurate. But even if we grant it to her, given that your objective is to identify areas of gender subordination, how come you do not want to consider that this duty has transformed Olosi men into women? Would you not say that these roles of *Olosi* men have made them "honorary women" or "female males" or "female sons"? After all, they have assumed the responsibilities and roles of daughters and are dutifully playing this role. Why are you reluctant to acknowledge that they are copying women and are using women as models? If your idea of equality is really to be meaningful, it should apply similarly to both women and men. You should take the same approach toward men that you do toward women. You use men as a measure for women and then tell us that women fall short. Yet, when men do things according to daughters' practices, rather than praising us, you tell us that women have lost ground. We are damned if we do, and damned if we don't. I'm not sure you are aware of it, but this male fixation is causing you to move the goal post in a most irregular manner.

OMU: Onowu, hold your steam. Let them tell us more about what they mean by this equality; perhaps we can then understand why they think motherhood and a career are mutually exclusive. *Ira n'ra anya* (being the same) and *ibu ofu* (being one): what is the predicate of these terms? What do they socially signify? You have taken men as the measure and seem to want women to be men. The question is which men are we talking about: Obi, *ndichie* (members of the Obi's cabinet), *ndi ozo* (*ozo* title holders), or *iregwu* (adult untitled men)? One? All of them? Why are these men defining your yardstick? Do you believe that men epitomize the best in life?

GREER: Our analysis shows they do. We discovered deeply entrenched inequality and deeply entrenched institutionalization of gender difference when we studied what men can do relative to what women actually do. For our conclusion to be wrong, a society should be one in which sexual difference carried no social signifiers, the sexes are equal in power, and "mothering" and "fathering" a child is evenly shared.[23]

ONYEAMAMA: I suppose we should also share the gestation period, the same labor pains, the same breast suckling duties. If we cannot share that, then they should place being a mother on the same level as being a father.

ONOWU: How many societies did you study? Of that number, how many did you patiently study? Of that number, how many are African? How many are Igbo? If your comments today are anything to go by, I would say very few.

End of Act IV

Act V: Fluid Identities and Shifting Hierarchies

OMU: Here in *obodo Onicha*, we have a complex system of identities that are defined by the practices and social roles and social location of people. No one social identity is fixed; men and women are constantly shifting between categories. *Di* (husband, consisting of both male and female members of a lineage) are in a dominant position in their lineage to *nwunye* (wife), who is in a subordinate relationship to them. But the same *di* is in a subordinate relationship to their *ogo* (wife's parent and lineage family). Then, in her natal village, that woman sheds her *nwunye* identity and becomes *ada* (daughter) that puts her in the dominant position of *di* to her lineage wives who relate to her as such. *Umunna* (both male and female) are in a subordinate position of *nwadiani* (grandchild) in the lineage and wards of their *ikwu nne* (maternal family) and have to defer to them as such. Also *umunna* are subordinate to their *diopka* and *isi ada*. These ever-shifting hierarchies and fluid identities means that no one is permanently stuck in a position of dominance. No one is in a permanently subordinate position or permanently dominant position. We agree we are biologically different from men, and men are different from women. But these biological differences are not rooted in power or ideological ranking and so the idea of sex differentiation does not imply the subjugation of women as a group, nor the subordination of one sex over the other.

ONOWU: You must understand that, when we speak of difference between women and men, we do not mean the same things that you do in your country, and we do not mean gender inequality which derives from your patriarchal structure. We, as Ikporo Onitsha, see ourselves as a pan-community group that negotiates political issues on the basis of our political category. As a political group, we are indomitable. Our strength is magnified and is much more than the number of people in the group. So when we speak of "having a voice," we mean having the right to participate in both political governance and political administration. Our role as community mothers gives Ikporo Onitsha powerful authority to influence our institutions. So, when we say that "being female" is important, we are not merely talking about our individual bodies, or nonpolitical issues or condoning states of affairs that are oppressive to women. We are talking about national powers and political and spiritual roles that accrue to us a result of who we are. We are talking about are social identities, commercial duties, and political and spiritual obligations that reflect our multiple situational roles as mothers, daughters, wives, and sisters.[24] Indeed, we derive from our overarching Council of Ikporo Onitsha the political right to shape the nation state. As Ikporo Onitsha, we sometimes see the world differently from men. When we do, we want that vision and the issues we identify factored into the smooth running of our community. Sometimes we see things the same as men, since we are all citizens of Onitsha. But we don't believe that men should take our voices and speak for us. We are adults. We feel pain, and we know where the thorn is thrust deep in our flesh. We don't need anyone to articulate our pain. Is that what you do in your country?

ONYEAMAMA: [*Butting in.*] Yes, that's what they do. And that is why they are wondering how our system can recognize difference between men and women, and yet we claim there is no sex inequality. My friend, being a woman does not mean living a life of oppression and being subordinate to men. The fact that you have a great need to emphasize your similarity to men, to be perceived as socially relevant, tells us that your society is anti-women. You do not see women as worthy. So when you want us to define ourselves by your perception of equality, you imagine us to be like you and your society. It is because we are different from you that we have no need to define equality and ourselves on male terms. We are not yearning to be men. We have a voice, and we are social complements of men in an interdependent complex.

DE BEAUVOIR: You speak of duties; what are they? What are these roles and responsibilities?

OMU: There are a number of them. At the family level, our society is organized on a kinship principle. The emphasis of our social interrelationships is family oriented. We are mothers, daughters, sisters, and wives. With the fathers, sons, brothers, and husbands, we hold the family together. But these diverse roles have political responsibilities in the context of the family and city-wide political groups.

In fact, every aspect of our lives is politically negotiated. We treat life as political, and organize ourselves accordingly. Our activities reflect this. For example, in the first half of the twentieth century, when agriculture was the dominant profession, the crops we planted held our families and the community together during the planting season, and those of the men during the bountiful harvest period. Today, in the context of wage labor, both women and men have professions, notably, teaching, nursing, law, medicine, engineering, and mass communication. They work to maintain their families together. At the national level, our matrifocused shrines of Obinamili, Olinri, Nne Nkisi, Uto, Ojedi, and Ebenebe and others guard the community. At the lineage level, *Ndi isi ada* (lineage priestesses) ritually cleanse and calm all the homes and the land of the patrilineage. They still do so today. As *umuada* (lineage daughters) we embody and preserve the community's female principle in our natal lineage.[25] But as mothers we preserve the community's maternal principle in our marital lineages. Our primary home is our natal home, and our identity is elaborated through our lineage. We view ourselves as "strangers" in our marital home, where we have a limited voice, because we are not part of that lineage. The fact that we agreed to live with "strangers" to assist them in the miracle of continuity does not mean that we have become a part of them. When we create our *akwukwa* (cooking hearth) in our marital homes, we keep in mind the purposive nature of that cohabitation, which is to bring life into the lineage and to nurture the spirit entities that have chosen to incarnate in that family. This is why motherhood is important.

ONYEAMAMA: Less than eighty years ago, our children used to be identified by their mothers' rather than their fathers' names. When you hear "Obeche Ozoena," "Umebe Nwayiuzo," and "Udegbuna Nwanyieke," you know immediately who the mothers are. But today it is no longer the case. *Eewu* (lament of sorrow), those catechists, those missionaries and school officials, really did something to us and we didn't know it! They forced our children to make us irrelevant!

HENDERSON: Even if what you say is true, it does not negate the fact that "children are primarily bound authoritatively by the *ofo* of their father's lineage priest, not their mother's" (1969, 140).

ONOWU: So what does that prove, that the father owns the child? No! What it shows is that in modern times descent is by the social father's lineage, but they are also under the protective custody of the *ofo* of the mother's lineage. I say social father, because he may not be the genitor. Many *diokpa* (lineage priests) are not the biological sons of their social fathers, but they were socialized to be such. Also there is a strong maternal consciousness, even as in modern times descent is traced through the father. So talk about "being bound authoritatively" is the kind of language that derives from a false picture of the society as male dominant and mothers as irrelevant. Remember that the crucial location of identity formation is by the hearth, where, through food and ritual prayers at her shrine, mothers instill a strong maternally focused consciousness in their children. A father's *ofo* is mediated by his mother's *oma* (maternal force). Sometimes the latter is stronger, and ill will towards a father is so strong that a son may choose to be subsumed by the *ofo* of his mother's lineage. When this occurs, and it has occurred, your argument that children are "bound authoritatively by father's *ofo*" is rendered false. Look closely to family ties and people's characters, and the dominance of maternal influence will become dominant.

Our roles as mothers and wives are vital to the continuity of life in our community. Our marital families know this and reciprocate by creating a space for us to provide resources for our children, and by always being there for our natal families, their in-laws. This is not to say that family conflicts do not exist; they do (signals Onyeamama to take over).

ONYEAMAMA: In the olden times, at the community level, Ikporo Onitsha farmed, traded, participated in administering the community, and kept the market open. Every woman was expected to have a profession, a trade, something that kept her productively engaged, contributed to her family's upkeep, and promoted her independency. This philosophy is still present today even though professions have changed and our daughters are now lawyers, doctors, professors, military officers, nurses, financial officers, and teachers. We dislike idleness; it encourages antisocial behavior. As members of Ikporo Onitsha, we adjudicate cases affecting women, we work with Obi and Council, *Agbalanze* (the titled men), *Ogbo na chi achi* (the ruling age grade), and *Agbala n'iregwu* (adult female and male citizenry). In the past, we accompanied soldiers to war with our protective spiritual shields. We traversed the hinterland and the waterways in our trading efforts. We propitiated the deities of the town, and in that role we were the spiritual channels through which the forces entered the community to heal it.

End of Act V

CHANGING STRATEGY: DE BEAUVOIR
CONFERS WITH GREER

Act VI: The Possibilities and Limits of Women's Lives

DE BEAUVOIR: Motherhood, mothering, and motherhood. Isn't this a case of "relegat[ing] the black to the rank of shoeshine boy; and he concludes from this that the black is good for nothing but shining shoes"?[26]

GREER: Ah, yes. Just like Gilligan. Justify an oppressed reality when other avenues are closed, and you can't get something better. It never ceases to amaze me, the lengths to which women will go to validate motherhood, sexuality, and spirituality, the triple factors of women's universal oppression. I wonder what the monarch will say to the modern Nigerian women's views that it is within marriage that women suffer the most oppression. Thanks to Omolara Ogundipe-Leslie, Buchi Emecheta, and Tola Pearce, we know about the marital disenfranchisement of African women: first they lose status by being married, then they become possessions, voiceless and often right-less, and finally they lose most of their personal freedom (Ogunidpe-Leslie, 1984).

DE BEAUVOIR: Well, you know people always present a rosy picture to strangers. As Cass Sunstein intimated, people will adapt their conduct and even their desires to what is presently available. In conditions such as this, it becomes a case of the fox not wanting the grapes, because he considers them to be sour, but we know that this belief is based on the fact that the grapes are unavailable (Sunstein 1992, 15). We are indeed fortunate to have alternative sources of information about the culture.

GREER: So what strategy shall we adopt? Humor them, or make them see the error of preferences that unjustly limit women's liberties and opportunities from the culture?

DE BEAUVOIR: We should prod them toward seeing the error of their perception. [*Resumes general conversation.*] Omu, all the things you've just mentioned are the same things women the world over normally do and are still oppressed. Is it not possible that you are seeing things incorrectly, that the roles you have described are inferior to those of men, and that Ikporo Onitsha are really subordinate?

OMU: You must not have been listening.

DE BEAUVOIR: What if women decided they want to plant men's crops?

OMU: What crops?

DE BEAUVOIR: Yams!

OMU: What about them? Women plant yams. Those who have "loan" of men's services or hired labor rapidly increase their acreage. Some don't, because tilling the ground to make earth mounds for yams requires an inordinate amount of labor. But why would they want to plant yams, when they have other avenues of obtaining the crop? What would they be proving? That they have excessive physical energy? Are they mad? Why is it important to prove that they have the same energy as men, when they may not? They have their trade, which can be expanded to increase their wealth.

GREER: Omu, the problem we have is that all the things you've enumerated are the same stereotypical things that women normally do. Marriage, motherhood, procreation, reproduction, nurturing—they are the same old things. We need to see that they can assume men's roles to accept that there is gender equality. That is the only way we can prove their sex is not a barrier to them.

OMU: And why do you believe doing men's tasks proves equality? How is equality proved or achieved by having women do things that disproportionately strain them? How is equality served by putting women at a disadvantage? And why do you believe cocoyam, legumes, vegetables, and cassava are unimportant in family sustenance and nourishment? They are the mainstay of our diet throughout the year, especially at the crucial time that yams have run out! You say that we've listed all the stereotypical things that women do. The difference, however, is that we assign value to what we do and we make sure that the whole community sees it as such.

GREER: We find it hard to believe that men do not make all the decisions in the town. Your society is patrilineal. Men control the bodies and labors of these women who are their wives and daughters. Don't you see that you are controlled by men, that your notions of liberty and female identity are still defined by men/patriarchs?

ONYEAMAMA: [*Muttering, as she taps her snuff box, and pours out a pinch.*] Here they come again, all knowing, all wisdom. Always peddling lies as truth. [*With her thumbnail, she deftly scoops up the tobacco, inserts it into each nostril, and momentarily pinches the nostrils shut. Inhaling sharply, and following with an audible sign of satisfaction, she intercepts a sneeze, wobbles her head to hold it, and successfully suppresses it with an audible "ah." Glaring blankly through the tobacco daze, she mutters in disgust at the visitors.*] Women who want to be men!

OMU: Onyeamama, do you want to respond?

ONYEAMAMA: Omu, no. I'm busy with an important matter.

OMU: [*Amused.*] Ah, yes, tobacco-snuffing, that profound task that nothing must disturb. You have mastery of the ways of childmaking; now you seek to possess that of tobacco-making.[27]

ONOWU: [*Interjecting to Omu.*] We seem to be talking at cross-purposes with our visitors; perhaps we should end this meeting. [*Turning to the visitors.*] You talk as one whose spirits have been stolen from you. You find it difficult to comprehend that women can be strong in being women. With all your knowledge, it is unclear why you do not understand that being female could be a systemic source of social advantage. Why do you assume any definition will necessarily be negative? It seems that in your society, being a woman, which implies being a daughter, mother, or a wife, is a negative and powerless thing, and so you are tragically consumed with sameness and with being men. But they need not be. Here, those roles embody social duties and responsibilities. You have to understand that this state of affairs is possible.

ONYEAMAMA: Onowu, ask them, why don't they understand that? Oyi'm (my friends), what did the men of your land give you to "turn" your head, so that you can no longer reason? What did they do, such that you are consumed by so much self-hate? That country of yours must be a "non-place." Don't you ever collectively call your men to task? Don't you ever ask them to propitiate you and the land when they have transgressed and devalued you?

[*Springing to her seat and sharply rapping her hips as she let out a derisive hiss.*] You call yourselves "women," but you do not even know what that means. [*Impatiently.*] How could you have allowed your men to trick you into subservience? They cannot survive on their own, and they know it. Men are weaklings! You must be fools not to know it, too. Now, in your hurt, you want to define the world of women through your fractured lens. Your anger is irrational. It is the anger of *onye mmuo* (the living dead). It is unhealthy and abnormal. Go. We don't feel it. We don't share it. *Ukumbu na aju aju, oda ekwe ekwe.* (The shoulder signs rejection, never acceptance.)

OMU: [*In amusement.*] You, white people, say we are primitive! [*The noisy audience breaks into laughter.*] Well, I'm sure there are some things we can teach you, if you will bring down your spirit, and let go of your all-too-knowing attitude. Here, we closely focus and live the precept *aka nni kwe aka epe, aka epe ekwe aka nni* (the right hand shakes the left hand, and the left hand shakes the right). Men make some decisions, women make some, and we confer together to make others. The important thing is that we both know it. We both acknowledge and validate what we each do for the good governance of our society. And so we aver: *egbe belu ugo ebelu; nke si ibiya ebena, nku kwapu ya* (let the hawk perch, let the eagle perch; whoever asserts that the other cannot perch, let its wing dislocate).

GREER: [*Piqued.*] Frankly, we didn't come here to discuss which culture is more advanced than the other. That wouldn't serve any purpose, since we know what the verdict would be. We came to see how we can help you participate in the new women's organization that we are building . . .

ONYEAMAMA: No, we don't want your organization of collective subordination.

GREER: Despite your attempt to paint a rosy picture of your society, it is clear, when we take a good look at it, that women haven't achieved much. They are overworked; they fetch water for the entire family, they gather the firewood, they cook, they farm, and they still look after the children. Omu, your women are oppressed. Their life is miserable; their options are limited. Worse still, they don't even know it.

OMU: Visionaries, you confuse material comfort and possession with emancipation. Much of the inequities you see today (1980s) are what your culture did to us. Our material reality may be harsh, but you are wrong to utilize men's life as a model of female identity, for that perversely presupposes that women are nothing. If you want to state that, do so directly. Don't keep treating women as nothing by characterizing their life and activities as irrelevant. Better still, ask yourself why you are so male fixated. Yes, Onitsha women cook. We cook for ourselves and our children; as wives we cook for our husbands; as daughters we cook for our fathers and mothers; and as senior daughters, we cook for our siblings, and . . .

GREER: But your husbands don't cook.

OMU: They cooked at the farm when they used to be farmers. They cook at ritual events; they cook as bachelors. Traditionally, they did not cook in their marital homes, but these days many do. Personally, I don't think husbands should be around the hearth, for that is where our medicines are kept. But if *azi* (young ones) say they do not mind, that is their choice. Our times are passing.

GREER: So you agree that men and women are not equal in your society, for if men and women were really equal, then husbands would also cook and share in the housework, and share everything equally.

ONYEAMAMA: *Eewuu!* [*A sound of pity.*] *Mmadu ka ekulu* (These are also human beings!) *Mm hu, nkita si na ndi nwelu ike amaro ano ani* (The dog said that those who have a behind do not know how to use it to sit—a metaphorical allusion that one is underutilizing a specific attribute, because one is unaware of its potentials). We are not disadvantaged because we do not participate in men's organizations. What you need to understand is the power and strength of our own organizations.

OMU: Visionaries, if you say that cooking is a measure of equality, then what does it say about equality, if you are in control of their stomachs? There is something you need to know. When you control the cooking, you control whatever life nourishment goes into the stomach; you control the man. Cooking is not simply the task of food preparation. It is a political location for negotiating what goes on in the home. It is a place for mounting control. For the wise women who were our mothers, who placed their *chi, okposi, ikenga,* and *oma* by the hearth, it is the location for the exertion of psychic force to control members' consciousness. You have to ask why, of all possible places, women kept the shrine to mothers by the hearth. If your "eyes" are clear visionaries, you will know the answer.
End Act VI

Analyzing the Docu-Drama

The dialogue may read as one of those nontheoretical, case studies from a time-bound, indigenous society from the Third World. Such a naïve reading misses the critical edge of the dialogue, which directly interrogates standard feminist assumptions about women and equality. Juxtaposing Western feminists assumptions to the turn-of-the-century Onitsha women's experiences reveals a society in which women's social advancement and empowered status far exceeds what any society, including contemporary First-World feminists, had achieved. The creation of a parallel political structure results in the empowered status of Onitsha women that undermines institutionalizing only men's interests. For starters, Onitsha women's agency and power were not simply a legal or judicial matter nor is it a set of formal rights contained in some legal document. Their power and agency was substantively secured by a sociopolitical system that conferred on them a series of rights that allowed them to wield political, social, economic, and spiritual power. The political, economic, and spiritual gains of Onitsha women at that time forces us to see that women's equality has to be secured by a formally constituted structure of power that accords them equal authority with men at all levels of society. Equality without structural reinforcement is not equality. In fact, the concept of equality that emerges from this position dictates a mutually reinforcing notion of power between men and women rather than one that comes from trying to wrest for women what men already have.

What emerged from the dialogue is that there are two ways of understanding equality. The model proposed by the Western feminist visitors, which construes equality to be about "sameness" between women and men such that both would have the same things; and the Onitsha view that acknowledges the biological differences between men and women and structures their relationship to be equal. The Western model uses men as the yardstick for determining what counts as equality and does not give adequate focus to the interests and aspirations of women. The Onitsha model constitutes its yardstick on the basis of equal worth between women and men and so accords focus to both women's and men's interests and aspirations. The Western model evolved from a societal structure in which men had been privileged over women as a result of their sex, and to correct the imbalance, men's life became the standard of assessment. The Onitsha model, by contrast, evolved from a societal vision that upholds the complementarity of women and men and sees both as equally vital to the well being of the society. I call the Western model, the restorative view of equality, because it is preoccupied in rectifying anomalies and correcting past wrongs by ensuring that women have whatever men have rather than in determining what equality really is when conceptualized from the interests of both men and women. The Onitsha view finds this restorative way of thinking about equality to be problematic. Not only is it too narrowly tied to correcting past mistakes, it is too restrictive of women's possibilities and does not provide adequate opportunity for thinking about equality when women and men are similarly empowered. Where women are the social equals of men and both are equally valued for the skills they bring to building the community, equality is differently conceptualized. It is conceived not in terms of some abstract notions of sameness but in terms of concrete sociopolitical duties and responsibilities that both sexes possess. Under this condition, equality implies comparable worth, and women and men have to sort out ways in which they are complements, and ways in which their duties, though different, are socially comparable.

Although the restorative view is understandable in light of the Western society's social and political history, the Onitsha spokespersons make the valid point that this view of equality is inherently damaging to women in that it still treats them as subordinate. When individuals are construed as the same, the restorative view continues tacitly to privilege men's life, ignoring conditions that are vital to women's lives as mothers and that are not duplicated in men's lives. To ignore these reproductive conditions and possibilities on the grounds that they speak too strongly about difference is to continue to treat women as unequal. This is what the Onitsha interlocutors kept identifying as the crux of the problem in the Western visitors' view of equality. Their resistance to this restorative notion of equality is a response to the deep-seated forms of discrimination that stacks the odds against women. The problem they have with its central idea of sex-neutrality is that it is false neutrality. Equality cannot be too concerned about leveling the inequality between women and men that it excludes legitimate differences of women from which issues that are vital to them arise. Any conception of equality must speak forcefully about women's reproductive capabilities and rights and their visions of reality that flow from them as it does about men's interests and rights. Because most of the political, legal, economic, and educational institutions of Western society were established on the grounds that women were lesser than men and lacked autonomy, it is foolhardy to seek equality in spaces and with concepts that were created with the devaluation of women in mind. A definition of equality cannot presume the legitimacy of only men's experiences of reality and their visions of life as that devalues women and forces them to live men's definitions of reality rather than of both.

From the Onitsha position, the visitors' urge to seek inclusion in the very alienating spaces that problematize women's lives signals a deep-seated psychological dysfunction that is passing off sex inequality as sex equality. The difference between them and their visitors' is drawn along the lines of historical experiences and structures of society. Where men are structurally dominant as in the Western society, structurally disadvantaged women would define equality in term of a level playing field with men. But where the structure of the society accommodates a sociopolitical scheme that accords equitable power to men and women, the emergent conception of equality would reflect a complementary social vision that both sexes had collaboratively chosen for their society. What this shows is that our conception of equality is really tied to the kind of society we have. It is only when this logical relationship is clearly articulated that we can then evaluate which of the models offer lesser conditions of inequality between the sexes. This will be the subject of the next chapter.

But before we commence that analysis, we need to discuss the other insights the docu-drama offers in pursuing social and legal reforms in modern-day Onitsha. To challenge the modern male-privileging values, we have to radically restructure the society to extend equality to men and women. Only then can the structural impediments be removed so that women can become the social complements of men they once were. Drawing on the insight that conceptions of equality are tied to the sociopolitical structure of societies, the goal of reform will be to use the values and structures of precolonial Onitsha society to ensure that modern Onitsha women's true interests and objectives are preserved in the reformed model. This is the only way that women's interests can become part of the ideology that defines the community.

Drawing insights from precolonial Onitsha society to respond to contemporary realities will result in certain shifts in the family. The following are a few examples. First, we will have to restore daughters' full rights of inheritance in their families so that they have the same rights as sons. This is crucial if daughters are to start at the same baseline with sons, and if they are to achieve

parity with sons in the current economic conditions of Nigeria. This restoration will have the following effects: Daughters will be socially and legally equal
to sons, a situation that will correct their present status of subordination. They
will have the right to either marry a male husband or become an *idigbe*. If a
daughter chooses the latter, her children will have the right to become part of
her consanguineal family, including having rights of inheritance to the family's
land as do the children of sons. This right of daughters will not nullify the right
of sons who could still choose to marry their own wives, and whose children
presently inherit from them. However, sons who choose to be the paramours
of an *idigbe* will be in the same position as daughters who marry male husbands.
Both their children will be socialized as members of their spouses' family rather
than their own. Because all sons and daughters will have full rights to family
land, even daughters who marry male husbands and males who are paramours
of *idigbe* can pass their share of inheritance to their children.

The rationale that currently prevents this from happening, which is that
family land would be transferred to other families through a daughter's marriage is no longer tenable. This is because every family will stand to gain in the
same way and no one family or set of children is necessarily the sole loser. We
are all mindful that the present situation that assigns family land only to sons
not only upholds a principle of inequality between children and impoverishes
daughters, it does not ensure that land is kept in the family. Ewelukwa's (2002,
443) point is still pertinent here. In the hot real estate market that exists in
many parts of Igboland, sons are disposing of family land through sales.

A further advantage of societal restructuring is also that woman–woman
marriages will be permitted, since marriage is fundamentally a social institution. Daughters can choose to marry whomever they choose. They can opt to
marry their own wives in order to have children or for companionship in just
the same ways that sons choose to have wives for companionship and to have
children.

Additionally, women of the community will have the right to strengthen
their own political institutions such that they will carry equal weight with that
of men. They could consider restoring the offices of Omu (female monarch)
and Otu Ogene since much of the contemporary male-privileging consciousness is fostered by the absence of a complementary female institution to equally
value the relevance of women. According equal rights to women will entail
restoring these institutions to create parity between the men and women and
to guarantee women access to power and control of resources. The importance
of a sociopolitical structure to women's equality is the redistribution of political powers along sex lines that will follow so that both sexes are equally ad-
vantaged. Other structural shifts will undoubtedly occur, but I will not be concerned with them here.

Conclusion

The docu-drama avoided any direct analysis of equality so as to highlight the multiple areas of conflict between the Onitsha view and the Western view of equality. It revealed the necessary conditions of equality when biological differences are factored into an understanding of human worth, and when males and females have political spheres of authority. The revelation shows what really counts as equality when equality is defined by women's and men's roles and objectives rather than by a privileged body. At a theoretical level this also shows that world travel, even with a loving objective, is fraught with conceptual problems. For "what it is to be them and what it is to be ourselves in their eyes" does not really work if one does not have the proper conceptual framework to imagine what it is to be them and to understand the practice and meaning of a different way of life. Imagining an alternative requires a radically different ways of being, which world travelers do not easily have. Not because they do not want to, or because they may not know how to think themselves out of their own society's conceptual box, but because of their heavy investment—conscious and unconscious—in their society's conceptual scheme. One needs sustained embeddedness in another society's cultural life to being to loosen one's own culture's conceptual scheme and to begin to grasp that culture's way of life in deep ways.

Equality is not a socially disconnected concept as is sometimes presumed. It requires supporting social structures, institutions, and practices to give it meaning. To argue for a socially disconnected notion of equality and rights is explicitly to advocate for the conventional social ideal that is constituted by a masculine eros. Whereas abstract philosophical analysis obscures this point, given that social reality is treated abstractly, the docu-drama directly exposes those intractable lines of conceptual difference and tenaciously held beliefs about women, gender relations, and equality.

Furthermore, the docu-drama makes the concept of equality seem culture dependent. This relativist tenor would be troubling to anyone who rejects the principle of cultural equivalence between the world's societies and who desires a globally, uniform definition of equality with compelling moral force and broad applicability. Such uniformists (including liberals, feminists, Marxists, and conservatives) cannot accept that there are varieties of equality since they fear what they see as the ethical chaos that the idea of equivalence entails.[28] However, on the other side of the divide are those whose social institutions are dismissed for promoting inequality. Noting that uniformists tend to associate cultural superiority with the West and cultural inferiority with others, they point to social practices in the West that are indicative of inequality.[29] As they see it, imperfection exists in the West as well, and it cannot arrogate to itself a morally superior stance.

By dragging the character of societies into the picture, the question we are forced to address is: How do we adjudicate between societies, knowing that the notion of equality derives from and prescribes a specific social vision? Onora O'Neill expresses the problem in a different way: "How do we know when cultural opportunities are equal, given the incomplete nature of the 'equal' predicate and the ambiguity of the concept of opportunity?" (1977, 177). The matter is simple and clear cut for those who insist that cultural opportunities are equal when they apply equally to both men and women. For relativists, however, the matter is not so simple, since they want to know who determines how equality is defined. If in a globalized, complex world, we want equality to conform to one uniform standard, then, who defines or which culture's social vision should prevail?[30]

The Onitsha social structure treats people as the bearers of rights and duties. Consequently, it raises problems for the underlying idea of equality as sameness, since the duties are not the same. The problem is, who defines the standard of sameness? If men's bodies and vision of the world constitute that standard, what happens when it encounters women's bodies and visions of the world? The local model exposes the male-privileging nature of the Western standard of equality, showing that such a standard shortchanges women. If a society can develop a dual-symmetrical structure of governance that gives women equal political voice and power, then there is something to be said for recognizing sex differences in our construal of equality. In the following chapter, I evaluate this notion of equality against the conventional notion of equality as sameness.

5

Structures of Equality

In Mono- and Dual-Sex Systems

But even those of us already defining ourselves as feminist thinkers and engaged in the process of critiquing traditional systems of ideas are still held back by unacknowledged restraints embedded deeply within our psyches.

. . .

So, for a long time, thinking women have refurbished the idea of systems created by men, engaging in a dialogue with the great male minds in their heads. . . . In accepting such dialogue, thinking woman stays far longer than is useful within the boundaries or the question-setting defined by the "great men." And just as long as she does, the source of new insight is closed to her.

—Gerda Lerner, *The Creation of Patriarchy* (1986)

As we saw in chapter 4, equality is shaped by the sociopolitical structure of the society within which is embedded. The prevailing notion of equality in liberal democratic societies of the West is informed by the values of the Western socio-political system in which biological sex is putatively ignored even though the society is fundamentally structured along male-privileging lines. By contrast, equality in the Onitsha sociopolitical system recognizes biological sex without affecting the social valuation of human worth. It rejects the view that sexual division of labor implies women's subjugation or patriarchy, and offers a conception of equality that rests on duty and responsibility. Concerned that the Western liberal notion of equality does not combat sexist oppression, and interested in discovering which sociopolitical system offers a better model of equality, this chapter examines the conception of equality in both systems.

Noting that true equality is attained when a society is ungendered, and power relations between women and men are equalized, I read A *Theory of Justice*. It was a brilliant book on the rational choice basis of equality, but it revealed nothing about the racialized, sexist reality of women of color in the United States and Canada that undermined true equality.[1] The liberal concept of equality in Rawls' authoritative book, and in the liberal democratic tradition of these two nations, fundamentally privileges middle- and upper-class white men. Not only are they the ones with the economic clout to avail themselves of the advantages of the system, but they are "by nature free and equal" to enjoy its privileges of whiteness and maleness. Contrariously, these are the very same features that stigmatize color, femaleness, and the economically disadvantaged, and that often make equality elusive.[2] The linchpin of Rawls' argument is that we can articulate an adequate conception of formal and substantive equality after individuals have entered into a social contract. They do so by imagining away their bodies, bodily states, status, class position, natural assets and abilities, intelligence, strength, conception of the good, rational plan of life, and other special features of their psychology.[3]

Feminists have challenged the legitimacy of this contract, arguing that the dematerialized self of the original position is really a privileged, materially solid, middle-class white male. It is not just that such men alone have the sociopolitical power to imagine away their body, but that they are able do so given that difference has never been a constitutive part of their self-image and identity. Zillah Eisenstein persuasively argues that the reason the male body is the normative body[4] is that it neither changes (since it is the paradigm) nor experiences the cyclical hormonal changes of menstruation, the protracted physical transformation associated with pregnancy, or even the meaning of being encased in a skin that differs from the norm. The normativity of the white male body situates white men at the center of the universe, allowing them to theorize about issues as if they shared everyone's paradigmatic position, and as if, like them, everyone were "the natural proprietor[s] of [their] own person[s] and capacities owing nothing to society for them."[5] Indeed, as Susan Moller Okin argued, this normativity obliterates the fact that the Rawlsian conceptualization of fairness, justice, and equality is based on the subjugation of women in the family. With white men as all-powerful beings in a white male-privileging world, theorists like Rawls could not see the systemic gender and racial inequalities that resulted in white men's advantage. Consequently, the universalization of a doctrine of equal rights from that standpoint severely falls short, as it occludes the social, political, legal, military, educational, and professional privileges of these men.

Contemporary Western feminists' critiques of the liberal sociopolitical system emphasize the fact that the language of equality inadequately addresses women's experiences in substantive ways. The main objective of this chapter, therefore, is to explicate a language and notion of equality that can secure women's right to equality outside of the current limitations of the liberal tradition. It does this, first, by highlighting the relation of equality to a specific theory of society, and then by explicating the nature of rights that arises therefrom. Because of the intricate relationship between equality and a societal vision, we cannot eradicate inequality without substantially altering the character of the society. Noting that both the docu-drama in the previous chapter and Catharine MacKinnon's work on sex difference have shown that gender inequality is tied to the way sex difference is conceptualized in sociopolitical systems, I consider that where sex difference is putatively ignored, as in Western societies, it has been smuggled back illicitly through the utilization of the male body as the normative paradigm. However, where it is publicly noted and the two sexes are equally valued, both bodies define and code societal values and set the parameters for an equitable treatment of the sexes. Drawing insight from this, I establish the ways in which the Western mono-sex system raises fundamental problems for equality. Next, I examine the dual-sex system to understand how it forces a society to deal more honestly with sex difference rather than ignoring it. The analysis of the two sociopolitical systems allows us to articulate a new theory of equality, after choosing the sociopolitical framework that best provides a more robust notion of equality. In the last section, I install the African dual-sex system in the United States to explore the possibility of creating a new model of society that offers a nonpatriarchal model of social relations.

PART 1: THE ONTOLOGICAL PROBLEM
OF LIBERAL EQUALITY

The Cultural Roots of Rights and Equality

In this contemporary age of globalization, the desire for a uniform theory of rights has often caused a section of the international community, consisting of Western-sponsored international agencies, nongovernmental organizations (NGOs), and globalists, to strive for a transcultural formulation of equality. This influential body, made up of what I call universalists, seeks to homogenize the world under one value scheme. By contrast, another section of the international community, made up of African, Asian, and Arab states, espouses a culturally oriented approach to issues. Being more tolerant of cultural diversity, they insist that *odi be ndi dilu fa* (that which is the custom of any society is rightfully theirs to preserve) and point out that *mba na su na onu na onu* (each society "speaks" in culturally inflected ways).[6] Although this culturalist stance appears to be relativistic, it is not necessarily so, because proponents of the position do not see cultures as irreducibly different. They agree that there are shared areas of overlap, but would insist too that salient differences persist between cultures, differences that are rooted in religion, community values, and family structures. In upholding uniformity, however, universalists seem to ignore that their proffered idea of rights and universality have cultural roots, even though they treat them as culturally neutral and absolute.[7] Although their urge for global collaboration leads them to act as if there is just one correct set of ethical standards applicable to all nations, irrespective of cultural differences, culturalists strive to resist moral absolutism and to assert their independence. Sometimes this prods them to react as if there can be no overlap in nations' value schemes.

Challenging the universalists' regime of absolutism, James C. Hsiung provides a reading of the culturally based nature of rights. He shows that the theory of rights and the transcultural model of equality sanctioned by the United Nations are inherently Western and reflect the cultural ideology of the West. In his view, the underlying theory of rights of liberal society with its autonomous adversarial individuals, contrasts sharply with the model of equality that emerges from the consensual family-centered structure of Confucian society. In the latter framework, individuals are socially interdependent, familial kin. The notion of equality and the corresponding theory of rights that emerges therefrom are not based on adversarial, autonomous individuals but on human beings who are dependent on their families (Hsiung 1985). Hsiung's point is that the attempted homogenization of the world under a uniform standard of equality erroneously universalizes the values and social vision of an autonomous individualism that embodies a fundamentally mistaken view of people. Yet, the universalist ignores the cultural specificity of the liberal democratic (Western) model of equality, its underlying ideology of adversarial individuals, its sacralization of the individual, and the competitive character of society it demands.

In their haste to set up a global uniform standard, proponents of the universalist approach often ignore the complex ways in which the prevailing liberal conception of equality presupposes a theory of society, gender relations, and idealized constructs of rights that are based on the Western political history and morality. In the process, they ignore the fact that these constructs may not necessarily cohere with other societies' notions of social good and their corollary regime of rights. The problem culturalists from other societies have with the liberal democratic model of equality is not simply that it is Western, but that it promotes a vision of society that is in conflict with their own. In the liberal vision, people are wholly individualistic, wholly self-sufficient, and, as C. B. Macpherson once put it, the "natural proprietors of their own persons and capacities owing nothing to society for them" (1962, 263). Macpherson explains that this doctrine of individualism "leans heavily on the justifying theory of the capitalist market," its market relations, and competitive individuals (1983, 45). Its theoretical tilt toward market and market values draws on and reinforces an abstract model of humanity known as "homo economicus," and it treats them as freely competing for scarce social goods. In his examination of the foundation of capitalist economy and its accompanying liberal society, Lester C. Thurow (1983) asserts that this view of homo sapiens is completely misguided. Whereas real societies are constituted by intelligent, contradictory, self- and other-motivated complex personalities, the liberal democratic principles promote a false image of society as a self-regulating marketplace, populated by self-directed, self-motivated beings whose rational purpose is "the pursuit of maximum material possessions" (Macpherson 1983, 54).

Responding to these critiques, theorists such as Rawls would agree that a more nuanced theory of society is desirable, but they would insist that the criticism does not undermine the universal applicability of their theory of rights and its underlying view of liberal equality. They would insist that whatever quirks there may be in their theory (including those disclosed by Okin) could be addressed so that liberal equality could apply to all nations and social situations. Of course, taking this stance implies rejecting the idea that their theoretical structure is culture bound, privileging individualism and valuing individual rights over group rights. They would also be tacitly prescribing a model of society as well as insisting on the epistemic priority of that model over other visions of society. Liberalism's approach to Hsiung's critique is to tinker with its model of equality, but is not clear is that the problem is amenable to an easy resolution. This is because the thrust of the critique goes beyond the mere identification of internal defects in the model to the vital area of differences and incompatibility of values.

The Problem of Cultural Incommensurability

First Nation legal theorist Aki-kwe/Mary Ellen Turpel cogently raises the problem of the incompatibility of values by contending that native communities in Canada do not share the market ontology, individualistic values, and corresponding vision of society underlying the liberal democratic state of Canada, which subscribes to the notion of liberal equality (1989, 149–57).[8] Most important for the objective of this chapter is Aki-kwe's argument that Aboriginal People do not have a conception of property and ownership on which the liberal conception of rights and equality can emerge. According to Aki-kwe, "there is no equivalent of 'right' . . . because there is no equivalent to the ownership of private property. The collective or communal basis of Aboriginal life does not really have a parallel to individual rights; they are incommensurable" (1989, 152). Attempts by the Canadian government to overcome this incommensurability by foisting its market-based worldview on them have resulted in the devastation of First Nation communities. The pertinent issue here is that the liberal model of equality and its social vision of market relations are not universally portable. They generate severe difficulties when they are extended to cultures that do not share that marketplace ideology of self-sufficiency and the principle of commodification. What the Aboriginal worldview is actually asserting is, first, that the cultural and ontological limits of the Canadian conception of right and liberal equality are much narrower and require a stricter set of conditions than the universality claims suggest; second, that this conception is based on a doctrine of individualism and a theory of society that violates the communal social vision and social logic of the Aboriginal culture; and (3) that the Canadian worldview cannot easily be reconciled with the conceptual scheme of the First Nation without the dissolution of the liberal equality principle and vision of society. The only way a resolution has been achieved is by domination, either by virtue of military power or by political clout.

Aki-kwe's critique shows quite clearly the substantive differences between the Aboriginal ethical scheme and the ethical scheme of the Canadian Charter of Rights. These differences are not just at the epistemic level but also at the ontological level, and include differences about life, society, and human nature that underlie the notion of equality in the Canadian Charter of Rights as well as differences that derive from the synergy of these ideas. When the concept of private property is absent, a synergy is created with other norms that devalue proprietal relations such as the commodification and ownership of land and the treatment of children as one's own. Insofar as the Aboriginal challenge is an ontological rather than an epistemological one, it cannot be addressed simply by modifying the idea of proprietal rights, reaffirming the ideal of individual rights, and massaging the principle of liberal equality. No viable solution can accommodate the salient differences between the Aboriginal view of reality and the liberal view. The incompatibility of the two ontological schemes is such that the only way the two can coexist in the same geographic space is for one to either totally dominate or completely marginalize the other. Whatever route is taken, liberalism cannot claim moral superiority, given that it lacks the grounds to do so.[9]

Hsiung provides a historical explanation for these flaws that forces us to take seriously the relationship between the theory of rights and the nature of the society. He contends that liberal equality emerged from the urge for freedom and the subsequent revolt of the European populace against the brutality of absolute monarchism.[10] Because this push for freedom has an adversarial basis, a model of equality arose to respond to the normative conflicts in the society. Equality was conceptualized to protect the right of the individual against an over-zealous state and an oppressive church. This resulted in the sacralization of the individual and the supremacy of the doctrine of individual rights in the modern nation state in Europe. The concept of individual rights was invented to counterbalance the invasive power and violence of the state. But because people are born into families rather than springing full-grown into the world, this historical account raises important questions: Why were people conceptualized simply as individuals? Why were they not conceptualized as members of families? And why were families of the time unable to offer protection to their members?

The explanation that Hsiung offers is that the emphasis on individuals was a result of European allegiance to a domineering church, which weakened and fragmented family bonds. This fragmentation left individuals vulnerable to the violent power of the state, and the atomized individuals turned to political associations outside of the family for protection and to gain personal autonomy. Within the political ideology of patriarchalism that developed, only males could gain autonomy and become individuals, and they could only do so when they became husbands or fathers.[11] The violence of the state and the vulnerable nature of atomized males laid the basis for the creation of the European modern state and civic society. This came about by means of a social contract theory in which autonomous (male) individuals came together to create a civic society in order to check the powers of an invasive state. The model of rights that emerged from this oppressive political condition differed in character from the one that emerged in the kinship-centered environment of Confucian China, which lacked similar antagonistic conditions. Hsiung describes the Eastern model of rights as groupist and consensual. Families rather than individuals were the autonomous groups that protected their members from the state and that checked the power of the state. Within this Confucian reality, families were the dominant political groups, and they shaped the character of their political society; hence, there was no need to develop a culture of radical individualism. Although the communal notion of equality emphasized group rights rather than individual rights, it did not imply that members of the family were not perceived as distinct and separate, nor that they lacked rights. They were individuals within the confines of the family, and they had rights that derived from their families, too.

The value of Hsiung's intervention is that it highlights the intimately close connection between the notion and character of equality and the history and structure of a society. In refusing to accept the rhetoric of universalists, he presents a different way of thinking about equality that destabilizes our assumptions about reality and society. He challenges us to take seriously in our theorization the links between social organization and the character of equality. The shortcoming of the Confucian model, however, is that, like the adversarial model of the West, it too construes only men as bearers of rights. As Aihwa Ong reveals, that framework did not uphold the rights of female members of the family as it did the rights of sons and fathers (2000, 1996). Consequently, the Confucian outlook created two layers of subordination for women: first, at the family level, and second, at the level of civic society.

The Problem of Race and Racism

Now that attention is legitimately focused on society, we can focus on another major moral problem that bedevils liberalism. Charles W. Mills contends that buried deep in the heart of American liberalism are racially configured pivotal concepts (1999, 1997). Any attempt to speak of freedom, right, and equality activates the person/subperson distinction on which the social goods and privileges of American liberalism are allocated. Although formally, all citizens within the state are individuals and constitutionally, all citizens have equal rights and are fundamentally the same, in reality, not all humans within the society are treated as individuals. In fact, Leon Higginbotham's (1996) work divulges the legal and judicial ways in which African Americans were denied their humanity. Because of the long, deep roots of the white supremacist worldview, the operative notion of equality in the United States post-Civil Rights society can still be invoked or retired at will to ensure that black people's access to resources are compromised and unequal. Much as we hate to admit it, concepts and sociopolitical frameworks are not value-neutral simply because theorists have stated them to be so. Mills's critique goes beneath the theoretical foundation of liberalism to expose its racist-loaded roots.

The issue at stake here is not the easily identifiable problem of misapplication of a sound model of liberal equality, but rather the problem raised by a defective theory of equality and an equally defective theory of society. The category of race in the United States does not merely cause misapplication of concepts, it causes their defect. It does this by structurally altering the constitutive nature of these concepts, theories, and political systems along white supremacist lines. Racism signals the existence of defective concepts that are relationally tied to a problematic theory of society that sustains them. Racist obstructions, therefore, emerge *naturally* to thwart the aspirations of those who are raced, while remaining invisible to those who are racially privileged. Because of its very constitution, the United States model of liberal equality valorizes whiteness and by this means exacerbates racial discrimination even as it publicly encourages social and political equality.[12]

Because racial imprinting occurs at a deep subterranean level, attempts to remedy racially based oppression must dismantle the structure.[13] The standard practice of extending a selected cluster of social goods to people of color does not solve the problem, because they are not and cannot be radical enough, given that they are mired in the miasma of white supremacist ideology. They leave untouched the deep roots of the problem because solutions are being conceptualized from a viewpoint that fails to appreciate the effects of racism on the self-image and perceptions of blacks and people of color in America. Although the egregiousness of racism is readily acknowledged and condemned, it continues to thrive because to uproot it completely would destroy the social privileges, economic interests, and social capital that have accrued and are still accruing to white Americans. The value of Hsiung's critique is that it shows how we have to re-envision the entire society from the ground up to achieve the necessary transformation. Without this, the promise of racial equality cannot be realized, since it would be constrained by the very sociopolitical structure within which liberal equality was created.

Everyday living or practical life in Canada and the United States yields a shifting alignment along race, class, and gender lines that does not radically alter the sociopolitical structure of the society. Contrary to liberalism's promise of objectivity and equal rights, people within these societies are neither all equal nor all the same. Although the Civil Rights Act in the United States and the Charter of Rights in Canada were introduced to remedy the problem of racial and gender oppression, racial and gender problems still exist today. Forty years after the passage of the Act and the Charter, there still exists a wide gulf between the attempts to remedy and the actual remedying of these problems. The slow progress of the Civil Rights Act has nothing to do with the complicated legacy of slavery but rather with the failure to systematically dismantle structures that reinforce white supremacy and impede the implementation of the compensatory provisions of the Civil Rights Act.

Mills locates the root of the Act's shortcoming in a white supremacist superstructure that provides the necessary criteria of identity, justification, and evaluation to every individual in the society. Without dismantling this superstructure, any attempt to redress racial inequality generates contradictions. The system's underlying, racially loaded notions of fairness, objectivity, and individualism thwart the compensatory provisions of the Civil Rights Act by representing them as antithetical to the promise of individualism and individual freedom that is at the heart of liberalism. The system also represents the Act as unfairly penalizing individual whites who bore no direct responsibility for the atrocities committed upon blacks and Native Americans. It exploits the idea that all Americans are equal and must have equal means of pursuing their objectives to undermine the redistribution of power intended by the Civil Rights Act.

White supremacy recasts racism as an individual matter rather than an institutional issue. It minimizes centuries-long history of exploitation of black labor and represents those exploited as having the same rights and constitutional protection as whites. It creates the illusion that systemic problems are superficial, and it represents blacks as unfairly being privileged. By avoiding structural scrutiny, the system deflects attention from how the present generation of white America, including white immigrants, are beneficiaries of an exploitative system that for over two and a half centuries represented blacks as properties. This subtle recasting of racism generates constitutional challenges against the compensatory provisions of the Civil Rights Act. The ameliorative strategies proposed to compensate the progeny of exploited blacks suddenly appear as reverse discrimination and as an illegitimate attempt to treat some Americans (i.e., blacks) as more special than others. The brilliance of the reverse discrimination argument is not simply that it works, or that it has been dismantling the provisions of the Civil Rights Act, but that it raises the bar so high that equality is not easily attainable by blacks. Thus, when legal challenges are mounted by proponents of the reverse discrimination idea on the grounds that all Americans are equal and that no one should be entitled to special privileges, they do a number of things. They cover up America's sordid history, they egregiously misread the provisions of the Civil Rights Act as demands for special privileges, and more importantly, they used the racially loaded concepts of liberalism to shore up white supremacy.

Like Hsiung, Mills's work on racial contract unsettles standard ways of thinking about racism, liberalism, and liberal equality. Often seduced by its ideals of fairness, objectivity, and justice, we fail to see that its central ideology of white supremacy takes black people's rights away at the moment liberalism seems to grant it. This is because the notion of individuals at the heart of the United States constitution stacks the odds against nonwhites, having defined the individual as white male. So while the state speaks of material progress for blacks and for everyone, a direct link is made between the abstract idea of the individual and the concrete manifestation of an individual as a white male. The linkage short-circuits the compensatory provision of the Civil Rights Act because the black recipient is not the same as the individual at the heart of the constitution. This forces the state to apportion out its largesse in ways that are consistent with the tenets of racialized liberalism and that do not undermine the material advancement and success of whites. Working under that impossible condition, the state then requires blacks to abide by the protocol of individualism and, as individuals, to prove in a court of law that they really have been discriminated against, that they satisfy the requirements of the Act if they are to obtain compensatory relief. The irony here is that blacks are forced to give individual accounts of the discriminatory experiences they had when they were not perceived or treated as individuals, and they lacked the necessary means to keep the sorts of individual records a liberal justice system requires. It is not surprising that most cannot take advantage of the Acts' compensatory packages, not only because they lack the resources to do so but also because the public pressures on individuals who have chosen to do so are daunting.[14] In effect, white America sets up matters to avoid collective responsibility for the centuries-long oppression of blacks by pitching the history of slavery as a matter of individual misfortune. This discourse of individuals and the ideology of individualism that sustains it enable white America to shift the blame of socio-economic failure onto the progeny of the enslaved, and then chastise them for their substantially lower quality of life.

The short summary of Mills's work on racial contract is that America's problems of equality cannot be corrected within a liberal framework and its conception of society. Constitutional amelioration fails to curb the validating concepts, structures, and institutions of the racialized American society or to limit the extension of equality to those who deviate from the normative standard of whiteness. It is the color bar that is buried deep within the Constitution's substructure that continues decades after the passage of the Civil Rights Act to reinforce racial inequality.[15] With rights continually circumscribed by a hyperbolized category of race, the possibility of blacks and people of color achieving equal treatment with whites remains slim, for the simple reason that the social paradigm still holds an essential part of who they are against them.

The Problem of Gender and Class

In *Feminism Unmodified*, Catharine MacKinnon lays out the gender limitations of the liberal notion of equality operative in the United States.[16] Similar to blacks and other people of color, white women are sometimes represented as asking for special privileges when they argue for their rights. MacKinnon reveals that gender inequality is the norm in America's "democratic" society and its legal justice system because of its white-male yardstick. As she puts it, "virtually every quality that distinguishes men from women is already affirmatively compensated" in the society:

> Men's physiology defines most sports, their needs define auto and health insurance coverage, their socially designed biographies define workplace expectations and successful career patterns, their perspectives and concerns define quality in scholarship, their experiences and obsessions define merit, their objectification of life defines art, their military service defines citizenship, their presence defines family, their inability to get along with each other—their wars and rulerships—defines history, their image defines god, and their genitals define sex. (1987, 36)

Even when constitutional provisions are introduced to correct the problem, little is achieved, because sex is treated as a matter of difference rather than of domination.

MacKinnon argues that the credibility problem women face when they insist on equality goes to the heart of the liberal system and its male-privileging vision of society. It exploits women's difference from men as a reason not to recognize the legitimacy of their difference.[17] Although she did not address the issue of race, the liberal system also exploits women of color's racial difference from white women to cast them as paradigmatically deviant. MacKinnon shows that according to the difference doctrine, "it is sex discrimination to give women what we need, because only women need it. It is not sex discrimination not to give women what they need because then only women will not get what they need" (1987, 36). This negation of the subjectivity and rights of women is an ingenious strategy that allows liberal democratic nations such as the United States and Canada to override women's rights. After an extensive study of the subject, Judy Fudge contends that those who uphold the doctrine of liberalism have to acknowledge that just because there is no white male beneficiary of needed legislation does not mean that there is no sex discrimination (1988). For if, indeed, equality implies that the only way white women and women of color can get things is to get them for white men, then this principle of equality is adding more to white men's advantage than dissolving their advantage over women.

The problem of liberal equality is that it pitches women's difference in ways that either minimize it or make it matter. When the latter is the case, it stigmatizes women, and when it minimizes their difference, it denies them equal treatment. Liberalism presents a society as race- and gender-neutral, although racist and sexist relations constitute it. When the category of race intersects with gender, additional layers of complication are added, and black women become double losers.[18] While the in-built male yardstick discriminates against both white and black women, the racial property of whiteness unites both white men and women. And although white women are privileged by their skin color, and black men can find common ground with white men on the basis of sex, black women have no such common ground with the normative individual of the yardstick. So, when symbolic advantages are won for women on gender or race grounds, the advantage goes principally to white women and black men, not to black women. Meanwhile, some white males are not above complaining that the gender equity provisions of the Civil Rights Act discriminate against them in that they give people of color and white women what they do not give to white men. This idea that white women and people of color are taking away from white men offers a window into the privileged male heart of white America. Ironically, white men's natural sense of entitlement and their natural presumption of privilege tell us that the standard of equality has long been skewed to their advantage, and that the society has always responded to their needs.

Before moving to articulate the nature of the society underlying liberalism, it is also worthwhile to note that there is a class dimension to the conception of equality in liberal democratic countries. The issue of class inequality comes from the capitalist market relations of the society. In the United States this inequity manifests in labor laws that privilege corporations and in the inadequate punishment for corporate malfeasance and white-collar crimes.[19] The judicial system's lenient treatment of rich criminals, fraudulent Wall Street analysts and accountants, and rapacious CEOs contrasts sharply with the harsh sentences that are handed down to lower-class burglars and robbers. This discrepancy in sentencing and in the punishment meted out to the rich and the poor tells us that the legal, political, and social rights of America's moneyed class routinely supersede those of the middle class and working poor. It also tells us that people are really neither "the same" nor equal before the law, since possession of capital buys political access and the best legal representation.

Liberal equality and its doctrine of individualism do not provide a particularly effective basis for equality because they value the moneyed class more than others. As Al Sharpton succinctly puts it, "all of us are created equal, but all of us don't end up equal" (2004, 15). The range of criticism from cultural, racial, and sexual positions exposes the structural flaws of liberalism. Liberal equality underwrites the doctrine of sex difference that reinforces the advantages and privileges of white men. Defenders of this notion of equality have tried to mute criticism by appealing to constitutional and legislative frameworks guaranteeing equality. But in recent times, critical race theorists and feminists have undercut the legitimacy of this appeal to formal and substantive equality on the grounds that it is ineffectual in delivering equality.[20] Despite attempts to present them as effective because of their cultural, racial, and gender neutrality, the ameliorative quality of these theories of equality is over-interpreted in ways that maintain the underlying inequities between males and females and between classes.

With all these critiques in mind, we need to determine if under a different sociopolitical structure, a notion of "individual" and "rights" would emerge that would foster a nonpatriarchal political ideology. However, before we undertake that task, we need to revisit the sociohistorical roots of liberalism to better understand its male-privileging contours and its preference for the patriarchal theory of state. This will enable us detect and avoid the pitfalls of the liberal view of equality and the society that defines it.

PART 2: LIBERALISM, PATRIARCHALISM, AND THE MONO-SEX SYSTEM

To conduct this examination, I shall use the term "mono- or single sex"[21] to characterize the sociopolitical system. The system's ideology is patriarchal, and the character of the system is mono-symmetrical. The mono-sex mode of identification allows us to draw attention to the single-sexed structure of society and to observe the sex that is privileged by it. Although liberalism emphasizes the individual, it would help to see that there is only one sex in the state and in the society, and that any divergence from this sex relegates one to a subordinate position. Centering the single-sex nature of the system allows us to think clearly about other possibilities to circumvent the inherent problem of gender inequality.

Feminists in the United States have correctly identified that both the state, the society, and the family are patriarchal entities. Their chosen strategy for solving the problem of gender inequality in these spheres is twofold. In the family, they call for wives to seek equality with husbands and to have equal weight in decision making and in running the family. Their rejection of the ideology of male dominance in this sphere attempts to underwrite a nonpatriarchal family model in which the two sexes, rather than just one sex, constitute the center of salience. In effect, feminists are advocating for a dual-sex mode of power sharing instead of the single- or mono-sex model of power distribution in the family. Interestingly, at the level of the state, they inexplicably refrained from pursuing a similar path. Instead, they are seeking integration in all the male spheres of government rather than working for a different model of governance by, for example, setting up a complementary chain of power distribution to secure their equality and autonomy. The question that is not sufficiently addressed is whether equality is possible in this male-privileging model. The short answer is no, given that women are forced to live by and meet the conditions of those formerly male spheres.

So what underwrote this push for integration? Feminists' reluctance to push for the creation of a distinct line of authority that parallels that of men seems to be the outcome of buying into the dream of "oneness" and "sameness" offered by liberalism. But we need to revisit the critical moments in the making of liberalism to determine if this course of action is worthwhile. From the seventeenth century onward to modern times, a single asymmetrical line of authority constituted the state in Britain, the United States, and Canada. A man was at the apex and other male actors were in key positions all the way down to the base of the political structure. Until the twentieth century, women did not exist within this political world. A woman could rule, as did Queen Elizabeth I, and Queen Victoria, and (Margaret Thatcher in the twentieth century), but they drew their power from their fathers, or from figures of authority in dominantly male political parties. One can say that their rule was masculinist in that they ruled in extremely masculine systems.

During the second half of the twentieth century, women began to appear in the political realm, but more as handmaidens than as architects of state policy. Up to the end of the twentieth century, the character of the political structures in the United States, Canada, and most European nations had changed somewhat visibly. But this still did not guarantee equal power to women. This remains true even under the reign of Margaret Thatcher. Although women increasingly moved into the public world of work and politics, men were still in all the dominant positions in government and the business world. The dominant ideology of the state remained very much masculine. Even after the ratification of the Civil Rights Act in the United States and the Charter of Rights in Canada, the legislative houses in both countries remained predominantly male. As a result of this male dominance in governance, the societies and political structures of their nations can be described as mono- or single sex. This is not because there were no members of the opposite sex to be found within its structures, but because humanity was ideologically defined in terms of the sex of the dominant group.

The sociopolitical ideology of the Western mono-sex system emerged from and derived its justification from a Christian cosmological scheme, a model that was viewed as made in heaven. Its legitimizing myths claim that the male creator of the universe had given men dominion over women. Eve, and by extension, all women, were subordinate to Adam and to all men. To subordinate their procreative powers to men, the legitimizing myths of the European and United States political state claimed that women had been created out of the rib of Adam, to keep him company. The seventeenth-century theoretician, Sir Robert Filmer, a contemporary of the empiricist philosopher John Locke and a defender of state patriarchalism, contended that God gave Adam the power to rule over the world and his wife. Upholding the political and familial subjugation of women, he stated that "her desires were to be subject to his" (Pateman 2001, 126). This divine grant of power to Adam was enshrined in the doctrine of coverture of English common law. It states:

> By marriage, the husband and wife are one person in law: that is, the very being, or legal existence of the woman is suspended during the marriage, or at least is incorporated and consolidated into that of the husband; under whose wing, protection, and cover, she performs everything: and is therefore called . . . a *feme-covert* . . . her husband [is called] her baron, or lord.[22]

Although this use of the Bible to justify women's domination by men rests on centuries of scholarly work in philosophy, theology, and political and legal fields, it was also used to establish the doctrine of the divine rights of kings (the idea that kings are God's representatives on the earth; Butler 2001, 59). But in the seventeenth century, the political paradigm of monarchical absolutism was under attack by the burgeoning merchant class and adult men who had been disenfranchised by the ideology of patriarchalism. Theorists such as John Locke championed the rejection of the doctrine of divine rights of kings. He attacked the idea that the natural ruler of civil society is the father—the king. In his rebuttal, Filmer argued that in the same way that the "natural" ruler of the family is the father, the king is the natural ruler or father of the society. Linking paternal power to political power, and vesting it in the king, Filmer cast kings and fathers as the dominant elements in the political and civic sphere of society and in the home. For him, all unmarried men are subject to the will of their fathers, and all fathers are subordinate to the king, who makes all the political decisions for his children. Women had no place in this sociopolitical scheme because "the man . . . is the nobler and principal agent in generation" (cited in Pateman 2001, 126).

According to Pateman, Filmer's doctrine of patriarchalism rests on an epistemological scheme in which unmarried men lacked relevance until they became fathers. However, women were trapped in a state that was "procreatively and politically irrelevant." They were perceived as "empty vessels for the excesses of men's sexual and procreative power" (2001, 127), and they had no autonomous sphere of existence within the moral universe. Philosophers like Locke attacked this doctrine of patriarchy not because it treated women as irrelevant, but because it stressed the dominance of the king over the landed gentry as well as the subjugation of sons to fathers (Pateman 2001, and Butler 2001). As constituted, patriarchalism and its political structure of monarchism robbed men (that is, adult sons) of their autonomy and political freedom, and so to liberate them, Locke articulated the concept of the individual. The concept was deployed to undermine both fathers' authority over sons and the legitimacy of the king's power over adult male citizens. First, Locke pried open the linkage between political power and paternal power by introducing a dichotomy between civil or political society and the family. He argued that although it may be true that fathers or patriarchs have dominance in the home, the granting of powers to Adam did not extend to the king in the political arena. The crux of Locke's argument is that because the private world of the family is distinctively different from the public world of the state, the derivation of power from the family to the political realm is untenable. Eventually, the passage of the English Bill of Rights of 1689 limited absolute monarchy.

As Hsiung has rightly pointed out, there is a one-to-one connection between the theory of rights and that theory of society. We see it in the provisions of the 1689 Bill of Rights that guarantees equality for men. Because the public-private dichotomy undercuts the derivation of political power from fathers to the king, a new theory of state and a new theory of rights and society were required. Locke presented the idea of a social contract that advanced the idea of autonomous individuals who are rational and capable of making decisions about morality and governance. In his *Essay Concerning Human Understanding*, he argued that such individuals were possible because reason is universal and not the exclusive preserve of the king. The thrust of his argument is that because individuals are rational and can make responsible decisions, they do not need a sovereign to do this for them.[23] They could come together to form a social contract and to contractually transfer to a public authority the duty to protect individual rights and freedoms. In the *Second Treatise of Government*, Locke used the social contract to secure the conceptual basis for the liberty of sons and the demise of absolute monarchalism. He did not secure the freedom of daughters and wives because it was not in the interests of men for this to occur. So despite his suggestion that women too are rational, Locke did not undermine the sexual contract upon which women's subjugation had occurred under patriarchalism (Butler 2001).

In the United States, Gerda Lerner contends that the "American Constitution embodied the patriarchal assumption, shared by the entire society, that women were not members of the polity" (Lerner 1998, 444). She draws on the 1776 letters between President John Adams and his wife Abigail to establish that the political culture of the time was patriarchal and to expose men's willful attempt to preserve women's subordinate status. In his view, granting women the code of laws Abigail sought would lead to social chaos. As he put it, "we know better than to repeal our Masculine systems" (Lerner 1998, 445). Carol Pateman and Mary Lyndon Shanley cogently argued that although the doctrine of patriarchalism of fathers was subsequently overthrown, it did not result in the overthrow of the masculine, male-privileging ethos that underpinned the Western political culture (Pateman and Shanley 1991). Patriarchal ethos, as defined by male dominance in civic society, continued unabated up until today. It sat well with the new population of liberated sons (the new individuals), who were primarily interested in protecting their new privileges at the expense of females. In very definite ways, this male-privileging tradition of Western political thought expanded and entrenched the character of women's subjugation. It rested on a conception of the "political" and of a society that excluded women as a group by structurally placing all men ahead of women.[24]

The theory of society and the theory of state that formed the bedrock of modern nation-states of liberal democratic dispensation promoted gender inequality. Even the civil society that emerged from the curtailment of the absolutist powers of the state and which contemporary African nongovernmental agencies (NGOs) are touting as a liberatory space is intrinsically a masculine male-privileging sphere. Although liberal democracy has been touted as the most progressive form of governance, this is true only if we underplay its mono-sex system of governance and the inherent gender inequality of its social contract theory. Whilst Locke and Rousseau cogently argued that individuals constituted the primary building blocks of society, they did not extend the notion of freedom and rights to women and enslaved peoples. Although women were not seen as individuals at the formative moments of the liberal political culture, proponents of that culture assumed that its benefits could be universalized to everyone. They imagined that its masculine bias and its mono-sex system could be separated from its advantages, and that it could equally promote the aspirations of the two sexes. But given the asymmetrical, male privileging political culture of liberalism, what makes feminists believe that opting for assimilation into that culture would result in a radically different state of affairs?[25]

MacKinnon questions how the advantages of liberal democracy can be separated from the advantages that accrue when masculinity and male privilege shape the constitutive structure of the system of governance. Feminist scholars in the West (and here I include women of color in the United States, Canada, and Western Europe) have convincingly argued that liberal democracy along with its theory of state and of society, is characterized by a domination ideology that represents as "natural" a condition in which only white men are rational beings and all others are irrational beings. If the embedded racial and sexual codes continue to recognize only white males as worthy, and all others (including white women and people of color) as legal minors,[26] how then can rationality, freedom, and equality be extended to women and people of color by the very system that denies their being? In the following discussion of liberal equality, I make no distinction between formal and substantive equality insofar as both are features of a mono-sex system.

The Mono-Sex System and Its Theory of Equality

The Western mono-sex system is designed around white men's interests, needs and expectations, and it institutionalized these as part of the state machinery. A cursory look at present-day upper echelons of political administration, the judiciary, the corporate world, and the military confirms this picture in the United States, Canada, and Western Europe.[27] Economic, political, judicial, and law-enforcement powers are concentrated in the hands of rich upper- and middle-class white men whose economic status as "heads of household" relationally quadrupled in importance. Unable to compete since the societal playing field is unfairly and unjustly tilted, white women have traditionally relied on marital ties, family connections, or male benefactors for support and survival.[28] Although the mono-sex nature of the system discriminates against women as a group, most women in the United States are averse to tying equality to groups rather than to individuals. Taken in by the promise of individual freedom, most take pride in the individualistic ethos of their society and point to it as the basis of America's global strength and well-being. But what is the nature of this individualistic model of equality to which most subscribe?

The American mono-sex political system propounds a theory of equality that putatively treats both women and men as equal. In actuality, it assigns a subordinate status to women. Mary Daly states in *Beyond God the Father* that the political implication of this subordinate status is that "women have had the power of naming stolen from us. We have not been free to use our own power to name ourselves, the world, or God" (1973, 8). The social and epistemological ramification of this lack of power to name one's reality is that it limits women's mental capacities which they should have developed along with their self-perceptions and their ability to understand their own social situations. For Daly, this devaluation of women's possibilities fosters an inadequate description of the world and presents it as an adequate one. It produces women whom Sheila Ruth describes as "male-identified" (1990, 81),[29] that is, women who are socialized to identify with men's power, security, omniscience, and might. Consequently, political alliance between women is undermined by the male-identified ideology that causes them to turn against one another. As Kate Millett explains, this "created a lively antagonism between whore and madam, and in the present between career woman and housewife" (1990, 498).

Gerda Lerner goes on to argue that the dominance of this male-identified ideology has "skewed the intellectual development of women as a group, since their major intellectual endeavor had to be to counteract the pervasive patriarchal assumptions of their inferiority and incompleteness as human beings" (1998, 446). Subjugation rather than equality for women is implicitly built into the mono-sex system. For white women, the situation is somewhat ameliorated by the white-male yardstick that rewards their subordinate status by ranking them as higher and superior to other racial groups in a world dominated by white men. Thus, racial superiority mitigates gender inequality, and the price of this advantage is tighter bonding with white male authority under the aegis of conjugality and patriarchy (Ruth 1990, 82–84).

As long as the polity remains dominantly mono-sex, white women find it difficult to transcend the imposition placed on their potentialities and power by the male-privileging aspects of the mono-sex system. Further complicating matters for gender equality is the public-private dichotomy that entrenches men's privilege. The emotional ties of marriage in the private sphere ameliorate the subjugation they experience in the public sector. Because the character of the sexual contract underpinning the liberal democratic theory of society is masked, white women do not easily see the ways the public sphere is connected to private, and their public disempowerment is made possible by the terms of their private life. As Okin revealed, the exploitative edge of that deep-seated sexual contract in the private sphere promotes inequality and injustice for women in the public domain. The emotional ties of nuclear-family living preserves the stability of the system by blocking the emergence of a woman-identified radical political consciousness required to challenge the patriarchal power of men. Attuned more to the benefits that have accrued to them from an imperfect system, white women are unwilling to jeopardize the familiar for an unfamiliar reality, regardless of the latter's promise of equality. There seems to be insufficient lack awareness that rejecting the traditional conception of marriage and the underlying sexual contract that comes with it need not imply the end of marriage *per se*. The rejection merely opens up the possibility of different forms of marital relationships, some of which need not be based on a sexual relationship. After all, social-contract theorists obtained the freedom of adult sons by rejecting the traditional model of father without nullifying the conception of fatherhood.

Unlike sons who sought to become part of the masculine ideology of the mono-sex system because of the advantage it conferred to them, feminists have to realize that gender equality cannot occur within a sociopolitical system that imposes subordination on women. They cannot obtain gender equality even if they devote their energies to removing the legal obstacles to gender equality. The only way women can become dominant in a mono-sex system is to overthrow the last vestiges of the patriarchal society and establish a matriarchal society, but that is equally not a desirable option. It is a mistake to replace one problematic system with another.

Because proponents of liberal equality are wedded to their social ideology, they may not realize the ways in which the constitutive ethos of mono-sex society is detrimental to the promise of equality. They cannot see that the mono-sex ethos helps conceal the fact that the individual represented as "the basic element of autonomy and sovereignty" is really a man whose rights are enforced by the very same system that undermines women's equality. Feminists would claim to know this fact, but this knowledge is not adequately reflected in their strategies. The sociopolitical structure within which relief is sought is the structural problem that continues to undermine the extension of rights to women in very complicated ways. Their subscription to the idea that everyone is equal and "similarly situated" undercuts any justification for change by obscuring the fact that the real problem is the social, economic, and political relations that make the female sex problematic. There is insufficient appreciation that in a context in which only one sex is privileged, the rights of the privileged group would override the material rights of the nonprivileged group. Legal remedies would not solve the problem for, as MacKinnon disclosed, a "law guaranteeing sex equality requires, in an unequal society, that before one can be equal legally, one must be equal socially" (MacKinnon 1989, 239). The fact of the matter is that women are not socially equal in a mono-sex system and the law cannot change that reality.

Of course, things can change but only if we restructure the society. Nothing says that this cannot be done and that women will forever remain subordinate to men. The very real hope of feminists is that change will come, but it is still a long way off. If feminists are really desirous of change they would have to take the radical step of withdrawing from the male-privileging system and push for another system that equally values the sexes as they did in the sphere of marriage (Fudge 1988: 485–54). The catch here is that the racialized, mono-sex system of the United States and Canada fosters the myth that this course of action is both unintelligible and impossible. The function of this myth is, of course, to deflect attention from, and prevent attacks against the asymmetrical line of power that ranks women as a group below men as a group. Its goal is to convince everyone through its discourse of individualism that the system is gender-neutral, and all self-affirming individuals are treated equally. To do this effectively, the mono-sex system uses doublespeak to conceal the vital fact that its assignment of rights and power is by route of groups.[30] The very problem of group inequality is difficult to overcome when the system impedes the effort of the subordinate group to see themselves as a group, and to name the nature of their oppression. The status quo is maintained when the subordinate group cannot form a politically conscious resistance group, because everything tells them that everyone is equal, and that individuals rather than groups must be the basis on which equality is defined and achieved. In an Orwellian sense, the mono-sex system asserts that all humans—both men and women—are equal, but in actuality men are "more equal" than others.

The shortcomings of liberal notions of equality have been extensively discussed by feminists who have noted that women in the United States and Canada are still struggling to achieve equality with their men (Fox-Genovese 1991, MacKinnon 1987, Fudge 1988). Structurally, women still end up at the lower rungs of the economic, political, and social ladder, even with the "guarantees" of the Civil Rights Acts and the Charter of Rights. There is growing recognition that a robust notion of equality is required to address the shortcomings of liberal equality (MacKinnon 2004; Koggels 1994, Fudge 1988), and that this requires changing the structures of the society. The shortcomings of liberalism make clear that it does not offer a viable way out of the morass. The question is, what can be done? How do we change a mono-sex society so that men cannot effectively dominate women? If, as has been argued so far, the sociopolitical system is a contributory factor to this state of affairs, then we need a context in which the two sexes are equally privileged. What sort of social reality would we have if instead of a single-sex system, we had a dual-sex system as occurs in families; one for women and the other for men? To ascertain whether or not this is a viable option, we now turn to a historical environment in which such a system was utilized in social organization.

PART 3: THE PRINCIPLE OF COMPLEMENTARITY AND THE DUAL-SEX SYSTEM

Some critics would assert that a dual-sex system is caught in the same difficulties as the mono-sex system, in that it defines a rigid gender system (Amadiume 1987a)[31] or precludes the possibility of a third gender (Herdt 1994).[32] These lines of critique may appear devastating, but they are, I believe, fundamentally misdirected, because the proposed dual-sex system does not arise from within the same conceptual parameters as the patriarchal, asymmetrical, mono-sex system within which these critiques are conceptualized and rooted.[33] The proposed dual-sex system does not presuppose gender or gender-based assumptions. Quite unlike the mono-sex system, the cultural scheme within which the dual-sex system is embedded publicly recognizes biological or sex differences, but unlike the former, it does not define those differences within a paradigm of domination and subordination. What gives the patriarchal mono-sex system its distinct sexual dimorphic characteristic is not its recognition of sexual differences, but the male-privileging principle of sex inequality that lies at the heart of the system. Underpinning the principle of equality is a rigid gender paradigm that maintains the inequality of the system. This ensures that within its value scheme, there can only be one dominant sex, which stands in a hierarchal relationship to the other sex.

We cannot overemphasize that although a dual-sex system recognizes sex differences, it rejects the paradigm of female subordination and inferiorization. Working within this system requires us to step completely outside of the mono-sex system *and to leave behind* its patriarchal values, asymmetrical mode of thought, and criteria of meaningfulness. When the dual-sex system is critiqued for its sexual dimorphism, it is a clear indication that the critique is coming from a gendered, mono-sex framework that is still translating biological sex differences using a value scheme that is both patriarchal and asymmetrical. In fact, one is invoking an inapplicable standard to understand and critique the dual-sex system. Stepping outside of the mono-sex system opens up a range of possibilities for other forms of social organization without erasing the differences between biological sexes. The challenge here is not to slide back to, and continually invoke the values of the old framework by confusing discussions about the sexes as proof of the continued reign of the patriarchal, asymmetrical, mono-sex system.

Once we step outside of the mono-sex scheme, the rigidity that Amadiume perceives between sex and gender dissipates. In fact, the entire language of gender dissolves! Why? Because we are no longer working within a paradigm that presupposes female subordination, and their assumptions are no longer being presumed.[34] In the nonpatriarchal world that emerges, we have the challenging task of rethinking all the normative ideas, assumptions, and values that derived from the mono-sex system. More importantly, we will have to understand the new ways in which sex is talked about without connoting gender. "Gender" carries epistemic and ontological connotations that do not belong to the social environment being discussed in which women are not structurally inferior to men.

A historical example of the dual-sex system is the Onitsha, Aboh, and Obamkpa political systems of the late eighteenth and nineteenth centuries.

They were structured along dual-symmetrical lines of male and female spheres of authority that Kamene Okonjo describes as dual-sex.[35] This bimodal structure operated trimodally.[36] Each sex had a modal sphere. The area of shared obligations and duties constitutes the third space of collaborative activity between the two groups. The mechanism for social and political action in the dual-sex system was the governing councils of the two spheres. Women and men (I am using these in the sense of adult females and males)[37] had their own autonomous governing councils to address the community needs and social obligations that arise in their spheres of influence, and to guide the nation's development.[38] In the trimodal state of action, the two councils and constituencies came together in conference sessions to address issues at a supra-national level.[39]

Prior to 1886, the Ikporo Onitsha (Council of Women of Onitsha) had the Omu as its leader. As was the case in Obamkpa and Aboh, the Onitsha political structure had two monarchs: the Obi (male) and the Omu (female). The Omu, along with her council of Otu Ogene, was the head of the female side of national administration. They complemented the role and duties of the male administrative side represented by the Obi and the Ndichie at the apex. With her council, the Otu Ogene, the Omu represented the interests of the nation of Onitsha in trade, economic matters, and certain political social and spiritual functions, as well as the interests of women.[40] The Obi did the same with the Ndichie in the male sphere of authority.

For most of the nineteenth century, the Obi was a politically weak, spiritual entity living in seclusion in his residence. His political powers were effectively circumscribed by the spiritual dimension of the office and the political powers of Ndichie. Once the Obi was installed, he emerged in public once a year, during his annual rededication ceremony.[41] By contrast, the Omu was a public figure, having attained her position by the power of industry, entrepreneurial skill, or spiritual force.[42] She ruled publicly and was not in seclusion, as was the Obi. It is important to state that no conjugal or familial relationship existed between the Omu (the community's maternal principle) and the Obi (the community's paternal principle). They both embodied spiritual powers. Each lived in his or her own palace, each underwent similar purification rites prior to installation,[43] each performed annual rededication ceremonies, and each possessed the Onitsha insignia of royalty. Both were nonautocratic rulers, since the administrative infrastructure of checks and balances did not support despotism. Each was responsible for maintaining social harmony in his or her specific spheres of authority and in the society at large.

Structurally, this political structure of sex differentiation is one in which women's and men's interests were institutionalized by the state so that the heads of the two administrative structures complemented rather than duplicated each other's powers and privileges.[44] They were not in an adversarial relationship. Predominantly, each council was responsible for the governance and administration of members of the respective sex.[45] Because the political structure defined an *inter*dependent relationship, they functioned in a complex weave to create a tight social fabric. Omu and Ikporo Onitsha had jurisdiction over matters of trade, and the men (adult young unmarried men) had the task of keeping the trade routes open. In riverine towns such as Aboh, the Omu played a vital part in military campaigns. Her canoe with its ritual mat, believed to make fighters invisible, led the men to battle. So although men were in charge of military campaigns, women were in charge of the rituals required to mobilize the deities and divinities as well as to fortify the moral resolve of fighters so that a favorable outcome could be achieved.[46] Both sexes had agricultural responsibilities: men planted and produced yams, the labor-intensive staple crops that sustain the community for half the year; and women produced vegetables, corn, and cocoyams, the staple food that sustain the family during the second half of the year when the yams ran out. The adjudication of disputes occurred in both the men's and women's spheres, and sometimes jointly. Lastly, both played key roles in spiritual matters, propitiating the nation's deities, purifying homes, and ensuring that the community maintained spiritual balance.

Because roles, responsibilities, and obligations fell equally under female and male spheres of influence, the administration worked in a complementary manner. Women's sphere of activities complemented that of the men, and vice versa. The notion of complementarity invoked here in no way parallels the notion advocated by conservative American women in the mono-sex system. In the latter system, gender domination and inferiorization of women are the norm, and so complementarity emphasizes gender inequalities that have arisen as part of the patriarchal division of labor. This is an entirely different framework from the dual-sex system. Thus, to state that the Omu and Ikporo Onitsha complemented the Obi and Iregwu (the rank and file of adult men) is not to imply that Ikporo Onitsha provided the "feminine," "caring," emotional side of the divide.

Additionally, sexual and reproductive capacities did not translate into a source of systemic disadvantage, as they did in the mono-sex system; rather they were loci of strength and advantage. Political interaction between the sexes was mediated by a conscious awareness of Iregwu and Ikporo Onitsha's respective social roles and responsibilities. Care was valued by both women and men as the hallmark of good family (lineage) and conjugal relations. It was also a part of their social roles. Women did not value care simply because they were women. They did so because they were mothers, sisters, daughters, wives, friends, good trading partners and so on. Men, too, valued care for similar reasons. The social ideology of the dual-sex system did not require women's entire existence to revolve around the care of children and others. Men were also required to be caring. Older children cared for younger children; parents, grandparents, and older lineage members cared for younger ones. Industriousness, assertiveness, and independence were valued attributes for all adult members of the society, given the duties they performed as part of their administrative roles. No one sex had a monopoly on these and other psychological attributes. Both men and women could be assertive, cowardly, fearless, bold, patient, and shrewd. Both women and men needed political acumen, foresight, and assertiveness to survive in the sociopolitical conditions of the times and to perform their tasks. Oratorical skills and intellectual acumen defined leadership and were possessed by leaders in either group.

Within the dual-sex system, the roles, responsibilities, and obligations of adult women did not pattern the feminine traits of the mono-sex system. Behavioral traits were not gendered. Like community fathers, community mothers or Ikporo Onitsha displayed traits and attitudes that appeared on both sides of the divide in the mono-sex system. They applied the relevant trait to the job at hand. They were shrewd, logical, and rational in matters of trade. They had a good head for calculation, and ably performed this task efficiently. They were eloquent speakers in the political arena and possessed moral integrity. Because roles and responsibilities were primarily social, anyone could perform the task should the need arise. Ikporo Onitsha (that is, married or divorced daughters, widows, and some wives) could plant yams, and community fathers (that is, married or divorced sons and widowers) could grow vegetables and cocoyam. Community fathers could trade, and Ikporo Onitsha could participate in keeping the trade routes open.

The social nature of familial roles and the institution of marriage made it possible for a female to be either a wife or a husband. As was explained in chapter 1, some daughters did not marry, some married and later divorced, and some became widows. These three sets of daughters could enter into *idigbe* relationships with male lovers, or they could marry wives, who bore children for them. Furthermore, as Amadiume indicated, in the absence of any male within the lineage or conjugal unit, the most senior daughter would end her marriage and assume the headship of the male side of the line, even as she remained the head of the female line. These kinds of headships occurred when a family sought to thwart the rotation of seniority rights out of their subfamily to a junior one, which would have extinguished their rights. However, contrary to Amadiume's claims, this has nothing to do with a daughter becoming male, as that suggests that membership in and valuation by a family is dependent on being male.

The basis for the national division of duties along lines of sex is administrative convenience, and was not gender-based. For this reason, the division did not preclude members of the opposite sex from participating in them. (The fact that Ikporo Onitsha was in charge of trade did not mean that men were barred men from trading in the market or they could not take on that duty).

The goal of the division was to allocate administrative spheres of control to both sexes so that they could function *as partners* in the management of the community at large. Under the dual/symmetrical arrangement, duties were conceptualized in ways that gave both sexes comparable measures of autonomy and independence. Because rights accrue to groups rather than to individuals, the political effect of this complementary principle is that both women and men had political significance and were valued, and that their worth was incorporated into the conception of ideals and attributes. None dominated the other. Acting collaboratively on national matters,[47] the heads of the two modal spheres and their councils formulated the nation's political stance on issues. This clearly defined, interdependent structure ensured that each sex group was viewed as a vital cog in the sociopolitical wheel. The consultative process of political rule also ensured that both the viewpoints of Ikporo Onitsha and Iregwu were well represented in decisions that affected the whole community.[48] No decision that affected the lives of women, their administrative area of control, or their status was made without the knowledge and agreement of the Women's Council.

Decision-making proceeded up and down and between the chains in a consultative manner until a satisfactory decision was reached.[49] Suggestions, ideas, and advice were informally elicited from the other side and from different sectors of the community. Heated debates and conflict might arise, but these were dealt with in a nonadversarial manner until a fair and judicious resolution that maintained group cohesion was obtained. It did not mean that consensus was arrived at all the time. It proved elusive on occasions, and sometimes it was not necessary. On the occasions when consensus proved elusive, those who deeply felt that their perspectives were sidelined could overturn the decisions, indicating the non-autocratic nature of policies. Sometimes there were serious consequences to these actions. These resulted in major sociopolitical disruptions that split the community into opposing camps. Nevertheless, after a period of time, peace was eventually restored.

At the national level, the interests of the entire community converged. Because the governing councils were a central unifying organization, they promoted pan-community values. They also built cohesion among Ikporo Onitsha and Iregwu and promoted a community-centered consciousness. The strength of the dual-sex system was that no one sex had a monopoly of power, authority, and privilege. Both sexes had blocks of power and authority, which ensured that women's presence and roles in community governance were not taken for granted. Both men and women were able to protect their collective rights and could respect what each brought to community administration and development. Denial of the other's rights and refusal to respect them led to disruptive social challenges and social withdrawals. Ikporo Onitsha exercised power in the same way that Iregwu did. Power and authority were built into social and political roles, allowing occupants of those positions to wield influence. Insofar as women and men occupied positions of authority, these attributes were perceived as human social attributes. The point here is that the societal conception of power captured the fact that Ikporo Onitsha exercised power and authority.[50]

The two parallel administrative structures and their trimodal space of consensus building and sociopolitical action also radiated downward through the nine village wards to the family level. As Hsiung described about the Confucian model of equality, the Onitsha model preserved the integrity and autonomy of the family, which in turn, acted as the bulwark against the state. But unlike the Confucian model, the Onitsha model did not frame the identity as one in which daughters were subordinate, and their interests were best represented by men. Even today, the head of the female line is the overall *isi ada* (the ward's head daughter) and on the male line is the overall *diokpa* or *di okpala* (the ward's head son). The pattern repeated downwards at the lineage and family level, with the *isi ada* and *diokpa* at the head of each line. Although the interests of the lineage daughters converge with those of the lineage sons, the parallel line of authority still exists. Both maintain their autonomy but they also come together for joint family meetings. However, the position of *inyemedi* (or lineage wives) is a separate matter. They are not part of the two parallel lines that terminate at the family level because, as wives, they are really not part of the marital family. Even though the interests of the two family groups converge in certain areas, *inyemedi* do not participate in *umuada* meetings, since there are consanguineal matters of interest to *umuada* that *inyemedi* do not share. Equally, there are conjugal matters of importance to *inyemedi* that are of no interest to *umuada*.[51] So what character of equality emerges from this sociopolitical system?

The Dual-Sex System and Its Conception of Equality

The theory of a dual-sex system society gives rise to a theory of rights that does not involve the extraction of entitlements and the assertion of rights against the state. Individuals are not pitted against the state, and the state is not seen as an adversarial entity. In nineteenth-century Onitsha, the state was a natural progression and extension of the lineage structure, which assimilated immigrants into the polity. The state reflected cultural values, notions, and philosophies about family, society, and the relation of various members of the family to the state. The state was characterized by loyalty to the citizenry, utilization of the principle of moral suasion, the integrity of selected leaders and spokespeople, and the participation of both men and women in the formulation of laws, rules, and norms that governed the wards. Because the political structure was non absolutist, there was nothing for freeborns to fear from the state, for each person was or reflected the state. One of the male monarch's roles was to take on the sins of the community and to spiritually purify the community; and the female monarch's role was to nurture and grow the community through ensuring the economic well-being of the town. That of Ndichie was to head the political and military units that made up the wards, and the Otu Ogene and Ikporo Onitsha assumed the maternal status as well as economic and spiritual responsibility of the entire community. In these roles, Ikporo Onitsha possessed political, judicial, and spiritual powers that enabled it to be a dominant political force in Onitsha.

Equality was defined on the basis of membership in a specific sex group. At its most basic level, the concept that *Nwa onye Onitsha adaro aka ibe ya* (literally, no Onitsha person is greater than another) encapsulated the idea that adult men and women are equal, and inherent in that idea is that this prerogative is accorded to all adult citizens. This basic notion of equality supports and empowers any adult to speak in any public forum, either in *ime obi* (the male monarch's meeting chamber), in the Omu's palace, at *ilo mgheleme* (Ikporo Onitsha's public meeting ground), in Ndichie's and Otu Ogene's reception chambers, or at family meeting houses. This notion of equality takes precedence over all political positions, and in this way, it safeguards the political, judicial, legal, and social right of anyone to be heard or to initiate action regardless of political status, and to participate in political deliberations. At a meta-level of distribution of responsibilities, equality is also attached to roles and duties, ensuring that the tasks of both biological sex groups are comparable and equal, even though they may be different. Equality is not accorded to individuals simply because they are individuals, but because they are bearers of rights that derive from social, political, and religious roles and offices. They have duties to perform, whatever they may be. Because of this link between equality and duties, equality can be exercised and enforced without interference from others. In a very basic sense, this notion of equality is attached to personhood and is secured by citizenship duties and rights. For example, while a stranger would have to obtain permission to assert his or her rights (given that he or she has no social duty), an indigene merely enforces his or her equality rights or duties by invoking them.

This notion of equality informs the political administration that was described in the last section. The idea that "no Onitsha person is greater than another" captures the properties of individuality and sameness that give meaning to equality. But this notion of "the individual" and "sameness" is different from one that exists in the mono-sex system. It does not presuppose that an individual is male or female, it does not see individuals as both socially independent and bearers of inalienable rights, it does not treat rights as disconnected from duty, and it does not construe individuals as self-sufficient, self-reliant, and self-realizing. It presumes and treats the individual as a socially dependent being, in interdependent relationship with others. The language reflects this gender neutrality by treating everyone as a human being and not marking the sex. This dual-sex conceptual scheme gives both sexes the same level of significance while accommodating their biological differences. At the substantive level, however, equality in terms of social duties and rights derives from the powers that accrue to groups as a result of their social responsibilities. Although groups are the primary political focus, it is crucial to note that individuals do not cease to exist.

Politically, each modal group is composed of individuals who are in varying kinds of relationships and subgroupings. These subgroupings provide other meaningful reference frames for members to live by, and for mutual support. It is not true that the notion of individuality is foreign to Onitsha culture, simply because emphasis is given to group relationships. The notion of individuality is very much in existence and is reinforced by the strength of the group.

People's right to equality is secured at the level of their biological group rather than as autonomous individuals. The extension of equality to groups rather than to undifferentiated individuals meant that no one group or sex was privileged or devalued. Sex difference led to equitable division of roles and responsibilities as a complement of the other, each group had community-wide duties and responsibilities that contributed to the well-being of the society and to the maintenance of the group's identity. Although these duties vary in type, they were weighted the same. The groups could periodically renegotiate their duties and the meaning of the roles, but once the renegotiations were complete, the duties socially interlock. For example, keeping the market routes open (a task that falls under the jurisdiction of men—Ndichie and Iregwu) is crucial to women, who are the principal agents of trade (and under whose watch falls both local and long-distance trade). If men fail to live up to their responsibilities, trade and commerce, the duties of Ikporo women, would suffer, and so would the quality of life of the community.

The dual-sex system values both sexes for the skills they bring to building community and shaping the culture. Again, this does not imply that the notion of individuality is nonexistent in the culture. Rather individuals are conceptualized as relationally tied to social groups. The underlying model of equality recognizes difference but treats and values the sexes as equal.[52] Both the adult-male group and the adult-female group were equal in relation to their service to the nation, and their contribution to the society's well being. Though this construal of equality operates at the group level rather than at the individual level, it nevertheless possessed the same traits valued at the individual level: autonomy, sameness, and difference.

The centrality of the sameness standard generates sex inequality in the mono-sex system, but not in the dual-sex system. In the mono-sex system, the idea puts women in the impossible position of asserting their difference from men even as they insist on similarity with them. Because women are compared to men under the similarity standard yet are judged by their distance from them under the difference standard (MacKinnon 1987, 34), Fox-Genovese wonders, "How can women, if they are different, ever hope to be equal? How can . . . they aspire to be equal, [if they] continue to insist that they are fundamentally different?" (Fox-Genovese 1991, 244). The dual-sex system resolves this problem by factoring difference into the system at the foundational level and tying equality to groups, and accepting that women and men can be equal but different. The conception of equality as comparable worth allows this to happen. It ensures, on the one hand, that both groups share vital similarities—administrative skills, psychological attributes, and temperament—that the dual-sex system positively values. The system positively values the fact that men and women share important physiological differences and captures this in what Pateman calls the "social conception of individuality" (Pateman 1987, 122). This conception recognizes that women and men are biologically differentiated but not unequal. In building sociopolitical cohesion, the physiological characteristics of individuals were politically unimportant in defining the ground rules for social and political respect. Respect was earned by the manner in which duties were tackled. Tying equality to the ideal of comparable worth vis-à-vis the duties performed by both groups meant that similar values were assigned to each group's contribution to society. This basis of value assignment extends to each individual member of the group the benefits, properties, and traits achieved at the group level.

Individual members of the two sex groups may occupy subordinate social roles at different moments of their lives, but the subordination is attached to the role, not to bodies. For example, women who are wives would be in a subordinate relationship to members of their marital family, including their children. But this is true only when they are in or playing the role of a wife. Role-playing or being in specific roles does not negate their other superordinate identities, such as their roles as mothers, their structurally dominant role of husband to the wives in their natal family, and their pan-national status as members of Ikporo Onitsha. Given that subordination is relationally tied to roles rather than to bodies or person, when one is no longer in that role (i.e., playing the role) one is no longer subordinate. This is how the fluidity of identities that Amadiume erroneously explained by reference to gender occur. Gender cannot explain this fluidity because it is locked in a rigid underlying framework of sex inequality. The fluidity of identities is a consequence of attaching rights and duties to roles. Given the multiplicity of social roles people have to play at any given time, no one is permanently locked into any one role, as occurs in the mono-sex system. The only enduring identity is the one people receive at birth as either a daughter or son of someone. Because equality is displaced from bodies to tasks and duties, individual women and men have the same rights, not because they are individually ranked, but because their duties, though different, are socially comparable at the group level. In a context where power and rights are distributed on the basis of duties, mutual respect develops between the sexes if these duties are performed in a satisfactory way. Women's and men's views are deemed critical, both because of the work they do and the special insights they bring to the running of the society. In this nurturing environment, both are their own persons, and women are unaccustomed to men's making decisions *for* them. In political matters, each group has a strong political voice, and it is as groups that people make and enforce political decisions. The dual-sex system incorporates the concept of individuals and embodies the trait of autonomy. In the following section, we will address the way this concept and its defining features differ from those of the mono-sex system by examining the problems and weaknesses of the mono-sex system's notion of individualism.

PART 4: THE PROBLEM OF MONO-SEX INDIVIDUALISM

A critical review of the mono-sex system reveals that the notion of the individual offers the false hope that gender equality is possible. Anyone can be an individual and equal to another, even though they are not. At the abstract level, "the individual [is] the repository of all legitimate rights and . . . the basic element of sovereignty" (Fox-Genovese 1991, 121). Theoretically, the doctrine of individualism envisions a society that is "composed of impersonal and interchangeable units of sovereignty with a model of human beings as rational, accountable and autonomous" (1991, 123). It presents people as distinct individuals isolated from each other with a sense of self as independent of family and community relationships, and as not constituted by social relations. Borrowing Frantz Fanon's description, this picture of individual is one in which "each person shuts himself up in his own subjectivity" (1966, 47). This mono-sex view of individuals is seductively powerful, given that the individual is presented as an objective and impersonal category. Theorists believe that it can easily be extended to include women, who would then benefit from it politically. This has led some feminist scholars to redefine the concept so that "women have the same claims as men on the role of individual" (Fox-Genovese 1991, 119). But Fox-Genovese notes that "the goal of 'the rights of women' has revealed itself as deceptive. Rights have not granted women equality with men, much less obliterated centuries of discrimination against women" (1991, 229). Colleen Sheppard argues too that "equality rights were acknowledged only to the extent that they left the *status quo* intact (1991, 415, her emphasis).

Lorraine Code has critiqued the idea of the autonomous man that redefines individualism—self-sufficient, independent, self-reliant, and self realizing. She views this idea as misguided because it prods a society to value independence and to undervalue relations of interdependence (trust, friendship, loyalty, and responsibility). It also construes the individual as atomistic bearer of rights, whose autonomy is compromised by social relations that stress cooperation and interdependence. Catorina Mackenzie and Natalie Stoljar acknowledge that this conception of atomistic subjectivity and its central idea of "hyperbolized autonomy" (Code 1991) that defines the autonomous man is the problem at the heart of individualism. Their work tries to repair the problem, contending that this defective conception of autonomy and autonomous agents does not render the basic idea of autonomy untenable. Rather it requires a replacement of the atomistic subjectivity trait with a relational view of subjectivity that understands that people are in relation with others and only become persons within this matrix of relationships. For Mackenzie and Stoljar, the relational view of subjectivity does not undermine philosophical accounts of autonomy or provide any compelling reason for rejecting it (2000, 8).

Under relational autonomy or a relational view of individualism, individuals' capacities are constitutively social and relational (Friedman 2000 and Barclay 2000). Social institutions, practices, relationships, and norms that affect agents' freedom can impede hyperbolized autonomy by limiting the range of available options, but this will be totally consistent with a relations view of autonomy. If this impact on relational autonomy occurs in an oppressive social context, such as a mono-sex system, autonomy would be antithetical to women's interests. Such a situation would explain why Fox-Genovese argued that socially imposed restrictions ultimately curtail women's freedom and autonomy. However, according to Friedman, a definition of autonomy in which social constraints limit women's autonomy is misguided, because autonomy *per se* is not antithetical to women's interests. In fact, for her, autonomy has the capacity to disrupt oppressive social relationships, not reinforce them. Linda Barclay provides support for this view by contending that although we cannot be autonomous in the absence of social relationships we can reject some social relationships, and choose new ones. For her, this element of choice proves that we are not so strongly constituted by social relations and shared values that we cannot change them. Susan Babbitt disagrees. The problem that she rightly identifies is that we cannot assume that marginalized and disempowered people living within the context of a coercive ideology can understand what is in their own true interest. They may not be able to reject problematic relations or choose new ones, even if the premise is that everyone has the right to choose freely and can benefit from these advantages (Babbitt 1996, 35). The disempowered ideology fostered by coercive structures limits the conceptual horizon and narrows the range of options for the disempowered and dispossessed.

This leads us back to where we were before, which is that voluntary rational choice and relational autonomy within an oppressive context would not get women anywhere. Fox-Genovese would argue that Barclay and Friedman do not take seriously enough the ways in which the doctrine of individualism is "explicitly fashioned by and for men" (1991, 119), and the ways in which that fashioning impedes their assumptions. Her point would be that they are too focused on the idea of the individual and not enough on the social, where the constraining structures lie. A critical part of this problem is that males who are privileged by the mono-sex system and who have developed a strong sense of group belonging are pitted against women who have not had the institutional space to develop a strong sense of self and collectivity. The main problem is that the inherent sexual inequality of the mono-sex system militates against gender equality.

Providing judicial support for Fox-Genovese's view, MacKinnon and Fudge present an array of judicial studies that detail the ways in which judicial interpretations are based on oppressive social norms to curtail the autonomy and freedom of women even after such rights are protected by the Charter or Bill of Rights. This routinely happens because socially situated justices are reluctant to recognize that the real justification for protective legislation to advance women's equality and autonomy is not the fact that they are female, but rather that social and economic relations have been used to curtail their rights.[53] Fudge contends that "the abstract and universal form of legal rights within liberalism has not proven to be amenable to the concrete, contextualized analysis which is a necessary first step for ameliorating women's systemic social subordination" (1988, 551). To argue as Friedman and Barclay have done, places the onus on the individual and provides justification for the argument that protective legislation is unnecessary. For if women have autonomy, which means they have rights, liberty, and voluntaristic contractual relations, then legislation that redistributes power is not required. Fudge points out that the root of the difficulty in incorporating women's difference into the notion of the individual is that it conceals a masculine ethos of male dominance. "Subjects appear free and equal before the law yet this formal legal equality and freedom is enabled in a social context of overarching inequality" (Fudge 1988, 534). As a result

> the very way in which rights are framed in constitutional documents such as the Canadian Charter of Rights poses another barrier. These rights are framed in abstract and general language, and although the equality provisions contained in the Charter are amenable to progressive interpretations offered by feminists, as the decisions issued to date clearly demonstrate they are equally amenable to formal and narrow interpretations which are antithetical to feminist struggles. (Fudge 1988, 533)

Unlike Friedman and Barclay, the issue for Fox-Genovese, MacKinnon, and Fudge is not whether women *can* have autonomy or *can* exercise their autonomy but whether the very real constraints in the society allows them to transcend the society's patriarchal structure. The issue is not whether women can reconstitute some of their personal relationships of love, friendship, and marriage along positive lines but whether they can remove the socially entrenched racial and gender discriminatory structure that are impediments to equality.

Whereas Barclay's and Friedman's reforms revolve within the boundaries of liberalism, MacKinnon and Fox-Genovese are challenging the very boundaries of liberalism that are responsible for gender inequality. Although, Mackenzie's, Stoljar's, Barclay's, and Friedman's reformulation of autonomy is pitched at the individual level, it is still epistemologically useful. The problem is not with their reformulations but with the sociopolitical structures within which their concept of autonomy is embedded. Because the mono-sex system within which the concept of autonomy and the doctrine of individualism are located is fundamentally a male-privileging system, it will reproduce the sorts of problem that Fox-Genovese, MacKinnon, and Fudge are highlighting. The only way to avoid the latter problem is to transfer the relational conception of autonomy and its notion of the individual to a sociopolitical system such as the dual-sex system that fundamentally treats both men and women as equal. Properly conceptualized, autonomy (as relational) and individualism are not problematic concepts, as Mackenzie and Stoljar indicated. They would function properly when situated in a system that treats the equality of men and women as a fundamental characteristic of its structure and that defines rights only after women and men are socially situated as equal to each other. This definition of autonomy and individualism overlaps neatly with that of the dual-sex system.

Fox-Genovese is correct to assert that "a feminist critique of individualism must simultaneously engage the strength and weaknesses of our [Western] tradition." That engagement, however, must leave us free to think outside of the box. Having correctly determined that the basis of this problem lies in feminists' difficulty in "reimagining the collectivity—society as a whole—in such a way as to take account of women's legitimate needs" (1991, 230), Fox-Genovese undermines her own insight by sliding back to restore a tradition that she should have let lie. She states: "To jettison them now means to forego the possibility of coming to terms with our history and perhaps the possibility of shaping our future as well" (1991, 243). But to come to terms with this history is to face it squarely, acknowledge its deficiencies, and then move beyond it. We cannot allow sentiments to trap us within it, given that, as Gerda Lerner reminds us, for millennia, for far longer than any other structured group in society, women "have lived in a condition of trained ignorance, alienated from their own collective experience through the denial of the existence of

Women's History. . . . [They] have . . . been forced to prove to themselves and to others their capacity for full humanity and their capacity for abstract thought" (1998, 446). Thus, Fox-Genovese was wrong to veer from the path to which her argument led. The questions she should have asked were: Why should there be just a male head and a male dominant line of power? Why should only one sex be privileged in the polity, and what is the legitimacy for an asymmetrical distribution of power and resources? To grasp the ideological nature of the mono-sex system is to see that the social collective can be reimagined differently, perhaps through the dual-sex frame. After all, there is nothing fixed and immutable about the mono-sex asymmetrical system. It could be radically restructured to create parallel structures: one for males and the other for females with a trimodal space of action.

It is important to stress that this structure will differ from the separate-but-equal policy of white supremacists in the post-Reconstruction era United States, when blacks were drained of resources and kept in perpetual penury. It will also differ from the radical feminist separatist stance that rejects collaboration with men, as it will differ from the conservative women's groups that define the subordinate role of women as "complementary" to the superordinate roles of men. Carol Gilligan (1982) had raised the possibility of a different value system. But her system is based on the attributes that patriarchal ideology assigned to women. Insofar as the ideology is the obverse side of the current male-privileging scheme, it has no emancipatory potential, and as MacKinnon observes, it is an insult to women's possibilities.

The critical point of all these critiques is not that the mono-sex system offers false hope of gender equality through peddling a gender-loaded conception of the individual as gender-neutral, but that a redefined notion of autonomy and individualism is consistent with the dual-sex system and would promote self-assured, independent women. We need to work for structural change and a social structure that positively values women. We need to see too that to recognize difference is not to open the door to inequality, as was the case during segregation in the United States, but to recognize the ways in which the ideology of "all people" promotes inequality.

PART 5: THE DUAL-SEX SYSTEM IN THE UNITED STATES

In concluding, I propose to examine how the dual-sex system could work in the United States, I propose a restructuring in which the male and female sides are equal and the duties of each side has equal value.[54] Although this is a hypothetical experiment, it points to a perfectly conceivable scenario. Before the idea is rejected as utterly preposterous, let us recall that change begins at the level of hypothesis. The model offers an equitable form of relationship between the sexes as well as insights for a new bill of rights for women. Certainly a lot of wrinkles need to be ironed out to make this system effective. In fact, the idea that the American sociopolitical system could become dual-sex is not so far-fetched in a political system that is already a diarchy, made up of the Republican and Democratic parties. This diarchy is imperfect, since one party controls either the executive arm of government and/or the Congress, rather than both controlling it at the same time, as the dual-sex system requires. Suppose for the sake of argument that the Republican Party is construed as the female side of the dual-sex symmetry, and the Democratic Party is the male side of the symmetry. The key difference from the present state of diarchy is that both sides are in power at the same time and are ruling in a complementary, interdependent manner. This raises certain questions: What kind of administrative arrangement should we expect, given the dual line of symmetry? What structures, social institutions, attitudes, and consciousnesses would change as a consequence of this system? How would these changes deal with issues of gender discrimination? How would equality be defined and understood? How would we understand the new American society? Many of these questions cannot satisfactorily be answered in this conclusion, but they chart the direction of future research.

Mindful of Babbitt's point that the oppressed may not know their true interests, we recognize that the long history of discrimination against people of color and women in general will be difficult to transcend. However, if the oppressed are able to form their own group, the first dramatic effect will be a shift in consciousness. We acknowledge that the dynamic of race has for a long time defined the basis of social and institutional ordering in the United States. This means that a shift to using biological sex will initially prove disorienting, since men of all colors will be on one side, against women of all colors. White will no longer be the normative color as all colors will have equal value. That shift in consciousness does not mean that race issues will be totally eliminated. They may be redrawn in other ways, but the equalization of color at the foundational levels and the nonprivileged status of the color white means that things will not function as in the old days. Part of the complication will come from de-emphasizing colors and giving a higher social priority to sex matters rather than to race. People will have to become accustomed to seeing themselves in other ways.

Privileged white men in particular will have a difficult time letting go, given their sense of entitlement in the American polity and their firm conviction that they know best. Of course, they will tender spurious arguments as to why this model can never work. But if we face down these complaints and move ahead, we will find that bereft of the institutional trappings that have for so long reinforced their privilege, white men will have to reorder their priorities to form meaningful alliances with men of color whose institutional esteem would be boosted by the dual-sex realignment. Although there has been a longer history of political collaboration between white women and women of color, white women will have to go through the same process with women of color in order to get over their reliance on white men for their privilege. What is clear is that along this sex line of division, the category of race will no longer have the force to confer institutional advantages on white men and women as it does in the present. Initially, all groups will have to refashion their identity, aware of the ways in which culture, consciousness, and lived experience are shaped by race and class. But as the sociopolitical experiment takes hold, other issues will undoubtedly arise as some of the familiar lines of division fade way.

It is natural that the initial stage will be marked by confusion, as people unlearn old and familiar habits and attempt to forge new principles and values. Let us suppose that everyone is able to work through the problems of the transition period. It will be clear to both groups that the objective of this equal distribution of responsibility is to avoid the present situation, in which women make up over half the population but are treated as minors, while men exclusively rule and dominate the society. Thus, for women to be valued as the social adults they are, they must have equal representation at judicial, political, economic, administrative, and social levels. Once this stage passes, and the dual-sex system becomes more familiar, we will notice a change in consciousness in which both men and women will increasingly become group-identified and openly so. Both men and women will increasingly become accustomed to seeing each other work with comparable authority in different and equally weighted positions of power. Adult women and adult men will occupy interdependent political and economic positions and spheres of authority. Women will have full authority and control over matters that fall under their jurisdiction in the same way that men have authority and power over matters in their own domain.

If the society is to work, both will have to negotiate collaboratively what duties and responsibilities each of the two groups will have. To ensure that this change progresses as it should, all economic and financial matters will initially be under the jurisdiction of women. Regardless of how the other duties are divided up, the economy, judicial matters, law enforcement, military affairs, labor, and employment will all have to come under the principles of the dual-sex system. To avoid perceiving any sector of the polity as male or female, there will be rotation of administrative duties. But such rotation will not affect the fact that some judicial matters that concern women (such as those that relate to their reproductive health) will come under their jurisdiction. They will no longer have to live in a world in which such matters are debated and decided by men who do not have the same experiences. This does not mean that they will ignore the medical contributions of men to the debate. It is more that since women are no longer minors, men cannot control and make the final decision because women will have a dominant voice of authority. In the new dispensation, men will not have dominance over all positions of power, leadership, and authority.

Let us suppose that under this new dual-sex system, leaders will be elected. The electoral decisions for the two groups may occur simultaneously, or the groups may opt for different electoral cycles. Whatever the preferred method, the decision to elect new representatives on the male side will not affect the status quo and nature of political decisions, elections, and representation on the female side. Both sides, however, will remain interested in the candidates of the other, since they would have to work together once elected. Although women cannot vote in men's elections and vice versa, nothing stops them from supporting and campaigning for preferred candidates.

At the apex of this dual-sex system will be two presidents—a male and a female—who will work collaboratively in ruling the nation. Whereas today the role of the Congress is to make laws and check the powers of the presidency, in the new political system, the powers of both and the duties that women and men do will each be structured to check the excesses of the other. As heads of the nation, the presidents will each have a governing council or cabinet to advise and assist in key tasks. Both spheres—female and male—will administer their affairs separately, but will regularly meet in conference sessions to deliberate on matters that require the perspective of both sexes. The prevailing spirit in these conference sessions and the entire administrative tasks will be based on consensus, since neither of them will have sole authority to overturn the other's work or to rule the nation alone. For example, if men controlled the armed forces and women controlled the treasury and the office of budget and appropriations, it would be foolhardy for the male president and his counselors to declare war on some country unilaterally. Without the endorsement of the female president, the treasury and office of budget and appropriation would not finance the war. The female president would refuse to authorize payments needed to mobilize, prepare for, and wage war. What this means is that the basis for declaring war must be very clearly defined, and the process for defining these grounds would naturally lead to a re-evaluation of national priorities and a rethinking of wars usefulness in solving problems.

On the basis of this debate, in which national priorities are ascertained, the distribution of funds to issues of women's greater priorities—commerce, education, justice, childcare, and social welfare—will have to be determined. Strategies will have to be devised to deal with and deter aggression and resolve conflicts. Depending on the national vision, the immediate strength of this system is that it introduces a different set of values that may curb adventurism. It will also stop a hawkish female or male president from unilaterally committing national resources to war without due consideration for the lives that would be lost and for the negative impact of such a war project on other aspects of national life.

By transferring substantive powers and equal authority to women, the new United States dual-sex system will foster a new value scheme that would correct the past history of women's minimal participation in governance. This political system will give them an important platform upon which to enter the political arena in large numbers, and to accord significant weight to issues they are passionate about, whatever they may be. With their enhanced authority and power, they can determine how much of the national budget will go to specific sectors of the economy. They will determine very clearly the lines along which society shall move, and will reshape national policy to meet the needs of various segments of the population. It is safe to say that world problems will not end, even if all societies adopted the dual-sex system. However, this system will eliminate the public-private dichotomy as well as the basis of gender inequality. When gender discrimination is eliminated, both parties are more attentive to family matters. As moral advances are made, and people begin to place a higher premium on life, stronger measures would be put in place to resolve and diffuse tensions long before opposition hardens into intransigence. One thing at least is certain; that under this dual-sex system, women would be the other half of the administration, and men would have to become accustomed to seeing them in positions of national significance and great responsibility.

Although divided along male and female lines, this political system would not promote antagonism but interdependency. This would begin by having one half see the other half as adults, possessing the requisite skills and ability to be in positions of authority. As a nation run by responsible adults, the country would continue to experience moments of conflict. But because each sex needs the other to survive, given that the services that each control would be integral to the smooth running of the government, they would have to reach compromises. In the same way that the armed forces today do not think about seizing power, men should not be able to encroach on the power and function of women. To attempt to do so would lead to serious political instability that would unravel social cohesion.

In present-day reality, the basis of political fusion is the market. Since the Reagan era, both political parties—Republicans and Democrats—have defined themselves in relation to where they stand on economic matters: for big business or for bigger business; for the rich or for the upper middle-class; for free enterprise and hefty government subsidies of corporations or for minimal government regulation of the market and subsidies for corporations. The dual-sex system provides an opportunity to rethink these market-oriented priorities and to introduce people-oriented, social justice goals. Ensuring that campaigns are publicly rather than privately funded will remove the corrupting influence of money and big business from elections and governance. Functioning as a countervailing force, women could advance causes and issues that are of concern to them, and like men, could bring them to national attention. In conference committees, where national and social goals would be reviewed, women would directly participate in defining what these goals are. By virtue of their group strength, they would initiate polices, in contrast to the present time where they have no clear sense of who they are collectively, and of what their group-identified objectives are. Unlike what presently occurs under the mono-sex system, women would not have to plead with men about the importance of certain issues, and hope for their goodwill; they would not have to spend years trying to justify and mobilize support for these issues. They would have the power to authorize change.

The new dual-sex system presupposes at the onset that the power men and women have would be of equal weight, which is why they would have equal responsibilities and power in the running of the nation. The "equal" here does not mean that the tasks and duties are uniform, but that they would have equal weight and that equal value would be assigned to them. For example, if women determined that childrearing issues were important to them, then this issue would become part of a comprehensive policy in which businesses would have to make adequate provisions for its female employees. Instead of giving perks that reward a male lifestyle (spending the most time at the office), the basis of giving perks would be re-evaluated such that women's multitasking style of work would be rewarded.

This system shift from a mono-sex to a dual-sex system would give women the opportunity and the right to be at the center of things—at the crucial point of decision making, rather than at the periphery. At the same time, the dual-sex system recognizes that there are important differences between men and women that must not be blurred. These differences would receive consideration in the formulation of policy and laws. Whereas women were once in a vulnerable position vis-à-vis legal matters, now they would have a strong voice, because laws would not only reflect their concerns, they would adjudicate them. Thus, just as men (in business, workers' organizations, and support services) safeguard and champion issues that are of importance to them, women could safeguard and champion issues that are of interest to women. This dynamic would bring about numerous changes at the philosophical, ethical, economic, social, and political levels.

Under the principle of equality as comparable worth, women's and men's groups would be autonomous and equivalent in terms of what they do for the state and for the survival of the community. As complements of each other, they would perform different tasks and function in different roles, and still be perceived as equal rather than unequal. Although the dual-sex system embodies a hierarchical relationship within groups, the social divisions would neither be rigid nor obstruct social mobility. One would attain social importance by virtue of one's accomplishments. When political power is no longer the exclusive preserve of a specific sex, as it has been in the past, a more equitable distribution of civic duties, privileges, influence, and political power would result. Women will be able to focus on their personal and community needs and communally enhance their visibility and respect.

Assuredly, it is empowering to know that, at the formal procedural level, all Americans are individuals and the same, but at the substantive level, the focus of equality would be on the two sex groups and the transference of the benefits of that group equality to members. Defining equality relationally at the level of groups rather than at the level of the individual enables each group member to have a focused vision and a clear sense of his or her roles and duties. The dual-sex system shows that factoring sexual difference into political relations need not result in sex inequality. This is especially true if the difference is taken seriously enough to achieve balance. In such circumstances, the context can be structured to affirm the sexes equally, but differently. Once comparable worth is inscribed into the context and forms of relationships, women and men will be equally valued in terms of their social roles. Although feminism has made important contributions to redefining gender relations, its individualistic commitment to the mono-sex system retards its progress. The built-in power imbalance between men and women allows gender inequity to be preserved and reinforced.

CONCLUSION
Toward a Balanced Society

"Our grievance is that the land is changed—we are all dying."
—A combatant of the Women's War at the Tribunal,
quoted in Sylvia Leith-Ross (1939), 38

As I come to the end of the book and reflect on its theme, I realize that indeed the land has radically changed. There is an urgent need for comprehensive reform of Igbo values if we are to restore women's former social relevance and combat the modern culture of violence with its dismissive treatment of human life. On Sunday, October 6, 2002, the *New York Times* printed a horrifying news item:

> Armed men waiting at the junction cornered Barnabas and Amaka Blessing Igwe, a couple who were prominent lawyers in this part of Nigeria. They pulled them out of their Mercedes, witnesses said. One of the attackers cut off the wife's left leg with a machete. He hacked at her back so that her body folded. She breathed her last right there. The men fired into the air to frighten away passers-by, though . . . people living in nearby buildings were able to tell the police later what they had seen. The killers pumped bullets into the husband's body. They got into the Mercedes and ran over him. But he was still alive and was taken to a nearby hospital. He died there.

Just how does one begin to theorize this killing and the new modern culture of violence in Igboland in discussions about the family? How does one make sense of these contemporary acts of lawlessness and the utter disregard for human life that is plaguing Igboland as well as Africa as a whole? Barnabas Igwe was the chairman of the Nigerian Bar Association for Anambra state, an organization very much concerned with law and order. With the support of his wife, Amaka, he was by all accounts, one of the fiercest critics of then state governor, Chinwoke Mbadinuju, who turned the state into his fiefdom and unconsciously preyed on the citizenry. According to *New York Times* media reports, Anambra had become "the most gravely mismanaged of Nigeria's 36 states. . . . Unpaid teachers were on strike for the full school year . . . state civil servants and court workers have been on strike for many months. The state's bar association accused state leaders of pocketing the money meant to pay the striking workers." Just before the Igwes were killed, the state Bar Association had demanded the resignation of the governor. Seven days from the expiration of the ultimatum, the Igwes were murdered.

The question of who killed the Igwes threw the state of Anambra into a quandary. Rumor had it that members of the state-funded Vigilante Services, the Bakassi Boys, had carried out the killing on the orders of the born-again Christian state governor. The Bakassi Boys were initially part of a homegrown resistance movement against armed robbers, who had instituted a reign of terror in the neighboring state of Imo. These murderous criminals had received protection from corrupt police officers with whom they shared the proceeds of their marauding activities. In a short space of time, the Bakassi Boys had acquired a contradictory fearsome reputation for inscrutable uprightness and uncompromising violence. The latter was for their gory trademark of publicly beheading notorious armed robbers and robbery suspects and leaving the decapitated bodies and heads on display for all to see. An exasperated Anambra state public decided to place its faith on the infallibility of the vigilante group's occult powers, which the group promoted with a Star Wars-type sword that allegedly glowed red in the presence of people of ill repute.

To dispel the rumors of the governor's culpability in the execution of the Igwes, the secretary to the government argued that the operation could not have been done by the state's vigilante services because "The head was not chopped off. Instead, after he [Barnabas] was shot, they ran over his body with a car" (*New York Times*). The defense defied logic. Not only did it embody an official admission that state employees actually chop off people's head as part of their regular day's work, but that the state government knowingly funded these activities. The secretary to the government seemed oblivious of the need to maintain a semblance of good governance and rule of law.

It is true that the entire population of the state had clamored for the hiring of the Bakassi Boys when the Nigerian police abdicated its law enforcement responsibilities to the people. Indeed, the Bakassi Boys had earned local respect for stepping in to provide a sorely needed service that the police were incapable of giving. They quelled the crime wave in bustling urban centers and, in case after case, they took back the cities from criminals. However, unlike police officers, the Bakassi Boys owed allegiance to no one, other than to their quasi-religious brotherhood. Psychologically battered by the continuous violence, rapes, and killings by armed robbers, the public eagerly welcomed the Bakassi Boys as crime-control agents and saviors. For quite a while, the Bakassi Boys cultivated an aura of impartiality and lived up to their reputation as a nonpolitical organization. To their credit, they successfully rid the city of Onitsha of armed robbers, violent criminals, and their patrons. But in the process of fighting crime, they also killed a number of innocent people who came to be considered criminals by virtue of having been killed by the Bakassi Boys. In a short space of time their crime-fighting goals became corrupt.

For the past twenty-five years or so, Anambra state and other parts of Igboland had been slowly sliding into moral degeneracy that highlights the ahistorical character of Rousseau's state of nature and the social contract theory. Following the end of the Biafran war, little attention has been paid to issues of morality and the moral and material welfare of families. The thirty-some years of military rule by an indelibly politicized army exacerbated the moral decay of both the nation and the region. Crime and corruption offered the fastest pathway to wealth and notoriety, which were soon confused with fame and success. With an economy mired in recession and contracting sharply, there was no shortage of recruits to a criminal life. Everyone saw the need to cut corners. (A people that had in the past applied a litmus test of moral integrity before honoring people discarded its moral compass and lionized anyone who was rich, regardless of how they acquired their wealth.) As the moral life of the people plummeted, more and more unspeakable deeds were committed in the mad rush for wealth by forces profiting from the chaos. Within this vortex of social decay, the legitimacy of using vigilante services to root out one order of lawlessness was an academic exercise most people were not interested in entertaining. The immediate question for most people was how to uproot the heinous activities of criminal gangs; the larger question of how the state and its people got to this state of affairs attracted little attention. On the few occasions when that question was tentatively raised, one recurring approach was to direct attention to the pathology of the people, and to strive to locate the defect in the psyche of Igbos. As with all psychologically oriented arguments, such a line of reasoning continually missed the very modern nature of the failure of the African state and breakdown of its rule of law.

So what is the connection of the case of the Igwe to the argument of the book? In an important way, the murders signal the culmination of a long progression of events that began with colonial policies and its institutionalization of violence. The state of affairs in Anambra, particularly its culture of violence, is a logical outcome of negative colonial and postcolonial policies and models of governance that are based on a total disregard for ethical norms that manifested in violent expression of male privilege. The murder of the Igwes shows how far Igboland spiraled out of control as it slid into despotic rule, political decay, and maladministration. The governing ideology disconnects leadership from the prime imperative of providing good leadership and governance and empowers state rulers to brutally exploit and prey on their citizens. In a very basic manner, the murders speak to the dispiriting failure of the modern African state, and points to the artificiality of these states that did not evolve naturally from their own indigenous political and social institutions. Some scholars argue that most of the violence in Africa today (in Uganda, Rwanda, Burundi, Congo, Sierra Leone, Liberia) can be traced to the divisive, factional policies that formed the basis of the colonial state, which the postcolonial states failed to root out. Mahmood Mamdani (1996) attributes it to despotic patrimonialism arising from a failure to detribalize the Native Authority system. Of course, as Frantz Fanon warned, corrections were impossible because in the realm of internal affairs, dictatorial tendencies do not get very far because they cannot halt their own contradiction. Part of the problem is the emergence of leaders who availed themselves of the nondemocratic offerings and structures of the state. Inevitably, the state sinks into stagnation and the vain attempts to hide its regression further exacerbates the decline (Fanon 1963, 165). That is the situation in Anambra today.

A large segment of the violence of the failed state is directed at women. The despotic tendencies of these states depend on a rigid masculinist consciousness that permeates the state and promotes a culture of violence towards women. While Anambra state in particular, and Igboland in general, remain trapped in the vicious grips of a brutalizing ideology, erstwhile colonizers are rapidly transforming and advancing their societies in ways that make a mockery of their earlier castigation of various African phenomena—the ideal of women's industriousness and empowerment, attitudes toward male and female sexuality, the concept of woman–woman marriage, and the institution of *idigbe*—as primitive and backward. These are the very same attitudes, practices, and concepts that the contemporary societies of former colonizers are touting as hallmarks of sophistication, progress, and tolerance. Imagine if the dual-sex systems had been allowed to flourish. While tolerance is elusive in Anambra state, Igboland is fast regressing into a state of patriarchal anachronism that once characterized pre-1960s Western societies. Meanwhile, the latter have embraced progressive values, and are working towards an emancipatory value scheme for women, having learnt that a forward-looking society must equitably integrate the creative energies and labor of its female sex into its sociopolitical structures.

The murders of the Igwes make it all the more pertinent that drastic social, political, and jurisprudential changes are required to transform the society. These changes must not be ones that leave intact sites of despotism and structures of violence, including the customary laws, that enthrone male dominance. Dismantling these structures is necessary to ensure that women are fully incorporated into the society with rights and social worth that are equal to the male members of society. The incorporation will then initiate discussions on what kind of society that people desire and how to secure women's equality within it. It is hoped that these will be guided by contemporary critiques of liberalism and civil society as well as by feminist insights on gender equality.

Because the primary concern of this book is not the political condition of governance but the state of the family, I will devote the rest of my concluding remarks to the status of female relatives. There is no question that Igbo women have made tremendous advances in education, and are to be found in all kinds of occupations both within and outside Nigeria. But the more pressing matter in this picture of progress is the issue of gender inequality both within families and in the society at large. Gender inequality that was introduced during colonialism and nurtured in postcolonial Nigeria, hamstrings women and translates into resource deprivation as well as the end of important decision-making positions to women at the larger societal level. Igbo societies today are characterized by a hardened patriarchal ideology that has resulted in women's loss of ground in defining the vision of their societies, and in gaining sociopolitical positions of importance that correspond to the high level of energy and labor they invest in nurturing and growing the society. As families increasingly evolved into male-privileging systems, male relatives were distributing resources in ways that further solidified the abrogation of the rights of female members of a family. Traditional ruling councils and local community councils replicate this male-privileging ideology by valuing only the opinion of men. At the pan-Igbo level, cultural and sociopolitical organizations such as the Igbo-wide Ohaneze group represents an all-male club whose deliberations and policies are oblivious to the views of women and totally insensitive to issues that concern and affect them.

Chapters 1 and 2 explored the nature of Igbo society at a specific historical period before radical modification by the patriarchal ideology of the colonial state. The idea that men are the measure of all things was not the Igbo cultural ideology prior to colonial modifications. This was very well captured by social institutions and by the male-generated transcriptions of combatants of the 1929 Women's War. Igbo women made it clear that they did not wish to be oppressed by their menfolk. They resented the fact that the colonial state was diverting resources only to men, and they disliked the fact that they were not in the loop of people to be consulted on matters affecting their communities. As I argued in chapter 2, women's insistence on self-representation early in the days of colonial rule could not have occurred if there had not been a tradition of women's participation in the political, social, economic, and religious administration of their communities. While historical events contain proof of women's political and social roles in their communities, the spurious traditions that contemporary Igbo men are constructing are deliberately designed to keep women down, even as they parade the length and breadth of Nigeria insisting on their rights and demanding that Igbos (i.e., Igbo men) be given their due.

On examining the manner in which women's rights are eroded, in chapter 3 I highlighted the convoluted way courts of law interpreted traditions to override women's rights. The fact that these interpretations violated the logic of their cultural intent as well as the repugnancy clause of the constitution raises a profound problem of adjudication of justice. When the judiciary is involved in the erosion of women's rights, how can women's rights be safeguarded? Faced with the paradox in which the courts are part of the process of the subjugation of women, the standard response would be to call for judicial reforms and to insist that scrupulous attention be paid to the rule of law to correct the problem. Such a response typically appeals to the Western society to argue that, where the law works well, such problems do not occur. It is unclear that this is true. Chapter 5 points to the fallacy in that viewpoint. Western feminists' investigation of the judicial process reveals that even in contexts where the rule of law is observed, women are still worse off. This is not to say that the practice of the rule of law is bad, but that the problem of sexism is much deeper than is ordinarily admitted. The problem is not so much the concept of equality, but the sociopolitical system within which that notion of equality unfolds. I showed why that sociopolitical system shortchanges women. Liberalism and a liberal democratic society do not secure gender equality, given that it has been founded on the basis of gender and racial inequality and that its notion of equality is constituted by a masculinist ideology. We have to re-envision society along the lines of a dual-sex society if we are to overcome the problem of gender inequality. The structural limitations of the liberal democratic system must be addressed if we are to have any hope of correcting the inequities that Igbo widows or daughters encounter in courts of law.

Women's knowledge can contest oppressive power. In 1974 Kamene Okonjo wrote about the dual-sex system of governance, but there was surprisingly little interest in the model and in its offerings for an alternative solution to one of the problems of equality. The dual-sex system holds the promise of a different way of configuring a society to incorporate the modalities of sex equality. Rather than claiming to ignore sex while utilizing men to build the structure the society, it would be better to accept the existence of biological sex, and build a society that reflects that fact. The dual-sex system provides a way to overcome some of the structural shortcomings of the present asymmetrical, mono-sex system and its notion of gender equality. The latter system claims to treat everyone as an individual, but in its promises to deliver equality to women it fails, because the social structure is designed to deliver formal and substantive equality only to one sex, men. Because the idea of two biological sexes is integrated into the dual-sex system, it can deliver substantive equality.

There is a serious political crisis in Igboland, just as there is a serious epistemological crisis within the Western intellectual scheme. The latter tries to define a new pathway following the disintegration of its old, Cold War worldview, while Igboland face the challenging task of rescuing its communities from moral degradation and political extinction. In the same way that the West is presently at a post-Cold-War crossroads, and new concepts are being articulated to define this epoch, Igbo societies will have to reinvent themselves if they are to emerge from their present ethical morass. The crucial question we now face is, how do we rethink present Igboland, given the moral decay that is spreading over the entire landscape? We could start by reintegrating women back into society as equal partners with men and channeling their creative energies into rebuilding the society. In order to build a balanced society in which men and women would function at their optimal level, gender equity and the rule of law must become the central pivots of society.

NOTES

Introduction

1. After studying some social institutions in the Onitsha and parts of northwestern Igboland, I have argued, against Ifi Amadiume, that Igbo culture was nongendered prior to colonialism. See Nzegwu 1998.

2. Very few studies have been done on the African family or African families. Among the most useful for our purposes here are Oppong (1974), Amadiume (1987a) and (1987b), and Sticher (1988).

3. This study recognizes that there are distinct differences between Marxist feminism, socialist feminism, radical feminism, and liberal feminism. But at the foundational level of culture, the differences are minimal in that they share the same history, cultural values, and ontological scheme. Although the four strands of feminism have different ways of accounting for women's subordination, they tend to be in general agreement about the history, nature, and character of patriarchy.

4. I have argued that there are different accents to racism, and that the sort that was unleashed in West Africa in the late nineteenth century and early twentieth century was directed to cultures rather than to bodies. See Nzegwu 1999.

5. I have also argued that patriarchy and matriarchy are two sides of the same coin, and that prior to colonialism both of these features were not part of Igbo culture. See Nzegwu 1998 and 2001.

6. Because I have explained in numerous articles why gender is epistemologically problematic, I will not go over this argument again. See Nzegwu 2003, 2002, 2001 and 1998.

7. Offering a different perspective on black families are texts by Collins (1990), hooks (1989), and Sudarkasa (1996) have portrayed African American families as nurturing spaces against the corrosive effects of racism. Historians Elsa Barkley Brown and Evelyn Brooks Higginbotham, and critical race legal theorists Angela Harris and Cheryl Harris, make a similar point in a va-

riety of ways. I have in mind Brown (1995), Higginbotham (1995), and Harris (1995).

8. Diop (1989) and Amadiume (1997) conducted lengthy archeological readings of Africa's sociology and history. In fact, Diop represented matriarchy as African and patriarchy as endemically European.

9. See Margaret Strobel's 1982 review of the social science literature on Africa. In 1987, Claire Robertson extended this initial effort by reviewing articles published between 1976 and 1985.

10. This becomes clear when we engage the work of Joseph Marie Thérèse Agbasiere, who depended on the male viewpoint of N. O. Olisa on the inheritance rights of women in Igbo societies. Agbasiere does not seem to understand that this dependence is problematic, since Olisa's account may embody gender biases. See Agbasiere 2000, 38 n. 2.

11. Edith Ike Mark-Odu, an Igbo female chief noted shortly before her death in 2003 that "the Igbo woman is [now] the most culturally marginalized." These changes must encapsulate even minor issues as the kolanut issue. According to her, "grassroots women . . . have identified it as critical to their empowerment . . . [because] that is where the youth learn that women are not really consequential." Excerpted from Abati 2003.

Chapter 1. Family Politics

1. Early ethnographers on the Igbo culture whose work I shall not be using include G. I. Jones and Daryll Forde, and M. D. W. Jeffrey.

2. See Amadiume's discussion of Cheikh Anta Diop's position and the elaboration of her own view of matriarchy (1997, 71–79).

3. After finally discerning the significance of the Asantehemaa in Asante political culture following years of study, Rattray asked his informants why he had not been aware of this fact. He was told: "The white man never asked us this. As you have dealings which recognize only men, we supposed the European considered women of no account, and we know you do not recognize them as we have always done" (Rattray 1969, 83 cited in Oduyoye 1995, 95).

4. See Mikell (1997), Stichter and Parpart (1988), Amadiume (1987a), Robertson and Berger (1986), Bosah (1979), Nzimiro (1972), H. Henderson (1969), Obi (1966, 1963). Also see the works of R. Henderson (1972).

5. Igbo women's historic revolts against disenfranchisement in the early history of colonial rule in Igboland provide compelling proof against claims of women's political irrelevance. These include the Nwaobiala Movement of 1918 (Mba 1982, 68–72) as well as their skirmishes with the United Africa Company as they protested their sharp trading practices (G. I. Jones 1989, 96). Furthermore, the anthropological work of Margaret M. Green and Sylvia Leith-Ross paints vivid and different pictures of Igbo women's assertiveness.

6. See "Social Anthropology and Two Contrasting Uses of Tribalism," which explores anthropologists' use of "tribe" and "tribalism" in African studies. Ekeh has noted that British social anthropologists have imprecisely defined African kinship terms and categories by treating them as static, and precluding the historical examination of societies to ascertain the nature and character of kinship (1990). He argues that these terminologies were kept because it was claimed that there were no available records of the past and because anthropologists of the time wanted to pursue a functionalist methodology that would make social anthropology relevant to the governance objectives of colonial administration. For confirmation of this see Lord Lugard's foreword in C. K. Meek's book, *Law and Authority in a Nigerian Tribe*. He states: "The result has been to place at the disposal of administrators in the Tropics invaluable information and suggestions which the meagre cadre of officials in the earliest years, had neither the training nor the time to acquire" (1937, v).

7. Jack Stauder also makes this point in the two essays he wrote discussing the role of anthropology in nineteenth-century colonialism and its aftermath. "The Relevance of Anthropology under Imperialism" was written for the Wenner-Gren Symposium on "Relevance" in Anthropology, held in March 1970. "Functions of Functionalism" was presented at a meeting of the American Anthropological Association in New York, November 1971. A shortened version, by Kath Levine, of the two articles were published in *The Racial Economy of Science* (1993), edited by Sandra Harding.

8. The rise of kidnapping bands and their destructive activities profoundly affected the nature of families over the course of two centuries. People who went to the stream to fetch water vanished; mothers who went to the markets never returned; widows who were alone in their homes with their children were kidnapped at night; men were kidnapped at the farms—nobody was safe. Olaudah Equiano's eighteenth-century story of his kidnapping profoundly reveals the emotional trauma of this period (1755).

9. See Don C. Ohadike's description of the founding of communities in the Igbo-speaking areas west of the Niger. Also see Amadiume's account of the founding of Nnobi and Nnewi (1987a), 40–41.

10. Oral histories from Olaudah Equiano and from different parts of Igboland as well as the conical *uno aja* security architecture confirm this assessment of social upheaval. The *uno aja* towers were security structure within which children were hidden when their parents went to markets or the farm. For an oral history account of the sociopolitical turbulence of this period, see the account of the slave trade by Mbagwu Ogbete, aged c. 80, in Umuokwara, Akokwa, 15 and 16 July 1972 and 9 July 1973 in Elizabeth Isichei 1978, 111. Also see the account of Joseph Nwose, aged c. 75, in Etiti, Alor, 10 July 1972, in Isichei 1978, 50–52. Furthermore, John Barbot's account of Bonny/Igbo relations in 1678–82 and John Adams's late eighteenth-century account leave us

in no doubt about the high volume of Igbo slaves who were sold in Bonny and Old and New Calabar (Isichei 1978, 10–11). The procurement of such a high volume of slaves radically destabilized the region from which these slaves had come. It also directs us to take seriously the ethos of the models preserved in the Caribbean not simply because they are interesting, but because they represent attenuated capsules of nineteenth century African family systems. African Diaspora scholarship in Bahia (Brazil), Cuba, Surinam, and Guiana reveal remarkable ways in which nineteenth century traditions, vocabulary, and language were preserved.

11. See R. N. Henderson's description of the influx of Igbo women and their male relatives into Onitsha (1972, 425–26). These persons attached themselves to individual families who gave them family land. For further reading on this practice in other areas of Igboland, see Isichei (1973, 62–63); and J. C. Nwankwo's account of the evolution of the Aro settlement of Ndikelionwu in Isichei (1978, 104–6).

12. The founding of Ndikelionwu community provides an example of this model of family and community formation. See Isichei (1978, 104–7). Also historical research of Onitsha families reveals the presence of unrelated bloodlines that today appear as members of the same family. There are two types of such bloodlines. The first type consists of families that have established their own autonomy after having constructed mythical genealogies, including inventing nonexistent offspring for the founder, to pass themselves off as part of the direct line of descent. The second type consists of families that did not separate from the family into which they had merged. They share the same names and history. It is only during ritual activities, when they are excluded from performing certain rites, that it becomes obvious they are part of the genealogical line. Investigation often reveals that the latter branches may have been the line of a domestic servant, a slave, or an immigrant who lived with the family.

13. I owe this analysis to Niara Sudarkasa.

14. Though she is to be commended for her insights, Amadiume fell afoul of this critical prescription by continually centering and using the conjugal unit to begin analysis of Igbo families.

15. It is no secret in Onitsha that some families today are descendants of children born from *idigbe* relationships, in which adult daughters had children who were absorbed into her kin group. Members of Ogboli Olosi ward of Onitsha are descendants of Olosi, the daughter of Obi Chimaevi and her non-Onitsha paramour (see R. W. Harding 1963, Henderson 1972, Bosah 1979, Nzimiro 1972). Some members of Obikporo too are descendants of Usse, daughter of Aroli and her child with an Igala man, and others are descendants of widows who constituted the rest of the ward (Henderson 1972, 86–88; Bosah 1979, 24). Igbo mothers founded towns and wards of towns even during the

highly volatile climate of slave raids, kidnappings, and depopulation of the Igbo hinterland. An example is Usse, whose return to Onitsha with Idoko, the child she had with the Igala warrior, Onojo Oboni, was a rare and celebrated phenomenon. Usse had been captured during a slave raid at a trading location by Onojo Oboni, with whom she later had a son. On his death, she returned to Onitsha with her son and some paraphernalia of governance. She brought the key institution, *ora okwute*, which contemporary Onitsha men laud as a symbol of their power.

16. *Nze* is a sacred protective force of a clan.

17. This occurred when his wife married a wife in which she was the "husband" to her wife. Another occasion was when his adult sons had their own children who treated him rather their fathers as *nna*.

18. This does not exclude the fact that some parents pawned their children—both males and females—and may have sold some to redeem the rest of their family from debt. But these were not the normal conditions under which marriage took place.

19. Evidence shows that during this period of post-Ogidi war in the 1850s and the war with Obosi, Onitsha contracted as families moved closer to the central core and away from their outlying settlement at the border of the town. It seems that this was when strictures about daughters' marrying Igbo emerged. Also see Basden on the state of insecurity during this period (1938), 104–11.

20. See C. N. Amadi's discussion of the marriage conditions people of Amaeze Obibi established with their neighbors to protect their daughters from egregious acts on the part of their husbands and their husbands' people (Isichei 1978, 98–99).

21. Because in the European and American nuclear family of the early twentieth century, women's sexuality and reproductive powers were controlled by husbands, scholars tended to think that the same sort of control was exerted on all women worldwide. Predictably, therefore, they exported inappropriate gender ideologies as they tried to find the strong hand of men lurking everywhere in the background, guiding, sanctioning, and directing social and political affairs. In the patriarchal scheme of the West, once the transactional rite of marriage is completed ("to have and to hold till death do us part"), a husband is guaranteed proprietary right over the wife. Another man cannot have access to her body or be responsible for her pregnancy. Because marriage transfers a wife to a groom completely, the concept of faithfulness is used to regulate a wife's autonomy, restrain her sexuality, and control of her body. Consequently, any violation of the norms of marriage activates deep feelings of betrayal and intense jealously in the husband. Charges of infidelity ameliorate this loss of control and are assuaged by the public stigmatization of the child as bastard and castigation of the mother as fallen.

22. Historically, husbands had to assist their in-laws in farm work of fishing in what was called *olu ogo* (in-law's work). In modern times, this consists in providing labor during celebratory and distressful family events such as engagements, weddings, medical issues, funerals, as well as in minutiae of other ways when material and moral support is called for.

23. Igbo marriages did not permanently transfer daughters to husbands, as occurred in European and Judeo-Christian forms of marriages. Should their marriages end, they returned to their natal kin; and on their death, their bodies were returned for burial with their kin group.

24. I have extensively argued this point in "Chasing Shadows" (1998).

25. This section was constructed from personal interviews and research carried over a period of thirty years about practices in the following areas— Onitsha, Aguleri, Nando, Mbaukwu, and Awka—as well as from critically reading of the works of Thomas, Basden, Margaret M. Green, Leith-Ross, Richard and Helen Henderson, and transcripts of the Women's War.

26. Historically, in some northeastern parts of Igboland wives had *agiri* (lovers—the terminology used in Aguleri, Umueri, Nteje, Awkuzu and other Anambara areas) or *nuno* (lover—in Onitsha dialect), *owhum* (friend/lovers in Awka, Amawbia). The practice appears to be much wider than acknowledged. In her study of the Ubang in Cross River State, Chinturu Uchendu (2003) notes that women had official *utin* (lovers).

27. That is, a relationship that is not necessarily "extra," but transcends or goes beyond the marital union. I am aware the Amadiume had represented marital sexuality as being monogamous for wives. Her descriptions that lineage daughters police wives and act as ritual specialists dealing with confessions of infidelity or adultery by wives (1987a, 16) is designed to show that extramarital relationships were not sanctioned for wives. The problem about the rituals, however, is that Amadiume did not determine when these confessions began. Rather she presented such relationships as if they were an integral part of Igbo custom from time immemorial. Given the heavy influence of Christianity in the region, and the fact that missionaries made fidelity a cardinal issue in marriages, it is important to determine whether or not this "tradition" owed its genesis to Christian influence. As she herself acknowledged, indigenous institutions were being abandoned and reinterpreted to the detriment of women (1987a, 123). Was it possible that lineage daughters were introducing some of these Christian ideals into their families by making it a part of their judicial tasks to maintain the "purity" of the family bloodline?

One way to determine whether or not the fidelity clause was of a recent nature is to reconcile it with the sanctioned practices of extramarital affairs that existed in numerous parts of northwestern Igboland, including Nnobi. What do we make of this fidelity clause when a bride has not conceived after two years and returns to her natal home to "seek" a child, or when a wife is married to a little boy and has relations with a partner or partners in order to conceive; or when a husband is impotent and the wife looks to lovers to fulfill the act of conception? These cases clearly contradict the fidelity rule that works to bring Nnobi women under the prescription of the Christian ethical scheme and present them as virtuous women. Structural impediments were not placed in the path of wives to become mothers. The ethical framework that sanctioned these activities is at odds with the Christian ethical framework that may have influenced these activities. One thing is clear, we cannot simply wish away historic practices that occurred under a different ethical framework simply because they do not accord with Christian morality that has since gained ascendancy.

28. This is by no means an exhaustive list of the sanctioned transmarital relationships. On another note, I should state that I will not be discussing cases where daughters have chosen to remain in, or return to, the homestead to continue the family line by having children. This is because the focus is on wives who are outsiders, who do not have any genealogical connection with the family. By contrast, by virtue of being a daughter, the daughter has direct ties to the family, to the father pole. Igbo legal theorist S. N. Chinwuba Obi recognizes this fact, but thinks that there is nothing significant about it. According to him, the fact that daughters may step in to continue a family line does not change anything, because it "does not disturb the normal rules of inheritance" (1963, 185). If a daughter dies without issue, the normal line of succession operates as if she never existed. If, however, she does bear sons, they will succeed in accordance with "the normal principle of primogeniture" (1963, 185). For someone who is exceptionally male-centered and father-focused, Obi fails, interestingly enough, to see that such a daughter can alter the male-father pole, since her sons and daughters would have a different father.

29. This is the period between engagement and the formal relocation of the bride to her marital home.

30. This latter option may lead to the break-up of the marriage if the wife is relatively young. However, it happens where the young wife is involved with a powerful man in the community. Other times that it occurs is with mature, older wives who are no longer having children. Though Igbo male scholars may be reluctant to discuss these examples, and may want to treat them as extremely rare cases, they are quite common practices in Igbo social life. This reluctance is misguided given that these practices evolved under a different ethical scheme than the one which is in operation today. For the traditional Igbo family, procreation was the raison d'être for marriage. Nothing required that the father had to be the genitor of the children. Consequently, Igbo fathers embraced all children that was born within their conjugal unit and contented themselves with the postreproductive role of caring for the children of

the marriage, as well as those of the lineage. They nurtured and emotionally bonded with them and shaped them to be full members of the lineage.

31. By limiting my claims to the nineteenth century, I do not mean to state that the phenomenon does not go further back in time. It simply means that my historical data only go that far back.

32. The practice is described as "*i ẓe t'agbo,* meaning "bringing in a genetic trait." It gave rise to the name Ezelagbo, that marks the fact. Information about this practice in the Awka region comes from the late Madam Margaret Egbunike, an indigene of Mbaukwu, and in Anambra region, from Madam Abumchukwu of Abube, Nando.

33. These abominable relations would be those between freeborns and *osu* (those dedicated to a shrine), or between freeborns and *Oru* (the enslaved), or between members of the same kin group.

34. See Obi, the section on "Husband's General Position vis-à-vis His Wife" (1966, 203–5). There, he discusses that a husband is entitled to respect and obedience from his wife. Obi may be wishing that this state of affairs was the norm, but after learning of the ways wives use food to force their husbands into submission, and of the high rate of divorce and runaway wives, it is clear that a husband's entitlement to respect and obedience is predicated on his meeting his wives' demands and his obligations as they see them.

35. Because Onitsha people had a history of migration from Benin, they do not see themselves as Igbos, even though they speak Igbo language. As such, the women accepted marriage offer from Igbos west of the Niger, but not from communities that lie eastwards.

36. In the blacksmiths' town of Awka, girls remain at home until the age of sixteen, when they marry (Thomas 1913–14, 13). This contrasts sharply with the poorer Agulu community, where Awka men were permitted to marry much younger Agulu girls and return to Awka with them. The effect of this practice was that Agulu had "fewer wives in proportion to the adult male population," resulting in the high number of "tenanted solitary males or bachelors."

37. For the kinds of marital conditions that Obibi community drew up for neighboring communities marrying their daughters see Isichei (1978, 98–99).

38. Igbo mothers had social and economic responsibilities towards themselves, their children, dependents, parents, and siblings. They traded; farmed; processed agricultural products; manufactured textiles, mats, and pottery; and engaged in a whole set of other activities. Socially and politically, they administered the community through their women's councils.

39. This is also called *mkpuke* by Igbos east of Onitsha.

40. Elsewhere I have argued that the implication of family interrelationship and the logic of constantly shifting superordinate/subordinate roles mean that no one is ever exhaustively defined by one identity or role. Autonomous spaces are created that are dependent on seniority, or some specific

duties that one performs. See Nzegwu "Chasing Shadows: The Misplaced Search for Matriarchy" (1998), 594–622.

41. This is a different kind of subjection that patriarchy insists upon.

42. It is important to state that the woman who is unable to bear a child can still have children by marrying a wife.

43. She passes on citizenship and her family's name to her children if she is in an *idigbe* relationship, and she passes on her husband's family name if she is married.

44. This is why in Igbo social scheme, wives are seen as responsible for all matters relating to the birth of a new child, including the sex of the baby. Again, this is why a wife has society's approval to leave her matrimonial home to seek a baby.

45. See the works of Basden, Thomas, Meek, Leith-Ross, Green, Obi, Nwakamma Okoro, Richard Henderson, Helen Henderson, and Agbasiere.

46. I have written about wives as agents of colonization. See "Chasing Shadows" (1998). When marriage is looked at from the perspective of wives, they appear as stouthearted travelers who move into other families to reshape both the genetic histories and values of "strangers." If we take that imagery seriously enough, we begin to understand why as mothers, wives are truly appreciated by affinal families. They make possible their expansion by giving birth to new members, and ensuring the survival of the family.

47. This occurs because the basis of inheritance is through the mother. In modern times, a father's wealth is divided in terms of the number of wives who are the mother of sons. The sons then inherit according to the allotment that goes to their mother. This principle of distribution of wealth is based on the *usokwu* or *mkpuke* (the hearth hold) that is defined by mothers. Children receive their allotment in terms of their mother line.

48. This is why unmarried men or paramours of married women are not seen as fathers.

49. Also it is interesting how Onwuejeogwu tries to minimize this power by means of unfortunate language such as "Women are reciprocally exchanged as wealth among about twenty-seven exogamous groups . . ." "exchang[ing] women among themselves . . ." (1980, 53).

50. Within Obi's framework, the smallest subdivision of a patrilineal family is the household, consisting of a man/patriarch and his wife or wives with their unmarried children and any other dependents such as wards and domestic servants.

51. The term "corporate" frames the family on a legal model that allows researchers to project into families traits and features of a corporation that may not necessarily reside in it. See Obi 1966.

52. It is interesting to see the ways in which Obi's description of Igbo family parallels Meek's description written in 1937.

53. Thomas (1913–14), Basden (1938, 1921), Talbot (1926), Meek (1957, 1937, 1936), Chubb (1948), G. I. Jones (1961, 1950, 1949), and Forde and Jones (1950).

54. Notably, A. K. Ajisafe (1924), Omoneukanrin (1942), Ekere (1944), Delano (1944), Esenwa (1948), Egharevba (1949), Akpan (1955), Arikpo (1955), Elias (1963, 1956, 1954), Udoma (1956), Ekeghe (1957), Folarin n.d., Ajayi (1960), Kasunmu (1962), and Coker (1966).

55. In an essay, "Philosophers' Intellectual Responsibility to African Females" (1996a), I examined some of the reasons why the theoretical works of Igbo scholars are marred by their inattentiveness to gender issues.

56. Feminist scholars have convincingly exposed the limitations of this methodology and the historical distortions it generates (Sandra Harding, Carole Pateman, Susan Moller Okin, and many more). Similarly, African historians have made the same point about European historians of Africa (Kenneth Dike, Adiele Afigbo, Adu Boahen, and others). In his own contribution, Jan Vansina has argued that such methodological strategies compromise the heuristic value of oral history and anthropological reconstructions that arise from them (1985, 107–8).

57. It is by means of this flawed methodology that Igbo male scholars can easily "prove" the patriarchal character of Igbo societies and vociferously assert male dominance over women. This proof is invalid, since it ignores the intended and unintended consequences of colonialism and its injection of western ideologies into Igboland. Unfortunately, many Igbos today present these reconstructions as "authentic" traditions.

58. Further complicating matters is Obi's reliance on the business model of corporations. The corporation analogy further secures the patriarchal definition of family and removes daughters/sisters and wives/mothers from scholarly consideration just on the basis of their sex. Fixing exclusive attention on the heads of units who are male further consolidates the patriarchal model.

59. Scholars who have written on the dynamic role of daughters in Igbo families include: Nzegwu (2002b) and (1998), Amadiume (1997), Ekejiuba (1995) and (1966). This switch facilitates the transposition unto Igbo families features that "flowed from the ideologies and myths invented by the bourgeoisie to consolidate their parcels of influence in the new Nigerian era (Ekeh 1990, 105).

60. We tend to think that the real line of continuity exists with fathers, because the practice of polygyny positions fathers as the constant factor in lineages. But the standard cases in which strangers were absorbed into a family are ones in which they were conceived within the socially sanctioned space of marriage.

61. To her credit, Ifi Amadiume has been the most prominent Igbo scholar to examine the role of motherhood in Igbo families (1997, 1987a, and

1987b). To argue the case against the patriarchal character of Igbo society with the institution of daughter is a fairly easy undertaking because daughters are part of the family and are descendants of the father. Because Igbo family ideology does not situate mothers as members of the affinal family, it is more difficult to argue the case of nonpatriarchal family with the role of mothers. In northern Igboland, the status of mothers is not necessarily coincident with their status as wives, even though both roles converge on the same body.

62. I have discussed this in another article "Philosophers' Intellectual Responsibility to African Females," (1996a, 130–35).

63. This transformation is a fairly recent one. We must pay greater attention to how it happened if we are to understand the processes of structurally shifting power to one group in a society. An understanding of the mechanics is crucial if we are effectively to halt and subsequently reverse the patriarchy process.

Chapter 2. Legalizing Patriarchy

1. This is justice that is guided by the adjudicator's ideas of political circumstances of the event rather than by the rules of law.

2. This concept has been more extensively explored in the article "Hidden Spaces, Silenced Practices and the Concept of Igba N'rira" (Nzegwu 2002b).

3. The fallacy is that "indigenous institutions, owing nothing to European political concepts, were the foundations upon which local government in Nigeria has been built" (Harris 1957, 1).

4. Richard Henderson did this when he described the *ofo* as a male spiritual symbol of authority (1972, 118–19).

5. Flora Kaplan discusses how the use of the term "dowry" in divorce cases had the effect of contracting and effacing a range of practices that are part of Benin and Igbo marriage process (Kaplan 1997, 263–64). In the European colonial scheme, "dowry" referred to the goods and property a bride took with her to her marital home. But this is different from the Igbo process where "bridewealth" and "bride service" are part of what the husband has to convey to the family of the bride. When dowry was used as a substitute, it changed the meaning of the Igbo marriage processes in the following ways: (a) it established a single dowry payment as what the groom gives to the bride's family; (b) it dispensed with the extended series of crucial interactions known as "bride service" (this component was utilized by families to bond the groom to their own family norms and traditions); and (c) when divorces occurred, men's claims for compensation were accepted.

6. Okosi was appointed following the conclusion of the judicial inquiry into the Obiship dispute by Commissioner Bedwell. He was crowned without

conforming to traditional protocols of coronation and in the face of nonacceptance by the majority of the population. See the 1963 Obiship Report of R. W. Harding, 177.

7. This is usually the oldest of the age-grade associations in the community. They are part of the ruling administrative structure.

8. See John Whitford's account of 1872 in Isichei (1978, 257); Bishop Ajayi Crowther's account of 1870 in Isichei (259); and Taylor's account of 1857 in K. Onwuka Dike (1962), 14.

9. What was the community's position on this abolition? Obi Samuel Okosi was a controversial figure who ruled without regard for Onitsha customs. As a Christian, he thought little of those customs, seeing them as morally reprobate. The community complained that he should not be the Obi, since he arbitrarily disregarded all traditional methods of selection of Obi and many of the traditional requirements of the office (see Harding 1963, 177).

10. NAE, CSO 26/3, 27002, "Report on the Igbo and Ezengbo Clan," cited in Adewoye 1977, 203.

11. Afigbo's commentary becomes intelligible within the context of the negative impact of the slave trade on Igbo political process and value scheme. Oral history accounts from the mid-nineteenth century to the early twentieth century revealed that large sections of Igboland were under the predatory rule of the slave-trading Aro theocracy. Members of communities such as Alor "turned the external crisis of the trans-Atlantic slave trade into an opportunity to gain wealth and powers" (52). The "bold and unscrupulous" ones among them readily accumulated capital by kidnapping women, children, and men whom they sold off to the Aro. The rise of men in society corresponds to more insecurity and bloodshed. In short, the prevalence of the Aro slave traders had sensitized numerous Igbo communities to the presence of brutal activities of foreign overlords (Isichei 1978, 50–52, 68–71, 104–7, and 108–38).

12. Chanock (1982) and Flora Kaplan (1997) provide examples of how these occurred in East Africa and in Benin City, Nigeria.

13. Chief Ngadi Onuma of Oloko, cited in Afigbo (1972, 256).

14. See Amadiume (1987a, 15). This issue will be dealt with in much greater detail in chapter 5.

15. The schools began in the compound of Orikagbue with 30 boys and 14 girls. They used Crowther's primer, the focus of which was learning the alphabet, reading, writing, and arithmetic (see Nwabara 1977, 49–50 and 65). Also according to Kenneth Dike, in 1858 when he toured Onitsha, Ajayi Crowther reported that Mr. Romaine had "little girls" among his pupils (Dike 1962, 13).

16. See Nwabara 1977 (chapter 3).

17. Figures are reproduced in Nwabara (1977, 68–69).

18. In numerous families, older sisters speak of having contributed an immense amount of labor and economic resources to put their younger brothers through school. Of course, they hoped for material reward when their brothers completed their education and gained employment in prestigious positions, but they did not always get it.

19. Beatrice Olie, nee Egbuna, speaks regretfully of the extensive sacrifice she made to contribute to her brother's school fees. The idea was that after he became a lawyer or doctor and began to generate wealth, he would take care of the extended family. Her hope was to live vicariously through her brother; she achieved wealth and prestige once her brother secured it for the family. Interestingly, when these brothers arrived back from England with their degrees, their values and lifestyle changed. The change switched the axis from the consanguineal structure of family that had benefited everyone to a nuclear family structure in which educated men's prime obligation was to their nuclear conjugal unit.

20. It is interesting that these legal fictions are today regarded as "living law" by law theorists who want to draw a useful distinction between lawyers law (the codified customary laws used by lawyers) and the customary laws of the community. See Ulrike Wanitzek (2003).

21. NAI, CSO 21/3264, comments on the native courts by Sir Hugh Clifford.

22. *Memorandum as to the Origin of the Recent Disturbances in the Owerri and Calabar Provinces* (Lagos 1930, 21).

23. They did this either because they were inattentively conflating "patriliny" and "patriarchy" and treating them as synonymous, or because their theoretical objectives did not require them to think critically about colonialism and to question the products they identified as traditional, or because they relied on and drew extensively from the research work of earlier European writers. But these reasons do not get to the root of the matter.

24. Between 1909 and 1930, no woman was a member of the native courts, as warrant chief, court clerk, interpreter, messenger, or police. After the Aba Inquiry, very few women were appointed to the posts.

25. For an example of how this is done see Ahudi's testimony in Aba Commission of Inquiry (1930, 114). Disputants are forced to borrow money so as to pay usury fees if their case is to be heard.

26. Other ways in which widows and young heirs loose their land occurs whenever there is an existing land dispute. The chiefs or court clerks would elicit bribes from both parties because they knew that a land case is an important matter (Ogwe, Aba Commission of Inquiry 1930, 738). After collecting from one side, he would ask the other party for the same amount or more, promising to settle the matter to the satisfaction of both disputants. If any of the par-

ties were unable to pay the requested amount, the chief or court clerk would direct them to his loan shark who would advance the stipulated sum to the litigants. Should they default in paying the loan they would automatically loose the land to the chief or court clerk. If one of the parties happens to be a young widow with a young heir, the chief or court clerk would marry her to gain control of the land.

Land registration was also used to dispossess the true custodians of the land. The acquisition of land titles became the route for legitimizing the importance of husbands and the rights of men to assume ownership of property. The idea that widows could own property may seem far-fetched to some who believe the current patriarchal rhetoric that widows had no property of their own. Victor Uchendu's father's mother was the owner of property referred to as the family property (Uchendu 1965, 7). His father's mother was wealthy and she inherited some of the property. In Onitsha, merchant queens such as Mgbogo Ifeajuna, Ileanwusi Egwuatu, Ogbeyanu Suzi, and others owned properties, and some of the family land that sons fight over today were acquired by their mothers. An example of the latter is the Enwonwu property in Umu Aroli, Onitsha.

27. Many of these Igbo brides were in their early teens.

28. Information about marital relations between Onitsha women and non-Onitsha women was collected over the years from a number of sources in Onitsha: the late Enyi Nwanyiuzo Nsowu, the late Madam Udegbuna Etuke, the late Chinyelugo Nneka Chugbo, the late Mrs. Rosa Nwokedi, the late Madam Margaret Egbunike, the late Mrs. Veronica Uwechia, Chibogu and Ebele Ejem, and others.

29. For a later version of this, see Nzimiro (1972, 108–9).

30. The bridewealth of Victor Uchendu's mother and her first husband, Jumbo, was shared by the judges of the Ayab Native Court (Uchendu 1965, 6).

31. *Ala* is the earth deity.

32. There was the prominent case of Odu Isaac Anieka Mbanefo who went to retrieve his son Okuefuna, born long after his mother and Mbanefo had separated.

33. The cases of Nneka Okolonji Akpe (wife of Chugbo) and Baby Isito, two strikingly beautiful Onitsha women, come to mind. Their marriages were beset by problems of conception. Subsequently, both women returned to their natal homes ostensibly "for medicinal treatment." Nneka succeeded in bearing at least three children with paramours before returning to her marital home. Baby did not conceive in the ten-year period she was away from her husband, who later requested her return while he was able to have children with his second wife.

34. I have examined elsewhere the interesting ways this institution forestalled the formation of patriarchal relations (Nzegwu 2002). Central to it is

the concept of *oyi* (friend) which connotes a process of *iyi oyi* (having a friend/lover).

35. On "eloping" from her marital home, the woman was received by the paramour, his family, and ward with great fanfare. On occasions, cannons were fired where the personalities involved were sufficiently prominent and affluent. Wards kept tallies as to which one was more successful in receiving "elopees." The relocation and return of the bridewealth to the former husband marked the formal end of the previous marriage and the beginning of the new. Wards with a high number of elopees prided themselves for being very attractive to women and in being good husbands. Both parties were forced to recognize that there was no permanence to marriage outside what both couples worked to achieve; permanence could only be ensured if one was a good husband, an idea that subjected the spouses to continuous scrutiny. *Igba n'rira* forced men to refine and highlight their skills as reasonable, cooperative, flexible, and affectionate men and to portray themselves as better husbands. Because *igba n'rira* was one of those social practices that proved that men did not have suzerainty over women, it was inevitable that it was one of the first casualties in colonial, missionary, and African men's construal of customs and tradition.

36. The customs became stultifying when the supportive environment changed. In eroding families' support of daughters, such customs caused them to ignore women's needs and rights. This closure meant that, whereas in the past, no family would condone the maltreatment of their daughters, since a family's integrity is affected by the treatment meted out to one of its members, they do so today. If a daughter was being abused in her marital home, the abuse and disrespect were also directed to, and shared by, all members of the family. It is for this reason that daughters were expected to come home if they encountered unfavorable marital conditions. Because no member of a family is an autonomous individual, the family relationally shares respect. The maltreatment of one is the maltreatment of all members, a situation that eventually necessitated ensuring that bridewealth be affordable, in case a daughter need to end her marriage in a hurry. This ensures that she is not trapped in an unhappy or disastrous marriage. The shift in consciousness brought about by colonialism means that integrity is no longer collectively shared. It opens up the possibility that daughters may be abused with impunity.

37. This was a particularly severe form of punishment for recalcitrant husbands exerted by contemporary Igbo wives. In places where the bridewealth was substantially heavy, men often found that they lacked the financial means to marry another wife, if their departing wife failed to return her bridewealth. When a husband demanded the bridewealth, the estranged wife usually sent him to her family, since they were the ones who shared the wealth. They, in turn, would inform him that they had spent the money. They would promise to pay once their daughter got a new husband who would pay bridewealth. In

the meantime, the former husband lacked both a wife and the means to marry another one.

38. Meek portrayed women as irrational only to belatedly admit that "there were other predisposing causes of discontent chief among these was widespread hatred of the corrupt system of native administration" (1937, ix).

39. See the analyses of G. I. Jones (1989), Victor Uchendu (1965), and C. K. Meek (1937).

40. Meek continually gave inaccurate accounts of Igbo women in his study. His errors may be seen as proof of his lack of awareness of the multiple identities of women and the sorts of social, political, and religious obligations that are attached to those roles. He often collapsed the duties of daughters with the duties of wives and then deployed his error to establish the minority status of women in general. See Meek (1937, 334).

41. Inflation and high cost of living was one of them. Walter Rodney makes this clear when he revealed that in 1929, the United African Company (UAC) and other trading companies in Eastern Nigeria had reduced the prices they paid for palm produce, principally produced by Igbo women. This price reduction was catastrophic for women since at the same time the cost of living was rising owing to the higher cost of imported goods (Rodney 1982, 158). G. I. Jones also explained why the tax issue was very pertinent to Igbo women. Because they had the only profitable commodity, oil palm produce, they had to contribute substantially to their husband's and sons' tax. Jones also disclosed that the region was already going through severe recession because of the 1929 global recession and the depressed prices companies were paying for palm oil. He believed that the protectorate government in Lagos was unaware of the economic realities in the region and hence treated it unfairly. According to him, no consideration was given to a region that was

> already contributing a disproportionate amount of the revenue of the country in indirect taxation through export and import duties. The duty on kernels and on palm oil was based on their weight and not on their value. A ton of kernels paid a duty of 22s 6d. In 1923 when it had been raised to this amount it represented an ad valorum duty of 8%. With the fall in world prices this had increased to 14%. The duty on oil increased similarly from 6% to over 11%. The only concession made by the government was to abolish the 15% ad valorum duty on imported foodstuffs. While this . . . benefited urban dwellers in Lagos and Port Harcourt and particular expatriates and middle class Africans, it had little relevance to the eastern provinces which were self-sufficient in their food supply and did not buy any of these imports except stockfish, a semi-luxury. (Jones 1989, 102)

42. In fact, in 1929, Assistant District Officer Captain John Cook called warrant chiefs together and told them they were to conduct a new detailed

count of wives, children, goats, etc. He added that the "exercise had nothing to do with the tax on women." But this statement was greeted with foreboding because the same ploy had been employed when men were counted. Warrant chiefs concluded that this would be the case and informed the community that this was a prelude to women's taxation (Afigbo 1972, 236). Reinforcing this interpretation, Nwabara reveals that the government's intention to tax women was also supported by the divisional officer of Nsukka, W. H. Lloyd (see Nwabara 1977, 198). On Lloyd's account they were already assessing women's crops—cocoyam, maize, livestock—and even apparel (1977, 176).

43. In the Commission of Inquiry investigating the causes of the uprising, women vented their frustration against the instrument of governance that required them to subsidize their men while refusing to recognize them.

44. Ogoja Province Annual Report, 1928; see also Mba. (1982, 72–73).

45. This occurred in 1928 (Mba 1982, 73).

46. Wives of the new burgeoning elite modeled themselves on the patriarchal framework and helped perpetuate the idea that men traditionally dominated Igbo societies. British colonial officials failed to grasp that the fact that these wives of the new elite deferred to their husbands and accepted them as their masters did not mean that the new lifestyle reflected the values of the older society. If anything, they were different.

47. In other areas women drew attention to road safety, insisting that the rapidly moving traffic on the tarred roads was creating fatalities.

48. She was one of the several women killed in this region.

49. The colonial government still found it hard to grapple with the idea of women as political agents, and so it refused to acknowledge the full implication of women's charges.

50. Afigbo 1972, Mba 1982, Amadiume 1987. Mba and Amadiume seemed to have subscribed to the feminist view of human development, and to the idea that patriarchy was pervasive.

51. For historical records on the uprising report see the official papers of the Birrell Gray Commission (1929), and the Aba Commission of Inquiry (1930).

52. See Mba (1982, 87–93). We should note that references to men are usually references to husbands, brothers, uncles, fathers, etc. The town and village setting in which people lived then was one in which references to "men" did not refer to faceless individuals.

53. It is important to realize that at this point in time affluent women could not utilize the services of banks—either bank their money or obtain loans in their own names.

54. A dead give-away in the Igbo situation is the failure to include the erosion of the rights of daughters to family resources in theorizing about the colonial impact on the culture. This happens because the focus is always on women as wives and their experiences in their marital homes, and because it

is assumed that marriages were permanent. But when we consider the life histories of women at the turn of the century and institutions such as *idigbe, igba n'rira* and *ikwu ngo* (paying back the bridewealth)—all of which speak of the termination of a marriage, we need to address how those women survived in the society. When we do, we will find that some returned to their natal homes, lived in their own dwellings or residential units, and engaged in economic activities. They did not necessarily live with their mothers, and they had their own farmland for their needs. This aspect of daughters' resource access is never highlighted in texts, and so we fail to see and subsequently preserve their rights.

55. We must not forget that in Nigeria's present economic state, land was a valuable commodity. It not only provided food (agriculture) and shelter (rent-free home), but it gave owners the requisite collateral to engage in higher-level economic activities. One of such phenomenon is the elimination of daughter's right of access to family land, which today is being explained in terms of "our patriarchal tradition." Yet, to focus on the processes of transformation would have allowed theorists to see the myriad land registration policy and the colonial Native Authority Administration shortchanged Igbo women.

56. Consider the earlier mentioned examples of Obi Oputa of Aboh, Okugo of Oloko, Okposi chiefs in Afikpo, and O'Connor in Onitsha.

57. A "head of household" was deemed to be the breadwinner. In the colonial patriarchal ideology, that individual is an exclusively a man, either a husband or father, with a passive, dependent wife. The error in using this concept in Igboland, at the time, was that wives were neither dependent on husbands nor passive beings (see Leith-Ross 1965, 230–32). They traded, farmed, and processed agricultural products. There was equal partnership in the maintenance of the family. Despite the important role of Igbo wives in the home, anthropologists and colonial officers automatically assumed that only husbands were breadwinners and all others in the households—wife, son, daughters, and others—were dependents. This definition did not accommodate the very real fact that Igbo wives were never economically dependent on husbands and were not maintained by them. In fact, Igbo wives maintained themselves and their children, and sometimes even the husband. In the subsistence economy that existed at the turn of the twentieth century, wives were equal and sometimes carried the burden of maintaining the family. Yet, because the pattern of Igbo marriage appeared virilocal, anthropologists and colonial officials erroneously assumed that since wives were not the owners of the house in the affinal compound, they must have been passive beings and economically dependent on the husband, which was not true. Yet, by this characterization, they effectively obscured from view Igbo wives' contributions to the marriage as well as began the undermining of the former equitable basis of marriage.

58. See S. N. Chinwuba Obi on "Types of Elementary Families" (1966, 90–92).

59. Such public policies include: the designation of a wife's property as marital property that the husband can lawfully control and dispose of without her consent; securing permission from the husband to receive medical treatment and be operated upon; securing permission from the husband to open and operate a bank account; securing permission to obtain a job, and so on.

60. See the special issue of the journal *Development and Change* (vol. 18, 1987), which is devoted to the concept of household in Africa.

61. See the works of Ekejiuba (1995), Sudarkasa (1996), and Fapohunda (1987).

62. See Thomas (1913–14), Basden (1966), Meek (1937), Jones (1989).

63. Targeting oil mill presses to men (Mba), presenting themselves as heads of households with the power shift that entailed, and effacing the contributions of women in the running of the society.

64. See Amadiume (1997), (1987a), and (1987b).

Chapter 3. Customs and Misrepresentations

1. This timeline follows that of Richard Henderson (1972, 90–102).

2. Also see Henderson 1972, 190. An example is Margaret Arimah of Umu Dei, wife of Joseph Ntephe of Umuaroli.

3. Section 2 of the Kola Tenancy Law of 1935 defines a "kola tenancy" as a right of use and occupation of any land which is enjoyed by a native in virtue of a kola, (a genus of a West African tree developing into a nut used in drugs and for flavoring of local drinks) or other token payment made by such native or any predecessor in title or in virtue of a grant from which no payment in money or any kind was enacted.

4. The success of Nwanyiemelie (the Triumphant Woman) Nwonaku, daughter of Adiebo Eseagba of Ofuluzo family of Umu Dei, lay in establishing personal relationships with the agents. While still married to Ifeajunna, she became a polygamist, marrying many wives of her own, whom she set up as companions to her male trading partners, especially the European and Sierra Leonean agents. This network of familial ties created a competitive edge for her trading operations, based primarily as it was on the *kwolu kwondi* (barter-trust) system of trade. Her wives, who were companions to her trading partners, created a context of recognition and trust for her, and in this sense functioned as her trading collaterals. She deployed her two sisters as key officers in her trade and investment operations. At her death in July 1919, she had established a trading empire in palm produce, fish, and trade goods, namely cloth, matches, and tobacco. She was a very wealthy woman, with wealth measured in cowries, brass rods, cloth, and land.

5. A notable entrepreneur, Lucinda Okwunne, daughter of Bachi Olodi Akpe of Ogboli Olosi, married an agent G. W. Christian, and used her

position as wife to control the firm's policy with whom to trade. As the link between the locals and the Europeans, Lucinda expanded her trading influence, setting up a parallel trading operation beside her husband's shop. Utilizing the *kwolu kwondi* (barter) method, she resold the share of goods personally allocated to her by her husband in smaller quantities to smaller traders. By this means, she built up a comfortable investment in cloth, cowries, and land before leaving her husband in 1915. Marriage to a European factory agent gave Lucinda an effective means of raising capital to purchase land, control trade, and earn her creditworthiness. For the agents, marriage was a critical way to secure their trading operations from fraud and defaulters.

6. Also see Kristin Mann on women and landed property in Lagos (Mann 1991a, 1991b).

7. Mann presents a case of such encroachment in which a brother disinherited his sister. The dying father had given the son (Pedro Feliciano) the crown grant to the land on which stood the family home, and after the death of their mother, the brother evicted the sister (Maria Theresa) and took over the house for his sole use (1991b, 695). The court ruled in favor of the brother when the sister took the case to court (*Maria Theresa v. Pedro Feliciano*, April 19, 1897). Though women had the right to share in the family estate, this was not always preserved by male relatives who typically appropriated the entire family resources for their personal use, and in this way put female relatives to economic disadvantage. Another case was that of a husband's punitive attempt to disinherit his wife. Unbeknownst to Mary Macaulay, her husband Collins D. Macaulay took the title of the property she inherited from her paternal aunt, Nancy Cole, and used it as security to obtain a loan. He defaulted on the loan and skipped out on the marriage. The moneylender foreclosed on the loan and sold the property. Mary was able to get her land back only because she was able to hire an attorney to fight in court (*Mary Macaulay v. Buari Apala and Faseke Olukolu*, 1894). Those who did not have the resources to hire a lawyer simply lost their property.

8. *Nwugege v. Adigwe & anor.*, Nigerian Law Reports (1934), 134.

9. See the 1963 official report of the inquiry of Obiship dispute.

10. This does not mean that only Igbo judges are discriminatory. Similar patterns can be found in other parts of the country, as reflected in cases such as *Ogamien v. Ogamien* (1967), and *Idehen v. Idehen* (1991). Essentially, *Nnezianya v. Okagbue & 2 Ors.* (1963) says that a daughter's children have no right to inherit their grandfather's estate because their mother, who is the only child of her parents, is female. *Onwuchekwa v. Onwuchekwa* (1991) dismissed as not repugnant to natural justice a wife's claim that to deny her interest in a jointly acquired property deemed her and her money the property of her husband. See also *Eze v. Eze*.

11. Justice Eze Ezobu, in a paper on law of succession and land law delivered at the National Workshop for Magistrates, Area and Customary Court Judges, June 15–26, 1992.

12. It is important to note that there have been extensive reforms of the British judicial system to make it more gender sensitive. A similar practice has not occurred in the Nigerian judicial system that seems to take pride in handing down gender insensitive rulings. For examples of such rulings, see Ewelukwa 2002.

13. My emphasis, WD/19/61 [unreported] cited in Kasunmu 1977. This was not unlike the 1987 case of Wambui Otieno, when the Appellate Court in Kenya dismissed the applicability of the Marriage Act that governed her marriage, and insisted that customary law must prevail. See Stamp 1991.

14. For versions of the founding of Nnewi see Amadiume 1987b.

15. It would make sense for Okakpu to stand by Caroline if she were the full-blooded sister of Caroline's deceased spouse. But the facts of the case state that Okakpu is Augustine's half sister; they share the same father, not the same mother. As we saw in chapter 1, the first unit of salience is the uterine unit which forges the most intimate bond of kinship. By virtue of having different mothers, Augustine and Okakpu are not bound by the most intimate *ibe nne* or *oma* even though they are bound by the *ibe nne* of their father's mother. But the latter *ibe nne* also binds them to Adina and Adina's interest within the family. Because the father's mother *ibe nne* is much weaker, and Augustine has already violated it by trying to void Adina's interests, Okakpu really was not breaking ranks with her family, as Oladapo presumed. She was working for the interests of her consanguineal family to ensure that all its extended branches are preserved. Her staunch support of Caroline also suggests that her mother and Caroline are probably from the same village or are related in some way, or belong to the same church.

16. It is noteworthy that the institution of *mmuo* (masked "spirits") and *ora okwute* (the judicial organization attached to the former), was brought to Onitsha by an Onitsha woman, Usse, daughter of Eze Aroli and wife of Onojo Oboni, and her Igala son, Idoko.

17. All women of Ogbeotu are considered initiates of the masquerade institution by virtue of their Igala lineage and in deference to Usse, who introduced the institution to Onitsha.

18. Cases abound in Onitsha in which widows whose marriages had been contracted under the Marriage Act are denied letters of administration on the ground that under customary law widows cannot administer their husband's estate even though the property has been acquired through the joint efforts and initiatives of both partners and is not in family compounds. In other cases, sons who were not known to exist during the marriage of the couple sur-

faced after the death of a husband to claim property. Other cases include those in which widows were denied letters of administration on the ground that they were not of good behavior. All kinds of obstacles are placed in the paths of widows at the time of their husbands' death to prevent them from being granted letters of administration to take care of the children of the marriage. See the essays of A. B. Kasunmu and Okey Achike in *Law and the African Family in Africa* (1977).

19. Ewelukwa points out that The High Court Law of Eastern Nigeria, Cap. 61, Laws of Eastern Nigeria, 1963 are based on English statutes as the Wills Act 1837 and the Married Women Property Act 1882. These operate as laws in Eastern Nigeria (of which Anambra state is a part) and affect the right of widows even though they may have been repealed or amended in England. This means that the rules governing the administration of estate in England before 1900 apply. Included in this rule are the English Statutes of Distribution of 1670 and 1685, but not the English Administration of Estates Act of 1925 and 1952. To make matters worse, the Supreme Court Ordinance states that the court has a duty, subject to certain requirements, to enforce native laws and customs. See footnotes 70 on p. 446 and 97 on p. 453.

20. Widows, especially young ones, are always under suspicion. The motives of brothers and their wives are never questioned. When the living male "protector" is alive, financially well off, and values the wife, she is accepted and can do no wrong. But as soon as the "protector" dies, the wife is cast in the role of a villain. She is then accused of killing the spouse. There is logic to this vilification. It creates the necessary public basis upon which preemptive attempts to appropriate a deceased's resources are launched.

21. The tensions between the two forms of marriages turned wives into a flashpoint of family disputes. In the past the consanguineal principle of family organization promoted a consciousness of inclusivity; however, modern nuclear family values and the exigencies of modern life undermined the effectiveness of wives organizations, which had acted as bulwark against members of the affinal family.

22. Joining male family detractors are married daughters (who have not been provided for by their own natal family) and other wives (who tomorrow may become "husband killers"). While there are tangible benefits for some male members of the family, the benefits for the women are always ephemeral.

23. It may be assumed that it is only marriages contracted under customary norms that face harrowing disputes over inheritance. But that is not the case. Although the Marriage Act is seen as minimizing the vulnerability of women and of reducing incidences of inheritance disputes, widows still undergo terrible experiences unless their children are sufficiently grown to stand up to their father's family. Despite the growing preference for companionate marriage, wives are still seen as outsiders who do not belong to the "family." As

economic times worsen, widows and children have to fight off their brothers-in-law/uncles intent on appropriating the property of "our brother."

24. It is interesting to observe the varying ways in which men endeavor to extend control over women, even when there is no traditional basis for such authority. My male witness referred to as PW1 and the defendant/appellant always tried to add provisos to make it seem that decisions were contingent only on male authority.

25. This is the same kind of legal maneuver that is presently ongoing in northern Nigeria. Sharia courts are handing down death sentences on poor women on the basis that they are adulterous, while their male partners avoid conviction because there are not six witnesses to the crime. Although concerned with truth and righteousness, it is interesting that DNA proof is conveniently rejected, not because it would not yield the truth, but on the basis that it is not in the Qur'an. That these acts are motivated by gender oppression becomes obvious when local customs that are favorable to women are quickly undermined as inconsistent with the norms of a modern society.

26. Given that the socioeconomic conditions that once made it imperative for land to reside with the family no longer exists, there is no reason for married daughters not to inherit their father's estate.

27. I see this as early evidence of the gradual adoption by consanguineal family of the Western proprietal framework and the transformation of the *di okpala* as a patriarch.

28. Daughters were entitled to live in their father's house until they married and moved to their marital homes. But should any of their marriages fail, they would move back to live with their mother, if she were still alive and residing in the home. If all these daughters married, and their mother subsequently died while they were still married, the property then became *oku diokpa* ("property for the oldest son").

29. I have in mind the Ezeoba v. Mozie Civil War; the 1899–1900 and the 1931–1935 Obi-ship disputes; the insurrection of Chief Odita, Ajie, and the impeachment of Obiozo, Onyia.

30. Another newer equity principle of division was that utilized by the Egbunike family after the Nigerian Civil War. They chose to dispense with the old principle of dividing on the basis of mother. Instead, they accommodated all the sons of the family, even though that meant that some, whose allotment would have been larger on the old principle (because they were the only sons of their mother), took a smaller share. The Obianwu family has also utilized a different model of inheritance division, in which all the children—both sons and daughters—received allocations. The point is that a lot of modifications are already in place in Onitsha.

31. So why did my counsel fail to explain the issue to the judges? The counsel who had conducted this case from the start, Chief Amanke Okafor,

had then suffered the most tragic blow of his life, the loss of his only child and son. Because I had authorized him to act in my interest regarding all legal matters, he handed the case to another counsel who was not as well versed in the intricacies of the case as Okafor, and who, for that reason, may have missed the fact that the contradiction was a false one.

32. The year was 1997.

33. The issue of contradiction is something that I dealt with extensively as part of an advanced course in logic during my doctoral program. For an entire semester I plowed through all manner of proofs from predicate logic with identity, modal logic, intuitionistic logic, theory of definite descriptions, set theory, to Godel's Theorem. That exercise trained me to see the lower threshold of proof that people often invoke to declare a set of statements a contradiction. Those declarations, strictly speaking, are logically inaccurate. What are normally referred to as contradictions are usually inconsistencies or oblique statements that *appear* to be contradictory because an inappropriately narrow frame of reference is utilized to understand the assertions, or one is bamboozled by metaphoric expressions and sees a contradiction where none exists.

34. In fact, the very real possibility that there could be miscarriage of justice because customs are misinterpreted by judges who are not members of a culture, is good reason for shifting from customary law to the constitution.

35. Note that in marriage a wife co-mingles her finances with her husband and they jointly invest in such big-ticket projects as buying land and building a home. However, when a divorce occurs, *she* has to move out of the jointly acquired real estate because it is *his* property.

36. Some wives have kept having more children in the hope that the next child will be a son. There are numerous cases where some have continued and failed only to have their husband bring anther wife into the home to produce what she obviously cannot.

37. See the concluding section of Amadime's *Afrikan Matriarchal Foundations: The Igbo Case* (1987b).

38. That section states that "a citizen of Nigeria of a particular . . . sex . . . shall not, by reason only that he is such a person —be subjected either expressly by, or in the practical application of, any law in force in Nigeria or any executive or administrative action of the government, to disabilities or restrictions to which citizens of Nigeria of other . . . sex . . . are not made subject" (Nigerian Constitution 1979).

39. This has certainly been my own experience. I filed the case in 1980 and by the time judgement was rendered in 1986, I had completed a two years master's program in philosophy in Nigeria, and I was two years into a doctoral program in philosophy in Canada. By the time the Federal Court of Appeals handed down its judgment in 1997, I had earned my Ph.D., taught for six years at a university in the United States, and received tenure. Had I stayed in the

house in the midst of hostile relatives-in-law, it is doubtful that I would have made significant progress in life.

40. Some feminists have argued that to avoid being discriminatory toward women, legal and institutional precepts must take into account such events in a woman's life as pregnancy, nurturing, and motherhood.

Chapter 4. The Conclave

1. Against a background of important texts about Onitsha, this chapter articulates a model of agency, rights, and political consciousness that once characterized women's reality in Onitsha. Richard Henderson (1972) and Helen Henderson's (1969) substantive study of Onitsha society, Ikenna Nzimiro's (1972) informative work on Onitsha political systems, S. I. Bosah (1979) and Sam Ifeka's (1973) social histories, and R. W. Harding's Report on the Obiship dispute (1963) collectively raise critical questions about sex equality and women's political roles in Onitsha. As valuable as these studies have become, they paint a gloomy picture of a society (except for Helen Henderson's study), in which women are absent in the political processes of community administration. In the depicted all-male terrain, social and political identities are presented as constitutively male and the exclusive prerogative of men. This corresponding presentation of women as second-class citizens raises the following question: How can men be the only political actors when the political, economic, social, and religious roles of women have not been examined?

2. She was the wife of Egwuatu of Ogbeotu and the last Omu. She died in 1886. See Orakwue (1953).

3. Helen Henderson is a white American female anthropologist. In 1962–1963, she carried out field research for her doctoral thesis in Onitsha. Her part was created after my reading of her dissertation. She was included more to give substantive weight to the opinion of the Western women than to make her out as a feminist. Her dissertation on Onitsha women is a major work that should have been published.

4. Uwechia and Chinyelugo Chugbo worked in this capacity from 1974 to 1990. With the demise of the Omu institution after colonialism, the office of Onye-Isi-Ikporo-Onitsha (Head-Of-Onitsha-Women) was revamped to replace that of the Omu.

5. I acknowledge that the environment in which Helen Henderson conducted her research in the early 1960s is different from the one in which an Omu ruled. Though the institution of Ikporo Onitsha existed and there was an Onye-isi-Ikporo-Onitsha in the period, the character of rule was low-keyed and radically different from the formal ceremonial rule of an Omu. The decline of the office of Omu was caused by the combined effect of Christianization, the monopolistic trade policies of the Niger Trading Company, colonial gender

policies of Western education, and the new prestigious role of "wife" that prevented the new generation of Onitsha women from going into commercial trading. The long-term effect of this changing ideological pattern was a growth in female dependency and a decline in the wealth-generating capabilities of Onitsha women. As the male-privileging policies of the colonial administration gained sway, few women had the financial resources to make a bid for the Omu-ship.

6. The male-privileging ethos has been highlighted by a number of scholars. For the purposes of this chapter, I am focusing on the works of the following scholars: Catharine MacKinnon in the chapter "Difference and Dominance: On Sex Discrimination" (1987 32–45); and Aki-Kwe/Mary Ellen Turpel's critique of Canada's individualistic notion of right and individual autonomy (1989, 149–57). It also emerged in the symposium among E. Dubois, M. Dunlap, C. Gilligan, C. MacKinnon, and C. Menkel-Meadow (1985, 11–87).

7. Although the literal translation of Ikporo Onitsha is Women of Onitsha, the translation Council of Community Mothers also captures the duties of women as community mothers. I shall use the terms interchangeably.

8. Most of what de Beauvoir says is in the form of direct quotes or paraphrases from *The Second Sex* (1990).

9. Some of these may in actual fact be uncles, and aunts.

10. This idea is taken from Juliet Mitchell (1987, 26).

11. To use as an attack implement.

12. The female sacred meeting ground.

13. It may be argued that the need to underscore women's value is a compensatory move that establishes the subordinate status of women. The view is that the same is not done for men, since it goes without saying that men are valued. This analysis is problematic. It presupposes the primacy of men, and reproduces patriarchy by ignoring salient aspects of the culture. Voicing and naming are important features in an orally structured conceptual scheme. You name and voice that which you want to underscore. It is this same principle that compels men in the prestigious Agbalanze society to take as their title *Akunne* (mother's wealth). This same affirmative and validatory spirit underpins the name "*Nwanyibuife*," a constant and joyous reminder of women's worth.

14. "*Nne Chiokwu*" means mother of Chiokwu, which is the preferred way of naming mothers. "*Nne*" means mother.

15. The "chi" referenced here is the personal spirit or guardian of each individual. Before birth, it is believed that all souls choose their fate in life, and that they live according to that prenatal life plan. Individuals cannot deviate from this plan, though they can modify some of the provisions of their choice.

16. What she is referring here as "men" are actually lineage sons who have their own meetings in the same way that lineage daughters have their own meetings.

17. For rich ethnographic material on this topic, see Helen Henderson (1970, 257–63).

18. The information the Onowu is responding to is contained in Henderson, (1969, 250–51).

19. For references on Omu Onyearo Nkechi, see Orakwue (1953, 59).

20. The information is from Taylor and Crowther (1864, 33) as cited in Henderson's Ph.D. diss. (1969, 244).

21. See excerpt of John Whitford's 1877 description in Isichei (1978, 257).

22. Women who tried to expose the secrets of masquerade have been executed, but that is not really an issue of female oppression. The same fate has been meted out to men who committed the same offense. It is difficult to attempt to use a masquerade for a widespread oppression of women. Members of a lineage and members of a mother's lineage will not stand by and watch a daughter's or a granddaughter's humiliation. It is not just that such an event is a negative mark on the family's reputation, but that the protection and well-being of every member of the lineage (both living and dead) is a sacred responsibility.

23. Ideas for the comments of the visitors in this section came from Susan Moller Okin's "Introduction" to *Justice, Gender, and the Family* (1989).

24. In the first half of the twentieth century, women would be long- and short-distance traders, herbalists, diviners, farmers, fisherwomen, cloth weavers, potters, and so on. In the second half of the century, these roles expanded to include the following professions: law, teaching, nursing, medicine, civil administration, engineering, journalism, judicial roles, trading, and so on.

25. It is important to stress that "female principle" does not mean the feminine as a patriarchal ideology suggests.

26. This quote is originally George Bernard Shaw's, which de Beauvoir (1990) used in the section "Woman as 'Other.'"

27. A proverb that not-so-politely hints that one has lost perspective and is acting irresponsibly. It refers back to the case of a woman, who in the process of snuffing tobacco, ignored the safety of her baby. When rebuked for nearly dropping her baby, she nonchalantly replied, "I know the root and ways of childmaking, but I have no clues as to that of tobacco production." The Omu's use of it informs Onyeamama that she understands her objective to trivialize and ridicule the visitors' concerns.

28. Specifically, conceptual uniformists worry about the prospects of adjudicating between right and wrong, if opposing ethical values are assigned to the same act. Horror scenarios are imagined: What if sex discrimination is presented as sex equality in a place like Saudi Arabia? What if female circumcision is construed as an instance of female equality in Somalia and Sudan, or *suttee* and female infanticide in India, or wearing the *burqa* in Afghanistan?

The very idea that these practices could have positive meaning under the doctrine of cultural equivalence reinforces the rejection of the idea that equality might have different meanings for many people. If these questions seem normal, carefully note the cultural direction in which the charge of sex discrimination seems "naturally" to lie. Would the questions have been normal if African, Indian, Chinese, or Japanese women were indicting the West for sex discrimination?

29. These would include the use of silicone gel in women's breasts, liposuctions, cosmetic facelifts, and the cutting away of body parts in the name of beauty. In their view, the pornographic marketing of anorexic teenage girls and women as objects of erotica is symptomatic of a diseased society and must not be tolerated under the idea of sex equality.

30. I should point out an important shift. Whereas in the past, the fear is not that some onerous practice may be viewed as acceptable, in the present age of globalization, the issue is that cultural differences should be eliminated.

Chapter 5. Structures of Equality

1. In her critique of Rawls' "Justice as Fairness: For Whom?" Susan Moller Okin argued that Rawls' dismissal of sex allowed him to present a theory of justice that assumes and rests on gender inequality in the family. Moreover, life as a person of color in Canada or the United States shows that the issue of equality does not lie in the creation of a set of perfectly neutral precepts but in with how these precepts are deployed.

2. For more detailed reading on this point see Razack (1998); Crenshaw (1995); Higginbotham (1995); Brown (1995); Harris (1995); Matsuda (1989); Eisenstein (1988); MacKinnon (1989); Fudge (1988); Thornhill (1985a, 1985b).

3. See Rawls's description of the "original position"; specifically pages 12 and 137. The weakness of this abstract experience is that others whose bodies have been the target of stigmatization and are given to monthly hormonal cycles cannot easily imagine away features that are constitutive of their body. The mere idea of a removal of these stigmas does not mean that the individual automatically enters a prestigmatization phase.

4. See Eisenstein (1988). She argues that with men as the norm, discussions of even biological sex privilege the male body (1988, 79–116).

5. The conflation of Rawls's and Macpherson's position may be seen as inherently problematic. It was done to highlight the basic assumptions of the individualistic principles underpinning the two positions. Macpherson's portrayal of the "possessive individual" underlying liberalism may be seen as no longer relevant to contemporary life, since later theorists have corrected earlier defects. However, when one is outside the conceptual framework and unconcerned with matters of detail, it becomes very relevant, since most of the

structural problems that Marxists and feminists have identified as flaws of the liberal-democratic tradition substantially retain the central ideas and assumptions of its seventeenth-century genesis. See C. B. Macpherson on individualism versus collectivism (1962, 255).

6. Note that this does not imply cultural stasis, since people are aware that change is a normal phenomenon in any society. What is being recognized here, too, is the right of any people to define and modify their concept of a good life.

7. This charge underlies the works of Kofi Buenor Hadjor (1998), James Hsiung (1985), and Makau Mutua (2002).

8. The fact that Aboriginal People have a different conceptual scheme does not mean that they cannot be forced to regulate their life under Canada's liberal scheme, but it will necessarily throw their life into chaos. However, the question is not whether or not they can adapt and change, but whether there is justification for forcing them to adapt. The answer that liberalism is a better model simply begs the question.

9. Today the United States and Canada's liberal frameworks have effectively marginalized the communal Aboriginal worldview. Nothing says that the social vision of liberalism is ethically superior or that it is the best possible model. This raises important questions: What moral arguments do proponents of liberalism draw upon to justify the violent overthrow of an incompatible ontological scheme? What makes liberal equality necessarily superior? Is it actually superior?

10. Makau Matua makes a similar point, contending that in the West, "the language of rights primarily developed along the trajectory of claims against the state; entitlements which imply the right to seek an individual remedy for a wrong" (2002, 71).

11. See Butler (2001) and Pateman (2001). European women could never become individuals because they were conceptualized as extensions of the dominant male figure in their lives.

12. Leon Higginbotham (1996) gave a chronological survey of how the system of justice exacerbated the problem. As well, the recent right-wing assault on affirmative action reveals that at its heart, whiteness is the norm and all others undeserving recipients. Also see Cheryl Harris's argument in "Whiteness as Property" (1995).

13. Although the main focus of the argument is on the sex/gender divide, the following theories make this pertinent point. See Catharine MacKinnon (1989, 1987); Christine Koggel (1994, 45–47); Judy Fudge (1988, 493–95).

14. In the recent case of African American farmers, for example, even after it became clear that the United States Department of Agriculture had discriminated against them in the disbursement of loans, getting restitution has not been easy. See K. Dewan (2004).

15. Blacks are frequently perceived as breaking the law when they drive, indicating that they were never part of the constituency the laws were designed to protect.

16. In *Sexual Contract*, Carole Pateman also provides a much more substantial explanation of the conceptual roots and character of this problem and also of how it affects women. See also Lenore J. Weitzman's research on the social and economic effects of divorce law reforms reveals how the rights of white men regularly override those of white women in the judicial system, with devastating political, social, and economic consequences (1990, 312–35).

17. Although MacKinnon does not say "white women," the logic of her argument captures the relationship of white women to white men rather than of black women to either white or black men. Harris (1990), Crenshaw (1995), Brown (1995, 39–54) and E. Higginbotham (1995, 3–24) have, in different ways, made the argument that race invidiously defines the reality of black women and that it is outranks sex in the definition of difference.

18. See Elizabeth Spelman on this point in *Inessential Woman* (1988).

19. According to Lee Drutman, "where the cost of corporate crime has been estimated, the numbers are staggering. Most credible estimates confirm that, in the aggregate, white-collar and corporate crimes cost the United States hundreds of billions of dollars annually—far more than conventional categories of crimes such as burglary and robbery." See "It's time to chart the toll of America's corporate crime," (2003, 16A).

20. See Crenshaw (1995), Harris (1995), Mills (1999, 1997), Eisenstein (1988), L. Gordon (1999, 1995), Koggel (1994), MacKinnon (1987, 2000), Fudge (1988), and Aki-kwe (1989). Gordon's concept of bad faith provides an existential argument as to why the extension of substantive equality to blacks falls short. It problematizes the humanity of blacks and challenges our assumptions of what it means to be human.

21. The mono-sex system is sexually dimorphic in nature even though it presents the society as single-sexed. The liberal democratic system of the Western society is basically a mono-sex system with two prominent spaces: the public and the private spheres. In the public sphere, we find all the various male-dominant organs of governance—the executive, judiciary, legislature—with different systems of governance—monarchical, parliamentary, presidential, socialist, or Soviet. The private sphere is the domestic realm, but the normative sex of that environment is inherently male. Only fathers who are inevitably always male have the authority to rule the family. No female—wife or daughter—has any structural powers.

22. Sir W. Blackstone, *Commentaries on the Laws of England*, 4th Ed., ed. J. DeWitt Andrews, 442. (Chicago: Allaghan and Co., 1899) Cited in Pateman 2001, 129.

23. For further reading, see Elizabeth Potter (1994, 27–50).

24. For further discussion of this point, see Pateman and Shanley 1991, 3.

25. It never greatly mattered that the social largesse of freedom and equality about which Locke and Rousseau waxed eloquent were both a product of slavery and the exploitative appropriations of the land of Aboriginal Peoples in Canada and the United States. For Locke and Rousseau, the benefits of freedom went unproblematically and exclusively to white men, who were the only ones recognized as capable of political action by the system. Men, as the sole citizens in the "democratic" mono-sex polis, were the beneficiaries of rights that were only minimally circumscribed. They used the law to secure many of the political, social, and cultural policies that implicitly and explicitly privileged them.

26. White men are presumed to have the requisite intellectual insight and emotional maturity to rule, while white women and racial minorities are regarded as lacking the necessary intelligence to run their lives.

27. We should avoid seeing the population in these areas as exclusively white given that Aboriginal peoples predate the arrival of Europeans in the United States and Canada, and Africans have been there too, including Europe, in large numbers since the eighteenth century.

28. It is not an accident that the spousal dependency of middle-class white women was the focus of second-wave feminism.

29. This is because the mono-sex system neutralizes women's power by fragmenting their consciousness. Such a system cannot hold the key to women's salvation. Ruth's point clarifies why the Omu requests her visitors: "Take a good look at me, and at the position I occupy: *Omu* (female monarch) of the community and *Onye-Isi-Ikporo Onitsha* (head of *Ikporo Onitsha*)." Her point is not the trivial one that a female can be the head of the structure, but that under a different theory of society, social equality is possible, and the major political positions will be occupied by both men and women.

30. Lester Thurow (1994) has pointed out the readiness of the liberal democratic system to accommodate corporations and business groups, which is at odds with the strong resistance an administration puts up when a marginalized racialized group demands an end to group discrimination. In the latter case, group arguments are treated as illegitimate, even though they are accommodated for corporations and business interests.

31. I have opted to use the term "dual-sex," which Amadiume declared is misconceived. Her claim that it references a rigid system in which "male attributes and male status referred to the biologically male sex—man—as female attributes and female status referred to the biologically female sex—woman" is true if and only if the patriarchal scheme of interpretation is presupposed (1987a, 15).

32. He conducts an investigation into the genealogy of the male-female dichotomy and the ways in which it is taken for granted. See Herdt (1994, 21–81).

33. It is a mistake to assume that to recognize sex difference is to allow sex inequality, since there is no entailment between the two. As argued earlier, an entailment relation exists only with a specific framework that rigs up the two in that manner.

34. For a full discussion of this point see Nzegwu 2001.

35. Okonjo's description of the Omu-ship in Obamkpa is particularly relevant since the institution is an Ika Igbo and Onitsha phenomenon (see Okonjo 1976, 45). Other descriptions offered are by the local community historian Sam Ifeka (1973) and by Richard Henderson, who also chronicled the institution in his 1972 book on Onitsha.

36. I owe this terminology to Chinturu Uchendu, 2003.

37. In this sense I differ from Amadiume, who defines men and women as biological and male and female as gender attributes. In my reading, there are no male and female attributes, because the social scheme allows for the development of these attributes across the board. Power, authority, prestige, privilege, etc., are not male attributes, as Amadiume assumes, but human social attributes that result from occupying hierarchical positions.

38. For a more extended description of the dual-sex system and of male and female responsibilities, see Okonjo (1976) and Nzegwu (1995).

39. This was what transpired during John Whitford's trip to Onitsha in 1872. The trade negotiation could only proceed when Omu Onyero Nkechi and her councilors arrived for the deliberations. See Isichei (1973).

40. The opinion of the other was respected, as the signature of the Omu on late-nineteenth-century historical records attest. At that time, much more so than now, women's authority in commerce and trade was very much respected and upheld. However, following the death of the last Omu in 1886, the powers and duties of the office devolved to *Onye-isi-Ikporo-Onitsha* (the head of the women's council).

41. This has changed over the years. The present Obi now travels out the region and outside of Nigeria frequently.

42. Past Omu have tended to occupy two main niches—the spiritual and the economic. Atagbusi, the senior daughter of Ogboli Eke ward of Onitsha was a powerful spiritual woman; Onyero Nkechi and Nwagboka were merchant queens.

43. At installation, the final rite was performed by the opposing sex. In the case of the Obi, the lineage priestess of Obio (one of the village wards of Onitsha) shaved his hair; while a non-indigene male priest from Nri performed the Omu's last dedication rite.

44. For example, and as Okonjo described for Obamkpa, matters relating to trade, market rules regulations, and price-fixing were under the jurisdiction of the Omu. Women controlled certain crops, farm animals, and economic trees; they acted as priestesses to the deities of the community, they were responsible for the propitiation of the communal deities; and certain judicial, social, and political matters of the community fell under their jurisdiction. Maintenance of trade routes, labor intensive agriculture, and certain judicial, social, and political affairs fell under the jurisdiction of the Obi and the men.

45. For further descriptions of this, see Okonjo (1976, 45–58).

46. As far as I have been able to determine, however, women were known to fend off attackers and slave raiders when their children were threatened. That they are not the ones who usually sallied off to war is not adequately explained on the grounds that they were women. It had more to do with their official status as peacemakers that is tied to the conception of motherhood and the role of mothers in the society. Mothers-as-women went to war as a last resort. As mothers, their responsibility of ensuring the continuity of the community means that they could not always afford to be in the midst of a military campaign.

47. I take here the definition of nationhood that is built on ethnicity, in which a cultural nation is equivalent to a political nation state. This is the case in European nationalism. See Oloruntimehin (1990, 565–79).

48. This relevant section of the historical document was cited in Isichei (1978).

49. It is unfortunate that this administrative feature has undergone radical transformations along male-privileging lines. This occurred in various ways. As the state and the church reinforced male dominance, the Obi of Onitsha expanded his sphere of authority to become the exclusive power in the community. Up until 1985, the last Obi of Onitsha, Ofala Okagbue, still sought out women's opinions before making policy pronouncements. This is hardly the case with the new Obi of Onitsha installed in 2001.

50. To state that a gender interpretation does not apply in this case is to admit that there are other forms of explanation that the phenomenon invokes. The same is true for the institution that Amadiume erroneously characterizes as "male daughters" and "female husbands." See Nzegwu (1998 or 2000) for a critique of such ideas.

51. Amadiume has made it seem that *umuada* police only wives. The truth is that as impartial arbitrators, they police both wives and their brothers. They chastise brothers when they feel they are over-stepping their bounds, or when they see them mistreating their wives. Although structurally, *inyemedi* is in a hierarchically subordinate position, it would be a mistake to portray the relationship between them and *umuada* as always antagonistic, and their in-

terests as always divergent. We must not forget that *umuada* are, after all, *in-yemedi* in their marital homes, and that all *inyemedi* are *umuada* in their natal homes. It is not far-fetched that within the community-wide sphere of the Women's Council, *inyemedi* would share a common interest with *umuada*.

52. De Beauvoir et al. would see themselves as freely making choices within a system that they believe offers them liberty. From another end of the spectrum, Omu et al. can see the inherent gender inequality in the Western feminist visitors' conceptual scheme and would surmise that the social structure is inherently structured to disallow sexual equality. Their resistance to the visitors' notion of equality should be seen as a response to its deep-seated discrimination that disingenuously disempowers women. Thus, while the visitors exalt their awareness of their condition and their belief in the progressive nature of their steps, the Onitsha audience is wondering why that system could not create the same type of empowering spaces for women that it had for men. Unfamiliar with the existential conditions of such a system, they would construe the women's failure to advocate for equality as lack of assertiveness on their part.

53. When judicial decisions deploy the doctrine of individual autonomy, reinforcing individualism, justices ignore that fact that individualism promotes a fragmented consciousness for women and a group-identified consciousness for men. It empowers judges and policymakers to interpret the compensatory provisions as extra rights for women and to gut them. As Fudge noted, the symbolic victories consisting in giving one's name to one's child do not fundamentally change the power structure. For example, the criminal codes and statutes remain unchanged, undermining any attempt to fully implement the provisions of the Canadian Charter of Rights or American Civil Rights Act.

54. This problem was posed to students of mine during a fall semester 1992 class called "African Women and Feminism." They were asked to transpose the dual-sex system to the United States and evaluate the result. The response of the students was surprising, for many reasons. First, there were racial and gender overtones in the answers. Black female students performed better on the exercise than black male students, who simply could not handle the implications of this reality. Black female students also did much better than their white sisters, who refused to address the question, primarily because they could not accept the fact that Africa is the origin of this model of inter-gender relations and they did not want to lose their privileges. The better performance of the black female students lies in the fact that they had a clearer idea of what needed to be changed and the sequence in which the change should proceed.

GLOSSARY

ada singular, daughter
agiri lovers
aka odo wooden pestle
akpa whulu uterus
Ala Earth deity
anasi first wife
chi the inner spiritual guardian of any individual
di okpala lineage senior son
dibia diviner
efuluefu ragamuffin
Ezelagbo one who came from and with the genealogical traits of another family
idigbe, adagbe, or *idegbe* which allowed a daughter to enter into a socially legitimate union with a man of her choosing
igba n'rira a swift process of divorce in which a woman simply relocated to a lover's home from her marital home
ije urie a practice where by a betrothed girl paid extended visits to the suitor and his family
ikporo ogbe women of the word
ikwu na ibe kith and kin
inyemedi lineage wives
isi ada lineage senior daughter
ize t'iagbo bringing in a genetic trait
mmadu human beings
mmuo spirit
ndi Igbo Igbo people
nna father
nnatambili immigrants
nne mother
nuno lover

nwa afo child of the womb
nwadiani grandchild
nwanne gender-neutral term, "child of the mother"
nwunye wife
ọfo Igbo symbol of spiritual authority
ofu afọ literally, one womb
ogbe ward
ogo in-laws
Ọgu Umunwanyi Women's War
ọma or *ibe nne* the spirit of mothers, mother's mother, and mother's uterine
    sisters
Ọmenazu one born at the back or after the demise of the father
omugo postpartum period
ọmumu principle of fertility and reproductive power
oso aka wastrel
ọwhum friend, lover
ozo spiritual title
ugom prison
uju menses
umuada plural, daughters/sisters
umu agbo young unmarried girls
umu aro little children
umu ikolobia young unmarried boys
umunne gender-neutral term, "children of the mother"
umunna gender-neutral term, "children of the father"
umu okpala sons/brothers
usokwu or *mkpuke* wife's dwelling unit and space within the marital compound

REFERENCES AND BIBLIOGRAPHY

Legal Cases

Animashaurun v. Onuta Osuma & Ors., 1972, 2 East Central State Law Report 274

Eze v. Eze, Suit No. C/S 31–59

Idehen v. Idehen, 6 Nigerian Weekly Law Report 382, 1991

Maria Theresa v. Pedro Feliciano, April 19, 1897, JNCC 18, 350

Mary Macaulay v. Buari Apala and Faseke Olukolu, April 9, 1894, JNCC 300–05

Mojekwu v. Mojekwu, 7 Monthly Judgments of the Supreme Court of Nigeria, 2004, 161–81.

Mojekwu v. Mojekwu, 7 Nigerian Weekly Law Report, 1997, 283–309.

Nnezianya v. Okagbue & 2 Ors. (1963), 1 All Nigeria Law Report, 352

Nwugege v. Adigwe & anor., Nigeria Law Reports (1934), 134

Nzegwus v. Nzegwu (1997), Judgment of Suit No. (CA/E/318/87)

Nzegwu v. Nzegwus (1986), Judgment of Suit No. (0/78/81)

Ogamien v. Ogamien, Nigeria Monthly Law Report 245 (1967)

Olumo & Ors. v. Okure & Ors., 1985, 3 Nigerian Weekly Law Report 372

Onwuchekwa v. Onwuchekwa, 5 Nigerian Weekly Law Report 739, 1991

Orakwue v. Orakwue, Suit No. E/33M/80

Overseas Construction Co. (Nigeria) Ltd. v. Greek Enterprises Co. Ltd., (1985) 3 Nigerian Weekly Law Report, 407

Ransome Kuti v. A. G. of the Federation (1985) 2, Nigerian Weekly Law Report 24E

Solomon v. Gbabo (1974) 4 East Central State Law Report 457

Books and Articles

Aba Commission of Inquiry. *Notes of Evidence Taken by the Commission of Inquiry Appointed to Inquire into the Disturbances in the Calabar and Owerri Provinces, December 1929*. London: Waterlow, 1930.

Abati, Reuben. "Letter from Edith Ike Mark-Odu," *The Guardian*, (Lagos, Nigeria), Friday, December 19, 2003.

Achebe, Chinua. *Hope and Impediments*. New York: Anchor Books/Doubleday, 1989.
———. *Things Fall Apart*. London: Heinemann, 1958.
Achike, Okey. "Problems of Creation and Dissolution of Customary Marriages in Nigeria." In *Law and the Family in Africa*, ed. Simon Roberts. The Hague: Mouton, 1977, 145–58.
Adewoye, Omoniyi. *The Judicial System in Southern Nigeria, 1854–1954*. London: Longman, 1977.
Afigbo, A. E. "Oral Tradition and the History of Segmentary Societies." In *Perspectives and Methods of Studying African History*, ed. Erim O. Erim and Okon E. Uya. Enugu. Nigeria: Fourth Dimension Publishing Co. Ltd., 1984, 54–63.
———. *The Warrant Chiefs: Indirect Rule in South-Eastern Nigeria, 1891–1929*. London: Longman, 1972.
———. "Revolution and Reaction in Eastern Nigeria," *Journal of the Historical Society of Nigeria*, 3, no. 3 (December, 1966): 541.
Afonja, Simi. "Changing Patterns of Gender Stratification in West Africa." In *Persistent Equalities: Women and World Development*, ed. Irene Tinker. New York: Oxford University Press, 1990, 198–209.
———. "Land Control: A Critical Factor in Yoruba Gender Stratification." In *Women and Class in Africa*, ed. Claire Robertson and Iris Berger. New York: Africana Publishing Company — Holms and Meier, 1986, 78–91.
———. "Women, Power and Authority in Traditional Yoruba Society." In *Visibility and Power: Essays on Women in Society and Development*, ed. Leela Dube, Eleanor Leacock, and Shirley Ardener. Dehli: Oxford University Press, 1986, 136–57.
Agbasiere, Joseph Thérèse. *Women in Igbo Life and Thought*. London: Routledge, 2000.
Aguilar, Delia D. "Third World Revolution and First World Feminism: Toward a Dialogue." In *Promissory Notes: Women in the Transition to Socialism*. ed. Sonia Kruks, Rayna Rapp, and Marilyn B. Young. New York: Monthly Review Press, 1989, 338–44.
Aidoo, Agnes Akosua. "Asante Queen Mothers in Government and Politics in the Nineteenth Century." In *The Black Woman Cross-Culturally*, ed. Filomina Chioma Steady. Cambridge, Mass: Schenkman Publishers Co, 1981, 65–77.
Ajayi, F. A. "The Interaction of English Law with Customary Law in Western Nigeria" *Journal of African Law* 4, 98 (1960).
Ajisafe, A. K. *The Laws and Customs of the Yoruba People*. London: Routledge, 1924.

Aki-kwe/Mary Ellen Turpel. "Aboriginal Peoples and the Canadian Charter of Rights and Freedoms: Contradictions and Challenges," *Canadian Woman Studies/Les Cahiers de la Femme* 10, nos. 2 and 3 (1989): 149–157.

Akpan, N. U. "Have Traditional Authorities a Place in Modern Local Government Systems?" *J.A.A.* 7, no. 109 (1955).

Akunne, B. A. "Ibè Nné Bond of Common Motherhood at Nri," *Odinani: Journal of the Odinani Museum*, Nri, Nigeria, no. 2, September 1977, 60–63.

Amadiume, Ifi. *Reinventing Africa: Matriarchy, Religion & Culture*. London: Zed Books Ltd., 1997.

———. *Male Daughters, Female Husbands*. London: Zed Books Ltd., 1987a.

———. *Afrikan Matriarchal Foundations: The Igbo Case*. London: Karnak House, 1987b.

Amos, Valeri, and Pratibha Parmar. "Challenging Imperial Feminisms." *Feminist Review* 17, 1984, 3–9.

Angelou, Maya. *I Know Why the Caged Bird Sings*. New York: Random House, 1970.

Appiah, Kwame Anthony. *In My Father's House*. Oxford: Oxford University Press, 1992.

Ardener, Shirley. "Introduction: The Nature of Women in Society." In *Defining Females*, ed. Shirley Ardener. Oxford: Berg, 1993, 1–33.

———. ed. *Perceiving Women*. New York: John Wiley and Sons, 1975.

Arikpo, Okoi. "The Future of Bride Price" *West Africa*, Oct. 29, 1955.

Assie-Lumumba, N'dri Thérèse. "Gender Biases in African Historiography." In *Engendering African Social Sciences*, ed. Ayesha Imam, Amina Mama, Fatou Sow. Dakar, Senegal: CODESRIA, 1999, 81–115.

Astell, Mary. *Some Reflections Upon Marriage*. New York: Source Book Press, 1970. Reprinted from the 4th ed. of 1730.

Awe, Bolanle, ed. *Nigerian Women in Historical Perspective*. Lagos, Nigeria: Sankore/Bookcraft, 1992.

Babbitt, Susan E. *Impossible Dreams: Rationality, Integrity, and Moral Imagination*. Boulder, Colo.: Westview Press, 1996.

Barbot, John. *A Description of the Coasts of North and South Guinea*. In Churchill's *Voyages and Travels*, vol. 5. London: 1746.

Barclay, Linda. "Autonomy and the Social Self." *Relational Autonomy: Feminist Perspectives on Autonomy, Agency, and the Social Self*, ed. Catorina Mackenzie and Natalie Stoljar. New York: Oxford University Press, 2000, 52–71.

Barnes, J. A. "The Politics of Law." In *Man in Africa*, ed. Mary Douglas and Phyllis M. Kaberry. London: Tavistock Publications, 1969, 99–118.

Bartky, Sandra Lee. "Towards a Phenomenology of Feminist Consciousness." In *Feminism and Philosophy*, ed. Mary Vetterling Braggin, Frederick A. Ellison, and Jane English. Totowa, N.J.: Rowman and Littlefield, 1977, 22–34.

Basden, George. T. *Niger Ibos*. New York: Barnes and Noble, 1938; reprinted in 1966.

———. *Among the Ibos of Nigeria*. London: Seeley, Service and Co., 1921.

Bastian, Misty L. "'Vultures of the Marketplace': Southeastern Nigerian Women and Discourse of the Ogu Umunwaanyi (Women's War of 1929)." In *Women in African Colonial Histories*, ed. Jean Allman, Susan Geiger, and Nakanyike Musisi. Bloomington: Indiana University Press, 2002, 260–81.

Bigge, David M. and Amelie von Briesen. "Conflict in the Zimbabwean Courts: Women's Rights and Indigenous Self-Determination in Magaya v. Magaya," *Harvard Human Rights Journal* 289–313 Spring, 2000.

Birrell Gray Commission. *Minutes of Evidence Taken by a Commission of Inquiry Appointed to Inquire into Certain Incidents at Opobo, Abak, and Utu-Etim-Ekpo in December 1929*. Public Record Office, Nigeria File Co 583/176/7.

Boahen, A. Adu. *African Perspectives on Colonialism*. Baltimore: Johns Hopkins University Press, 1987.

Bosah, Nnayelugo S. I. *Groundwork of the History and Culture of Onitsha*. Apapa, Nigeria: Times Press Ltd., 1979.

Bridenthall, Renate. "The Family: The View from a Room of Her Own." In *Rethinking that Family: Some Feminist Questions*, ed. Barrie Thorne and Marilyn Yalom. New York: Longman, 1982, 225–39.

Brown, Clari Vickery. "Home Production for Use in a Market Economy." In *Rethinking that Family: Some Feminist Questions*, ed. Barrie Thorne and Marilyn Yalom. New York: Longman, 1982, 151–67.

Brown, Elsa Barkley. "'What Has Happened Here': The Politics of Difference in Women's History and Feminist Politics." In *"We Specialize in the Wholly Impossible": A Reader in Black Women's History*, ed. Darlene Clark Hine, Wilma King, and Linda Reed. Brooklyn, N.Y.: Carlson Publishing Inc., 1995, 39–54.

Burdo, Adolphe. *The Niger and the Benueh*, trans. Mrs. Sturge. London: Richard Bentley and Son, 1880.

Butegwa, Florence. "Mediating Culture and Human Rights in Favour of Land Rights for Women in Africa: A Framework for Community-Level Action." In *Cultural Transformation and Human Rights in Africa*, ed. Abduhalli A. An-Na'im. London: Zed Books Ltd., 2002, 108–25.

Butler, Melissa A. "Early Liberal Roots of Feminism: John Locke and the Attack on Patriarchy." In *Feminism: Critical Concepts in Literary and Cultural Studies*, Vol. 1, Feminism and the Enlightenment, ed. Mary Evans. London: Routledge, 2001, 55–81.

Callaway, Helen. *Gender, Culture and Empire: European Women in Colonial Nigeria*. London: Macmillan Press (in association with St. Antony's College, Oxford), 1987.

Chanock, Martin. "Human Rights and Cultural Branding: Who Speaks and How." In *Cultural Transformation and Human Rights in Africa*, ed. Abduhalli A. An-Na'im. London: Zed Books Ltd., 2002, 38–67.

———. "Paradigms, Policies, and Property: A Review of the Customary Law of Land Tenure." In *Law in Colonial Africa*, ed. Kristin Mann and Richard Roberts. Portsmouth, N.H.: Heinemann, 1991, 61–84.

———. "Making Customary Law: Men, Women, and Courts in Colonial Rhodesia." In *African Women and the Law: Historical* Perspectives vol. 7, ed. Margaret Jean Hay and Marcia Wright. Boston: African Studies Center, Boston University, 1982, 53–67.

Chubb, L. T. *Ibo Land Tenure*, 1st ed. Zaria: Gaskiya Corporation, Ibadan, Nigeria: Ibadan University Press, 1961.

Code, Lorraine. *What Can She Know? Feminist Theory and the Construction of Knowledge*. Ithaca, N.Y.: Cornell University Press, 1991.

Cohen-Almagor, Raphael. "Between Neutrality and Perfectionism," *The Canadian Journal of Law and Jurisprudence* 2, July 1994: 217–36.

Coker, G. B. A. *Family Property among the Yorubas*. London: Sweet & Maxwell, 1966.

Cole, Patrick. *Modern and Traditional Elites in the Politics of Lagos*. London: Cambridge University Press, 1975.

Collier, Jane, Michelle Z. Rosaldo, and Sylvia Yanagisako. "Is There a Family: New Anthropological Views." In *Rethinking That Family: Some Feminist Questions*, ed. Barrie Thorne and Marilyn Yalom. New York: Longman, 1982, 25–39.

Collins, Patricia Hill. *Black Feminist Thought: Knowledge, Consciousness, and the Politics of Empowerment*. Boston: Unwin Hyman, 1990.

Coltheart, Lenore. "Desire, Consent and Liberal Theory." In *Feminist Challenges: Social and Political Theory*, ed. Carole Pateman and Elizabeth Gross. Boston: Northeastern University Press, 1986, 112–22.

Convention on the Elimination of all Forms of Discrimination Against Women (CEDAW). In *Twenty-Five Human Rights Documents*. New York: Center for the Study of Human Rights, Columbia University, 1994, 48–56.

Corlett, J. Angelo. "The Problem of Collective Moral Rights," *The Canadian Journal of Law and Jurisprudence* 2, July 1994: 237–59.

Cossman, Brenda J. "Turning the Gaze on Itself: Comparative Law, Feminist Legal Studies, and the Postcolonial Project." In *Global Critical Race Feminism: An International Reader*, ed. Adrienne Katherine Wing. New York: New York University, 2000, 27–41.

Cranston, Maurice. "What are Human Rights?" In *The Human Rights Reader*, ed. Walter Laqueur and Barry Rubin. New York: New American Library, 1997, 17–25.

Crenshaw, Kimberlé Williams. "Mapping the Margins: Intersectionality, Identity, Politics, and Violence Against Women of Color." In *Critical Race Theory: The Key Writings That Formed the Movement*, ed. Kimberlé Crenshaw, Neil Gotanda, Gary Peller, and Kendall Thomas. New York: The New Press, 1995, 357–83.

Crowther, Samuel and J. C. Taylor. *The Gospel on the Banks of the Niger*. London: 1895.

Cutrafelli, Maria Rosa. *Women of Africa: Roots of Oppression*. London: Zed Press, 1983.

Daly, Mary. *Beyond God the Father*. Boston: Beacon Press, 1973

Daniels, W. C. Ekow. "Problems in the Law Relating to the Maintenance and Support of Wives and Children." In *Domestic Rights and Duties in Ghana*, (Legon Family Research Papers, no. 1), ed. Christine Oppong. Legon: University of Ghana Institute of African Studies, 1974, 285–91.

Davies, Carole Boyce. "Feminist Consciousness and African Literary Criticism." In *Ngambika: Studies of Women in African Literature*, ed. Carole Boyce Davies and Anne Adams Graves. Trenton, N.J.: African World Press, 1986, 1–23.

Davis, Kathy and Jantine Oldersma. "The Gender of Power: An Introduction." In *The Gender of Power: A Symposium*, ed. Monique Leijenaar, Kathy Davis, Claudine Helleman, Jantine Oldersma and Dini Vos. Leiden: Vakgroep Vrouwenstudies FSW, Vrouwen en Autonomie, 1987, 13–24.

de Beauvoir, Simone. "Woman as Other" In *Issues in Feminism: An Introduction to Women's Studies*, ed. Sheila Ruth. Mountain View, Calif.: Mayfield Publishing Company, 1990.

Delano, I. O. *An African Looks at Marriage*. London: United Society for Christian Literature, 1944.

di Leonardo, Micaela. "Introduction: Gender, Culture, and Political Economy." In *Gender at the Crossroads of Knowledge: Feminist Anthropology in the Postmodern Era*, ed. Micaela di Leonardo. Berkeley: University of California Press, 1991, 312–36.

Dewan, Shaila K. "Black Farmers' Refrain: Where's All Our Money?" *The New York Times*, National Report, Sunday August 1, 2004, A14.

Dike, Azuka A. *The Resilence of Igbo Culture: A Case Study of Awka Town*. Enugu: Fourth Dimension Publishing Co. Ltd., 1985.

Dike, Kenneth Onwuka. *Trade and Politics in the Niger Delta, 1830–1885*. Oxford: Clarendon Press, 1965.

———. *Origins of the Niger Mission: 1841–1891*. Ibadan: Ibadan University Press, 1962.

Dike, Kenneth Onwuka and Felicia Ekejiuba. *The Aro of South-Eastern Nigeria, 1650–1980*. Ibadan, Nigeria: Ibadan University Press Limited, 1990.

Diop, Cheikh Anta. *The Cultural Unity of Black Africa: The Domains of Matriarchy and of Patriarchy in Classical Antiquity.* London: Karnak House, 1989.

Dolphyne, Florence Abena. *The Emancipation of Women: An African Perspective.* Accra Ghana: Universities Press, 1991.

Douglas, Mary. "Is Matriliny Doomed in Africa?" In *Man in Africa*, ed. Mary Douglas and Phyllis M. Kaberry. London: Tavistock Publications, 1969, 121–35.

Drutman, Lee. "It's Time to Chart the Toll of America's Corporate Crime," *The Press and Sun Bulletin*, Binghamton, NY. Sunday, November 9, 2003, 16A.

Dube, Leela, Eleanor Leacock, and Shirley Ardener, eds. *Visibility and Power: Essays on Women in Society and Development.* New Delhi: Oxford University Press, 1986.

Dubois, E., M. Dunlap, C. Gilligan, C. MacKinnon, C. Menkel-Meadow. "Feminist Discourse, Moral Values, and the Law—A Conversation," *Buffalow Law Review*, 34, no. 2 (1985): 11–87.

Dunlap, M., E. Dubois, C. Gilligan, C. MacKinnon, C. Menkel-Meadow. "Feminist Discourse, Moral Values, and the Law—A Conversation," *Buffalow Law Review*, 34, no. 2 (1985): 11–87.

Edeh, Emmanuel M. P. *Towards an Igbo Metaphysics.* Chicago: Loyola University Press, 1985.

Egharevba, J. U. *Benin Law and Custom*, 3rd Ed., Port Harcourt, Nigeria: C.M.S. Niger Press, 1949.

Eisenstein, Zillah. *The Female Body and the Law.* Los Angeles: University of California Press, 1988.

Ejiwunmi, Akintola, Olufemi. *Nzegwus v. Nzegwu*, Court of Appeal Judgment to suit no. CA/E/318/87, April 22, 1997.

Ekeghe, O. O. *A Short History of Abiriba.* Aba, Nigeria: Nigeria International Press, 1957.

Ekeh, Peter P. "Social Anthropology and Two Contrasting Uses of Tribalism in Africa," *Comparative Study of Society and History* [Imperialism and Political Identity] 32, no. 4 (Oct 1990): 660–700.

———. "Colonialism and the Two Publics in Africa: A Theoretical Statement." *Comparative Studies in Society and History* 17, no. 1 (Jan 1975): 91–112.

Ekejiuba, Felicia. "Down to Fundamentals: Women-Centred Heathholds in Rural West Africa." In *Women Wielding the Hoe*, ed. Deborah Fahy Bryceson. Oxford: Oxford University Press, 1995, 47–61.

———. "Chiefs, Elders, and Leaders: An Examination of Power and its Legitimation in Traditional Ibo Society." Unpublished Paper, 1974.

————. "Omu Okwei: The Merchant Queen of Ossamari," *Nigeria*, Sept 90 (1966): 213–20.

Ekere, C. A. "Ibibio Indigenous Legal System" *West Africa* 28, no. 5 (Feb 1944): 103.

Elias, Taslim Olawale. *The Nigerian Legal System*. London: 1963. *Nigerian Land Law and Custom*. London, Routledge and Paul, 1962.

————. *The Nature of African Customary Law*. Manchester: Manchester University Press, 1956.

————. *Groundwork of Nigerian Law*. London: Routledge & Kegan Paul, 1954.

Elshtain, Jean Bethke. "Politics Sanctified and Subdued: Patriarchalism and the Liberal Tradition." In *Feminism: Critical Concepts in Literary and Cultural Studies*, vol. 1, Feminism and the Enlightenment, ed. Mary Evans. London: Routledge, 2001, 82–117.

————. "Against Androgyny." In *Feminism and Equality*, ed. Anne Phillips. New York: New York University, 1987, 139–59.

Equiano, Olaudah. *The Interesting Narrative of the Life of Olaudah Equiano, or Gustavus Vassa, The African*. New York: Norton, 2001.

Esenwa, S. E. "Marriage Customs in Asaba Division" *Nigerian Field* 13, no. 2 (1948): 71.

Ewelukwa, Uche U. "Post-Colonialism, Gender, Customary Injustice: Widows in African Societies," *Human Rights Quarterly* 24 (2002): 424–86.

Fanon, Frantz. *The Wretched of the Earth*. New York: Grove Press, 1966.

Fapohunda, Eleanor R. "The Nuclear Household Model in Nigerian Public and Private Sector Policy: Colonial Legacy and Socio-Political Implications," *Development and Change* 18 (1987): 281–94.

Folarin, Adebesin. *The Laws and Customs of Egbaland*, Abeokuta, E. N. A. Press, 1928.

Forbes, Ian. "Equal Opportunity: Radical, Liberal and Conservative Critiques." In *Equality Politics and Gender*, ed. Elizabeth Meehan and Selma Sevenhuijsen. London: Sage Publications, 1991, 17–35.

Forde, Daryll and G. I. Jones. *The Ibo and Ibibio-Speaking Peoples of South-Eastern Nigeria*. London: International African Institute, 1950.

Forde, Dayll and Scott F., *The Native Economies of Nigeria*. London: Faber, 1946.

Fox-Genovese, Elizabeth. *Feminism without Illusions: A Critique of Individualism*. Chapel Hill: University of North Carolina Press, 1991.

Friedman, Marilyn. "Autonomy, Social Disruption, and Women." In *Relational Autonomy: Feminist Perspectives on Autonomy, Agency, and the Social Self*, ed. Catorina Mackenzie and Natalie Stoljar. New York: Oxford University Press, 2000, 35–51.

Frye, Marilyn. *The Politics of Reality: Essays in Feminist Theory*. Trumansburg, N.Y.: Crossing Press, 1983.

Fudge, Judy. "The Public/Private Distinction: The Possibilities of and the Limits of the Use of Charter Litigation to Further Feminist Struggles," *Osgoode Hall Law Journal* 25, 1988: 485—54.

Gamble, Sarah, ed. *The Routledge Critical Dictionary of Feminism and Postmodernism*. New York: Routledge, 2000.

Gatens, Moira. "'The Oppressed State of My Sex': Wollenstonecraft on Reason, Feeling and Equality." In *Feminist Interpretations and Political Theory*, ed. Mary Lyndon Shanley and Carole Pateman. Cambridge: Polity Press, 1991, 112–28.

Gilligan, Carol. *In a Different Voice: Psychological Theory and Women's Development*. Cambridge, Mass: Harvard University Press, 1982.

Gilligan, C., E. Dubois, M. Dunlap, C. MacKinnon, C. Menkel-Meadow. "Feminist Discourse, Moral Values, and the Law—A Conversation," *Buffalow Law Review*, 34, no. 2 (1985): 11–87.

Goode, William J. "Why Men Resist." In *Rethinking that Family: Some Feminist Questions*, ed. Barrie Thorne and Marilyn Yalom. New York: Longman, 1982, 131–50.

Goody, John R. *Production and Reproduction*. Cambridge: Cambridge University Press, 1976.

Gordon, April. "Gender, Ethnicity, and Class in Kenya: 'Burying Otieno' Revisited," *Signs* 20, 4 (Summer 1995): 883–912.

Gordon, Lewis R. "Fanon, Philosophy, and Racism." In *Racism and Philosophy*, ed. Susan Babbitt and Sue Campbell. Ithaca: Cornell University Press, 1999, 32–49.

———. "Race Pan-Africanism, and Identity: Antiblack Philosophy in Kwame Anthony Appiah's *In My Father's House*," Paper presented at the 1996 African Studies Association, Orlando, Florida.

———. *Bad Faith and Antiblack Racism*. Atlantic Highlands, N.J.: Humanities Press, 1995.

Gordon, Linda. "Why Nineteenth-Century Feminists Did Not Support 'Birth Control' and Twentieth-Century Feminists Do: Feminism, Reproduction, and the Family." In *Rethinking that Family: Some Feminist Questions*, eds. Barrie Thorne and Marilyn Yalom. New York: Longman, 1982, 40–39.

Gray, Leslie and Michael Kevane. "Diminished Access, Diverted Exclusion: Women and Land Tenure in Sub-Saharan Africa," *African Studies Review* 42, no. 2 (1999): 15–39.

Greene, Beth. "The Institution of Woman-Marriage in Africa: A Cross-Cultural Analysis." *Ethnology* 37, 4 (Fall 1998): 395–413.

Green, Margaret M. *Ibo Village Affairs*. London, Frank Cass and Co. Ltd., 1964.

Greer, Germaine. *The Female Eunuch*. London: Paladin, 1972.

Griffith, William B. "Equality and Egalitarianism: Framing the Contemporary

Debate," *The Canadian Journal of Law and Jurisprudence* 7, no. 1 (January 1994): 5–26.

Gross, Elizabeth. "Conclusion: What is Feminist Theory?" In *Feminist Challenges: Social and Political Theory*, ed. Carole Pateman and Elizabeth Gross. Boston: Northeastern University Press, 1986, 190–204.

Gyekye, Kwame. *Tradition and Modernity: Philosophical Reflections on the African Experience*. Oxford: Oxford University Press, 1997.

———. *An Essay on African Philosophical Thought*. Philadelphia: Temple University Press, 1995.

Haaken, Janice. "Field Dependence Research: A Historical Analysis of a Psychological Construct," *Signs: Journal of Women in Culture and Society* 13, no. 2 (1988): 311–30.

Hadjor, Kofi Buenor. "Whose Human Rights?" *Journal of Asian and African Studies* 33, no. 4 (1998): 359–68.

Haggis, Jane. "The Feminist Research Process: Defining a Topic." In *Feminist Praxis: Research, Theory and Epistemology in Feminist Sociology*, ed. Liz Stanley. London: Routledge, 1990, 67–79.

Hammar, Inger. "From Fredrika Bremer to Ellen Key. "Calling, Gender and the Emancipation Debate in Sweden c. 1830–1900." In *Gender and Vocation. Women, Religion and Social Change in the Nordic Countries, 1830–1940*, ed. Pirjo Markkola. Helsinki: Suomalaisen Kirjallisuuden Seura, 2000.

Hansen, Karen V. and Anita Ilta Garey. *Families in the U.S.: Kinship and Domestic Politics*. Philadelphia, PA: Temple University Pres, 1998.

Harding, R. W. *The Dispute Over the Obiship of Onitsha 1961–63*, Report of the Inquiry, Official Document No. 6, 1963. Enugu: Government Printer, 1963.

Harding, Sandra. "Introduction: Eurocentric Scientific Illiteracy—A Challenge for the World Community" *The Racial Economy of Science: Toward a Democratic Future*. Bloomington: Indiana University Press, 1993, 1–29.

———. "Is There a Feminist Method?" *Feminism & Science*. Bloomington: Indiana University Press, 1989, 17–32.

Harris, Angela. "Race and Essentialism in Feminist Legal Theory" *Stanford Law Review* 42 (1990): 581–616.

Harris, Cheryl I. "Whiteness as Property." In *Critical Race Theory: The Key Writings That Formed the Movement*, ed. Kimberlé Crenshaw, Neil Gotanda, Gary Peller, and Kendall Thomas. New York: The New Press, 1995, 226–91.

Harris, Philip J. *Local Government in Southern Nigeria: A Manual of Law and Procedure under the Eastern Region*, Cambridge: Cambridge University Press, 1957.

Hartsock, Nancy C. M. *Money, Sex and Power: Toward a Feminist Historical Materialism*. New York: Longman, 1983.

Hassan, Riffat. "On Human Rights and the Qur'anic Perspective." In *Human Rights in Religious Traditions*, ed. Arlene Swidler. New York: The Pilgrim Press, 1982, 51–65.

Hayek, Friedrich A. "Equality, Value, and Merit." In *Liberalism and Its Critics*, ed. Michael Sandel. New York: New York University Press, 1984, 80–99.

Held, Virginia. *Feminist Morality: Transforming Culture, Society, and Politics.* Chicago: University of Chicago Press, 1993.

———. "Liberty and Equality from a Feminist Perspective." In *Enlightenment, Rights and Revolution: Essays in Legal and Social Philosophy*, ed. Neil Mac-Cormick and Zenon Bankowski. Aberdeen, Scotland: Aberdeen University Press, 1989.

Henderson, Helen K. "Onitsha Woman: The Political Context for Political Power." In *Queens, Queen Mothers, Priestesses, and Power: Case Studies in African Gender*, ed. Flora Edouwaye S. Kaplan. New York: New York Academy of Sciences, vol. 810, 1997, 215–43.

———. *Ritual Roles of Women in Onitsha Ibo Society.* Ph.D. diss., University of California, Berkeley, 1969.

Henderson, Richard N. *The King in Every Man: Evolutionary Trends in Onitsha Ibo Society and Culture.* New Haven: Yale University Press, 1972.

Herdt, Gilbert. "Introduction: Third Sexes and Third Genders." In *Third Sex, Third Gender. Beyond Sexual Dimorphism in Culture and History*, ed. Gilbert Herdt. New York: Zone Books, 1994.

Higginbotham, A. Leon Jr. *Shades of Freedom: Racial Politics and the Presumption of the American Legal Process.* New York: Oxford University Press, 1996.

Higginbotham, Evelyn Brooks. "African-American Women's History and the Metalanguage of Race." In *"We Specialize in the Wholly Impossible": A Reader in Black Women's History*, ed. Darlene Clark Hine, Wilma King, and Linda Reed. Brooklyn, N.Y.: Carlson Publishing Inc., 1995, 3–24.

Himonga, Chuma N. "Women and Law in Southern Africa Research Project: Bridging the Divide between Scholarship and Action." In *Gender and Identity in Africa*, ed. Mechthild Reh and Gudrun Ludwar-Ene. Münster: Lit Verlag, 1995, 197–214.

hooks, bell. *Talking Back: Thinking Feminist, Thinking Black.* Boston, Mass.: South End Press, 1989.

Hopkins, A. G. "Property Rights and Empire Building: Britain's Annexation of Lagos, 1861." *The Journal of Economic History* 40 (1980): 777–98.

Horton, Africanus. *Black Nationalism in Africa 1867*, ed. Davidson Nicol. New York: Africana Publishing Corporation, 1969.

Hsiung, James C. "Human Rights in an East Asian Perspective," In *Human Rights in East Asia: A Cultural Perspective*, ed. James C. Hsiung. New York: Paragon House Publishers, 1985, 3–30.

Ibeziako, S. M. B. *The Nigerian Customary Law.* Nsukka, Nigeria: Etudo Ltd., [Onitsha] 1964.

Ifeka, Sam. *Onicha Kingship Institution.* Onitsha: Herald Books Ltd., 1973.

Ifeka-Moller, Caroline. "Female Militancy and Colonial Revolt: The Women's War of 1929, Eastern Nigeria." In *Perceiving Women,* ed. Shirley Ardener. New York: John Wiley & Sons, 1975, 128–32.

Igbafe, Philip A. "Tradition and Change in Benin Marriage System," *Journal of Economic and Social Studies,* 12, no. 1 (1970): 73–102.

Imam, Ayesha M. "Engendering African Social Sciences: An Introductory Essay." In *Engendering African Social Sciences,* ed. Ayesha Imam, Amina Mama, Fatou Sow. Dakar, Senegal: CODESRIA, 1999, 1–30.

————. "Towards an Adequate Analysis of the Position of Women in Society." In *Women in Nigeria,* ed. WIN Collective. London: Zed Press, 1985, 15–27.

Isichei, Elizabeth. *Igbo Worlds: An Anthology of Oral Histories and Historical Descriptions.* Philadelphia: Institute for the Study of Human Ideas, 1978.

————. *The Ibo People and the Europeans.* New York: St. Martin's Press, 1973.

Jacobs, Lesley A. "Equal Opportunity and Gender Disadvantage, *The Canadian Journal of Law and Jurisprudence* 7, no. 1(January 1994): 61–71.

Jaggar, Alison. "Political Philosophies of Women's Liberation." In *Feminism and Philosophy.* ed. Mary Vetterling-Braggin, Frederick A. Ellison and Jane English. Totowa, N.J.: Rowman and Littlefield, 1977, 5–21.

James, Wendy. "Matrifous on African Women." In *Defining Females,* ed. Shirley Ardener. Oxford: Berg, 1993, 123–45.

Johnson, Cheryl. "Class and Gender: A Consideration of Yoruba Women during the Colonial Period." In *Women and Class in Africa,* ed. Robertson, Claire and Iris Berger. New York: Africana Publishing Company–Holms and Meier, 1986, 237–54.

Johnson-Odim, Cheryl and Margaret Strobel, eds. *Expanding the Boundaries of Women's History.* Bloomington: Indiana University Press, 1992.

Johnson-Odim, Cheryl and Nina Emma Mba. *For Women and the Nation: Funmilayo Ransome-Kuti of Nigeria.* Urbana and Chicago: University of Illinois Press, 1997.

Johnson-Odim, Cheryl. *Common Themes, Different Contexts: Third World Women and Feminism.* Bloomington: Indiana University Press, 1991, 314–27.

Jones, Christina. "Concepts of Equality in Cases of Discrimination Against Women: Examples from Africa." In *Gender and Identity in Africa,* ed. Mechthild Reh and Gudrun Ludwar-Ene. Münster: Lit Verlag, 1995, 169–86.

Jones, G. I. *From Slaves to Palm Oil: Slave Trade and Palm Oil Trade in the Bight of Biafra.* Cambridge African Monographs 13. Cambridge: African Studies Center, 1989.

———. "Ecology and Social Structure among the North-Eastern Ibo" *Africa* 31, 117(1961).

———and Daryll Forde, *The Ibo and Ibibio-Speaking Peoples of South Eastern Nigeria*. London: International Africa Institute, 1950.

———. "Ibo Land Tenure" *Africa* 19, 309 (1949).

Jones-Quartey, P. W. "The Effects of the Maintenance of Children Act on Akan and Ewe Notions of Paternal Responsibility." In *Domestic Rights and Duties in Ghana* (Legon Family Research Papers, no. 1) ed. Christine Oppong. Legon: Institute of African Studies, University of Ghana, 1974, 292–304.

Karanja, Wambui wa. "The Phenomenon of 'Outside Wives': Some Reflections on its Possible Influence on Fertility." In *Nuptiality in Sub-Saharan Africa*, ed. Caroline Bledsoe and Gilles Pison. Oxford: Clarendon Press, 1994, 194–213.

Kaplan, Flora E. S. "Runaway Wives: Native Law and Custom in Benin, and Early Colonial Courts, Nigeria." In *Queens, Queen Mothers, Priestesses, and Power: Case Studies in African Gender*, ed. Flora Edouwaye S. Kaplan. New York: New York Academy of Sciences, vol. 810, 1997, 245–313.

Kasunmu, A. B. "Economic Consequences of Divorce: A Case Study of Some Judicial Decision in Lagos." In *Law and the Family in Africa*, ed. Simon Roberts. Mouton: The Hague, 1977, 129–43.

———. *Marriage and Divorce Among the Yorubas*, L.L.M. Thesis, University of London, 1962.

Koggel, Christine M. "A Feminist View of Equality and Its Implications for Affirmative Action, *The Canadian Journal of Law and Jurisprudence* 7, no. 1 (January 1994): 43–59.

Lahey, Kathleen. "Until Women Themselves Have Told All That They Have to Tell . . ." *Osgoode Hall Law Journal* 23 (1985): 519–41.

Lee, Durtman. "It's Time to Chart the Toll of America's Corporate Crime," *The Press & Sun Bulletin*, Binghamton, New York, Sunday, November 9, 2003, 16A.

Leith-Ross, Sylvia. *African Women: A Study of the Ibo of Nigeria*. London: Routledge & Kegan Paul Ltd., 1965.

Lerner, Gerda. "Men's Power to Define and the Formation of Women's Consciousness." In *Issues in Feminism*, ed. Sheila Ruth. Mountain View, Calif.: Mayfield Publishing Company, 1998, 442–47.

———. *The Creation of Patriarchy*. New York: Oxford University Press, 1986.

Lewis, Barbara. "The Impact of Development Politics on Women." In *African Woman South of the Sahara*, ed. Margaret Jean Hay and Sharon Stichter. London: Longman, 1984, 170–87.

Lloyd, Genevieve. "Individual, Responsibility, and the Philosophical Imagination." *Relational Autonomy*. New York: Oxford University Press, 2000, 112–23.

Lugard, Frederick John Dealtry. *The Dual Mandate in British Tropical Africa*. London: Frank Cass, 1965.

———. *Political Memoranda, Revisions of Instructions to Political Officers on Subjects Chiefly Political Administration, 1913–1918*, 3d ed. London: Frank Cass, 1970.

———. Foreword. In C. K. Meek, *Law and Authority in a Nigerian Tribe: A Study in Indirect Rule*. London: Oxford University Press 1937, v-vi.

Mabogunje, Akin. *Urbanization in Nigeria*. New York: Africana Publication Corporation,1968.

MacGaffey, Janet. "Evading Male Control: Women in the Second Economy in Zaire." In *Patriarchy and Class*, ed. Sharon Stichter and Jane Parpart. Boulder, Colo.: Westview Press, 1988, 161–96.

Mackenzie, Catriona and Natalie Stoljar. "Introduction: Autonomy Refigured." In *Relational Autonomy: Feminist Perspectives on Autonomy, Agency, and the Social Self*, ed. Catorina Mackenzie and Natalie Stoljar. New York: Oxford University Press, 2000, 3–31.

MacKinnon, Catharine A. *Toward a Feminist Theory of the State*. Cambridge, Mass: Harvard University Press, 1989.

———. *Feminism Unmodified*. Cambridge: Harvard University Press, 1987.

MacKinnon, C., E. Dubois, M. Dunlap, C. Gilligan, C. Menkel-Meadow. "Feminist Discourse, Moral Values, and the Law—A Conversation," *Buffalo Law Review* 34, no. 2 (1985): 11–87.

Macpherson, C. B. *The Real World of Democracy*. Toronto: CBC Enterprises, 1983.

———. *The Political Theory of Possessive Individualism: Hobbes to Locke*. London: Oxford University Press, 1962.

Maitun, Mary I. D. I. E. "Women, the Law and Convention: A Uganda Perspective," *Journal of Eastern African Research and Development* 15 (1985): 151–64.

Mamashela, Mothokoa. "Women and Development in Africa: With Special Reference to the Legal Disabilities of Married Women in Lesotho," *Journal of Eastern African Research and Development* 15 (1985): 165–70.

Mamdani, Mahmood. *Citizen and Subject: Contemporary Africa and the Legacy of Colonialism* Princeton, N.J.: Princeton University Press, 1996.

Mann, Kristin. "The Rise of Taiwo Olowo: Law, Accumulation, and Mobility in Early Colonial Lagos." In *Law in Colonial Africa*, ed. Kristin Mann and Richard Roberts. Portsmouth, N.H.: Heinemann, 1991a, 85–107.

———. "Women, Landed Property, and the Accumulation of Wealth in Early Colonial Lagos." *Signs: Journal of Women in Culture and Society*, (1991b): 682–706.

———. *Marrying Well: Marriage, Status and Social Change among the Educated Elite in Colonial Lagos.* Cambridge: Cambridge University Press, 1985.

———. "Women's Rights in Law and Practice: Marriage and Dispute Settlement in Colonial Lagos." In *African Women and the Law: Historical Perspectives*, vol. 7, ed. Margaret Jean Hay and Marcia Wright. Boston: African Studies Center, Boston University, 1982, 151–71.

Mann, Kristin and Richard Roberts. "Introduction: Law in Colonial Africa." In *Law in Colonial Africa*, ed. Kristin Mann, and Richard Roberts. Portsmouth, N.H.: Heinemann, 1991, 3–56.

Manuh, Takyiwaa. "Wives, Children, and Intestate Succession in Ghana." In *African Feminism: The Politics of Survival in Sub-Saharan Africa*, ed. Gwendolyn Mikell. Philadelphia: University of Pennsylvania Press, 1997, 77–95.

———. "Law and Society in Contemporary Africa." In *Africa*, eds. Phyllis M. Martin and Patrick O'Meara. Bloomington: Indiana University, 1995, 330–43.

March, Kathryn S., and Taqqu, Rachelle L. *Women's Informal Association in Developing Countries: Catalyst for Change?* Boulder, Colo.: Westview Press, 1986.

Mark-Odu, Edith Ike. "Letter from Edith Ike Mark-Odu," by Abati, Reuben. *The Guardian*, (Lagos, Nigeria) Friday, December 19, 2003.

Matsuda, Mari. "When the First Quail Calls: Multiple Consciousness as Jurisprudential Method." *Women's Rights Law Reporter* 2, no. 1 (Spring 1989): 7–10.

Matua, Makau. "The Banjul Charter: The Case for an African Cultural Fingerprint." In *Cultural Transformation and Human Rights in Africa*, ed. Abduhalli A. An-Na'im. London: Zed Books Ltd., 2002, 68–107.

May, Joan and Joyce Kazembe. "Beyond Legislation," *Journal of Eastern African Research and Development* 15 (1985): 171–79.

Mba, Nina Emma. *Nigerian Women Mobilized: Women's Political Activities in Southern Nigeria, 1900–1965.* Berkeley: Institute of International Studies, University of California, 1982.

Mbanefo, Isaac Anieka. *Isaac Anieka Mbanefo: A Friend of the Gods: An Autobiography.* Onitsha, Nigeria: Etukokwu Publishers Ltd., 1990.

Meehan, Elizabeth, and Selma Sevenhuijsen. "Problems in Principles and Policies." In *Equality Politics and Gender*, ed. Elizabeth Meehan and Selma Sevenhuijsen. London: Sage Publications, 1991, 1–16.

Meek, C. K. *Land Tenure and Land Administration in Nigeria and the Cameroons.* Colonial Research Studies, No. 22. London: Her Majesty's Stationary Office, 1957.

———. *Law and Authority in a Nigerian Tribe: A Study in Indirect Rule.* London: Oxford University Press 1937.

———. "Marriage by Exchange: A Disappearing Institution." *Africa* 9, 64 (1936).

Memorandum as to the Origin of the Recent Disturbances in the Owerri and Calabar Provinces. Lagos, 1930.

Menkel-Meadow, C., E. Dubois, M. Dunlap, C. Gilligan, C. MacKinnon. "Feminist Discourse, Moral Values, and the Law—A Conversation," *Buffalo Law Review*, 34, no. 2 (1985): 11–87.

Merry, Sally Engle. "The Articulation of Legal Spheres." In *African Women and the Law: Historical Perspectives* vol. 7, ed. Margaret Jean Hay and Marcia Wright. Boston: African Studies Center, Boston University, 1982, 67–89.

Mikell, Gwendolyn. "Introduction." *African Feminism: The Politics of Survival in Sub-Saharan Africa*, ed. Gwendolyn Mikell. Philadelphia: University of Pennsylvania Press, 1997, 1–50.

Miller, Pavla. *Transformations of Patriarchy in the West.* Bloomington: Indiana University Press, 1998.

Millett, Kate. In "Sexual Politics." *Issues in Feminism*, ed. Sheila Ruth. Mountain View, Calif.: Mayfield Publishing Company, 1990, 496–502.

Mills Charles W. "The Racial Polity." In *Racism and Philosophy*, ed., Susan Babbitt and Sue Campbell. Ithaca: Cornell University Press, 1999, 13–31.

———. *The Racial Contract.* Ithaca: Cornell University Press, 1997.

Minogue, Kenneth. "The History of the Idea of Human Rights." In *The Human Rights Reader*, ed. Walter Laqueur and Barry Rubin. New York: A Meridian Book, New American Library, 1997, 3–17.

Mitchell, Juliet. "Women and Equality." In *Feminism and Equality*, ed. Anne Phillips. New York: New York University, 1987, 24–43.

Mohanty, Chandra Talpade. "Cartographies of Struggle: Third World Women and the Politics of Feminism." In *Third World Women and the Politics of Feminism*, ed. Chandra Talpade Mohanty, Ann Russo, and Lourdes Torres. Bloomington: Indiana University Press, 1991, 1–47.

Moore, Sally Falk. "From Giving and Lending to Selling: Property Transactions Reflecting Historical Changes on Kilimanjaro." In *Law in Colonial Africa*, ed. Kristin Mann and Richard Roberts. Portsmouth, N.H.: Heinemann, 1991, 108–27.

Mugo, M. M. G. "African Orature and Human Rights," *Human and Peoples' Rights Monograph Series*, No. 13. Institute of Southern African Studies, Roma: National University of Lesotho, 1991.

Murdock, George Peter. *Social Structure.* New York: The Macmillan Co., 1949.

Musisi, Nakanyike B. "Colonial and Missionary Education: Women and Domesticity in Uganda, 1900–1945." In *African Encounters with Domesticity*, ed. Karen Tranberg Hansen. New Brunswick, N.J.: Rutgers University Press, 1992, 172–94.

Mutua, Makau, "The Banjul Charter: The Case for an African Cultural Fingerprint." In *Cultural Transformation and Human Rights in Africa*, ed. Abdullahi A. An-Na'im. London: Zed Press, 2002, 68–107.

Narayan, Uma. *Dislocating Cultures/Identities, Traditions, and Third-World Feminism*. New York: Routledge, 1997.

Nelson, Hilde Lindemann. "Introduction." In *Feminism and Families*, ed. Hilde Lindemann Nelson. New York: Routledge, 1997, 1–9.

Nesiah, Vasuki. "Toward a Feminist Internationality: A Critique of U.S. Feminist Legal Scholarship." In *Global Critical Race Feminism: An International Reader*, ed. Adrienne Katherine Wing. New York: New York University, 2000, 42–52.

Newbury, Colin. "Credit in Early Nineteenth-Century West African Trade." *Journal of African History* 13 (1972): 81–95.

Nicholson, Linda. "The Myth of the Traditional Family." In *Feminism and Families*, ed. Hilde Lindemann Nelson. New York: Routledge, 1997, 27–42.

Nicholson, Linda J. *Gender and History: The Limits of Social Theory in the Age of the Family*. New York: Columbia University Press, 1986.

Noah, Monday Effiong. "The Role, Status and Influence of Women in Traditional Times: The Example of the Ibibio of Southeastern Nigeria," *Nigeria Magazine* 53, no. 4 (1985).

Nwabara, S. N. *Iboland: A Century of Contact with Britain, 1860–1960*. London: Hodder and Stoughton, 1977.

Nzegwu, Nkiru. "Feminism and Africa: Impact and Limits of the Metaphysics of Gender." In *The Blackwell Companion to African Philosophy*, ed. Kwasi Wiredu. Cambridge, Mass.: Blackwell Publishers, 2004.

———. "The Epistemological Challenge of Motherhood to Patriliny." *JENDA: A Journal of Culture and African Women Studies* 5 (2003), http://www.jendajournal.com/issue5/nzegwu.html.

———. "O Africa: Gender Imperialism in Academia." In *African Women and Feminism: Reflecting on the Politics of Sisterhood*, ed. Oyeronke Oyewumi. Trenton, N.J.: Africa World Press, 2002a, 99–157.

———. "Hidden Spaces, Silenced Practices and the Concept of Igba N'rira," *West Africa Review* 3, no. 2. 2002b, http://www.westafricareview.com/war/vol3.2/nzegwu.html.

———. "The Politics of Gender in African Studies in the North." In *Women in African Scholarly Publishing*, ed. Cassandra Veney and Paul Tiyambe Zeleza. Trenton, N.J.: Africa World Press, 2001, 111–168.

———. "Colonial Racism: Sweeping Out Africa with Europe's Broom." In *Racism and Philosophy*, ed. Susan Babbitt and Sue Campbell. Ithaca: Cornell University Press, 1999, 124–156.

———. "Chasing Shadows: The Misplaced Search for Matriarchy," *Canadian Journal of African Studies*, 32, no. 3 (Fall 1998): 594–622. Reprinted in *West Africa Review* 2, no. 1 (August 2000).

———. "Philosophers' Intellectual Responsibility to African Females," *American Philosophical Association's (APA Newsletter)* 90, no.1 (1996a): 130–135.

———. "Questions of Identity and Inheritance: A Critical Review of Anthony Appiah's *In My Father's House*." *HYPATIA: A Journal of Feminist Philosophy* (Special Issue on Feminist Theory and the Family) 2, no. 1 (Winter 1996b): 176–99.

———. "Recovering Igbo Traditions: A Case for Indigenous Women's Organization in Development." In *Women, Culture and Development*, ed. Martha Nussbaum and Jonathan Glover. Oxford: Clarendon Press, 1995, 444–65.

———. "Gender Equality In a Dual Sex System: The Case of Onitsha," *Canadian Journal of Law and Jurisprudence* 7, no. 1 (1994b): 73–95. Reprinted in *JENDA: A Journal of Culture and African Women Studies* 1, no. 2 (2001a) http://www.jendajournal.com/vol1.2/nzegwu.html.

———. "Confronting Racism: Toward the Formation of a Female-Identified Consciousness," *Canadian Journal for Women and the Law* 7, no. 1 (1994a): 15–33.

Nzimiro, Ikenna *Studies in Ibo Political Systems: Chieftaincy and Politics in Four Niger States*. Berkeley: University of California Press, 1972.

Obi, S. N. Chinwuba. *The Ibo Law of Property*. London: Butterworth, 1963.

———*Modern Family Law in Southern Nigeria*. London: Sweet & Maxwell and Lagos: African Universities, 1966.

Oduyoye, Mercy Amba. *Daughters of Anowa: African Women and Patriarchy*. Maryknoll, N.Y.: Orbis Books, 1995.

Ogunidpe-Leslie, Omolara. *Re-Creating Ourselves: African Women and Critical Transformations*. Trenton, N.J.: Africa World Press, Inc., 1994.

———. "Women in Nigeria," *Women in Nigeria Today*. London: Zed Books, 1985: 119–31.

———. "Nigeria: Not Spinning on the Axis of Maleness." In *Sisterhood is Global*, ed. Robin Morgan. New York: Anchor Books, 1984, 498–504.

Ogunyemi, Chikwenye Okonjo. *African Wo/man Palava: The Nigerian Novel by Women*. Chicago: Chicago University Press, 1996.

Ogwu, Joy. "Perspectives of the Critical Impediments to Women in the Decision-Making Process." In *Nigerian Women in Politics, 1986–1993*, ed. Clara Osinulu & Nina Mba. Lagos: Malthouse Press Limited, 1996, 35–42.

Ohadike, Don C. *Anioma:A Social History of the Western Igbo People*. Athens, Ohio: Ohio University Press, 1994.

Oheneba-Sakyi, Yaw. *Female Autonomy, Family Decision Making, and Demographic Behavior in Africa*. Lewiston, Penn.: The Edwin Mellen Press, 1999.

Okin, Susan Moller. "John Rawls: Justice as Fairness — For Whom? In *Feminist Interpretations and Political Theory*, ed. Shanley, Mary Lydon and Carole Pateman. Princeton: Princeton University Press, 1991, 181–98.

———. "Families and Feminist Theory: Some Past and Present Issues." In *Feminism and Families*, ed. Hilde Lindemann Nelson. New York: Routledge, 1997, 13–26.

———. *Justice, Gender, and the Family*. New York: Basic Books, 1989.

Okonjo, Kamene. "Women's Political Participation in Nigeria." In *The Black Woman Cross-Culturally*, ed. Filomina Chioma Steady. Cambridge, Mass.: Schenkman Publishers Co, 1981, 79–106.

———. "The Dual-Sex Political System in Operation: Igbo Women and Community Politics in Midwestern Nigeria." In *Women in Africa*, ed. Nancy Hafkin and Edna Bay. Stanford, Calif: Stanford University Press, 1976, 45–58.

Okoro, Nwakama. *The Customary Laws of Succession in Eastern Nigeria*. London: Sweet and Maxwell, 1966.

Oladapo, Toro. "Inheritance Judgement Spurs Women Activism in Nigeria" *Panafrican News Agency*, Nigeria, Lagos. February 9, 1998.

O'Laughlin, Bridget. "Myth of the African Family in the World of Development." In *Women Wielding the Hoe: Lessons from Rural Africa for Feminist Theory and Development Practice*, ed. Deborah Fahy Bryceson. Oxford: Berg Publishers, 1995, 63–91.

Ollennu, N. A. *The Law of Testate and Intestate Succession in Ghana*. London: Sweet and Maxwell, 1966.

Oloruntimehin, B. O. "African Politics and Nationalism, 1919–35." In *Africa under Colonial Domination 1880–1935, UNESCO General History of Africa*, vol. 7, ed. Adu Boahen. Oxford: James Curry 1990, 565–579.

Omoneukanrin, C. O. *Itshekiri Law and Custom* Lagos, Nigeria: Ife-Olu Printing Works, 1942.

O'Neill, Onora. "How Do We Know When Opportunities Are Equal? *Feminism and Philosophy*, eds. Mary Vetterling-Braggin, Frederick A. Elliston, and Jane English. Totowa, N.J.: Rowman and Littlefield, 1977, 177–90.

Ong, Aihwa. "The Gender and Labor Politics of Postmodernity." In *Globalization and the Challenges of a New Century: A Reader*, ed. Patrick O'Meara, Howard D. Mehlinger, and Matthew Krain. Bloomington: Indiana University Press, 2000, 253–81.

———. "Strategic Sisterhood or Sisters in Solidarity? Questions of Communitarianism and Citizenship in Asia." *Indiana Journal of Global Legal Studies* 4 (Fall 1996): 107–35.

Onwuejeogwu, Michael Angulu. *An Outline of an Igbo Civilization: Nri Kingdom, and Hegemony AD 994 to Present*. Nri, Nigeria: Odinani Museum, 1980.

Onwuamaegbu, Obunneme. High Court Judgment to suit no. 0/78/81, *Nzegwu v. Nzegwus & Ors.*, July 24, 1986.

Oppong, Christine. *Middle-Class African Marriage.* London: George Allen Unwin, 1974.

Orakwue, J. I. *Onitsha Custom of Title-Taking.* Onitsha, Nigeria: Renascent Africa Press, Ltd., 1953.

Oriji, John N. "Igbo Women From 1929–1960," *West Africa Review* 2, no. 1 (2001), http://www.westafricareview.com/war/vol2.1/oriji.html.

Osinulu, Clara. "Preface." In *Nigerian Women in Politics, 1986–1993*, ed. Clara Osinulu and Nina Mba. Lagos: Malthouse Press Limited, 1996, 11–17.

Outshoorn, Joyce. "Power as a Political and Theoretical Concept in 'Second-Wave' Feminism." In *The Gender of Power: A Symposium*, ed. Monique Leijenaar, Kathy Davis, Claudine Helleman, Jantine Oldersma, and Dini Vos. Leiden: Vakgroep Vrouwenstudies FSW, Vrouwen en Autonomie, 1987, 25–33.

Oyĕwùmí, Oyèrónké. "Conceptualizing Gender: The Eurocentric Foundations of Feminist Concepts and the Challenge of African Epistemologies." *JENDA: A Journal of Culture and African Women Studies* 2, no. 1, 2002, http://www.jendajournal.com/jenda/vol2.1/oyewumi.pdf.

———. *Invention of Women: Making an African Sense of Western Discourses on Gender.* Minneapolis: University of Minnesota Press, 1997.

———. "Ties that (Un)Bind: Feminism, Sisterhood and Other Foreign Relations," *JENDA: A Journal of Culture and African Women Studies* 1, no. 1. 2001, http://www.jendajournal.com/jenda/vol1.1/oyewumi.pdf.

Parvikko, Tuija. "Conceptions of Gender Equality: Similarity and Difference." In *Equality Politics and Gender*, eds. Elizabeth Meehan and Selma Sevenhuijsen. London: Sage Publications, 1991, 36–51.

Pateman, Carole. "Genesis, Fathers and the Political Theory of Sons." In *Feminism: Critical Concepts in Literary and Cultural Studies*, vol. 1 (Feminism and the Enlightenment) ed. Mary Evans. London: Routledge, 2001, 118–53.

———. "'God Hath Ordained to Man a Helper': Hobbes, Patriarchy and Conjugal Right." In *Feminist Interpretations and Political Theory*, eds. Mary Lyndon Shanley and Carole Pateman. Cambridge, Mass.: Polity Press, 1991, 53–73.

———. *Sexual Contract.* Stanford: Stanford University Press 1988.

———. "Feminist Critiques of the Public/Private Dichotomy." In *Feminism and Equality*, ed. Anne Phillips. New York: New York University, 1987, 103–26.

———. "Introduction: The Theoretical Subversiveness of Feminism." In *Feminist Challenges: Social and Political Theory*, ed. Carole Pateman and Elizabeth Gross. Boston: Northeastern University Press, 1986, 1–10.

Pateman, Carole and Mary Lyndon Shanley. "Introduction." In *Feminist Interpretations and Political Theory*, ed. Mary Lyndon Shanley and Carole Pateman. Cambridge Mass.: Polity Press, 1991, 1–10.

Pearce, Tola. "Women, the State, and Reproductive Health Issues in Nigeria," *JENDA: A Journal of Culture and African Women Studies* 1, no. 1, 2001, http://www.jendajournal.com/jenda/vol1.1/pearce.html.

———. "Population Policies and the 'Creation' of Africa" *Africa* 19, no. 3 (1994): 61–76.

———. "Importing the New Reproductive Technologies: The Impact of Underlying Models of the Family, Females, and Women's Bodies in Nigeria." Paper presented at the WIDER conference on *Women, Equality and Reproductive Technology*, Helsinki, August 3–6, 1992.

Peters, Pauline. "Uses and Abuses of the Concept of 'Female-Headed Households' in Research on Agrarian Transformation and Policy." In *Women Wielding the Hoe*, ed. Deborah Fahy Bryceson. Oxford: Berg Publishers, 1995, 93–108.

Phillips, Ann. "Introduction." In *Feminism and Equality*, ed. Anne Phillips. New York: New York University Press, 1987, 1–23.

Postel-Coster, Els. "Women's Autonomy." In *The Gender of Power: A Symposium*, ed. Monique Leijenaar, Kathy Davis, Claudine Helleman, Jantine Oldersma and Dini Vos. Leiden: Vakgroep Vrouwenstudies FSW, Vrouwen en Autonomie, 1987, 34–40.

Potash, Betty. "Widows in Africa: An Introduction." In *Widows in African Societies*, ed. Betty Potash. Stanford: Stanford University Press, 1986, 1–43.

Potter, Elizabeth. "Locke's Epistemology and Women's Struggles." In *Modern Engendering: Critical Feminist Readings in Modern Western Philosophy*, ed. Bat-Ami Bar On. Albany: State University of New York Press, 1994, 27–50.

Rattray, Robert Sutherland *Ashanti*. New York: Negro University Press, 1969.

———. *Ashanti Law and Constitution*. Oxford: The Clarendon Press, 1956.

Razack, Sherene H. *Looking White People in the Eye*. Toronto: University of Toronto Press, 1998.

Rawls, John. *A Theory of Justice*. Cambridge: Harvard University Press, 1971.

Rioux, Marcia H. "Towards a Concept of Equality of Well-Being: Overcoming the Social and Legal Construction of Inequality, *The Canadian Journal of Law and Jurisprudence* 7, no. 1, (January 1994): 127–47.

Roberts, Richard and Kristin Mann. "Introduction: Law in Colonial Africa." In *Law in Colonial Africa* ed. Kristin Mann and Richard Roberts. Portsmouth, N.H.: Heinemann, 1991, 3–58.

Robertson, Claire. "Developing Economic Awareness: Changing Perspectives in Studies of African Women, 1976–1985," *Feminist Studies* 13, no. 1 (Spring 1987): 97–135.

————. "Women's Education and Class Formation in Africa, 1950–1980." In *Women and Class in Africa*. ed. Claire Robertson and Iris Berger. New York: Africana Publishing Company—Holms and Meier, 1986, 92–113.

————. "Ga Women and Socioeconomic Change in Accra, Ghana." In *Women in Africa*. ed. Nancy J. Hafkin and Edna G. Bay. Stanford: Stanford University Press, 1976.

Robertson, Claire and Iris Berger. "Introduction: Analyzing Class and Gender —African Perspectives." In *Women and Class in Africa*, ed. Claire Robertson and Iris Berger. New York: Africana Publishing Company— Holms and Meier, 1986, 3–24.

Rodney, Walter. *How Europe Underdeveloped Africa*. Washington D.C.: Howard University Press, 1982.

Rogers, Barbara. *The Domestication of Women: Discrimination in Developing Societies*. London: Tavistock, 1980

Rorty, Amélie Oksenberg. *Mind in Action: Essays in the Philosophy of Mind*. Boston: Beacon Press, 1988.

Rosaldo, Michelle Zimbalist "Women, Culture, and Society: A Theoretical Overview." In *Women, Culture, and Society*, ed. Michelle Zimbalist Rosaldo and Louise Lamphere. Stanford: Stanford University Press, 1974, 17–42.

Rothman, Barbara Katz. "Motherhood Under Patriarchy." In *Families in the U.S.: Kinship and Domestic Politics*, eds. Karen V. Hansen and Anita Ilta Carey. Philadelphia: Temple University Press, 1998, 21–31.

Rowbotham, Sheila. "The Trouble with 'Patriarchy.'" In *People's History and Socialist Theory*, ed. Raphael Samuel. Boston: Routledge and Kegan Paul, 1981, 364–69.

Ruddick, Sara. *Maternal Thinking: Toward a Politics of Peace*. Boston: Beacon Press, 1989.

Russell, Jennifer M. The Race/Class Conundrum and the Pursuit of Individualism in the Making of Social Policy," *Hastings Law Journal* 46, no. 5 (July 1995): 1353–1455.

Ruth, Sheila, "Images of Women in Patriarchy: The Masculist-Defined Woman." In *Issues in Feminism*, ed. Sheila Ruth. Mountain View, Calif.: Mayfield Publishing Company, 1990, 80–91.

Scott, Joan Wallach. *Gender and the Politics of History*. New York: Columbia University Press, 1999.

Shanley, Mary Lydon and Carole Pateman, eds. *Feminist Interpretations and Political Theory*. Princeton: Princeton University Press, 1991.

Shanley, Mary Lyndon. "Marital Slavery and Friendship: John Stuart Mill's *The Subjection of Women*." In *Feminist Interpretations and Political Theory*, ed. Mary Lyndon Shanley and Carole Pateman. Cambridge, Mass.: Polity Press, 1991, 164–80.

Sharpton, Al. *The New York Times Magazine,* Section 6, July 18, 2004, 15.

Sheppard, Colleen. "The 'I' in the 'It': Reflections on a Feminist Approach to Constitutional Theory." In *Canadian Perspectives on Legal Theory*, ed. R. Devlin. Toronto: Edmond Montgomery, 1991, 415–31.

Slocum, Sally "Woman the Gatherer: Male Bias in Anthropology." In *Issues in Feminism: An Introduction to Women's Studies*, ed. Sheila Ruth. Mountain View, Calif.: Mayfield Publishing Co., 1990, 198–204.

Sow, Fatou. "The Social Sciences in Africa and Gender Analysis." In *Engendering African Social Sciences*, ed. Ayesha Imam, Amina Mama, Fatou Sow. Dakar, Senegal: CODESRIA, 1999, 31–60.

Spelman V. Elizabeth. *Inessential Woman: Problems of Exclusion in Feminist Thought*. Boston: Beacon Press, 1988, 3–56.

———. "Simone de Beauvoir and Women: Just Who Does She Think 'We' Is?" In *Feminist Interpretations and Political Theory*, ed. Mary Lyndon Shanley and Carole Pateman. Cambridge, Mass.: Polity Press, 1991, 199–216.

Stamp, Patricia. "Burying Otieno: The Politics of Gender and Ethnicity in Kenya," *Signs: Journal of Women in Culture and Society* 16, no. 4 (Summer 1991): 808–45.

Stanley, Liz and Sue Wise. "Method, Methodology and Epistemology in Feminist Research Processes." In *Feminist Praxis: Research, Theory and Epistemology in Feminist Sociology*, ed. Liz Stanley. London: Routledge, 1990, 20–60.

Stauder, Jack. "The 'Relevance' of Anthropology to Colonialism and Imperialism." In *The Racial Economy of Science*, ed. Sandra Harding. Bloomington: Indiana University Press, 1993, 408–27.

Steady, Filomina Chioma, ed. *Black Women, Globalization, and Economic Justice: Engendering Racism in Africa and the African Diaspora*. Rochester, Vt.: Schenkman Books, Inc., 2001.

———. "The Black Woman Cross-Culturally: An Overview." In *The Black Woman Cross-Culturally*, ed. Filomina Chioma Steady. Cambridge, Mass.: Schenkman Publishers Co, 1981, 7–41.

Stichter, Sharon and Jane Parpart. "Introduction: Towards a Materialist Perspective on African Women." In *Patriarchy and Class*, ed. Sharon Stichter and Jane Parpart. Boulder, Colo.: Westview Press, 1988, 1–26.

Stoeltje, Beverly J. "Asante Queen Mothers: A Study in Female Authority." In *Queens, Queen Mothers, Priestesses, and Power: Case Studies in African Gender*, ed. Flora Edouwaye S. Kaplan. New York: New York Academy of Sciences, vol. 810, 1997, 41–71.

———. "Asante Queenmothers: A Study in Identity and Continuity." In *Gender and Identity in Africa*, ed. Mechthild Reh and Gudrun Ludwar-Ene. Münster: Lit Verlag, 1995, 15–32.

Stoljar, Natalie and Catorina Mackenzie. "Introduction: Autonomy Reconfig-ured." In *Relational Autonomy: Feminist Perspectives on Autonomy, Agency, and the Social Self*, ed. Catorina Mackenzie and Natalie Stoljar. New York: Oxford University Press, 2000, 3–31.

Strobel, Margaret. "African Women," *Signs: Journal of Women in Culture and Society* 8, no. 1 (1982): 109–29.

Sudarkasa, Niara. *The Strength of Our Mothers: African and African American Women and Families: Essays and Speeches*. Trenton, N.J.: Africa World Press, 1996.

———. "Female Employment and Family Organization in West Africa." In *The Black Woman Cross-Culturally*, ed. Filomina Chioma Steady. Cam-bridge, Mass: Schenkman Publishers Co, 1981, 49–63.

Sunstein, Cass, "Gender, Caste, Law." Paper presented at the WIDER confer-ence on *Women, Equality and Reproductive Technology*, Helsinki, August 3–6, 1992.

Taiwo, Olufemi, "Appropriating Africa: An Essay on New Africanist Schools," *Issue: Journal of Opinion* 23, no.1 (1995): 39–45.

Takaki, Ronald. "Reflections on Racial Patterns in America." In *From Differ-ent Shores: Perspectives on Race, Ethnicity in America*, ed. Ronald Takaki. New York: Oxford University Press, 1994, 24–35.

———. Takaki, Ronald. "To Count or Not to Count by Race and Gender?" In *From Different Shores: Perspectives on Race, Ethnicity in America*, ed. Ronald Takaki. New York: Oxford University Press, 1994, 241–42.

Talbot, Percy Amaury. *The Peoples of Southern Nigeria* vol. 4. London: Oxford University Press, 1926.

———. *Woman's Mysteries of a Primitive People, the Ibibios of Southern Nigeria*. London: Cassell and Company, Ltd., 1915.

Thomas, Northcote Whitridge. *Anthropological Report on the Ibo-Speaking Peoples of Nigeria*. London, Harrison and Sons, 1913–14.

Thorne, Barrie. "Feminism and the Family: Two Decades of Thought." In *Rethinking the Family: Some Feminist Questions*, eds. Barrie Thorne and Marilyn Yalom. Boston: Northeastern University Press, 1992, 3–30.

———. "Feminist Rethinking of the Family: An Overview." In *Rethinking that Family: Some Feminist Questions*, eds. Barrie Thorne and Marilyn Yalom. New York: Longman, 1982, 1–24.

Thornhill, Esmeralda. "Focus on Black Women!" *Canadian Journal of Women and the Law* 1 (1985a): 153–62.

———. "Black Women's Studies in Teaching Related to Women: Help or Hin-derance to Universal Sisterhood?" In *Black Women: Double Dilemma*. Montreal: Quebec Human Rights Commission, Education Department, 1985b.

Thornton, Merle. "Sex Equality is Not Enough for Feminism." In *Feminist Challenges: Social and Political Theory*, ed. Carole Pateman and Elizabeth Gross. Boston: Northeastern University Press, 1986, 77–98.

Thurow, Lester C. "Affirmative Action in Zero-Sum Society." In *From Different Shores: Perspectives on Race, Ethnicity in America*, ed. Ronald Takaki. New York: Oxford University Press, 1994, 235–40.

———. *Dangerous Currents: The State of Economics*. New York: Random House, 1983.

Tinker, Irene. "The Making of a Field: Advocates, Practitioners and Scholars." In *Persistent Inequalities: Women and World Development*, ed. Irene Tinker. Oxford: Oxford University Press, 1990, 27–53.

Tobi, Niki. Judgment to suit no. CA/E/318/87, *Nzegwus v. Nzegwu*, April 22, 1997.

Toungara, Jeanne Maddox. "Changing the Meaning of Marriage: Women and Family Law in Côte d'Ivoire." In *African Feminism: The Politics of Survival in Sub-Saharan Africa*, ed. Gwendolyn Mikell. Philadelphia: University of Pennsylvania Press, 1997, 53–76.

Turpel, Mary Ellen/Aki-kwe. "Aboriginal Peoples and the Canadian Charter of Rights and Freedoms: Contradictions and Challenges," *Canadian Woman Studies/Les Cahiers de la Femme* 10, nos. 2 and 3, (1989): 149–57.

Uchendu, Chinturu. Equal Encounters: Gender, Language, and Power in an African Society—The Case of Ubang-Obudu, Nigeria. Ph.D. Diss, University of Maryland, Baltimore, 2003.

Uchendu, Victor. *The Igbo of Southeast Nigeria*. New York: Holt, Rinehart and Winston, 1965.

Udoma, E. Udoma. *A Memorandum Submitted by the Ibibio State Union to the Jones Commission of Inquiry into the Position, Status and Influence of Chiefs and Natural Rulers in the Eastern Nigeria*. Aba: Ikemesi and Co., 1956.

Van Allen, Judith. "'Aba Riots' or Igbo Women's War?" In *Ideology, Stratification, the Invisibility of Women*, ed. N. J. Hafkin and Edna Bay, Stanford, Calif.: Stanford University Press 1976, 59–86.

———. "Sitting on a Man: Colonialism and the Lost Political Institutions of Igbo Women," *Canadian Journal of African Studies* 6, no. 2 (1972): 168–81.

Vansina, Jan. *Oral Tradition as History*. Madison: University of Wiscosin Press, 1985.

Vellenga, Dorothy Dee. "The Widow among the Matrilineal Akan of Southern Ghana." In *Widows in African Societies: Choices and Constraints*, ed. Betty Potash. Stanford: Stanford University Press, 1986, 220–40.

Vogt, Margaret. "The Military and Women in Politics." In *Nigerian Women in Politics, 1986–1993*, ed. Clara Osinulu and Nina Mba. Lagos: Malthouse Press Limited, 1996, 64–76.

Walby, Sylvia. *Theorizing Patriarchy*. Oxford: Basil Blackwell, 1990.

Walker, Alice. *The Color Purple*. Boston, Mass.: G. K. Hall, 1986.

Wallace, Michelle. *Black Macho and the Myth of the Superwoman*. New York: Verso, 1990.

Wanitzek, Ulrike. "The Power of Language in the Discourse on Women's Rights: Some Examples from Tanzania," *Africa Today* 49, no. 1 (2003): 3–19.

Warren, Charles. *The Supreme Court in United States History* 2, rev. ed., Boston: Little, Brown, and Company, 1926.

Weitzman, Lenore J. "Women and Children Last: The Social and Economic Consequences of Divorce Law Reforms." In *Issues in Feminism*, ed. Sheila Ruth. Mountain View, Calif.: Mayfield Publishing Company, 1990, 312–35.

Willer, Heid. "Women Industrialists: A Potential for Economic Development in Nigeria?" In *Gender and Identity in Africa*, ed. Mechthild Reh and Gudrun Ludwar-Ene. Münster: Lit Verlag, 1995, 99–134.

Wing, Adrien Katherine. "Introduction: Global Critical Race Feminism for the Twenty-First Century." In *Global Critical Race Feminism: An International Reader*, ed. Adrienne Katherine Wing. New York: New York University Press, 2000, 1–23.

Wiredu, Kwasi. "An Akan Perspective on Human Rights." In *Human Rights in Africa: Cross-Cultural Perspectives*, ed. Abdullahi Ahmed An-Na'im and Francis M. Deng. Washington D.C.: Brookings Institution, 1990, 243–60.

Wollenstonecraft, Mary. *A Vindication of the Rights of Women: With Strictures on Political and Moral Subjects*. Buffalo, N.Y.: Prometheus Books, 1989.

Woodman, Gordon. "Basic Questions in the Task of Inheritance Law." In *Changing Family Studies*, Legon Family Research Papers, No. 3, ed. Christine Oppong. Legon: Institute of African Studies, University of Ghana, 1975, 139–46.

———. "The Rights of Wives, Sons and Daughters in the Estates of their Deceased Husbands and Fathers." In *Domestic Rights and Duties in Ghana*, Legon Family Research Papers, No. 1, ed. Christine Oppong. Legon: Institute of African Studies, University of Ghana, 1974, 268–84.

Young, Iris Marion. "Is Male Gender Identity the Cause of Male Domination?" In *Mothering: Essays in Feminist Theory*, ed. Joyce Treblicot. Totowa, N.J.: Rowman and Allanheld, 1984, 129–46.

Zaretsky, Eli. "The Place of the Family in the Origins of the Welfare State." In *Rethinking the Family: Some Feminist Questions*, ed. Barrie Thorne and Marilyn Yalom. New York: Longman, 1982, 188–224.

Zeleza, Paul Tiyambe. "Gender Biases in African Historiography." In *Engendering African Social Sciences*, ed. Ayesha Imam, Amina Mama, and Fatou Sow. Dakar, Senegal: CODESRIA, 1999, 81–115.

———. *Manufacturing African Studies and Crises*. Dakar, Senegal: CODESRIA Book Series, 1997.

INDEX